BRESCIA UNIVERSITY COLLEGE LIBRARY

3 6277 00029174 2

BERYL IVEY LIBRARY

PR
585
.W6
B42
2009

D1600226

*British Women Poets and the Romantic
Writing Community*

British Women Poets and the Romantic Writing Community

STEPHEN C. BEHRENDT

The Johns Hopkins University Press

Baltimore

BRESCIA UNIVERSITY
COLLEGE LIBRARY

© 2009 The Johns Hopkins University Press
All rights reserved. Published 2009
Printed in the United States of America on acid-free paper

2 4 6 8 9 7 5 3 1

The Johns Hopkins University Press
2715 North Charles Street
Baltimore, Maryland 21218-4363
www.press.jhu.edu

Library of Congress Cataloging-in-Publication Data

Behrendt, Stephen C., 1947–
British women poets and the romantic writing community / Stephen C. Behrendt.
p. cm.
Includes bibliographical references and index.
ISBN-13: 978-0-8018-9054-3 (hardcover : alk. paper)
ISBN-10: 0-8018-9054-3 (hardcover : alk. paper)
1. English poetry—Women authors—History and criticism. 2. English poetry—19th
century—History and criticism. 3. English poetry—18th century—History and
criticism. 4. Women and literature—Great Britain—History—18th century. 5. Women
and literature—Great Britain—History—19th century. 6. Romanticism—
Great Britain. I. Title.
PR585.W6B47 2008
821'.7099287—dc22   2008013752

A catalog record for this book is available from the British Library.

*Special discounts are available for bulk purchases of this book. For more information, please
contact Special Sales at 410-516-6936 or specialsales@press.jhu.edu.*

The Johns Hopkins University Press uses environmentally friendly book materials,
including recycled text paper that is composed of at least 30 percent post-consumer
waste, whenever possible. All of our book papers are acid-free, and our jackets and
covers are printed on paper with recycled content.

For Stuart Curran

CONTENTS

ACKNOWLEDGMENTS

A book like this one evolves over many years, and it accumulates many debts along the way. I have long enjoyed conversations in person and in correspondence with colleagues engaged in the recovery and reassessment of Romantic-era writers, both women and men. Being part of this collective activity, which seems to be pursued in every instance with uncommon energy and ingenuity, has been invaluable to me as I have tried to think my way through the issues that I discuss in this book. These issues have been central to my own scholarship for many years now, as they also have been to my teaching. Both of these activities, I have come to realize, have been dramatically and irreversibly altered by what I have learned in the process of discovering writers to whom I was never introduced in my own formal education, whose acquaintance I only made subsequently, and whose works opened up wholly new vistas on the landscape of the diverse and dynamic writing community that existed in the British Isles between the outbreak of the war with the American colonies and the accession of the youthful Queen Victoria. The result, for me, has been a wholesale rethinking of what I understand by the Romantic writing community and an appreciation of what is to be learned and gained when we reexamine from new perspectives and with new information things with which we had long been fairly confident we were familiar.

Some of the results of these explorations have previously appeared, in much abbreviated fashion, in essays and articles. Some of the preliminary details about women and war, for example, appeared in a chapter in Philip Shaw's collection, *Romantic Wars* (Ashgate, 2000); some thoughts about Scottish women writers appeared in my own introduction to *Scottish Women Romantic Poets* (Alexander Street Press, 2002); and some early musings on Irish women poets appeared in "Irish Women Poets of the Romantic Period: A Different Sort of Other" (*Women's Writing* 12. 2 [2005]).

This book, then, is indebted to many friends and colleagues, as well as to students with whom I have worked in courses at all levels over the years and with whom

I have explored many of the problems and perceptions that are to be found in the pages that follow. Among the many friends and colleagues, too numerous to mention, I need to extend special warm thanks and appreciation for many favors, many suggestions, and many insights over the years: Stuart Curran, Paula Feldman, Diane Long Hoeveler, Harriet Kramer Linkin, Mark Lussier, Anne Mellor, Joseph Wittreich, and Susan Wolfson. I thank, too, the anonymous reader for Johns Hopkins University Press who read parts of the manuscript with care and whose insightful comments have contributed to this book's final form. At the University of Nebraska I have benefited from the patience and expertise of a wonderful interlibrary loan staff, headed by Brian O'Grady, that has helped me pursue materials from every quarter during the course of my research. I am also grateful for the steady support provided by the office of the Vice Chancellor for Research here at Nebraska, and for a summer stipend some years ago from the National Endowment for the Humanities. I have also appreciated the clear interest and care with which Michael Lonegro at the Johns Hopkins University Press has treated this project from the outset.

Finally, and as always, I owe a special debt of gratitude and love to my family: to my wife Patricia especially and eternally, who has read draft after draft, patiently, perceptively, and with an unfailing sense of why this entire project has been so important to me for all these years; and to my daughters Maia and Mei Grace, who have occasionally marveled that their dad could–and would–spend so much time writing, and who have been patient, too, when that writing had to come first.

As more and more of the literary work of British women from the Romantic era has been published in modern editions, often with scholarly apparatus, and as these writers have also begun to appear in anthologies intended especially for college and university students, the world has gradually begun to be reacquainted with writers and texts that had long been neglected or marginalized for a whole host of reasons. But anthologies can provide only a piecemeal sampling of this vast body of diverse writing, and too often anthologies tend to repeat one another when it comes to selections, so that most of this writing remains largely invisible. At the same time, specialized scholarly editions of some of the poets have begun to appear, but economic considerations largely restrict such editions to those writers whose recuperated reputations make editions of their works financially feasible for publishers. Inevitably, this leaves the majority still on the outside, looking in.

Many of the texts I discuss in this book are quite scarce; certainly most of them are not immediately available in most academic libraries, and some exist in only a handful of major libraries like the British Library and the National Library of Ireland, which makes them relatively inaccessible to many scholars and most students who might wish to consult the originals. Happily, some of these are starting to become available as a result of advances in digital and electronic technology. There is of course no substitute for examining original paper copies of books, both for appreciating their physical nature *as books* and for discovering the additional materials they contain in the form of marginalia, annotations, and corrections. Still, electronic versions of the originals at least provide one with access to the writing itself.

For books published before 1800, a particularly valuable resource is the electronic archive, Eighteenth Century Collections Online (ECCO), where digital images of the original texts are available in PDF format. For books published after 1800, there is also the Chadwyck-Healy electronic archive, Nineteenth-Century Poetry, although it is far more selective and contains relatively few works by lesser-known writers. Two electronic archives, published by Alexander Street Press and available through libraries (primarily academic research libraries) by subscription, contain electronic versions of complete volumes of poetry by women whose work is central to my book: Scottish Women Poets of the Romantic Period (2002) and Irish Women Poets of the Romantic Period (2008). Although these two archives consist of keyed-in transcriptions of the originals rather than digital images of them (as in ECCO), the texts are nevertheless complete, accurate, and easily searchable.

Several additional online archives and projects offer valuable resources for the further study of Romantic-era women poets. The first, housed at the University of California, Davis, and called British Women Romantic Writers, is still being developed and will eventually include all the Romantic-era volumes of poetry by women from the spectacular Kohler Collection of Nineteenth-Century British Poetry, which is held at the university's Shields Library. A second archive, with broader chronological parameters, is the pioneering British Women Writers project at Brown University, which took an early and influential lead in making primary resources accessible in electronic format. In addition to these university-sponsored initiatives, many individual scholars around the world have begun to prepare and to post on their Web sites electronic editions of primary texts.

The consequence of all this activity, which shows no sign of abating, is that we now enjoy increasing access to writers and works with which many–even most–of us have historically been unfamiliar. Many of the authors and works that I discuss in this book may be found in some of these resources, although, unfortunately, many are still to be found only in specialized libraries or through copies prepared from those originals.

*British Women Poets and the Romantic
Writing Community*

Introduction

We have all of us one human heart.

> —*William Wordsworth, "The Old Cumberland Beggar"*
> *(1800; comp. 1798)*

Ay, fair as are
The visions of a poet's solitude,
There must be something more for happiness;
They seek communion.

> —*Letitia Elizabeth Landon, "Erinna" (1827)*

What We Know and What We Thought We Knew

At the beginning of *A Christmas Carol*, Charles Dickens insists that we bear in mind that Jacob Marley's death is a fact. "There is no doubt that Marley was dead," the narrator tells us. "This must be distinctly understood, or nothing wonderful can come of this story" (39). Any effective tale relies on the ability of its hearer—and its teller—to distinguish between what is and what merely seems to be: Ebenezer Scrooge must learn this as surely as Hamlet had to learn it. When it comes to assessing the poetry written and published by women in the British Isles during the Romantic period, it is useful to separate what we know from what we only think we know. For this is not a tale simply about the Romantic literary canon or about the cultural wars that have during recent years attended the interrogation of that canon, at least in the academic world. Several decades of scholarship and numerous waves of theory have brought us to the present moment in which a wholesale reassessment of "British Romanticism" is occurring, as scholars, teachers, and students rethink a literary and cultural "movement" that was for nearly two centuries stereotyped in terms of a small group of male poets. The consequences of this oversimplification were many, as we now realize. For one, while the male poets were lionized, the other literary genres were routinely overlooked—or simply depreciated—by institutional academe, so that even so central a novelist as Walter Scott was eclipsed while Jane Austen was typically categorized—her composing and publishing dates notwithstanding—as an "eighteenth century" novelist in the comedy of manners tradition. So neglected was Romantic-era theater that even today it remains largely unexamined except by the most committed specialists, despite the immense interest—a *paying* interest at that—demonstrated by the contemporary public in all forms of theatre and theatrics, "legitimate" and otherwise. So too has the expanding field of literature for children and young readers generally been overlooked, although publishers of the early nineteenth century quickly realized the economic rewards of producing cheap editions for this market that the spread of literacy (combined with the moral earnestness promoted by the evangelical movement no less than by the reactionary political right) was creating. The historical reality is that the Romantic literary community was more diverse and more dynamic than could possibly be intuited from the old six-poet model of British Romanticism with which generations grew up.

What is true of Romantic literary genres is no less true of Romantic-era ideology. It is instructive to remember, right from the start, that in terms of both politics and poetics the majority of the Romantic era's writers did not occupy the left-of-center ground on which we usually think the canonical writers stood. For one thing, literary history (like cultural history) has always been fond of retrospectively heroizing its radical, liberal, or otherwise oppositional figures. Frequently myopic when it comes to genuine talent and enduring value, the "popular" critical establishment represented in the mainstream mass media (then as now) often lionizes what eventually proves to be ephemeral and mediocre at the expense of greater talents that are permitted to languish under inattention or, perhaps more often, withering criticism. Afterward, when time sorts out what contemporary professional critical opinion is seemingly so loath to do, things change and praise is forthcoming—often, paradoxically, when the artist is no longer alive to appreciate it. Canonical and noncanonical writers alike understood that the odds were almost always against them; for the few—like Scott or Byron, Hemans or Landon—who attained fame during their lifetimes, there were always the many who labored in ignominy and obscurity, consigned alike by public whim and critical disapprobation to history's dustheap.

The private and public writings alike of Romantic authors reveal how many of them chafed at the critical depreciation of their talents in the face of the praise regularly accorded to other, often considerably lesser, writers. That subsequent literary history has in many cases redressed the balance should not distract us, however, from the frequently unremarked presence and influence of those many other writers whose work represents what might seem at first glance to represent a very different vision of "Romantic literature." Indeed, when one considers the broader literary scene that includes the era's literally thousands of active writers, it becomes hard any longer to tolerate—much less to justify—monolithic terms like "Romantic literature," "Romantic poetry," or even "Romanticism," all of which presume a uniformity or consensus far beyond what facts will support. We would all do well to pay closer attention to Jerome McGann's point about the elusiveness of single, all-encompassing ideological categories: that all such categories are themselves illusory constructs formulated by the participants "to hold back an awareness of the contradictions inherent in contemporary social structures and the relations they support" (134). A quarter of a century old, McGann's admonition is still valid today.

William Stafford's recent insightful study of British women writers of the 1790s underscores McGann's point more specifically in terms of the historical and cultural milieu in which women writers—in all the genres—did their work during that volatile decade. Stafford reminds us, for instance, how few women writers can be labeled as unqualifiedly "Jacobin" or "anti-Jacobin," to use two familiar category descriptors. Rather, he demonstrates, we find in the work of writers as far left of center as Mary Hays and as far right as Jane West evidence of the authors' thoughtful engagement with—and frequently their sympathetic presentation of—ideas and actions that are at variance with standard oversimplified assessments of their political, social, or moral agendas. Women writers, as we are coming ever more completely to appreciate, were fully attuned to the actual, practical realities involved in public behavior, among which was of course publication. They knew about the limits as well as the opportunities involved in making their thoughts and words public—because they *had* to if they wished to pursue that option. Susan Wolfson has recently observed of women who wrote that for them to address the public sphere highlighted "the complication negotiated by any woman author, and it was a hot zone if her writing advanced the new philosophies of rights and liberties" (*Borderlines,* 15). Their knowledge of the risks involved consequently played a large part in aesthetic and intellectual considerations when they came to write and publish. For them, as Stafford observes, "there was a gap between ideology and lived reality" (*English Feminists,* 45). Indeed, the failure of traditional literary history to consider the practical consequences of this gap for Romantic-era women's writing is inextricably bound up in the historical inattention to the nature and substance—as well as the art and craft—of that writing. Historians, Stafford observes, are typically more aware of this disjunction *and its practical effects on writing* than are literary scholars, whose primary interest is in texts as expressions of ideas rather than as descriptors of historical and cultural circumstances. This is one reason why, Stafford suggests, literary scholars may be surprised when they look closely and with unprejudiced eyes at prose writers who are typically categorized readily and narrowly—Hannah More and West on the right, Mary Hays and Fanny Burney on the left—only to discover that frequently "these writers with one voice propose a separation of spheres, and then with another undermine it" (152).

Stafford's point is as relevant to Romantic-era women's poetry as it is to their prose. The women whose poetry I consider in the chapters that follow represent a variety of "shadings" of Romanticism that seldom conform to the familiar outlines of what we have customarily regarded as the male Romantic poetic tradition in Britain. But they are nevertheless *in conversation* with that tradition, as well as with one another, and this conversational aspect in fact characterizes far more of Romantic literary production—by women and men alike—than has commonly been appreciated. Writers of both genders, and from across the economic, political, and ideological spectrum, understood themselves to be participants in an active—even an interactive—*community* of writers and readers. Theirs was a common, shared enterprise, as they saw it, and not the solitary, introverted activity caricatured in the images of the flower-sniffing Wordsworthian wanderer, on the one hand, and the rebellious Byronic misanthrope, on the other. C. R. Johnson has noted that even those ostensibly "minor" (or "provincial") poets who published at a distance from the major population centers "did not exist in a vacuum" but were in fact "powerfully influenced by those who preceded and surrounded them" and that many of them (and their works) were known by their subsequently more famous contemporaries ([vi]). Throughout the period, Romantic poets committed their lives and their art to a collective, community-building activity that was sometimes patently nationalistic, sometimes intensely local and personal, and at other times universally humanitarian in its impulses. Always we find in this poetry the fundamental assumptions represented in the two passages that serve as epigraphs to this introductory chapter. Wordsworth's humanitarian plea, voiced in "The Old Cumberland Beggar," that his readers recognize and respect the human dignity of even the most humble citizen, reflects his conviction of the inescapably shared nature of all human experience. We are to recognize ourselves in the beggar, of course, but we are also to recognize ourselves in the acts of benevolence that his presence elicits from a diverse citizenry whose gestures are activated not by the calculating mind but rather by the "one human heart" that unites beggar, poet, and reader in this larger community. Landon, writing toward the end of the era, makes the related point that the value of art lies not in solitary acts of contemplation and creation but rather in the shared activities of consciousness raising that come with *consuming* art—with reading—as part of an interactive community. For Landon, "communion" is the objective of the artistic activity (and the aesthetic experience), an activity that implicitly includes also reading, and it is surely no accident that Landon's noun also names a sacrament. For both poets, writing is more than an occupation: it is a vocation, much as the term is understood among religious communities.

What we discover when we move beyond stereotypical views and look with care and discrimination at the full range of Romantic poetry is that it undermines the sort of facile categorizing that the academic and scholarly world can make so seductive to beginning students and to senior scholars alike. We like the security of knowing the ground, and it is instructive to contemplate how we humans have for eons anthropomorphicized the natural world as a means of simplifying it and making it more comprehensible and therefore more comfortable. Neatness and cleanliness are preached to us as literary and cultural scholars no less than they are to us as children whose rooms (and as academics whose offices) are frequently a shambles. But "cleaning up" often means "putting away," and not infrequently it means also *throwing* away. Such operations may be well meaning; certainly they are expedient. But expediency ignores the discontinuities, the dissonances, the failure to "fit" that characterizes real life no less than the real literary landscape of Romantic-era Britain, and responsible scholarship (like responsible teaching) requires that we rethink our paradigms. If, as frequently happens, both the poetics and the politics of the writers who have been canonized are liberal and progressive rather than conservative and reactionary, that does not give us license to ignore what was happening in other writing. For that other writing traces the broader sociopolitical and cultural scene occupied by the majority, and that scene both defines the nonconforming authors and delineates the nature of their nonconformity. Indeed, that ideologically conservative writing—and the cultural conditions to which it points—often provided the enabling device that provoked literary expression of the sort of alternatives that inform many of our most cherished (and sometimes most mistaken) Romantic stereotypes.

The reality, then, is that British Romanticism is a richly inflected cultural phenomenon, both in its artistic productions and in the cultural circumstances that surrounded those productions and their consumption. It is a community populated by a familiar few and by a multitude whose works, voices, and persons have been lost (some of them irretrievably) to literary history for much of two centuries. This community is characterized by complex ideological and intellectual gradations and shadings represented in the remarkable array of their literary works. Paradoxically, popular portraits of British Romanticism have historically tended simultaneously to resist and to reinforce paradigmatic assumptions about the period that this cultural movement encompasses, about the writers—and genres—we associate with this movement, and about the works that serve to define its leading characteristics— and hence the canon(s) of works we think of as "Romantic." I say "paradoxically" because, despite all that has changed in Romantic literary and cultural studies in recent years, what the "general public" (and a good many academics) understand by "British Romanticism" is still defined largely in terms of five (or six) canonical male poets and a rough idea that the period followed the French Revolution.

Philip Cox suggests that "the powerful narrative of Romanticism appears to sub- vert [most] attempts to redirect our critical attention towards other literary (and nonliterary) productions of the same period" (153). Indeed, the five canonical male poets (six if we add Blake to William Wordsworth, Coleridge, Byron, Percy Bysshe Shelley, and Keats) are so firmly associated with the traditional paradigm of British Romanticism that for many that movement has historically been assumed to be almost exclusively (1) male oriented or otherwise masculinist in outlook and ethos, and (2) grounded in and oriented toward poetry more than any of the other liter- ary genres. This familiar model of British Romanticism is, however, the product not so much of objective historiography and cultural scholarship as of the post- Romantic—and more particularly the twentieth-century—tastes of the times and of the academy that produced the paradigm. The persistence of this faulty vision of the literary landscape is evident from a century or more of academic scholarship and classroom teaching and from innumerable commercial textbook anthologies that even in the final decade of the twentieth century continued to ignore, elide, or otherwise minimize poetry by women.[1] That these assumptions about women's place in British Romanticism have proven to be entirely misleading, if not wholly incorrect, has not prevented their nevertheless becoming part of a cultural con- sciousness that has been properly challenged by revisionist scholarship of the past decade in particular.

The disappearance of British women poets of the Romantic era is largely a twen- tieth-century phenomenon, though, one that was attended in the earlier part of the century by Romanticism's loss of stature generally in the face of modernism and then New Criticism. As late as 1861, after all, Jane Williams's *Literary Women of England* devoted a full twelve chapters to women poets from the Romantic period. She had begun with a plan to write about Felicia Hemans, Williams tells us in her introduction, and, finding no extant study of Hemans's female contemporaries, felt compelled to compose that account herself. In doing so she set out to redress the conspicuous injustice she saw in British literary history, in which "our country has . . . been content, throughout long succeeding centuries, to leave the names of her most eminent daughters faintly discernible and often overshadowed on chance monuments" (11). Indeed, she lamented her unhappy discovery that standard references like the *Biographia Britannica* recorded relatively few women writers; consequently, "excepting the dates of their productions, furnished in books of reference, very little is known of them by the public, and Englishwomen generally are deprived of the benefit and satisfaction of forming a real acquaintance with their lives and characters" (6).

It took more than a century for the recovery that Williams imagined to begin in earnest. Textual scholarship is making available again works that have been effectively lost for most of two centuries, while critical and theoretical scholarship has set in motion a revisionist reassessment of those works and their place in the long history of British literature and culture. One need only glance at the contents of today's literary journals and the catalogues of academic and commercial publishers alike to recognize the considerable place that studies of women writers—including Romantic-era ones—now occupy. It has been more than twenty years since Stuart Curran published the groundbreaking essay that reacquainted contemporary scholars, students, and readers of British Romanticism with some of the women poets whose works had over the course of some two centuries largely disappeared from anthologies and academic curricula—and consequently from modern scholarship and modern classrooms.[2]

Happily, we no longer need to be reminded that many women were active on the literary scene in England during the years that literary history has customarily designated as the Romantic period: 1789/98–1832.[3] J. R. de J. Jackson's 1993 survey of women poets, for instance, established that no fewer than four hundred women were actively writing *and publishing* poetry in England during this period, a number that rises to well over five hundred when one also includes Scotland, Wales, and Ireland. Among these, several were in their lifetimes as popular as—and in some cases more popular than—their subsequently canonized male contemporaries. According to the contemporary press in 1793, for example, "no living poet could hold a candle to Lady Catherine Rebecca Manners, and Mrs. Mary Robinson was probably the greatest poet of all time" (Werkmeister, 311), When the *True Briton* hailed Robinson as "the *first Poet* now living," the *Oracle* (which had published her poetry as early as 1789) and the *Morning Post* (for which she would serve as poetry editor in 1799–1800) trumped that praise by calling her simply "the *first Poet*" (Werkmeister, 311–12). Meanwhile, the *Elegiac Sonnets* of her contemporary Charlotte Turner Smith had by the time of Smith's death in 1806 progressed through some nine editions since its first appearance in 1784. Moreover, Smith—whose poems had occasionally appeared in the *Morning Chronicle*—was in turn lauded in print, both before and after her death, by numerous poets—male and female alike—who acknowledged her skill and celebrated her reputation, both of which they sought (with varying degrees of success) to emulate.

When it comes to the latter part of the period, we still frequently encounter the mistaken public notion that narrowly regards Byron as the era's preeminent poet. Such a view conveniently forgets (or simply ignores) the great contemporary popularity of the poetry of Sir Walter Scott (whose *Lay of the Last Minstrel* [1805] and *Marmion* [1808] were immediate commercial successes) and Thomas Moore (whose *Irish Melodies* [1807–34] were widely admired in England while their author was lionized at home as an Irish national bard). It overlooks, too, Robert Bloomfield's enormously popular *The Farmer's Boy* (1800), which sold more than forty thousand copies over the course of its various editions. But women poets achieved their own successes during this period. Both Byron's sales and his popularity were subsequently rivaled and occasionally eclipsed by the immensely popular poems of Felicia Hemans, the nineteenth century's most published woman poet (whose total book sales exceeded eighteen thousand during her lifetime) and Letitia Elizabeth Landon ("L. E. L.," whose astonishing literary output earned her a fortune). Furthermore, it is instructive to note that just as many of these women poets read, learned from, and responded in their own poems to their male contemporaries (both Hemans and Landon, for example, engaged Byron), so too did those male poets clearly read, learn from, and respond in *their* poems to the women poets (Byron engaged both Hemans and Landon).

The literary community of the Romantic period in England was in fact precisely that: a *community,* and the works that emanated from it were often characterized by a complex and sophisticated intertextuality that was apparent to contemporary readers. Moreover, while gender undeniably played a considerable part in the literary and cultural politics of the period, it is an error to assume, as has often been done, that the activities of men and women were therefore wholly delineated and separated on the basis of notions about the "separate spheres" that have become commonplaces in twentieth-century criticism and theory.[4] For the truth is much more complicated than any such simplistic gender casting suggests. Indeed, more recent scholarship has suggested that instead of separate spheres there were in fact both overlapping and competing (or alternative) spheres, and that a good deal of discursive ground was actually defined by the no-person's-land that lay within the intersections and interstices among these variously configured spheres.[5] Leonore Davidoff has suggested (239), and Anne Mellor has reiterated, that the explanation of the rise and dynamic of the later eighteenth-century "public sphere" that has been proposed particularly in Jürgen Habermas's influential work presumes a consistently "masculine" and masculinist construction of both the private individual and the public agent. Such a proposition misreads historical reality, though, for the very reason Mellor states: it erases the fact that "women writers participated in the *same* discursive public sphere and in the *same* formation of public opinion as did their male peers" (*Mothers of the Nation*, 2–3).[6]

As is apparent both from its often conspicuous rhetorical "signs" and from the evidence of its deliberate intertextuality, women's published writing of the Romantic period in England was for the most part a designedly self-reflexive part of a *public* conversation carried on in print concerning issues of real national cultural, intellectual, political, and moral significance. "[I]nsofar as they represented the interests of women, children, and the family," Mellor writes, "they also saw themselves as particularly *responsible* for defining the future direction of public policy and social reform." In their public discourse, Mellor continues, women writers "asserted both the right and the duty of women to speak *for* the nation" (*Mothers of the Nation*, 9). But it is important to note further that they took it also as a right and a responsibility to speak *to* that nation, as Anna Letitia Barbauld did in 1793 when she published *Sins of Government, Sins of the Nation,* signing herself "A Volunteer." Although nineteenth-century women writers were increasingly constrained by the expectation that they should "civilize" a "fractious citizenry" by providing both models and exhortations of harmony, tranquility, and feminine submissiveness, according to Marlon Ross, this was much less the case during the early part of the Romantic era (192). By the end of the eighteenth century, women poets like Hannah More and Anna Letitia Barbauld, Anna Seward and her bête noir Charlotte Smith, Mary Robinson and Amelia Opie were taking an active role in a very public discourse on matters of genuine social, political, and economic importance, and their activity was in fact welcomed in many quarters. As Paula R. Backscheider observes, activist women poets "had become a deliberative body, a group that perceived in their writing, and were perceived themselves, as having a right to intervene in national life and its debates" (*Eighteenth-Century Women Poets*, 8).

Although it may have been largely invisible to much of twentieth-century scholarship, the intertextuality of women's writing during the Romantic era was in fact often noted, remarked, and appreciated within the period—as a survey of contemporary critical reviews reveals. Partly because charges of plagiarism and derivativeness played a large part in the politics of Romantic-era reviewing, authorial prefaces to volumes of poetry frequently contain the poet's apparently ingenuous declaration that she or he had not *intentionally* quoted, paraphrased, or otherwise appropriated the work of a contemporary or precursor without acknowledgment. In his preface to *Prometheus Unbound,* for example, Percy Bysshe Shelley famously made the argument to which many of his contemporaries undoubtedly subscribed: that in an era of seemingly universal composition, unintended similarities and unremarked influences are inevitable:

> It is impossible that any one who inhabits the same age as such writers as those who stand in the foremost ranks of our own, can conscientiously assure himself that his language and tone of thought may not have been modified by the study of the productions of those extraordinary intellects. It is true, that, not the spirit of their genius, but the forms in which it has manifested itself, are due less to the peculiarities of their own minds than to the peculiarity of the moral and intellectual condition of the minds among which they have been produced. Thus a number of writers possess the form, whilst they want the spirit of those whom, it is alleged, they imitate; because the former is the endowment of the age in which they live, and the latter must be the uncommunicated lightning of their own mind. (*Shelley's Poetry and Prose,* 207)

Less eloquently but perhaps more directly, the obscure Mrs. B. Finch had written in 1805, in the preface to her *Sonnets, and Other Poems:*

> I am not conscious of having been guilty of plagiarism, in any of my performances; tho' on this subject I speak cautiously, knowing how difficult it is for those who are much conversant with books, to steer clear of that error. Mr. [Richard Brinsley] Sheridan remarks, that "Faded ideas float in the fancy like half-forgotten dreams; and the imagination, in its fullest enjoyments, becomes suspicious of its offspring, and doubts whether it has created, or adopted." (vii–viii)

The point is the same in each case: within a dynamic literary community—whether one takes part in it via direct personal interaction or through a conversation mediated through printed texts—all participants tend to some extent to accumulate and to employ a common language and set of referents, and indeed a whole shared discourse field. Charlotte Smith's copious use of Shakespeare—whose words she reproduces but more often paraphrases or entirely recasts in her poetry and prose alike—demonstrates the freedom with which Romantic-era writers drew on the works of their predecessors and contemporaries, often without attribution, as part of their active engagement in this discourse field whose terms and dimensions they likewise expected their readers to appreciate.[7]

When he wrote his preface to *Prometheus Unbound,* Shelley was writing about what William Hazlitt would in 1825 call "the spirit of the age," in his long essay of

that name. But it is the elusive Mrs. Finch who supplies the detail that is of particular significance for this present book when she observes that opportunities for
unintended plagiarism are particularly numerous "for those who are much conver-
sant with books." Conventional literary criticism has always been fond of source
hunting, although what in our own time passes for objective scholarly inquiry into
"influence" (with or without anxiety) usually appeared during the Romantic period
in the form of far more hostile and ideologically motivated critical exposés bent on
defaming authors by revealing their intellectual and artistic (and therefore presumably also their moral and political) dishonesty. What Finch reminds us of, in her
preface, is the fact that the writers of the Romantic period did in fact read a great
deal, and not just the established, canonized works of their predecessors but also
the eminently *current* and therefore as yet uncanonized works of their immediate
contemporaries. Even canonical poets like Wordsworth did so, nor were they particularly shy about acknowledging the fact.[8]

Recognizing this frank acknowledgment of a writing *community* helps us to ap-
preciate why so many poems of this period explicitly engage *with other poems,* as well
as with their authors. For example, there is Martha Hanson's "Sonnet 40: To Mrs.
Charlotte Smith; Occasioned by Reading Her Very Pathetic and Beautiful Sonnets
'Written in the Church-Yard at Middleton' and, 'To Night'" in volume 1 of her
Sonnets, and Other Poems (100):

> A tear, if pitying Sympathy e'er shed
>> O'er suff'ring Excellence, 'tis due to thee;
>> Whose strains, each aching heart, from anguish free,
> Though Grief's dark tempest gathers round thy head.
> Yet as the Nightingale's, thy strains of grief
>> In notes of such soul-soothing sweetness flow,
>> That rapt, we listen to the tale of woe,
> Nor, lest we break thy music, bring relief.
> Oh! did I rove, like thee, among the flow'rs
>> Cultur'd by Poesy with tender hand,
>> To crown thy temples, I would weave a band,
> Whose buds, with Fascination's magick pow'rs,
> Should like thy lays, a lenient charm impart,
> And sooth [sic], to sweet Tranquillity, thy Heart.

Especially—but not exclusively—in sonnets of sensibility we find the authors engaging explicitly in community building, as Hanson does here. The precursor poet
supplies a stimulus in the form of a poem, a document that is rendered "public"

by virtue of its formal "public-ation." That poem, in turn, provides the medium for a transaction that links the successor poet (and her personal experience) with the precursor poet (and *her*) experience. But the successor's *poem* is also tied to the precursor's poem(s) through a complex act of community that involves, first, the private act of reading that enables Hanson to establish her own personal empathetic bonds with Smith, second, the likewise private act of poetic composition by which she gives physical *and aesthetic* form to her emotional and intellectual responses, and, third, the public act of publication through which she submits the record of her own transaction with Smith's sonnet (and experiences) to other readers. Of course, Hanson's overt signaling of her (and her poem's) relation to Smith (and *her* poems) invites readers to recognize their own comparable responses to these several poems and to the records of human experience that are given aesthetic form in them.

This pattern of overt reference is repeated in many ways throughout the Romantic period, sometimes through direct reference (either in the main text or in the accompanying apparatus) to names, titles, incidents, characters, and so forth and sometimes through more complex means. Shelley and Byron, for instance, carried on an intellectual and artistic conversation in their published works, in which it is possible to read, on one level at least, each poet's deliberate and systematic response to the other.[9] That Shelley, in particular, made such intertextual references to Byron, his works and ideas, a feature of his poems indicates his confidence that substantial numbers of his readers knew their Byron well enough to appreciate the intellectual substance—and not just the fact—of those references. Evidence of widespread intertextuality abounds in the works of others, of course, in the form of both semicovert allusions and the more obvious ones signaled especially in titles that refer to specific works and authors (like Hanson's poem that alludes to Smith's sonnets or verse letters that identify both parties in the correspondence). Indeed, in the early portion of the period, Smith's *Elegiac Sonnets* themselves often function as contextual, experiential markers in the poems written by other women in particular. Such works engaged in intellectual and aesthetic "conversation" with other poems and, indeed, with other artifacts of their culture that were not properly "literary" but nevertheless served as "texts" in the broader sense in which Roland Barthes (in "From Work to Text") and others understand them.

Moreover, because so much of it appeared routinely in the daily and periodical press, dozens of which publications routinely printed both poetry and short fiction, it is safe to conclude that poetry was both widely read and widely known among its public readerships. All but one of the poems contained in Southey's *Metrical Tales* (1805), for instance, had already appeared previously in the *Morning Post*, Mary Robinson's poems in the periodical press are "literally countless (uncountable because they are so widely disseminated under multiple pseudonyms)," and the number of Landon's poems that appeared without attribution (and have more often than not remained so) in periodicals and annuals is very large.[10] The visibility and prominence that poetry enjoyed within this widely disseminated and accessible public medium of print lent it a cultural centrality—as well as a currency in public discourse—that it has not enjoyed for nearly two centuries in the wake of the subsequent academic sequestering of poetry that has largely removed it from contemporary public awareness—and consequently has prevented it from having genuine public impact or influence. When it comes to poetry's place in the cultural mainstream today, as opposed to two centuries ago, Backscheider puts the case succinctly: "Few of us would read poetry as a means of social advancement, as a source of news, or as mass entertainment, but eighteenth-century people increasingly did" (*Eighteenth-Century Women Poets,* 9). That this is so is evident from the spectacular productivity of poets of all stamps of genius (or foolishness) whose output over the course of some sixty years (1770–1830) numbers to well over ten thousand *volumes,* even by conservative estimates.[11]

The plain fact is that it was a poetry-mad era, what Stuart Curran has called "one of the greatest ages for poetry in the nation's history," a period of conspicuous consumption in which seemingly everyone could participate both as consumer and creator. One result was an extraordinary range of aesthetic quality in poetry that ranged from the splendid to the truly wretched. "Like most passion," Curran continues, "that for poetry was oblivious to common sense, even perhaps transcendentally so." Indeed, in discussing Francis Hodgson's 1818 satirical rejoinder to canto 4 of Byron's *Childe Harold's Pilgrimage* (1818), *Childe Harold's Monitor,* Curran observes that "Hodgson's vision of a democratic melee of poets, rushing to the marketplace in search of the fame and fortune to be accorded by an ever-expanding publishing industry, testifies to a wholesale shift in cultural values" (*Poetic Form,* 15–17).[12] This shift had as much to do with the economics of literary production—for authors, publishers, and consumers—as it did with taste and aesthetics. The extraordinary literary response to Byron's works (especially *Childe Harold's Pilgrimage* and *Don Juan*), like that to Smith's *Elegiac Sonnets* earlier in the period, eloquently testifies to the conspicuous intertextuality that figured especially large in Romantic-era writing and that subsequently became largely invisible to nearly two centuries of literary history (and its associated scholarship) that was content to accept the simple—and wholly inaccurate—picture of "British Romanticism" represented by the names, lives, and works of the five or six canonical male poets. Far more than it is at the dawn of the twenty-first century, poetry was at the end of the eighteenth century and the beginning of the nineteenth a dynamic literary form whose targets could legitimately be said to include both an emerging "mass audience" and an array of more specialized, select, and often elite readerships.

The picture of a largely anarchic literary marketplace that appears in Hodgson's poem is not wholly inaccurate, however. Both writing and publishing experienced a remarkable explosion during this period, when the cost of producing books began to decline—especially after the paper shortages of the late 1790s—at the same time that literacy was increasing exponentially among a broad range of previously nonreading publics. These new readerships represented both the evolving cultural preferences (and assumptions) and the literary (and artistic) tastes of the emerging middle classes as well as the entirely democratic entrepreneurial impulses that motivated individual authors to enter the public sphere themselves. In terms of women's writing, one result was a proportionate increase in works actually written by laboring-class authors. The examples of Anne Yearsley ("Lactilla, the Poetical Milkwoman") and Janet Little ("the Scotch Milkmaid") are well known. Less well known are poets like Elizabeth Hands ("born in obscurity and never emerging beyond the lower stations in life," according to the preface to her *The Death of Amnon* [1789]), Christian Milne (the ship's carpenter's wife who published *Simple Poems on Simple Subjects* [1805] to raise a sum as a hedge against impoverishment should she be widowed), Ellen Taylor (the indigent Irish cottager and teacher, author of *Poems* [1792]), and Charlotte Richardson (the shoemaker's widow and schoolteacher who was befriended by Mrs. Newcome Cappé, with whose assistance she published *Poems Written on Different Occasions* [1806]).

Publication—including self-publication—as an avenue to both public notice and public influence was a strong attraction to two generations of Romantic poets who apparently found a ready audience (or, more properly, a multiplicity of audiences) for their verse. But this very productivity—some might say profligacy, as contemporary critics often did—and the associated plethora of venues for publication combined to doom many of these poets to obscurity, if only by virtue of the sheer numbers involved. That more than ten thousand volumes of poetry were published during the period makes it all the more remarkable that unostentatious little collections like *Lyrical Ballads* (which went practically unremarked in 1798) found their way into the canon while best sellers like *Marmion* later gradually dropped out of that canon, eclipsed by the greater (or at least hotter) sun of Byron's poems. Meanwhile, the spectacular success (and influence) of Smith's *Elegiac Sonnets* faded with her death in 1806, while the subsequent runaway successes of Hemans and Landon were elided by a gendered literary-historical establishment that lauded what it perceived as the delicate femininity of their works and then first minimized and next excluded those works (and their authors) for being precisely what that establishment had impercipiently branded them. The democracy of the literary marketplace that had given women their public poetic voices over the course of the eighteenth century turned against them in the new exclusionist, masculinist marketplace of the capitalist nineteenth century, taking away that voice when it could no longer either suppress it or misrepresent it. In any literary culture, the bottom line among writers who must publish to support themselves is always "what will sell." Moreover, as our own contemporary culture continues to remind us, commercial success is often regarded as something that both taints and trivializes the efforts of more privileged writers who fancy themselves superior to those who need to make a living by the pen. How effectively women were able to negotiate the treacherous ground on which their often precarious circumstances placed them—what Wolfson calls the "hot zone"—frequently determined their contemporary success or failure. Either way, not a few of them rued (sometimes in print) the decisions that were forced on them by these circumstances, decisions that often entailed compromising both their convictions and their art in the interest of readerly approbation and commercial success.

In her assessment of Felicia Hemans's career, Susan Wolfson offers a good example of the dynamics of this sort of exercise in navigation. Both Francis Jeffrey and Frederic Rowton, Wolfson reminds us, regularly damned Hemans with faint praise, as when in 1853 Rowton described "the delicacy, the softness, the pureness, the quick observant vision, the ready sensibility, the devotedness, the faith of woman's nature" that found in Hemans "their ultra representative" (386). Jeffrey had earlier encouraged Hemans to stick to women's "proper and natural business," which for Jeffrey was "private life." When she chose to do so her male commentators were effusive in praising her; when she explored and contested assumptions about women's life and experience, as she did in *Records of Woman* (1828), they fumed and fulminated. Wolfson's point is that "nineteenth-century honors to Hemans as 'most feminine' always imply a double negative . . . [according to which] what Hemans was 'not' was an unfilial, defiant, denatured, Amazonian, unpatriotic, immodest spawn of Wollstonecraft" (introduction, xx). Hemans herself admitted ruefully, late in her life, that she regretted what it had cost her as an artist to have invested so much time and effort in what she regarded as essentially "popular" works: shortly before her death she wrote, "My wish ever was to concentrate all my mental energy in the production of some more noble and complete work."[13] Hemans's comment, which undoubtedly expressed what many of her sister poets felt as well, suggests why it is so important for us to today to reassess their poetry within the context of the historical and cultural circumstances in which it was composed, published, and read.

Another complicating factor in the picture of Romanticism in Britain that solidified during the twentieth century becomes apparent when we consider that several of the period's women poets were also novelists, something that cannot be said about the familiar canonical male poets (although Shelley did try his hand at the genre, as did "the Ettrick Shepherd" James Hogg and of course Scott). Indeed, Robinson and Smith were commercially successful novelists who supported themselves and their dependents through their writing, a fact that was widely known among their readers (in fact, Smith mounted a considerable publicity campaign—especially in her prefaces—to call attention to her straitened circumstances), while Landon established her literary credentials early on with *The Improvisatrice* (1824) and secured them with her novel *Ethel Churchill* (1837). Amelia Opie published both poetry and fiction but attained her greatest fame in the latter genre, though she returned to poetry for her abolitionist poems, *The Negro Boy's Tale* (1824), and, after she became a Quaker, for both *How to Make Sugar* (1826) and her elegiac *Lays for the Dead* (1834). The Sheffield writer Barbara Hofland, who published nearly seventy books, mostly of fiction, that are usually (and probably inaccurately) described as predominantly "children's books," began her publishing career in 1805 with a volume of poems. The most obvious *male* poet to have accomplished a comparable feat is Sir Walter Scott, who largely abandoned poetry once the great popular success of poetic efforts like his *Lay of the Last Minstrel* (1805) and *Marmion* (1808) was eclipsed by the sensational public response to Byron's *Childe Harold's Pilgrimage* and subsequent poems. In the face of this clearly insurmountable poetic rival, Scott turned to the hugely successful series of novels for which he is now better remembered—and that he initially published, with considered determination, *anonymously.*

Just as the literary activity of the Romantic women poets (and writers in other genres) complicates our received notions about British Romanticism, so too does the situation of Scott, whose stock has declined so dramatically in our own times that he is seldom included in any but the most limited fashion (if at all) in academic courses (and the associated textbooks) devoted to that period of British literature. In this he shares the fate both of many of his fellow Scots (including Scottish women poets) and of their contemporaries in Ireland, whose works are typically absent from academic courses (and textbooks) ostensibly dedicated to "British" literature. This routine exclusion of much—if not all—literature not just by women poets but also by *Scottish* or *Irish* women poets is the primary reason I have devoted two chapters of this book to their works.

An author's selection of literary genre has of course historically been tied to gendered notions about the literary forms peculiarly appropriate to men and women and about the achievements of which each might be capable within them. Gendered assumptions of this sort—which had been culturally conditioned by custom within a literary marketplace increasingly dominated in the nineteenth century by a male (and masculinist) economic, social, and political establishment—are disturbingly apparent in the pointed rhetoric of Jane Williams's chapter on "the Poetesses" in her midcentury (and therefore largely retrospective) review of Romantic women writers, *Literary Women of England:*

> In poetry may be perceived the peculiar character of the author, the principles by which he is actuated, the habits of his daily life, the knowledge which he possesses, the thoughts which direct, and the feelings which agitate him; the social spirit of the age, and its influence upon his ideas, and upon their mode of expression. . . . The women of every age take its spirit from the men, and their share in the national poetry is like their part in a concert, to which men's voices give fulness and power, and of which men are the musical composers and directors. (141–42)

Not only are the efforts of women poets (and presumably women in general) secondary at best, according to the clear implication of Williams's logic, but those works must inevitably reflect the identities and perceptions of the masculinist establishment rather those of their authors. The men compose and direct (musical activities that are less flexible and more prescriptive than "conduct") what women perform, and the men's voices supply "fulness and power" in these performances. Women's contribution is largely light and decorative apparently, not substantial or substantive. Furthermore, because according to Williams poetry reveals an author's aggregate character (including the author's habits, knowledge, thoughts, and feelings), then the poetry of *women*—who "take its [the age's] spirit from the men"—must itself inevitably reveal the character not of the women themselves *but rather of the men* who "compose" and "direct" both their creative work and the women themselves. It is not a pretty picture, but it is one that was both common and pervasive already in the middle of the nineteenth century, when Mary Shelley was only recently dead and the age's two most celebrated "poetesses," Hemans and Landon, lay less than a generation in the past.

In rhetoric of this sort it becomes easy to see why Romantic poetry has historically been viewed as a male province. Women who sought to work in the more formal and esoteric genres traditionally associated with male poetry (e.g., the ode, the elegy, the epic) were often met with hostility, as was famously (but certainly not exclusively) demonstrated by Richard Polwhele's *The Unsex'd Females.* Polwhele had already in 1788 decried the "contempt of the domestic duties" that struck him as "the prevailing vice of our modern women" ("On the Dissipation of Fashionable Women," *Discourses,* 2:90). For Polwhele and others, women's increasing visibility as serious writers at the end of the eighteenth century could be construed—and denounced—as an assault on the family (and by extension the nation) and especially on a home-centered construct of the feminine that everywhere defers to male pre-rogative and male expertise. Given the volatile political climate of the revolutionary 1790s, the perceived antiestablishment perversity of the politics embraced by many literary women was easily linked to assumptions about gender perversity.[14] What is "unnatural" is not so much the *content* of women's writing as *the gesture itself:* the public-ation of the otherwise cloistered female voice.

It was expected that, if they chose to write poetry at all, women poets should confine themselves to the lyric and the sentimental modes, so that when Anna Le-titia Barbauld published her gloomy picture of England's future, *Eighteen Hundred and Eleven,* the negative critical response was ostensibly mounted as much on gen-dered principles of poetic decorum as on the poem's politically unpopular stance. Hemans was one of the first to appreciate how the marriage of sophisticated formal poetic *craft* and culturally sanctioned subject matter might produce a poetry that defied complaints about the "unnaturalness" of women's writing like those voiced by Polwhele. Hemans's early work participated almost from the first in a new (and ultimately troubling) sort of poetry that had, finally, to be "contained" by means of the sort of enforced gender stereotyping we see in the "critical" writing of male reviewers like Rowton and his ilk.

In fact, the Romantic-era male critical establishment was for the most part sim-ply incapable of treating women's writing in what today we would think of as a fair-minded fashion, and this was true often from sheer force of mental habit rather than from deliberate malevolence. Because women were routinely excluded from formal education, for instance, many male critics assumed that they were therefore incapable of writing in informed fashion on "intellectual" subjects, including not just philosophy and history but also politics, economics, and science. For women to publish on these subjects seemed to such critics a violation not just of decorum but also of nature: without rigorous formal experience in empirical reasoning, of which many eighteenth-century men believed women were not just temperamentally but *constitutionally* incapable, they could have nothing of value to say. To speak (or write) was therefore both improper and unnatural. This is why Romantic-era critical discussion of women's "learning"—especially as it applies to the more sophisticated forms of poetry—necessarily involves a larger ideological argument about women's education that reveals the widespread anxiety among the male literary and critical establishment over the possibility that such education might open up avenues for incursion into traditional bastions of male prerogative—including "serious" poetry. The assumption was that women should write about "what they knew," which implied that their writing must inevitably be essentially autobiographical (and "his-

torical," in Aristotelian terms) in nature, while men's writing was "naturally" imaginative (and "poetic," in Aristotelian terms).

To see how this sort of gendered thinking functioned in practice, we can consider the review of Hemans's *The Restoration of the Works of Art to Italy* and *The
Sceptic* that appeared in the *British Review* in 1820, which reflects assumptions about
women poets and their works that had been bandied about in the public press for
the preceding several decades. Of Hemans's poems, the reviewer writes:

> We know not whether the Authoress of these Poems will consider it a compli-
> ment, or otherwise, when we state that in examining her "Modern Greece" for
> review (see our work for August, 1817) . . . we conceived it to be the production of
> an academical, and certainly not a female, pen. It is not to disparage either sex to
> say that as they usually live in different worlds, so they must naturally write in dif-
> ferent styles. . . . From being early and deeply imbued with the elegant literature
> of Greece and Rome, the poetry of men of education, even when it does not rise
> much above mediocrity in other respects, often evinces an elaborate finish which
> does not usually fall to the lot of female writers. . . . [W]e have been surprised to
> observe how few female poets adorn our national collections, and how little really
> first rate versification has come from a quarter so fertile in other fruits of elegant
> literature, especially fictitious narrative.[15]

The full extent of the reviewer's bias becomes apparent when he reverts to the conventional gendered notions of intelligence, education, and feeling or sensibility:

> We might perhaps add . . . that the mind of women is not usually favourable to
> that deep-toned emotion which constitutes the very essence of the higher kinds of
> poetry. Tenderness, which is a very necessary quality of poetry, will not of course
> be denied to that sex, one of whose characteristic epithets, in common parlance,
> is that of "tender;" but poetry is in truth a thing of study; strong feeling is indeed
> necessary to its perfection; but it is the feeling of *a spectator* rather than of *a suf-
> ferer*. Those who feel most acutely, are least able to analyse their sensations; nor are
> the ladies usually in the habit of examining so closely into the springs of human
> emotion as to touch them at their pleasure. (300)

In other words, it is his opinion that a woman is governed principally by feeling rather than discrimination—by heart rather than head, sensibility rather than
sense—and that she can therefore write only what she feels, unlike the male writer
who is implicitly credited in this formulation with both a more comprehensive
imagination and an exemplary emotional detachment.

This review reflects a gendered stereotype of the poet (male and female alike) and denigrates that sort of poetry whose objective and aesthetic differs from that which the critic associates with the dominant poetic patriarchy represented in the educated, leisure-class male poet. By the middle of the Regency the emerging bourgeois culture was visibly reinforcing the gendered expectations about male and female writers and their themes, subjects, and even poetic forms. In the opinion of the *Quarterly Review,* for instance, women's appropriate province is obvious:

> Delicacy of feeling has long been, *and long may it be,* the fair and valued boast of our countrywomen; but we have had too frequent reason of late to lament, both in female readers and writers, the display of qualities very opposite in their nature. Their tastes, at least, have not escaped the infection of that pretended liberality, but real licentiousness of thought, the plague and the fearful sign of the times. Under its influence they lose their relish for what is *simple and sober, gentle or dignified,* and require the stimulus of excessive or bitter passion, of sedition, of audacious profaneness.[16]

The manner in which the conservative *Quarterly* melds social politics with gender politics anticipates the smug security with which Frederic Rowton some thirty years later ticks off "the delicacy, the softness, the pureness, the quick observant vision, the ready sensibility, the devotedness, the faith of woman's nature" as those qualities that in his opinion find "their ultra representative" in Hemans, whose works he characterizes as "a perfect embodiment of woman's soul" (386).

What They Knew and What We Forgot

Sweet songstress! whom the melancholy Muse
    With more than fondness loved, for thee she strung
    The lyre, on which herself enraptured hung,
And bade thee through the world its sweets diffuse.
Oft hath my childhood's tributary tear
    Paid homage to the sad harmonious strain,
    That told, alas! too true, the grief and pain
Which thy afflicted mind was doom'd to bear.
    Rest, sainted spirit! from a life of woe,
    And though no friendly hand on thee bestow
The stately marble, or emblazon'd name,
    To tell a thoughtless world who sleeps below:
    Yet o'er thy narrow bed a wreath shall blow,
Deriving vigour from the breath of fame!

So wrote Thomas Gent in a poem that first appeared in 1808 in the second edition of his *Poetic Sketches.*[17] Gent's poem was one among many memorials to Smith, whose death in 1806 did not reduce her impact on British poetry; indeed, her influence may be traced in the literary record of the entire Romantic period.

A quarter of a century later, in 1833, Wordsworth penned his memorable judgment that Charlotte Smith was "a lady to whom English verse is under greater obligations than are likely to be either acknowledged or remembered" (note to "Stanzas Suggested in a Steamboat off Saint Bees' Heads," *Poetical Works,* 4:399). Meanwhile, in 1826 the *Monthly Magazine* concluded its review of Louisa Stuart Costello's new collection, *Songs of a Stranger* (1825), by observing that

> It has lately been said, that since the death of Byron our poetry is at a low ebb. It is an error. Let us look at the band of women who still live, and write, and reflect honour on our age, and prove its intellectual refinement. Their names must grace our pages: Joanna Baillie—Dacre—Fanshawe—Hemans—Mitford—Costello. The authoress of "The Veils" [Emily Porden] and that *splendid epic,* "*Cœur de Lion,*" has only lately winged her way to a higher world. Miss Porden's epic has been neglected. Every noble whose ancestors fought in the Holy Land is bound in honour to see their deeds recorded; and when they have been nobly sung by a woman, let chivalry save her poetry from perishing unnoticed and unknown.[18]

Charlotte Smith was not the only woman poet, then, to whom English verse was, as Wordsworth put it, "indebted." There were more, many more.

Even so, women's poetry was often treated with condescension, as it was by the Rev. Alexander Dyce, in his 1825 *Specimens of British Poetesses.* Dyce observed that women's relatively low visibility as poets owed much to "their concealment in obscure publications," by which he meant both "minor" books and the literary market represented especially by those recent innovations, the literary annual and the nonce anthology. But like the reviewer for the *British Review* whose remarks on Felicia Hemans were clearly intended as applicable to women poets generally, Dyce assesses women's literary production along conventionally gendered lines. He remarks that

> the grander inspirations of the Muse have not been often breathed into the softer frame. The magic tones which have added a new existence to the heart—the tremendous thoughts which have impressed a successive stamp on the fluctuation of ages, and which have almost changed the character of nations,—these have not proceeded from woman; but her sensibility, her tenderness, her grace, have not been lost nor misemployed: her genius has gradually risen with the opportunities which facilitated its ascent. (iii–iv)

Literary anthologies published on both sides of the Atlantic during the remainder of the nineteenth century regularly included the poetry of British women, but that poetry invariably was bracketed by gender-inflected editorial comments like those of Dyce or, later, the notorious Frederic Rowton.[19]

A different sort of editorial bracketing that is morally exhortatory in nature is represented by comments like those of the American Sarah Josepha (Buell) Hale, who opened the preface to her *Ladies' Wreath* (1837) with the declaration that "the office of Poetry is to elevate, purify, and soften the human character; and thus promote civil, moral, and religious advancement." The particular talent of women poets, according to Hale, lies in their unique ability to "reveal the glories and mysteries of Nature, and teach that 'true self love and social are the same;' that there is no pursuit really noble and good, that does not aim to promote the good of others, and no dignity and purity in man, that is not derived from his spiritual likeness to his Saviour. In this, the best and most exalted office of the muse, woman is *morally gifted* to excel" (3–4; Hale's emphasis). Hale's nod to the concept of separate spheres notwithstanding, however, her insistence that selflessly promoting the good of others is a leading characteristic of women's poetry constitutes her recognition of the heightened cultural valuation of the human *community*—and the salutary and even redemptive nature of community building—that is the hallmark of the Romantic enterprise in Britain. Indeed, Hale's rhetoric clearly implies that women are uniquely suited to do this work that men are unable (or unwilling) to accomplish. This constitutional suitability, significantly, she attaches explicitly to women's particular moral gift.

When I began to think about this book I had in mind a broad study of the dynamics of literary and cultural marginalization during the Romantic period in England. But thinking about the phenomenon of periodization reminded me that the customary dating of the Romantic "period" in England itself reveals both a historico-critical methodology and a literary-cultural paradigm that have been profoundly influenced by the traditional canonical authors, by the ideas embodied in their works, by their influence (or conspicuous lack of it) on their times, and by an inherited, hierarchical, and historically masculinist academic cultural establishment. The critical, intellectual, and ideological values and procedures of this male-oriented cultural establishment have in turn historically reflected an array of gender- and class-based assumptions that went largely unquestioned for the better part of two centuries and that informed both intellectual *and aesthetic* judgments about Romantic-era authors for much of that same period. Paula Feldman remarks that virtually every Romantic-era woman poet had to deal with "a personal struggle with patriarchal constraints," which required her to negotiate a cultural environment in which "artistic expectations were highly gendered" (introduction, xxviii). That so many women poets nevertheless effectively challenged these expectations in works that were widely read, and whose influence can often be judged from the stridency with which they were attacked in the press, reminds us again of their historical presence not at the periphery of literary culture but rather—and for most of the Romantic era, too—at its center.

The reason why it remains so difficult to achieve any sort of consensus—however tentative—about British Romanticism's historical and chronological parameters, even today, is tied to an aspect of Romantic culture that remains curiously under-explored: its participants' pervasive awareness of the period as one of *transition.* At few other moments in Western history have the players in the cultural and social scenes (and in the politics that drive both) been so acutely conscious as they were during the Romantic era of how rapidly *and irreversibly* things were changing. The beheading of Louis XVI, in its terrible finality, epitomizes in many ways the profound changes that were transpiring not just in the political order but also in social, cultural, intellectual, and artistic institutions generally. Again and again, literary works call their readers' attention to paradises lost, found, or imminent—to the past or the future—at the same time that they remind them of the extraordinarily fluid nature of the present moment and of the impossibility of going back to some prior state whose features have been erased both by industrialization and urbanization and by a parallel psychological and spiritual alienation. Thomas Wolfe declared in 1940 that "You Can't Go Home Again," but Letitia Elizabeth Landon had made the point with devastating effectiveness already in 1824:

> I left my home;—'twas in a little vale,
> Sheltered from snow-storms by the stately pines;
> > . . . Years past by,
> But still that vale in silent beauty dwelt
> Within my memory. Home I came at last.
> I stood upon a mountain height, and looked
> Into the vale below; and smoke arose,
> And heavy sounds; and through the thick dim air
> Shot blackened turrets, and brick walls, and roofs
> Of the red tile. I entered in the streets:
> There were ten thousand hurrying to and fro;
> And masted vessels stood upon the river,
> And barges sullied the once dew-clear stream.

Where were the willows, where the cottages?
I sought my home; I sought and found a city,
Alas! for the green valley!   ("Home," *The Improvisatrice,* 2:323–24)

Landon's language captures with remarkable clarity both the external facts and the internal realities of the changes that were transforming England. The edenic valley, "little" and "sheltered," is replaced during the poet's absence by the urban excrescence of crowds, noise, and the industrial pollution ("heavy sounds," "blackened," "sullied") that is a metaphor for the spiritual pollution of that fancied past that is irretrievably lost.

At the same time, the literature of the British Romantic era reflects an intense awareness of the *historicality* (or historicity) of the contemporary experience. We see it both in the self-reflexive monumentality of much of the writing (and the parallel explosion of monumental sculpture in public spaces) and in the expanded cultural consciousness—the increasingly cosmopolitan worldview—which that writing prescribes with increasing urgency to its readers as the key to survival and success in the emerging modern world. According to James Chandler, "much of Romantic 'literature' inclines to organize itself around the topics we have associated with historical specificity" (78). This impulse Chandler regards as particularly symptomatic of "the 'history-making' function of all cultural work" (93). The literature of the Romantic period is insistently about *becoming,* and that dynamic process of change (whether it be progress, regress, maturation, evolution, or whatever we choose to call it) dictates that author and reader alike recognize that every moment is both potentially and actually one of those "spots of time" of which William Wordsworth wrote. Moreover, within this paradigm, nothing stands still: at every moment something is being altered, lost, or forgotten. "It is not now as it has been of yore," Wordsworth wrote ruefully, for "there hath pass'd away a glory from the earth" ("Ode" [1807]). The cost of existence in such a world—in which humanity's innate bonds with nature and with the rest of humanity are increasingly subjected to stress, rupture, and alienation—is steep for everyone involved.

The challenge faced alike by Romantic-era writers and citizens had fundamentally to do with the strength and resilience of the human spirit, which, in a world of such volatility, was forced more and more to rely on the individual rather than the group, the private rather than the public, and the heart rather than the head. That quality of "individualism" which scholars used to regard unhesitatingly as Romanticism's definitive characteristic proves, on closer inspection, to be not a "rugged" individualism but rather a negotiated, mediated, and ultimately precarious one that places a writer—and her or his fundamental identity—at almost continual risk of exclusion, alienation, and annihilation. This theme appears again and again, both overtly and covertly, within the work of women and men alike and in both traditional canonical and extracanonical writing. For example, Mariann Dark included in her 1818 *Sonnets and Other Poems* two sonnets that dealt explicitly with Charlotte Smith. In the first, subtitled "On Reading Mrs. Smith's Sonnets," she recounts how reading Smith's account in those poems of her personal "woes / Warbled in melancholy's plaintive tone" enables Dark to "lose remembrance of mine own" (40, ll. 2–3). Discovering in Smith a kindred spirit both as woman and as poet, Dark continues, she herself "dar'd aspire to feelings such as thine" (41, l. 10) that she might in turn reasonably set out to embody in sonnets of her own.

The next sonnet, subtitled "On Reviewing the Preceding," however, reveals the chastening experience of rethinking the matter of ambition, fame, and ignominy. Not only does Dark brand as "presumptuous" the ambition from which her fanciful comparison had proceeded; she also recognizes that her own unnurtured and unappreciated talent—cultivated in private but seemingly rendered invisible within the public sphere—brings its own curse: "I strike the lyre unknown! My very name / Will soon be blotted from this wretched earth" (43, ll. 13–14). Her exclamation seems to acknowledge the psychological death that comes with doing the unthinkable, which insight provides a useful perspective on why so many Romantic-era male critics were simply incapable of opening themselves up to receiving a variety of poetic discourse for which neither their cultural institutions nor their personal circumstances had prepared them. Ironically, as happens so often in Romantic poetry, when it comes to expressing one's own silencing, one's inability to write meaningfully, that expression takes the form of a completed, published poem.

On the other hand, any lesser-known poet is always conscious of the daunting odds involved in competing with a better-known one, as Martha Hanson had already observed in one of the several sonnets that she addressed to Smith in her 1809 collection:

> Sweet Poetess! around thy honour'd brow,
>   A wreath of simple flow'rs, I fain would twine;
>   But when its blooms are intermix'd with thine,
> (Where Poesy's most cultur'd blossoms glow)
> To thee, its wild buds could no praise impart.   (1:112, ll. 9–13)

This anxiety about being not just eclipsed but annihilated in the inevitable comparison is, of course, a recurring theme in Romantic poetry; among the canonicals Shelley's worries about Byron, like Keats's about Shelley, testify to its pervasive nature, and the theme recurs among women poets writing in the presumed glow of more famous women like Smith, Mary Robinson, and, later, Letitia Elizabeth Landon and Felicia Hemans.

Neither Dark nor her contemporary John Keats, then, were the only poets who arrived at the sobering realization that to write, to speak, to live, was for the Romantic individual to render oneself especially subject to neglect and dissolution. Therefore the Romantic artist often proceeds ruefully, knowing that introducing into a literary work her or his own private thoughts, feelings, and person (or personhood) necessarily and inevitably subjects her or him to misunderstanding or hostility when the result is not simply neglect, something that the often resoundingly negative critical response to Smith's prefaces to her novels underscores. Alternatively, the artist may adopt the sort of defiant posture we associate most often with Byron, proclaiming with bravado (or at least appearing to do so) that she or he is wholly unconcerned with public response and that she or he will have a say come what may. Yet (as the example of Byron also reminds us), even the most defiant and seemingly nonchalant writer seldom proceeded without an eye focused on the bottom line—profit, whether of fortune or of reputation.

This defiant note, relatively uncommon among male poets, is even more rare among women. Martha Hanson, however, put the case plainly:

> To the favour of an English Publick, literally speaking, I well know it were vain to aspire. Britain, jealous of the exactitude with which her laws literary, as well as civil, are administered, recognises not her Writers, as worthy of regard, till long consigned to the silent tomb; when the voice of partiality, which might recommend to favour, is hushed; and Time returns his verdict of honour, for those, whose merit resists his noiseless, but conquering arm. . . . [W]hile memory recalls an Otway starving, a Collins dying in the most melancholy state of mental suffering, and a Chatterton reduced to the dreadful alternative of perishing from want, or shortening his existence, by an act of which the desperation freezes the blood with horrour; if I reflect, at the same time, on the brightness of genius, which characterizes their works . . . Reason tells me, the absurdity of expecting to obtain the suffrage of publick approbation. (ix–xi)

In other words, the poet had best admit that she writes for her own enjoyment—and perhaps that of her friends and acquaintances—because the living poet most often finds her work (or his) badgered rather than praised, even when it is offered to the public as a *gift:* "To apologize for offering the present work to the World, would be tacitly to say, I felt myself wrong in doing so; which as these Poems are only *offered* to its notice, not *obtruded,* on it, I do not conceive to be the case" (vii–viii; Hanson's emphases). Such authorial pluckishness is as rare as it is engaging.

And therein lies another of the difficulties involved in assessing (or reassessing) the literature of the Romantic period, both as it has historically been represented within the model associated with the educational academy (and the anthologies and critical discourse that support and reflect it) and as the very different entity that it actually was in its own time. Much of contemporary twenty-first century culture remains sentimentally fond of an ideal of the artist (in whatever medium) who proceeds with grit and determination, doggedly pursuing what Percy Bysshe Shelley called "beautiful idealisms" that entertain no compromise with the ordinary, the pedestrian, the commercial. "That which can be made Explicit to the Idiot is not worth my care," William Blake announced in a letter to the unappreciative Dr. Trusler in 1799, electing instead to devote himself to "What is Grand" because it "rouzes the faculties to act" (*Complete Poetry and Prose,* 702). The implication is that what is grand cannot be embodied in "lesser" forms, which is much the same point that Dyce makes a quarter century later (employing the same terminology) in his comments about why men—not women—are preeminent in literary production. The point involves not just gender, however, but also class and economic intention. "Art for profit," it seems, is tainted art—if it is art at all; we have invented subcategories like "commercial art" or "popular art" to document our modern squeamishness with artists whose financial success undermines our culturally conditioned sentimental visions of uncompromising starving artists. Yet the rapid growth of the publishing industry, together with the associated expansion of literacy, during the Romantic period made it increasingly possible for writers to support themselves through direct interaction with readerships willing to pay (whether directly or, more often, indirectly through institutions like circulating libraries) for access to their work and for the pleasure to be found there. More and more, knowing what would sell—and why—came to be as important to an author as possessing either innate brilliance or acquired skill. Audiences were also *markets,* and authors (and their publishers) grew increasingly skillful at assessing those markets and manipulating the forms and the content of their own literary efforts in order to maximize their effectiveness—and their sales. Especially in the cases of women authors like Charlotte Smith or Mary Robinson early in the period, who came to depend on the profits from their writing to support themselves and their families, this matter of commercial viability was of no small consequence.

It was equally consequential, later, for Felicia Hemans, whose success was the more remarkable because it came in poetry. Literary production was "a business proposition" for the professional woman writer, as Paula Feldman notes. Hemans routinely asked her publishers—John Murray (who had published Byron's *Childe Harold's Pilgrimage* after it had been turned down by Longman, Constable, and others) and later William Blackwood (who had begun publishing her poems in 1818)—for advice about subjects that would have greatest market appeal. Indeed, as Feldman says, Hemans's great success "owed much to her shrewd business acumen and her ability to use her poetic talents to create an appealing product for the marketplace" (The Poet and the Profits," 149, 176). But success in the broader market had its costs, too, as traditional literary history makes clear. The extraordinarily prolific and versatile Letitia Elizabeth Landon remains a vexed subject among academics who are put off by precisely the formulaic elements of her art and her aesthetics that made her a commercial success and a cultural influence. In reality, though, the persistent image of the defiant and fiercely independent Romantic writer (like Byron, whose relative financial stability freed him from any need to "satisfy" his readers) represents the exception to the rule. In practice, as William St. Clair has demonstrated, "most authors were obliged to operate within a commercial system in which they, their advisers, and their publishers attempted to judge what the market wanted and how best to supply it" (161). The canonical writings of the British Romantic period represent an astonishingly *small* percentage of the period's total literary production, and yet they stood for well over a century both as a monument *and as a measure* by which other writings of the era were judged and, typically, found wanting. Why this was so, and how the situation has been modified in consequence of recent developments like the recovery of historically neglected or marginalized writers, forms part of the subject of this book.

The more I thought about the book I wanted to write, then, the more it became clear to me that the road lay through a literary and cultural landscape that is still being remapped in a number of important ways. Part of the challenge lies in the fact that this new map has not yet been completed—nor is it likely to be in the near future. This is so in part because there remain so many writers whose works need first to be recovered and reassessed on their own merits. One important step has already been taken by Paula R. Backscheider, whose extraordinary study of eighteenth-century women poets offers both a paradigm for, and a lesson in, one way in which such a revisionist examination might proceed. Backscheider examines her poets especially in terms of forms and genres, considering how and why women poets during the century preceding Romanticism chose the particular forms they did for their poems. At the same time, she considers both the designedly public pieces (like poems on public occasions and long verse narratives intended for general audiences) and the intentionally semiprivate ones (like verse correspondence and friendship poetry), both of which assume audiences of intended recipients that their poets specifically envision. In the process, she also begins for eighteenth-century women poets a significant reassessment of aesthetics that is instructive also for their Romantic successors.

Any informed reassessment of both the recovered *and the canonical* authors of the Romantic era requires of us a fuller appreciation of the full range of Romantic-era writing in all the literary and extraliterary genres. This reassessment needs to jettison the unreliable and increasingly contested standard(s) that are themselves predicated on the received judgments about a critically or ideologically filtered—and vastly restricted—subset of authors and works, whether we call it "the canon" or not. In the chapters that follow I try to open up the literary landscape by focusing on po-etry written by women in the British Isles during what I liberally demarcate as the Romantic era: c. 1770–1835. The terminal date is one of several, all from the 1830s, that are now frequently used for the period. The beginning date, which is a less conventional choice, is arguably on the early side, but I have selected it to include the early works of poets (like Mary Robinson, Anna Seward, and Eliza Ryves) who were already active before the more familiar starting dates in the 1780s.

Reimagining the British Romantic literary landscape means repopulating it with lives and works that have long been absent from conventional accounts. In a very real sense, they represent what might be called the *shades* of Romanticism, shades in the double senses of both "shadows" and "shadings" or hues. The shadows—the ghostly "visible but impalpable form[s] of . . . dead person[s]" (*OED*)—are those of the literally hundreds of women who wrote, published, and were discussed, both in the everyday discourse of the coffee house, the circulating library, the salon, and the street and in the more formal discourse of the reviewing press. Their works were emulated and contested, too, in the literary productions of their contemporaries, some of whose names and works are already familiar to us and some of whom com-prise an as yet relatively undiscovered country. It is possible to give greater form and substance to some of these shadows by revisiting their works, as I do here, making them "visible" again even when it is no longer possible to trace the details of their lives with the certainty we might wish.

It hardly needs restating at this late date that for most of the twentieth century literary historians routinely minimized the poetry of Romantic women poets (if they noted it at all), just as they did to a lesser extent that of male poets outside the familiar "Big Five" (or "Big Six"). Feldman writes that Romantic-era women "ap-peared in literary history as best as footnotes and at worst solely in familial relation to the 'major' male writers" (introduction, xxxii). Mary Tighe, for example, was often consigned to a footnote indicating the influence of her immensely popular *Psyche* (1805) on Keats and on works like his "The Eve of St. Agnes." As Harriet Kramer Linkin suggests, we need to investigate the "psychological and sociological aspect of criticism" that accounts for the troubling fact that for most of a century "the recognition of Keats's greatness required the disparagement of a poet like Tighe" ("Recuperating Romanticism," 146). Tighe's case is but one of many that one might cite in this respect. Observing the failure of women's poetry for the most part to conform fully and satisfactorily to the intellectual and aesthetic models represented in England by Wordsworth, Byron, and company, many literary historians deemed that "failure" to be *failure* in its other, wholly pejorative sense. Routinely relegating such poetry to secondary status at best at the dawn of the Information Age, they pursued a policy of streamlining and simplifying literary history from which would emerge a narrowly stereotypical—and significantly inaccurate—sketch that would come finally to be characterized as "the Romantic ideology."[20] Even now, the definite article "the" implies a monolithic construct that implicitly resists and excludes consideration of alterity—of "otherness"—and of diversity. Increasingly accustomed to the more "manageable" but artificially narrowed group of writers represented within this streamlined, mainstreamed, and profoundly male (and masculinist) canonical definition of Romantic poetry, literary historians, scholars, *and the students they trained* first passed over and then simply *forgot* this large and diverse body of poetry, which consequently fell into ever greater obscurity. Read less and less frequently, and typically dismissed as inferior when it was, it gradually disappeared from view.

This unfortunate history cannot be blamed simplistically on deliberate and malicious design by a coterie of misogynist male critics, however. True, the marginalization and subsequent exclusion of Romantic-era women poets owed much to a historical prejudice against women's efforts (and successes) in the public forum, whether in politics, education, or the arts. Richard Polwhele's 1798 *The Unsex'd Females* is a particularly notorious—though not atypical—contemporary example of a pointedly gendered attack on the (often effective) attempts of women writers to enter the public discourse on social, political, and economic topics traditionally reserved for men; William Gifford's *Baeviad* of the previous year offers another instance of this sort of attack. These critics typically grounded their argument on the notion of the "separate spheres" occupied by women and men, arguing that women's participation in the public sphere was inherently unnatural:

> Survey with me, what ne'er our fathers saw,
> A female band, despising NATURE's law,
> As "proud defiance" flashes from their arms,
> And vengeance smothers all their softer charms.
>   (*The Unsex'd Females,* ll. 11–14)[21]

Nor was this bias uncommon among the period's professional reviewers, whose responses tended to follow one or another of two distinctive tacks—outright renunciation or manipulative flattery—when they did not ignore women's writing entirely. Intolerant thinking of this sort was in fact endemic in later eighteenth-century Britain, and it reflects an intellectual and a moral conservatism that is the largely inevitable product of the culture's inherited notions of gender. That is, the intellectual and aesthetic structures for receiving and assessing poetry are inherited from the past, and like all inheritances they seem to the inheritors to be so wholly "natural" as to preclude questioning—much less revising.

The first type of critical reaction is typified by Polwhele's or Gifford's knee-jerk resistance; it takes the form of often withering reviews that not only castigate the writing itself in ostensibly objective critical terms but also engage in deliberate misrepresentation and defamation of the authors' characters, as happens in *The Unsex'd Females*. We glimpse a related, and common, version of this approach in the *Eclectic Review*'s comments about Mary Leadbeater's 1808 *Poems*. After reminding its readers that there are three strictly delimited levels of Parnassian poetry, the *Eclectic* accuses Leadbeater of "trespass" on "interdicted ground" in her poems. After quoting several passages from Leadbeater's occasional poems, the critic declares them to be "specimens of the middle order of poesy," remarking further that "[w]e may say of Mrs. L., what cannot be said of every modern poet, that she seldom sinks below the tame, insipid, and neutral style displayed in the above citations. Now and then, however, she does become very ridiculous."[22] In other words, while Leadbeater is not nearly so bad a poet as others, she is nevertheless "ridiculous," and in choosing that particular word the critic may well have been thinking of Henry Fielding's famous observation that "affectation appears to me the only true source of the ridiculous" (30).

The *Eclectic*'s reviewer appears subsequently to swerve in the direction of compliment when he announces that the poem "most deserving of attention" is Leadbeater's metrical version of her father's prose translation of the "thirteenth book" of the *Æneid*, composed by the fifteenth-century Christian humanist Maffeo Vegio (Mapheus Vegius) to describe Æneas's ultimate destiny.[23] But the seeming approbation quickly vanishes when he explains that what really matters is not Leadbeater's effort but rather the access that this effort has furnished to the otherwise little-known Latin text, which is printed side by side with Leadbeater's translation. Of Leadbeater's text, he says only that it "resembles the other compositions of Mrs. Leadbeater: it is void of spirit and elegance."[24] Interestingly, the *Critical Review* seized on the same poem as "the longest and worst of the poems in the present volume," although the reviewer quickly adds, with perverse wit, that the translation "is as good as the original deserves." The brief notice concludes with the sort of damning with faint praise that is so often the lot of the era's women poets: "The fair author certainly possesses considerable talents, which we are sorry to find she employs on subjects too trivial to be pursued by indifferent readers, and which claim attention only from those who have the pleasure of her intimate acquaintance."[25] Leadbeater's poems, the critic would have us agree, are dull, their language unsuitable, their subjects trivial, their intended audience inappropriate. Other than that, Leadbeater is a commendable poet. What makes Leadbeater (and others) "ridiculous," in all such formulations, is the "affectation" involved in presuming to join a community of discourse from which both cultural custom and institutional law seemed "naturally" to bar them. Occupying the ostensibly objective and therefore superior ground of the professional *critic,* the reviewer dismisses and excludes those works that deviate from the inherited aesthetic and ideology for which he speaks. Overwhelmingly, these works were by women and/or working-class writers; frequently they were both, and their exclusion exposes the habitual sexism and classism of much of traditional literary history and criticism.

The other variety of critical response, seemingly milder in manner but no less pernicious in effect, is visible in the many sugarcoated reviews that effusively praise an author for precisely those aspects of her work that embody the model of the subservient, sentimental, chaste and domestic woman who posed no threat to the masculinist status quo but instead largely affirmed it. Thus, as we have seen, the poetry of the enormously popular Felicia Hemans was presented in the mid-nineteenth century as the "ultra representative" of woman's soul, and women's writing was lauded for characteristics like tenderness or piety. Such commentary usually either misrepresented or ignored altogether those writers—including Hemans— and works that might seem to (and in fact often *did*) contest prevailing gendered attitudes, assumptions, and institutions.

The *Eclectic Review*'s 1813 response to the third edition of Tighe's *Psyche* offers a paradigmatic early illustration. Discussing the poem's Spenserian stanza format, the critic observes that

> Mrs. Tighe yields to none of her predecessors or contemporaries in general facility and felicity of handling this difficult measure. . . . Her diction is perfectly modern, yet highly poetical when the subject demands it. Her style is richly attired, and ordered with female taste and neatness. If her sentiments are sometimes too rapturously expressed, they are only alarming for a moment, and are softened away with such tenderness and modesty, that it would be more difficult for us to

establish a charge of indelicacy against her in any case, than to pass over unblamed the deliciousness of a few lines, escaping in reverie.[26]

Evident here is a familiar gendered aesthetic privileging in a *woman's* writing of "female taste and neatness," augmented by "tenderness and modesty," which are presented as characteristics that outweigh more empirically quantifiable aspects of the work. It is the absence of precisely these "female" characteristics, and the presence instead of openly contestatory social or political critique, that Polwhele and others take as evidence of what they most consider to be "unnatural" in women's poetry, whose subject matter their own cultural heritage conditions them to expect to be "delicate," not assertive.

At the same time, however, it is also reasonable—although perhaps less politically attractive—to attribute Romantic literary women's marginalization at least partly to a related phenomenon: to modernity's curious obsession with simplification, reduction, and compartmentalization, not just of knowledge or art but of human enterprise of whatever sort. Put simply, as the professional study of literature came ever more to reside within academic institutions, and in traditionally elite and male-dominated postsecondary ones (colleges and universities) especially, it seemed to many faculty that the range and scope of "British Romanticism" had to be reduced ever more in order to accommodate it to the time and space limits imposed by academic terms of study: by academic years, semesters, quarters, and so on. By the last third of the twentieth century, a "Romantic poetry" that tried to encompass not merely a "Big Five" (or six, including Blake) but also even so few as half a dozen other prolific contemporaries often proved too unwieldy for scholars, teachers, and students alike in an age of diminishing time, resources, and attention spans. The end result of all this reducing and homogenizing was of course a monodimensional "Romanticism" largely stripped of its diversity, its complications, and its complexity; the shortcomings of this simplifying are evident in electronic-age "resources" like the *Encarta Dictionary and Encyclopedia*'s definition of it.[27] The academic cultural establishment that had generated an almost exclusively male Romantic literary canon in the first place proceeded from a set of a priori cultural assumptions that privileged male authorship and male readership. This sort of circular reasoning dictated that when something had to be eliminated for the sake of exigency, what went was, of course, what that establishment regarded as the least important, the least necessary, to its own values and interests. Not surprisingly, this was the writing—and thus the literary voices—of women. Cultural entrenchment did not accommodate (or facilitate) change: it shut the door to it.

Recent scholarship is recovering the historical reality of a wide and diversified Romantic literary community. That community involves more than just numbers, however, which is why this book is also about "shadings" of Romanticism. That is, traditional conceptions of British Romantic literature historically revolved around two principal paradigms: the contemplative Wordsworthian poet of nature and nation and the defiant Byronic poet of worldliness and weltschmerz. The instant fame that attended the publication of the first cantos of *Childe Harold's Pilgrimage* established Byron as the preeminent poet of European Romanticism for most of the nineteenth century, while Wordsworth's more gradual accession to fame and influence justifiably enshrined him firmly within the evolving canon of British literature. Post-Romantic literary history arranged their contemporaries around them, in one way or another, not in the fashion of mere satellites but rather as "brother stars" whose light and heat may be perceived as related to one or the other of these models, sometimes in terms of similarities of form, content, or personal association (as Coleridge has been linked with Wordsworth and Shelley with Byron) and sometimes in terms of particularly striking differences (Keats, for instance).

Such formulations, which were produced almost exclusively by a male academic establishment, steeped in inherited gendered assumptions about writers and authorship, historically elided women (and their writing) from the picture. Not surprisingly, then, "feminist theory has exhibited sustained dislike for the romantic," according to Julie Ellison, who argues that, this antipathy notwithstanding, "feminism and romanticism share an anxiety about aggression and violence; a critique of authority; a commitment to the cognitive validity of feeling and atmosphere; an identification with the victim; an intrigue with the construction and deconstruction of subjectivity" (11). Pursuing this point, Anne Mellor some years ago proposed loosely categorizing the Romantics in terms of a masculine Romanticism and a feminine Romanticism. For Mellor, feminine Romanticism is "based on a subjectivity constructed in relation to other subjectivities, hence a self that is fluid, absorptive, responsive, with permeable ego boundaries," a self that "typically located its identity within a larger human nexus, a family or social community" (*Romanticism and Gender,* 209). The "masculine" and "feminine" poles, however, Mellor contends, "are finally not binary opposites but rather the endpoints on a continuum that ranges not only through the entire range of literary Romanticism but also through the corpus of individual writers" (11). The crucial distinction between these varieties of Romanticism hangs on the extent to which the writer (as thinker and therefore as philosopher) is committed to an essentially nurturant, humanitarian agenda whose central tenet is that no one should be injured, rather in the sense in which Sarah Josepha Hale suggested. The more prominent this communitarian view is in a writer's work, the more that work (and its author) may be designated as "feminine," regardless of the author's gender. Sorting writers in this fashion is interesting and often fruitful, to be sure, but the model remains largely binary and dialectical in nature: one belongs, more or less, to one category or the other, even when one is moving about on the gender continuum. Nevertheless, Mellor's formulation is especially valuable for its recognition that writers of both sexes clearly could—and did—frequently occupy the same discursive ground.

But the fact remains that alternative constellations of writers, however we choose to configure them, still populate only a part—and indeed a small part at that—of the starry sky of British poetry during the period. The groundbreaking work of scholars like Ellen Moers and Mary Poovey in Romantic fiction and Anne Mellor, Stuart Curran, Paula Feldman, and Susan Wolfson in Romantic poetry provided the initial impetus for the reassessment that has begun on both sides of the Atlantic.[28] Marlon B. Ross's important study of Romanticism and women's poetry, for example, applied the concept of "desire" (which, following Deleuze and Guattari, he sees as differing significantly between men and women) to account for what he regards as the particular historical and cultural circumstances that led women writers to place their own work (and the ideology that informed it) within self-restricting bounds that hindered their contemporaries and successors as much as (if not more than) it enabled them (see especially 6–14). Detailed studies of individual poets like Hemans, Mary Tighe, and Landon have added new insights even as they have helped us to refine the critical and cultural lenses we train on all the era's poets.[29] Even so, much remains to be done. Paula Backscheider's recent revisionist survey of eighteenth-century women's poetry eloquently illustrates the sort of inclusive approach that can dramatically reconfigure the poetic landscape, and this present book follows in several important respects the lead represented in that book.

I have chosen here to examine the work of Romantic-era British women poets in an analogous fashion, approaching them from several perspectives. I begin by looking at women writers' involvement with the rhetorical and ideological agendas of British radicalism, a subject that has not been investigated at any length in previous studies and one that underscores the commitment of women poets to public politics. This is followed by a chapter examining women's poetry on the subject of war, a topic that relates in important ways to the one on women and radical writing. Then I turn to matters of genre to discuss several individual poetic forms, first in a chapter on the sonnet and then in a second examining a combination of long forms (especially the verse narrative tale) and shorter ones (primarily occasional or "personal" poems). Finally, I look at two bodies of national poetry that have seldom been examined in their own right and that are typically—when their poets are considered at all—simply subsumed in an undifferentiating manner into "British" poetry: first Scottish poets and then their Irish contemporaries. I have deliberately adopted these multiple perspectives to show how they reveal somewhat different— but nevertheless complementary—views of the poets and their works. Even in an extended study like this one, there is not space to examine everything by everyone, nor do I wish in any event to risk suggesting yet another hierarchy by trying to rank poets, themes, or poetic forms. Rather, my objective in being selective rather than exhaustive is to open up the field to still more scrutiny than it has received even in these recent, more receptive and enlightened decades.

The chapters that follow, then, represent three alternative ways of constituting critical and contextual cross-sections of the body of women's poetry during the Romantic era. Each chapter is essentially preliminary, even when it constitutes the fullest discussion of its subject or its individual poets to date. Approaching this body of poetry by three different but complementary routes further demonstrates the point I wish to make about how Romantic poetry is far more nuanced—far more *shaded*—than we have typically given it credit for being. Each chapter therefore represents both a necessarily filtered "survey" of its constituent writers as well as a detailed examination of the work of many women poets. This examination covers some works that have already begun to enter the canon (witness their inclusion in commercial anthologies) and at some works that deserve wider recognition and discussion than they have so far received. Considering poetry of the period within altered and expanded parameters necessarily raises issues of aesthetics and poetics that have themselves gone too long unquestioned in Romantics scholarship, issues with which that scholarship needs to wrestle anew.

Women Writers, Radical Rhetoric, and the Public

Women and the Radical Temper

When it appeared in 1979, the volume of the *Biographical Dictionary of Modern British Radicals* that encompassed the Romantic period listed 214 figures representing various occupations and avocations. Of these only four—Mary Hays, Catherine Macaulay, Helen Maria Williams, and Mary Wollstonecraft—were women, and they made up a mostly eighteenth-century coterie. Macaulay had died already in 1791 and Wollstonecraft in 1797. By the turn of the century Hays had turned from the overt social and political radicalism of her early fiction (roughly through *The Victim of Prejudice* [1799]) toward the largely pedagogical fiction of her later years. And Williams published virtually nothing between 1803 and 1815, though she remained faithful to the republican cause until her death (Baylen and Grossman). Mary Darby Robinson is conspicuously absent from the list of radicals, although the leader of the circle of Della Cruscan writers with which she was for some time associated, Robert Merry, is counted among them. Nor is Robinson's exclusion the exception, for other women are missing, too, including poets like Charlotte Smith and the Irish writers Mary O'Brien and Henrietta Battier. Modern scholarship has until relatively recently been reluctant to acknowledge either the nature or the extent of Romantic-era women writers' involvement in radical politics.[1] Despite the increasingly reactionary climate that developed in Britain toward the end of the eighteenth century, many women writers nevertheless labored against it, deliberately entering into what was for most of them an often risky involvement with oppositional public politics whose dissenting nature was in their own time readily apparent to their contemporaries. Robinson had, after all, replied immediately and enthusiastically to Merry's republican poetic celebration of the French Revolution's achievements, *The*

Laurel of Liberty (1790) with *Ainsi va le Monde* (1790). There, with an unmistakable reference to Thomas Paine's work, she writes:

> Who shall the nat'ral Rights of Man deride,
> When Freedom spreads her fost'ring banners wide?
> Who shall contemn the heav'n-taught zeal that throws
> The balm of comfort on a Nation's woes?   (*Selected Poems,* 112, ll. 293–96)

Like her radical contemporaries, Robinson makes the point that France's lesson is not likely to be lost on other nations. Concerning Freedom, she continues:

> Nor yet, to GALLIA are her smiles confin'd,
> She opes her radiant gates to *all mankind;*
> Sure on the peopled earth there cannot be
> A foe to Liberty—that dares be free.   (113, ll. 301–4)

As if Robinson's own italicized indication of Freedom's universal audience did not already sufficiently embrace Britain, the next two lines—with their citation of that abiding Liberty which Romantic-era discourse among all parties celebrates as particularly *British*—cement the connection that radicals and reformers alike perceived in the revolution's early stages.

Robinson's subsequent affiliation with the *Morning Post* (especially during Daniel Stuart's tenure as manager and editor, when she served as poetry editor), brought her into closer contact with Coleridge and Southey, neither of whom had as yet entirely renounced his earlier republicanism. Furthermore, not only did this professional connection involve her in the day-to-day workings of a liberal paper but also her position as poetry editor (a position she held from 1799 until her death) lent her immediate access to an audience receptive to many aspects of the progressive agenda she encoded in her poems for that paper and that were encoded in others whose publication likely resulted from her editorial decisions. For a vastly popular poet who had already as early as 1793 been publicly touted as not just "the *first Poet* now living" but indeed "the *first Poet,*" her easy access to the *Morning Post's* readership was an additional advantage in advancing her agenda, even though her "radicalism" was far less direct and conspicuous than the sort that we associate with male contemporaries like Thomas Spence or John Thelwall.[2]

Mark Philip has reminded us that for the most part early radicalism in Romantic-era Britain was "without doubt reformist rather than revolutionary in character" (22), and the point is especially relevant to the works of the period's women writers. Radical writing took on a keen edge that itself reflected the violent rhetoric that was directed against British advocates of republicanism (French and otherwise) by

Edmund Burke and others. J. G. A. Pocock characterizes British responses to the French Revolution as "the most counter-revolutionary in Europe" (304), and the acrimonious public discourse that ensued became known as the "Pamphlet Wars." In volatile revolutionary times, the government had a large stake in maintaining the status quo and discrediting the opposition, whose antiauthoritarianism Burke and others characteristically branded as "unnatural." The intransigence of the government in dealing with opposition publishers and booksellers, one aspect of which culminated in the notorious Treason Trials of 1794, forced many radicals to realize that they could no longer rely on traditional methods for promoting reform and would consequently "have to find new tactics to advance their course" (Philip, 22). Indirection, rather than traditional frontal attack, became a preferable avenue, and literature offered an especially useful vehicle.

Mary Robinson's situation was in some respects analogous to that of Charlotte Turner Smith, who by the time she published her first novel, *Emmeline, the Orphan of the Castle,* in 1788 already enjoyed ready access to an interested readership by virtue of her considerable reputation as the author of the *Elegiac Sonnets,* which went through nine increasingly large editions during her lifetime and whose fourth edition had appeared already in 1786, only two years after the slim first edition of 1784. Both women significantly enlarged the size of their contemporary readerships— and their public influence—through their widely known novels. Thomas Cadell's edition of Smith's *Emmeline,* for example, sold out quickly and was immediately reprinted. Novels like Robinson's *Walsingham* (1797), Smith's *Desmond* (1792) and *The Young Philosopher* (1798), and Hays's *Memoirs of Emma Courtney* (1795) and *The Victim of Prejudice* (1799)—as well Hays's important protofeminist collection of biographical studies, *Female Biography; or, Memoirs of Illustrious and Celebrated Women of All Ages and Countries* (1803)—could serve as effective vehicles for advancing political, social, and economic ideologies no less than poems like Robinson's *Ainsi va le Monde* or Smith's *The Emigrants* (1793). As Adriana Craciun, Kari Lokke, and Judith Davis Miller have demonstrated, while modern scholars have typically discounted Smith's connections to radical culture, her contemporary readers *and critics* (including Smith's own sister, Catherine Dorset) had no doubts about the strength of her ties with "the reformers, and the revolutionists" and indeed with "some of the most violent advocates of the French Revolution."[3]

Paula Backscheider has effectively documented the growing public acceptance and approbation that eighteenth-century women writers had achieved in Britain. By the middle of that century, Backscheider observes, women found it increasingly easy to publish their poetry, especially in the century's ever-growing number of periodicals; moreover, "periodicals carefully framed poetry by women in a discourse of gratitude and respect for their talents and gender" (3–4). By the 1780s, she reports, periodical publishers actually worked to draw their readers' attention to the fact that their pages featured "the latest or most discussed poem" by women poets like Smith, Robinson, or Anna Seward, so that by the 1790s women poets were widely considered within the public consciousness to constitute "a deliberative body, a group that perceived their writing, and were perceived themselves, as having a right to intervene in national life and its debates" (8). Robinson, who was always attuned to the public temper, fully understood that excluding women from the public sphere (and consequently from the power of speech) would likely prove counterproductive in the long run. She was right. She and other women writers turned to the new opportunities for public activism that the explosion of the literary marketplace during the 1790s opened up to them, both as consumers *and as producers* of literature. Moreover, Robinson's own affiliation with the *Morning Post* and the readership to whom it gave her access only reaffirmed the conviction she shared with contemporary women radical reformers that because a free press inherently promoted both liberty and reform, "confidence in a free press became a frankly polemical position" (Gilmartin, 24–25).

At the same time, however, the climate of public discourse changed in the 1790s as Britain reacted both to the political dimensions of the French Revolution and to the leveling republican principles that informed its initial phases. Perceiving women's increasing determination to play a significant role in national social and political debate (as indicated by their increasing—and increasingly public—involvement in issues like abolition, education, women's rights), a more reactionary cultural establishment—in which men still enjoyed both economic and ideological dominance—began to erect new barriers to prevent women from contributing to the public discourse and to resuscitate some of the old ones. William Stafford observes, for instance, that despite women's continued access to publication, the areas to which their contributions were thought "proper" actually diminished: "The space where women were most likely to be denied access was the bitterly contested terrain of public controversy in politics and religion" (*English Feminists,* 8). Indeed, the periodical press, through the chorus of its reviewers, frequently seemed determined to steer (or to confine) women to the production of poetry and fiction. Stafford's extraordinary study is one of the first to examine in detail the inadequacy of most of the sweeping generalizations with which literary history has customarily approached women's writing of the Romantic period. For, as he demonstrates with respect to all the literary genres in which Romantic-era women were active in the 1790s, there were in fact no "universals" governing the production or the assessment of women's writing. Women whom literary history has traditionally labeled as "Jacobin" or "anti-Jacobin" writers frequently exhibit the features of *both* positions in their works, for instance, just as poems treating the same politically or socially volatile subjects are sometimes praised and sometimes vilified, depending upon who is doing the criticizing. What *was* true, though, was that the assessment of *all* writing—by women and men alike—was colored by political and ideological biases that regularly trumped any sort of objective aesthetic considerations. It is important to keep this in mind as we examine the relation of women poets to Romantic-era radicalism.

Poetry has come in our own age to be regarded as peripheral at best: some contend that it is kept alive today only by academic curricula and by creative writing programs, without both of which it would supposedly disappear. Others point to its absence from the "mainstream media," whether in traditional print forms or in their modern electronic counterparts, and to its segregation within literary journals whose readerships seldom represent anything like the demographics of the reading public as a whole. Such a view, of course, completely overlooks the flourishing state of poetry in the form of lyrics for popular music, from the socially committed lyrics of the 1960s "folk" revival to the hard-edged contemporary stuff of rap and hip-hop. In these popular culture iterations, poetry continues to serve as a forum for debate on the most pressing issues confronted by contemporary society, something that can hardly be said about the lyrics for more conventional "popular" music—or even about a considerable amount of the verse that is generated by the academically based creative writing industry. The point is especially relevant here, because two centuries ago in Britain poetry stood at the center—not the periphery—of public discourse. As Backscheider aptly says about the later eighteenth century, "poetry was consumer news in a century now recognized as obsessed with novelty and timeliness." "Few of us," she writes of our own age," would read poetry as a means of social advancement, as a source of news, or as mass entertainment, but eighteenth-century people increasingly did" (9–10). Moreover, we know both from the historical record and from modern scholarly studies that the contents of periodicals of all sorts reached a far greater number of citizens than is indicated merely by the number of copies printed, for in addition to their presence in circulating libraries, their contents were read out in coffeehouses, pubs, and other meeting places, so that one single copy might have served literally dozens of readers. The same is true for books, especially after the advent of the highly successful (and profitable) circulating libraries. Moreover, as William St. Clair has documented, the rapid expansion of reading that coincides with the Romantic period in Britain "occurred across all strata of society, whether categorised by income, by occupation, by educational attainment, by geographical location, by age, or by gender" (11). Indeed, the Romantic period may mark the last time in British literary and cultural history in which poetry stood in this fashion at the crossroads of cultural discourse, reflecting contemporary thought on a broad array of important issues even as it served to shape and direct that thought. This is why it is so important for us to be alert to the ways in which women poets of the period incorporated the elements of radicalism in the works they composed and published.

When we look at the poetry (especially) published by women of the Romantic period—whether they identified themselves actively and explicitly with the radical agenda or whether their association was more covert—we discover a remarkably consistent involvement with radical social and political subject matter and ideology. The *vehicle*—poetry—may strike modern readers as an unlikely one for articulating radical, oppositional subject matter, especially when we consider how widely such subject matter was considered to be off limits owing to widely entrenched "gender- and class-inflected strictures" governing propriety and publication (Cole and Swartz, 162). Moreover, its activating *agency*—often grounded in sentiment—may be distasteful to critical opinion that (then and now) expects from poetry a "loftier" style and "an official literary language" grounded in the discourse of the sublime. Nevertheless, there is no mistaking the elements of radicalism that drive this counterestablishment poetry. One common theme is a determined resistance to the state's impingement on individual prerogative, an interference that is routinely characterized as both unwarranted and "unnatural" (the writers pointedly turning the reactionary institution's own terminology against it). Sometimes this resistance is expressed as opposition to war and at others as protest against the economic tyranny maintained by the aristocratic establishment over the population at large and over their ordinary commercial interests, a tyranny that is widely replicated on the domestic scene within the individual British family. More often still, this poetry traces the consequences for the family unit in particular—whether it be the elemental nuclear family or the expanded national "family"—of the disruption of "natural" companionate relationships. Sometimes the poems articulate their radicalism explicitly, as happens in Mary Robinson's "January 1795," Elizabeth Moody's 1798 "Thoughts on War and Peace," or the 1795 "Lines Written by a Female Citizen!" attributed to the unidentified "F. A. C." Sometimes they take a slightly more indirect approach, as in Moody's "Anna's Complaint; or, The Miseries of War" (1795), Amelia Alderson Opie's "Ode on the Present Times" (1795), or the militaristic but deeply ambivalent "The Spanish Mother" (1809) attributed to "a Young Lady." This poetry resists and even renounces the hierarchical social and political structures of the embedded dominant patriarchy and substitutes for them a more egalitarian, companionate community whose leading values are respect, tolerance, affection, and shared experience. In this respect, the poetry reflects some of the traits that Anne Mellor associates with what she has called "feminine Romanticism," an ethos grounded in the notion that none should be harmed or injured when it can be prevented.[4]

Much British radical rhetoric, especially in the 1790s, features appeals to historical precedent, to the cultural memory of the old Anglo-Saxon compact and Magna Carta, and to an increasingly mythologized conception of the British constitution that was being forged in the popular consciousness in relation to the politics of that distant period. In this respect the radical movement, like the Glorious Revolution of a century earlier, aimed to demolish the prevailing order not as a means of instituting something entirely new but rather in order to restore what its advocates believed had been eroded and ultimately lost in a political usurpation by an unsanctioned power elite that ruled without the full consent of the governed. The inherent *nostalgia* involved in such notions of some golden era of earlier charters and compacts, and of the at least seemingly less exclusive governing structures associated with them, initially made Romantic radicalism especially appealing to working-class citizens, whether they were peaceable, God-fearing traditionalists or frame-breaking Luddites. For these were the people who felt most profoundly that they had been left out of the transition to the industrialized, capitalistic modern world. Trapped by the emerging competition between machines and their own human labor, these were the laboring masses toward whose improvement Robert Owen, for example, directed the reformist schemes he articulated in his *New Vision of Society* (1813) and in utopian communities like New Lanark and New Harmony. They are also the "Bees of England" whom Shelley dreamed in 1819 of rallying against "the lords who lay ye low" ("Song to the Men of England," *Complete Poetical Works,* 572). A generation earlier, they are the dehumanized and desensitized Britons whom Robinson describes as trapped in the nightmarish state in which "the Rich are upheld, and the Poor doom'd to pay" ("Stanzas," *Selected Poems,* 291, l. 34) and where the rich can process grandly and without compunction through a London in which "the wretch whom poverty subdues / Scarce dares to raise his tearful eye" ("The Birth-day," *Selected Poems,* 339, l. 29–30).[5] Lacking either effective spokespersons for their interests or direct access to economic and political power on their behalf, these suffering citizens understandably indulged in the "good old days" discourse that is the familiar recourse of those who feel most disenfranchised and excluded by a society—and its institutions—that appears to be passing them by without sufficient regard or, worse still, exploiting them unconscionably.

Curiously, little critical attention has been paid until fairly recently to women's presence and function within the radical culture. Most women were, after all, unlikely to derive solace from the prospect of reinstating an ancient order that had held no more place for them than the contemporary sociopolitical structure seemed to hold. Governed without their consent they surely were, unless they happened to be among that fortunate few, the women of independent means. Many of these comfortably self-sufficient women—like the aristocrats whose unconcern Robinson unmasks in poems like "The Birth-day" (1795)—were, in any event, unlikely to infuse their witty and often Whiggish writing with either the heat or the steel of radical sentiment; they preferred to fret, along with the more numerous men whose sympathies they generally shared, over the threat to their comfort and complacency posed by radical discourse and all it portended for the privileged. For the great majority of women, then, the mythic past offered no glimpses of some golden age during which they had possessed greater prerogative. Claims for women's rights, as James Epstein observes, were "problematically situated within popular radical discourse" of the period because the historical fact of women's legal and cultural exclusion meant that their claims could not easily be legitimated by the sort of appeal to England's past that could be mounted by the radical movement on behalf of men (23). Their best hope for empowerment and enfranchisement appeared to lie with the improved sociopolitical and cultural situation foreseen by melioristic eighteenth-century thinkers like the feminist historiographer Catharine Sawbridge Macaulay and the political philosopher William Godwin. Writers like these envisioned a fundamentally egalitarian and companionate arrangement in which men and women would be not competitors but partners, not unlike that in which the wives of many printers and other artisans found themselves profitably employed (and acknowledged) with their husbands. According to this paradigm, bettering the lot of "man" must inevitably improve matters for both sexes: a more enlightened (male) establishment would be far more likely to extend to women what had historically been denied them.[6]

This is one reason why education is accorded such a central place in the plans of feminists like Mary Wollstonecraft and Mary Hays, as it had been in those of Macaulay before them, for education seemed to offer one viable avenue into the political and cultural prerogatives routinely available to men. Macaulay read in the history of England the record of the gradual loss of the fundamental rights of man and the growing indications, in her own times, of substantive progress toward reattaining those rights "in a more perfect state" (Withey, 59). Not all women writers adopted Macaulay's optimistic view of sociopolitical renovation, of course, even given the climate of millenarian excitement that characterized the 1790s. Indeed, feminists like Wollstonecraft and Hays did not hesitate to employ calculated flattery when they argued that granting women greater access to education, for example, would make them better and more suitable wives and companions for men by reducing the artificial and *unnatural* gulf in status that had resulted from their exclusion. What was good for women, according to their rhetorically shrewd argument, was good for men as well. And if it was valid for education, the argument was no less so for other areas of activity and accomplishment—like politics and public policy.

At the same time, Macaulay's reversion to the venerable Anglo-Saxon paradigm is instructive in its reflection of the ways in which women writers were constrained in their writing, to a significant extent, by a masculinist historiography *and rhetoric* that they had to adapt for their own often subversive and oppositional purposes. For if the written records of women's experiences and perspectives are themselves a priori circumscribed and misshapen by the inherently male-centered nature of the language and discourse field that female authors are forced to employ and to manipulate in order to communicate their experiences, as some modern feminist theorists claim, then hypothetically their progress is blocked already at the most basic level of language and signification. But the reality was considerably less bleak, and the available language and rhetorical strategies less wholly circumscribed. Moreover, there was also considerable ideological diversity. Although Wollstonecraft and Hays are often lumped together in modern thinking, for instance, Hays's *Appeal to the Men of Great Britain in Behalf of the Women* (1798) actually faults Wollstonecraft for tactlessness and presumption. In publishing the *Appeal* anonymously, therefore, Hays strategically concealed her identity and her known association with Wollstonecraft (and Godwin) and thereby distanced herself from the ideological baggage that association involved. In fact, the greatest obstacles may not have been those of language and rhetoric after all. William Stafford claims that "the most intractable evils, the ones they could do least about, were not discursive and generic conventions but unequal political and civil rights and lack of access to money" (*English Feminists,* 221). As I argue here and elsewhere in this book, when it comes to the poetry written and published by women of the era, the issue is less one of language itself than of how that language is manipulated. And how it is manipulated has very much to do with those very considerations Stafford identifies.

British women involved in the radical movement had in any case to negotiate a complicated cultural passage if they were to participate in—and reap the rewards of—a movement designed to redress institutionalized social, political, and economic inequities. They needed in particular to resist the masculinist paradigm implicit in the nostalgic beau ideal that was the putative objective of contemporary radical politics. There *were* no "good old days" for them; any good days that were to be had necessarily lay in the future. As Adriana Craciun writes, British women had to reject notions of a "nostalgic golden age of the patriarchal 'free-born Briton'" and look instead across the channel for new models of liberty and empowerment (*British Women Writers,* 62).

In fact, Donna Landry has argued that even what we usually think of as radicalism, "with its roots in artisanal culture," was largely closed to women (*Muses of Resistance,* 268). This may be overstating the case, however, in light of what we are learning about the extent to which the wives of artisans frequently served as virtually full partners to their husbands, often taking over from them upon the husband's demise. Certainly it is fair to say, though, that women's very different circumstances meant that the ground for which, and over which, they struggled was not precisely the same ground with which their male counterparts were principally concerned. Not even E. P. Thompson, in his monumental *Making of the English Working Class,* fully appreciated the extent to which both his history and the manner of telling it were overwhelmingly masculinist. As Caroline Steedman has observed, in that work "class was constructed as a masculine identity in both its origin and expression, even when not all the actors were male" (112).[7] Steedman's point is like Anne Mellor's more recent observation that the work of the influential theorist Jürgen Habermas concerning the evolution of a "public sphere" in the later eighteenth century presumes a consistently masculine and masculinist construction of both the private citizen and the public agent (*Mothers of the Nation,* 2–3). Socioeconomic class reflects the literary communities to which various authors belonged and at the same time it underscores the conventions that governed both what was published and who published it—as well as who read it. When those conventions are overwhelmingly masculinist, the constraints for women are many and their consequences dramatic, as we learn from the work of scholars like Landry, Terry Lovell, and Cheryl Turner on the economic conditions under which women authors worked and their implications for class-oriented valuations of their works.[8] It is hard to disagree with Eleanor Ty's important observation that while Romantic women writers frequently contested, rebelled against, or repudiated them, they nevertheless often "inadvertently participated in the perpetuation of existing cultural, social, and linguistic categories of women and assignments of gender" (14). Although she has in mind novelists of the 1790s, Ty's comment is no less relevant to the work of female poets and no less applicable to much of the period that we think of as the Romantic era.

Poetry, Radical Sentiment, and Sympathy

Tracing the evidence of radical thought among women poets of the Romantic period can involve a circuitous journey, for the texts in question are not always where the modern inquirer might expect to find them. Vivien Jones offers an instructive illustration where she observes that a poem on the fall of the Bastille ("The Bastille: A Vision" [reproduced in Williams, *Letters Written in France,* 204]) intrudes conspicuously into the sentimental environment of Helen Maria Williams's novel, *Julia* (1790). When Williams published her *Poems on Various Subjects* in 1823, she claimed that this poem was one of only four among the entire volume that possessed "any reference to public events" (x). Quoting Sir James Mackintosh's response to Edmund Burke, Williams says of the taking of the Bastille that "it was an action not to be excused but applauded; not to be pardoned but admired: I shall not descend to vindicate acts which history will teach the remotest posterity to admire, and which is destined to kindle in unborn millions the holy enthusiasm of freedom" (xii).

The poem that appears in *Julia,* we are told by Williams's male intermediary character Mr. F., has just arrived in a letter from an English friend in France who had been immured in the Bastille as a political prisoner until his liberation through the agency of an influential acquaintance. Williams's poem treats the Bastille in the familiar fashion, as a symbol of the ancien régime's injustice:

> Bastille! within thy hideous pile
> Which stains of blood defile.—
> Thus rose the captive's sighs,
> Till slumber sealed his weeping eyes—
> Terrific visions hover near!
> He sees an awful form appear!
> Who drags his step to deeper cells,
> Where stranger wilder horror dwells.   (ll. 17–24)

The radical feminist sociosexual ethic that informs the narrative of Williams's popular novel culminates in the tale's dramatic "reconciliation," a resolution that mediates and resolves the tension that has been building throughout the novel between "illicit" sexual desire and the chastening influence of woman's inherent ingenuous nature. Interestingly, this dramatic crisis coincides with the appearance in the text of Williams's poem, whose subject is the renovatory purpose of revolutionary violence. Jones remarks that "this conjunction of sentimental sexual narrative with historical event" suggests one way in which Williams is able to liberate herself from the role of "acceptably decorous female poet and novelist" that the contemporary reader *expected* to encounter in a work whose author was known to be a woman (178–79) and thereby introduce her more radical agenda to an unprepared and therefore susceptible reader. That agenda involves her beautiful protagonist Julia's internalization of the political lesson the American and French Revolutions taught her, that opting for independence rather than marriage (and dependency) is a viable and even heroic alternative for women.[9] Mixing genres in this fashion (which in some respects anticipates the historical novel) enables authors to thematize radical arguments in terms of historical events. G. Gabrielle Starr has identified this mixing of genres as a distinctive feature of eighteenth-century fiction, which she has demonstrated contains abundant examples of "generic heterodoxies ranging from the literary influence of newspapers and political tracts to the cross-pollination of high literary species" (2).

No such mixing of genres occurs in a 1790 poem by the Dissenting polemicist Maria de Fleury celebrating the earliest stages of the French Revolution. In her poem, *British Liberty Established, and Gallic Liberty Restored; or, The Triumph of Freedom,* the author welcomes the newly liberated France to the enlightened world of freedom and liberty that has long been Britain's heritage:

> Britons rejoice, no chains are forg'd for you,
> To break your spirit, and your minds subdue;
> No dreary caves exclude the beauteous light,
> And bury heroes in perpetual night;
> No IRON CAGES, no BASTILES [sic] arise,
> To curse the groaning earth, insult the skies;
> No Widows weep, no Orphans mourn in vain
> Husbands and Fathers snatch'd away, or slain,
> By cruel Policy. Here FREEDOM reigns,
> And law and justice hold the sacred reins
> Of ENGLAND's government.   (13, pt. 1, ll. 143–53)

Although this sort of verse appears in one light to be fiercely loyalist, it can be seen in a somewhat different light if one reads the final lines as carrying an ironic inflection. Indeed, critical responses to this poem in the contemporary press were mixed; some reviewers in fact objected to what they perceived as violent and overzealous sentiments, perhaps because they suspected irony. For if France's newfound liberty was cause for celebration, then at least among those who perceived England as less free it could also serve as an inspiration—or a motivation—for domestic action:

> Thus bold, thus firm, when a whole People rise,
> Breathing one spirit, valiant, ardent, wise,
> What can resist?—The mighty torrent sweeps
> Guilt and Oppression to their native deeps;
> Plucks Usurpation from her ancient throne,
> And all the tools of Despotism down:

While Virtue, Law, and Justice, once again
Call'd to new life, begin their happy reign.   (24, pt. 2, ll. 223–30)

De Fleury's inflammatory rhetorical tactics were not lost on contemporary readers on both sides of the issue, nor were those tactics especially uncommon during the volatile first years following the Revolution.

The less explicitly contestatory tactic that Williams employs in *Julia* in mixing historical details and sociopolitical commentary with prose fiction—and especially the subversive tactic of "planting" that commentary within poems that interrupt the prose narrative—at once insulates the author (because the historical event is "real" and therefore part of the common cultural currency) and underscores the philosophical or political point being made (for the very same reason). The tactic is a familiar one in novels of the period, and Charlotte Smith was particularly adept in the way she used it. As Starr explains, almost every character at some point composes poems of perception and reflection that are then introduced into the narrative. "The novel's surrounding prose sets the stage for the production of both poetic vision and poetry itself, and lyric emerges in the novel as a special form of speech with its own particular context" (168). Smith's *Desmond* (1793), though it does not include any of Smith's poetry, nevertheless emerges as a "Jacobin" novel in part because its epistolary nature empowers its readers to think for themselves: political views of all stripes fill the letters, and no authorial voice intervenes to mediate or to judge those views.[10] This narrative procedure enables the author to convey ideologically radical ideas without seeming to do so herself—that is, in "her own" voice. In a politically dangerous time—which the last decade of the eighteenth century surely was—this appears a reasonable enough subterfuge. But was anyone fooled?

Richard Polwhele was not, for one, nor were those anti-Jacobin contemporaries who nodded approvingly over their copies of *The Unsex'd Females,* published in 1798, or over the pages of its lengthier predecessors, Thomas James Mathias's *Pursuits of Literature,* from which Polwhele borrowed his title, and William Gifford's *Baeviad.*[11] Polwhele had complained in print already a decade earlier about the "contempt of the domestic duties" that he regarded as "the prevailing vice of our modern women" who "prefer an intercourse with those who have little concern for her happiness, to the conversation of her family and friends, who must be necessarily interested in her welfare" ("On the Dissipation of Fashionable Women," *Discourses,* 2:90). What offended Polwhele most was the new spirit of personal and social independence that was prompting women to venture outside the tight family circle in which their role and activities were constrained by culturally enforced expectations about their domestic duties. It is not just that Polwhele was by 1798 worried about some women's admiration for French republican principles (and hence their interest in politics) or about "their sexually liberated notions" (Ty, 13). After all, by 1798 enthusiasm in England for the revolution had cooled considerably; even many of its most committed early enthusiasts had already embarked on face-saving campaigns of recantation. A reactionary social pragmatist, Polwhele believed that women's public endeavors—whether in politics or in print (and they were in fact often one and the same)—threatened the traditional patriarchal family, which he regarded as the foundation of societal stability. Thus he dismissed the argument advanced by so many radical women writers that it was in fact the prevailing establishment's appetite for international and domestic domination (including the domination in the private home that Polwhele took for granted), like the warmaking that was the inevitable consequence of that appetite, that posed the greatest and most immediate physical threat to the family unit.[12]

Nor were forward-thinking women immune to attacks by other women, as we learn for instance from Anne Macvicar Grant's caustic remarks in "A Familiar Epistle to a Friend" (*The Highlanders* [1808]). There Grant fulminates about Helen Maria Williams's efforts in poetry and prose alike to teach the lessons of French republicanism from her residence in France during the previous decade and a half. In *A Farewell, for Two Years, to England* (1791), Williams had contrasted the dawning promise of revolutionary egalitarianism with the fading promise of an England mired in materialism, privilege, and the inhumanity of the slave trade in a passage that culminates in a pointed reference to Paine:

> May other Lands the bright example show,
> May other regions lessen human woe!
> Yes, GALLIA, haste! tho' BRITAIN's sons decline
> The glorious power to save, that power is thine;
> Haste! since, while BRITAIN courts that dear-bought gold,
> For which her virtue and her fame are sold,
> And calmly calculates her trade of death,
> Her groaning victims yield in pangs their breath;
> Then save some portion of that suff'ring race
> From ills the mind can scarce endure to trace!
> Oh! whilst with mien august thy Leaders scan,
> And guard with jealous zeal the rights of man,
> Forget not that to all kind Nature gives
> Those common rights, the claim of all that lives.   (13, ll. 183–96)

Grant's incensed response to Williams and others like her shares much with those of her fellow loyalists:

To the passion for liberty giving loose rein,
At length [she] flew off to carouse on the Seine;
And growing inebriate while quaffing the draught,
Equality's new-fangled doctrines she taught;
And murder and sacrilege calmly survey'd;
In the new Pandemonium those demons had made;
Seine's blood-crimson'd waters with apathy ey'd,
While the glories of old father Thames she decried.　　(153, ll. 174–85)

In her poem, Grant tropes her contempt for Williams's radical egalitarianism through the metaphor of the public "drunkenness," a familiar tactic of loyalist rhetoric aimed at discrediting the opposition. It carries particular force here in its application to a woman, in whom "drunkenness" of any sort is presumed to be especially scandalous since it understood to be so unwomanly. Moreover, Grant's gendering of the Thames—and hence of the English political and intellectual entity—in male terms reminds us of the tendency within reactionary discourse to cast women's opposition in terms of a would-be independence that is unnatural because it is both antipatriarchal and antiauthoritarian.

As Catherine Decker has written, culturally sanctioned patriarchal codes promote "the correlation of public behavior with morality" by making women's obedience to prevailing social codes a moral duty. One such code, of course, is the proscription of women from participating in the public (male) discourse on matters of state, politics, religious doctrine, and so forth. To enter that discourse is to be "wrong" (because it is "unnatural"), and women who offend in this fashion are therefore *expected* "to punish *themselves* for such insinuations . . . [by] retirement from public life" (17–18, my emphasis). Interestingly, this formulation places women in an impossible position in which complete *silence*—which constitutes self-punishment—is presented as the only option: to speak (or to publish) requires demeaning exercises in self-censorship and self-silencing that are predicated on the woman's acceptance of the notion that her utterance is not just transgressive but also immoral.

Over and over, therefore, attacks on the *politics* of radical women writers are couched in post-Burkean tut-tutting about the shocking violations of *decorum* constituted by their writings, which are treated as unwelcome *and unnatural* intrusions into a discourse that historically excludes their voices. This helps explain Sarah Spence's pious and thoroughly gendered iteration of men's and women's roles in a 1793 pamphlet commenting on the impending war: "As a Woman, I would seek Peace and domestic felicity; relying on the Judgement of my Husband in all political affairs; conscious that it is not the province of my sex to investigate the various sources from which political information may be derived" ("A Fragment Taken from a Piece Written about 28 Jan. 1793," *Poems and Miscellaneous Pieces,* 91). This sort of gendered deference to the wisdom and authority of the male establishment—frequently presented explicitly as referencing the domestic household but implying thereby the nation-family—underlies much of the reactionary writing that followed in Britain in the wake of the French Revolution. In fiction, one may trace it in the many novels that set out to demonstrate through their vigorous lessoning the destructive (and often self-destructive) consequences of forward-looking feminist arguments about gender and public action that recur in novels like Williams's *Julia,* Wollstonecraft's *Mary, A Fiction* (1788), Eliza Fenwick's *Secresy* (1795), or Hays's *Victim of Prejudice.* Paradoxically, a much-reprinted novel like Amelia Alderson Opie's *The Father and Daughter* (1800) could be harnessed in support of both sides of the argument. Unlike the many readers who saw in it a moral parable about the terrible retribution visited upon a woman *and her poor father* by her unconventional sexual behavior (she is seduced by a charlatan suitor who jilts her after impregnating her), many others saw there a social lesson about the stifling and degrading nature of oppressive contemporary attitudes (and laws) concerning women, their circumstances, and the choices forced on them by the want of options and alternatives.

Reactionary readers recognized the danger inherent in smuggling radical principles into works intended for popular readerships. Like the gothic novel and the gothic drama, with which it shared many features, the Jacobin novel held great potential for subversion, and not just because radical poems could be embedded there or because their characters—and even their supposedly objective narrators—could function as spokespersons for politically radical views. In this light it is instructive to recall Dr. Johnson's criticism of Milton for having put exceptionable sentiments into Satan's mouth in *Paradise Lost.* For something of the same sort occurs with Charlotte Smith's five French Revolutionary novels (*Desmond* [1792]; *The Old Manor House* [1793]; *The Banished Man* [1794]; *Marchmont* [1796]; *The Young Philosopher* [1798]), in each of which, in one way or another, she "reveals herself to be the philosophical companion of Godwin and Condorcet" in both the radical orientation of the novels and in their linking of gender and politics (Miller, 338). Much the same is true of the radical politics relating more specifically to sexual relations that informs novels like those I have already mentioned.

Significantly, as G. Gabrielle Starr has demonstrated with respect to Romantic poetry's relation to eighteenth-century fiction, works of this mixed sort typically also draw, in one way or another, on the intellectual and aesthetic features of sentimental fiction, one of whose chief objectives is to generate feelings of "sympathy" in the sense in which David Hume, Adam Smith, and others had understood it: as that distinctly moral force by means of which "we enter into the sentiments of the rich and poor, and partake of their pleasures and uneasiness" (Hume, 362). When we sympathize with "the passions and sentiments of others," Hume had written in *A Treatise on Human Nature* (1739), those passions and sentiments first manifest themselves in our own minds "as mere ideas" which are "conceiv'd to belong to another person" (319). But on further contemplation the distance between stimulus and responding mind lessens: the resemblance and proximity of those apparently external passions and sentiments to others of which we are ourselves the authors and possessors leads us to convert what are essentially neutral "ideas" of passion into emotionally and intellectually charged "impressions," with the result that at length "we are convinc'd of the reality of the passion" (320). It is precisely in this intellectual *and emotional* space, in which that separation between what is merely observed and what is deeply felt is dramatically reduced, that the danger to established institutions was seen most especially to lie, for the pull of that emotional complex was itself frequently likened to "inebriation" and to a loosening of the governing and moderating powers of the rational intellect.

Samuel Jackson Pratt explored this humanizing power in *Sympathy: A Poem* (1781), whose popularity had resulted in a "corrected and much enlarged" fourth edition within its first year.[13] Pratt requested his reader to consider his poem as a "sketch" of "the Sympathetic Principle, or Social Principle" (iii). According to Pratt, "The bias SOCIAL, man with men must SHARE, / The varied benefits of earth and air; / Life's leading law, my friend, which governs all" (13, bk. 1, ll. 221–23). "The laws of Sympathy declare" that heaven's first maxim is "BORN TO SHARE," Pratt writes, noting further that "Instinct, Sympathy, or what you will" functions actively as "a great first principle" through the agency of "th' affections" for this purpose:

> Man's favour'd soul then tracing thro' each state,
> Behold it fitted for a social fate;
> Behold how ev'ry link in nature tends
> One chain to form of relatives and friends.
> One chain, unnumber'd beings to confine,
> 'Till all assimilate and all combine.   (15–16, bk. 1, ll. 257–62)

This universal interrelationship and natural reciprocity is most fully elaborated in these lines:

> This then is clear, while human kind exist,
> The social principle must still subsist,
> In strict dependency of one on all,

As run the binding links from great to small.
Man born for Man some friendly aid requires,
The contract strengthening till the soul retires;
Nor then, even then it breaks, for still we pay
A brother's homage to the breathless clay,
Jealous of destiny the heart would save
Its favored object from the closing grave,
Its favored object chosen from the rest,
In grief, in joy, the monarch of the breast;
To earth we trust what fondness would retain,
And leave the corpse to visit it again;
Nay, unconfined by partial ties of blood,
We brave e'en peril for a stranger's good.   (51–52, bk. 2, ll. 443–58)

The writers I am considering here fully understood the import of this sort of language, which lent philosophical *and moral* weight to radical ideals of social and political equality and responsibility that are inextricably linked with revolutionary republicanism. It was both natural and inevitable that such thinking would animate and inform not just fiction but also—and perhaps especially—poetry.

For poetry's great strength, historically and actually, has to do with its power to move and evoke, to manipulate in a very special way how the reader responds to its subject matter. The most effective poetry appeals to the reader's instinctive desire to participate with the author in the "making" of the work; it is an essentially performative process that reduces the separation between the author (and the author's characters or personae and what they say and do) and the reader in a manner analogous to what Hume describes as the way we reduce the distance between an idea and impression. Polwhele, Mathias, Grant, and their like worry that readers will so fully *sympathize* with what is conveyed in the text's words that they will be unable—or unwilling—to distinguish their own ideas from those the author has embedded in the text. The logical conclusion is that such "impressionable" readers, as Hume might call them, will come to regard the words—and the radical ideas—contained in the text as impressions that they, rather than the author, have produced. According to this scenario (which I am of course oversimplifying—but only a little), the reader will find in the text reinforcement for impressions—and convictions—that that reader will be seduced into believing are her or his own; they will seem, to such a reader, to come from within herself or himself rather than from without. The text becomes corroboration and verification, not mere suggestion, casting the reader rather than the author in the role of sower of radical seed. It is against just this sort of rhetorical seduction that the establishment and its spokespersons direct their fire, as Hannah More did in countless exercises in propaganda conducted in prose and in verse.

As well they should. In poems like "January, 1795" or "The Birth-day" Mary Robinson deliberately destabilizes the system by dramatizing for her readers the suffering of those who are excluded under an established system of callous privilege:

> Pavement slippery, people sneezing,
> Lords in ermine, beggars freezing;
> Titled gluttons dainties carving,
> Genius in a garret starving.
>
> Lofty mansions, warm and spacious;
> Courtiers cringing and voracious;
> Misers scarce the wretched heeding;
> Gallant soldiers fighting, bleeding.   ("January, 1795," *Selected Poems*, 365, ll. 1–8)

Robinson's poem shares in the sentiment expressed in a poem by Sarah Spence, "Poverty," that was roughly contemporary with it.[14] That poem, a meditation on the lack of charity to the poor, contains passages of devastating irony:

> . . . Some on the giddy brink
> Of Fortune stand; a mountain oft so high,
> That men below dwindle to ants, and moles;
> Born to be slaves, and not to *them* allied!
> 'Can the poor sooty boy, whose morning cries
> 'Are heard in beds of down, or wound our ears
> 'Returning from the Masque, the brother be,
> 'Of men of wit, of dignity, and rank!
> 'Distracting thought—the little dirty wretch!
> 'Can *he* claim kindred with the titled Lord!
> 'Is Heav'n for *him,* may *he* sit high as kings,
> 'Or rise to joys superior.—Begone the thought!
> 'Must men of *wealth* be thus debas'd!'   (*Poems,* 13)

Spence's poem replicates, as radical discourse frequently does, the thinking of the privileged minority who regard their own comfortable status as entirely natural and appropriate and who believe that the impoverished status of the majority is no less natural or appropriate: hence the aggrieved tone of the loftily positioned who regard as an insupportable, vulgar imposition the aspirations of the underprivileged to what is their rightful human share under God. Ironically, the usually reactionary Hannah More had already commented on this class distinction and its potential implications—positive and negative—for England. In her *Thoughts on the Importance of the Manners of the Great to General Society* of 1788, More offered the following observation:

> But vain will be all endeavours after *partial* and *subordinate* amendment. Reformation must begin with the GREAT, or it will never be effected. *Their* example is the fountain from whence the vulgar draw their habits, actions, and characters. To expect to reform the poor while the opulent are corrupt, is to throw odours into the stream while the springs are poisoned. (114)

Coming at the matter by means of an appeal to the supposedly "better nature"—or at least the sheer self-interest—of "the Great," More presciently implies that the failure to redress present wrongs may carry a heavy price in the future.

Neither Spence's nor Robinson's poem, however, is a simple exercise in the sort of unambiguous dialectical dualisms of the "haves" and the "have-nots" that More's rhetoric implies; although they invoke the binary oppositions typical of radical writing, both are rhetorically nuanced. Robinson's poem reminds the reader that subtle gradations exist within both the positive and the negative categories itemized there, even as it laments the unavoidable timelessness and universality of the terrible state of affairs it starkly and unblinkingly depicts. This stark verbal representation of "what is" functions as a means of rhetorically highlighting the more pressing issue of "what is *not.*" The tactic typifies Romantic radical discourse in general, from early authors and publishers like Paine and Thomas Spence and Eaton to later ones like Hone and Wooler, in all of whose works the procedure is readily apparent.

This sort of polarized, binary discourse appears also in the works of agrarian and working-class poets, as well as in those of women, well into the Regency. Mary Anne M'Mullan's 1816 poem "The Welcome," for instance, from her collection *The Naiad's Wreath,* contains these lines:

> The high may shine in glitt'ring state,
> The low must bend to humble fate;
> The great may boast of sov'reign sway,
> The little tremble and obey. . . .   (16, ll. 36–39)

Paradoxically, this is not a poem of outright social protest like Robinson's but instead apparently an examination of a universal psychological phenomenon: each individual's (in this case each *man's*) conviction that no one else could be more warmly welcomed home after an absence than he. The poem traces this sentiment among four groups of British men: sportsmen, field-workers, sailors, and soldiers—in that order. The poem's appearance in the immediate aftermath of Waterloo and the war's end would have lent particular weight to the situations of the sailors and soldiers. M'Mullan, the widow of a Royal Navy doctor, reduces the various social ranks rhetorically to only two and then states their differences just as starkly as Robinson had done two decades earlier in "January, 1795." Moreover, the relative privilege enjoyed by each rank is subtly conveyed in the auxiliary verbs that M'Mullan has chosen. While the high *may* shine and the great *may* boast, the low *must* bend to their lesser status and presumably also *must* tremble and obey (although the auxiliary verb is shrewdly elided).

The rhetorical strategy of the negative definition is evident, explicitly or implicitly, within both the texts *and the titles* of Jacobin novels like Robert Bage's *Man as He Is* (1792) and *Hermsprong; or, Man as He Is Not* (1796) and William Godwin's *Things as They Are* (subtitled *Caleb Williams* [1794]). It also figures widely in radical poetry of the entire period, from works like Merry's "Ode for the Fourteenth of July" (1791), Wordsworth's *An Evening Walk* (1793), and Southey's *Wat Tyler* (1794) to the radical squibs of T. J. Wooler and William Hone a generation later. That it is there as well in the writings of Williams, Robinson, Smith, Anna Letitia Barbauld, and a host of other women was until fairly recently relatively unnoticed, as may be deduced from Stuart Curran's remark that by the later eighteenth century poetry had been "sealed off as a male, upper-class fiefdom, requiring for its license not simply birth and breeding but a common education and exclusive standards of shared taste" ("Women Readers," 182). Women were not entirely shut out, however, as Backscheider, Mellor, Feldman, and others have demonstrated.

Anne Janowitz, for example, reminds us that one body of verse that has received insufficient attention consists of those poems that "attempt to *intervene in* rather than *represent* political and social movements (85). It is in relation to this category that poems like "January, 1795" and "The Birth-day," together with a host of others like Spence's "Poverty" and Opie's "Ode on the Present Times" (1795), need to be examined. This interventional impulse governs the eighth line of Robinson's "January, 1795," for example: "Gallant soldiers fighting, bleeding." Such a conventional line may evoke a predictable pathos, but we need to contextualize it, trying to forget in the process the extent to which our continual exposure via the modern media to an omnipresent and seemingly universal violence has largely anaesthetized us to that violence and to its effects. A generation that dined for a decade with televised images of carnage in Vietnam, for instance, or another that daily faces the appalling results of domestic gang violence and international terrorism, may have some trouble fully sympathizing (to use Hume's word and his sense), whatever their ideological convictions, with the actual lived reality that informed the experiences of, especially, the women who composed lines like these in the 1790s and afterward and of the women who read and intimately understood them. On the local and personal level, however, in the lives of those whose families pay the ultimate price (then and now), this pathos is not just a rhetorical effect but a stark reality.

Again and again in poems that can be attributed with some confidence to women and that address war and the death of "gallant soldiers" we find a mixture of anger, helplessness, and inevitability, laced with authentic pathos. Elizabeth Moody's ballad is typical:

> Ah, William, wherefore didst thou go
> To foreign lands to meet the foe?
> Why, won by war's deceitful charms,
> Didst thou forsake thy Anna's arms?
>
> ("Anna's Complaint; or, The Miseries of War," ll. 13–16)[15]

Here Moody enhances the universality of the speaker's experience by rendering it in conventionally domesticized, gendered fashion through the traditional Christian names, the trope on seduction, and the apparently innocent pun on "arms" in the stanza's final line. The argument that poems of this sort mount against war—that it is actively and inevitably destructive to that most basic of human objectives (Rousseau's *Second Discourse* notwithstanding), interpersonal community—is inherently also an argument against the contemporary government and the values and priorities that undergird it. That establishment engages in war at the expense of countless victims whose numbers include not just the wounded or killed men but also the multitude of emotionally and economically mangled "survivors"—the families for whose welfare that same government responsible for their mutilation cares not one whit. In this light it is not surprising to discover that Moody's poem, which first appeared in 1795, was subjoined in 1796 to a remarkable sixty-four-page pamphlet by "Humanitas" (George Miller) called *War a System of Madness and Irreligion.*[16] This matter of war and women's poetry forms the subject of the next chapter, but the typical treatment of war in that poetry is also inseparable from the discourse of Romantic radicalism, with its concern for issues of social injustice and class exploitation.

The Family and the Nation

Images of the home, of the family, of the hearth and the domestic circle—all of which regularly stand in for implied figurations of the nation—constitute a large and powerful presence within the Romantic ethos in the 1790s. This presence shares much with what Anne Mellor calls a "feminine Romanticism" that advocated a *pro-gressive* change in the political and social order, a change grounded on "the trope of the family-politic" or the concept of "a nation-state that evolves gradually and ratio-nally under the mutual care and guidance of both mother and father" (*Romanticism and Gender,* 65). Ironically, this sort of gradualism recalls Burke's anxieties about the precipitous alteration of power structures and social constituency in the aftermath of the French Revolution. War is merely the most dramatic and dangerous threat to the shared caregiving that characterizes that "feminine Romanticism."

In poetry written by women—as well as in many poems written by men that speak through the rhetorical personae of women—these images of the domestic and the national community are jeopardized by the looming, predatory shadows of warfare. A poem called "The Dying Soldier," whose unknown author may be male or female, appeared in 1798 in the *Lady's Magazine* (reproduced in Bennett, 224–25); it reverts to this theme in the voice of the soldier, who ruefully wonders

> Why did I wander from my native vale,
> And leave my cottage, where Contentment smil'd?
> Where all was happiness and peace.—Ah! why
> Did I e'er mingle in the strife of kings,
> And change the sickle for the gleaming sword,
> The low-fenc'd garden for th' embattled plain,
> Deep-ting'd with blood?   (ll. 2–8)

The speaker in Opie's "Ode on the Present Times" (reproduced in Bennett, 140–42), composed and published in the wake of Kosciusko's defeat by the Russians at Ma-ciejowice in 1794, likewise invokes the image of an omnivorous Death who levels all distinctions of nation, party, and ideology in a bloodbath of universal and indis-criminate destruction.[17] Who are those, the speaker asks of Freedom,

> . . . that madly bear
> Against thy sons the venal spear?
> Are they not men?—then say, what power
> Can bid my bosom mourn no more;
> O where's the fiend-delighting ban
> Forbidding MAN to weep for SLAUGHTERED MAN!   (ll. 43–48)

It is not a matter of French, British, Prussian, Russian, or Polish; it is simply men killing men, brothers slaying brothers, Cain destroying Abel. In this orgy of senseless mutual slaughter the female voice attempts to intervene.

Women's traditionally gendered role in the domestic sphere of course lends a particular moral and ethical legitimacy to the concerns they express in their own writing, whether on war or on other social issues. Speaking as wives, mothers, sisters, and "guardians of family and community values" (Epstein, 23), they can articulate elements of the radical agenda in ways that at least partially insulate them from the sort of criticism leveled against the more explicit radical discourse of the men. What is especially distinctive about radical poems in this mode is their tendency explicitly to identify the government (and, less frequently, the nation) as one of the threats. As is characteristic of radical rhetoric generally, the established government is figured as posing as much of a threat to the domestic circle—the family—as to the national family that is often emblematized in the contemporary caricature print in the female figure of Britannia, the "mother" country, beset by companies of males whose garb identifies them both with foreign nations and with traditional domestic institutions of power. Interestingly, by the end of the Regency, under the very different circumstances of post-Waterloo radical/reform agitation, the significations of this same iconography came to be almost entirely reversed, as we see in George Cruikshank's astonishing and sexually charged melding, in *Death or Liberty!* (1 December 1819), of this familiar image with the iconography of *The Rape of Lucretia* (as for instance in Titian's version). Cruikshank's powerful and troubling image presents a Britannia who is being sexually assaulted not by representatives of Government (domestic or foreign) but rather by the skeletal figure of Death, from behind whose neck flares in the wind a cape bearing the words "RADICAL REFORM" (reproduced in Vogler, 17).

Michael Scrivener has written that the reform movement that began to coalesce in the 1780s and that culminated most visibly in the formation in 1792 of the London Corresponding Society had by 1797 begun to disintegrate as a result of both government suppression and the diminution of public support for the reformist agenda. Not until after Waterloo did the reformist movement as it had initially been known reappear, and then it was short lived, surviving barely longer than the Queen Caroline affair of 1820–21 (Scrivener, *Poetry and Reform,* 12–13). That the Pitt government took the lead in suppressing both moderate reformism and more active radicalism, and that the Foxite Whigs even participated to some extent, is not surprising given the volatility of the 1790s. And because the issues at the heart of national debates often differed, both in temper and in details, from those of individual regions in Britain, the government often exploited these regional differences to stymie systematic opposition.[18] Moreover, radicals and reformers alike were further undermined by additional ideological fractures that fell along class lines. For one thing, the middle classes feared the poor, seeing in them a threat that was in many respects as great a danger to their own stability and prosperity (because the poor constituted an implicit threat to their *property*) as that which was posed by scheming ministerial climbers and entrenched aristocrats alike. For the emerging middle classes, this was a Scylla and Charybdis defined on one hand by the incipient anarchy embodied in the uneducated and impoverished masses and on the other by the defiant corruption epitomized by the entrenched sociopolitical establishment. "'Old Corruption' meant religious discrimination, aristocratic domination of parliament, disabling restrictions on trade and business, and overall a government that did not adequately represent the society" (Scrivener, *Poetry and Reform,* 15). The locus of this corruption, in the view of the middle classes, lay largely at the ministerial level and at that of the privileged aristocracy whose interests parliament and ministries alike seemed determined to advance at the expense of all others.

Part of the appeal of the more radical thinkers therefore lay in the skill with which they managed to remind their public(s) of the "good old days" of Magna Carta, conjuring up a nostalgic scenario built on the idea of a compact that existed between the monarch and "the people" without the middling interference of ministers and civil servants. Hence one element of radical verse from the 1790s can be seen in strident anti-Pittite poems like those that Mary O'Brien published in Ireland in the late 1780s and the 1790s in the wake of the Regency crisis. During this period, British citizens had good reason to fear the consequences of the king's incapacitation, which seemed to open the way for aggrandizers like Pitt. Indeed, For O'Brien the issue is clearly one of ministerial usurpation of power and prerogative. Without actually naming him, O'Brien refers to Pitt in *The Political Monitor; or, Regent's Friend* (1790) as "that ambitious minister whose aspiring hand had, on the melancholy occasion [of George III's illness] nearly subjugated to his pleasure the whole executive power of the state" (vi). Even the Prince Regent, who would have been granted full authority to rule in his father's stead had the Regency Bill of 1789 passed,[19] appears in O'Brien's view to be co-opted by Pitt:

> The Regent you form'd
>   Our nation supposes,
> Is a bond Prince of Egypt;
>   A captive like Moses.   (14, ll. 33–36)

In another poem from the same volume, "Thoughts on a Modern Prodigy," the spectral figure of Pitt arrives, Satanlike, to menace the nation:

> What means yon spectre that athwart mine eye,
>   In voice terrifick, strikes th' abstracted ear?

Forth from the bosom of yon dusky sky,
    In form gigantic, view the shade appear.

Deep roused, I see the shadow near the throne,
    A sacred terror now inverts my sight,
His puny arm, stretch'd forth, attempts the crown;
    Britons prepare to guard your Prince's right.

And art thou, trifler! of that sacred band,
    Rais'd by thy country far above thy sphere;
Chief of those rulers placed by Wisdom's hand,
    Who watch their country's rights with awful care?
.   .   .   .
Think not to mount on Falsehood's painted plumes,
    The visionary summit of Ambition's tower;
For ere thy imperious hope that state assumes,
    Virtue shall bar thee from the seat of power.   (18–19, ll. 13–24, 33–36)

Both poems situate the real threat to the nation in the power-hungry ministers who intrude themselves between the people and their sovereign. Nor was O'Brien alone in her sentiments; her Irish countrywoman Henrietta Battier took a comparable position in poems published at about the same time (as chapter 6, on the period's Irish women poets, demonstrates).

Writing as "Tabitha Bramble," Mary Robinson, whose radical sentiments were never in doubt, attacked Pitt and his ministers on more than one occasion in the *Morning Post*. In "A New Song," published in the *Morning Post* on 19 February 1798, Tabitha Bramble explicitly links Pitt with the subversion of British liberty:

While, with taxes on taxes, this fathomless Pitt,
Still palsies our virtue, and bids us submit;
Tho' we starve and go naked, we dare not complain,
For the devil that drives holds the T[reasur]y's *rein!*

The poem's structure and style echo those of a poem that had appeared in the third volume of her novel, *Walsingham* (1797), where it bore the title "Stanzas, on the World." Robinson expanded that poem's six stanzas to nine when she published it separately under the simple title of "Stanzas" in the *Gentleman's Magazine* in 1797.[20] In keeping with radical verse's fondness for wordplay, Robinson plays wittily on words like "rein," which inevitably melds for the reader into the implied "reign," and with the emblematic name of Pitt, who was frequently represented in contemporary caricatures as a gaping hole in the ground.

Of particular interest for their overt radicalism are the poems attributed to the unidentified "F. A.C." that appeared during the 1790s. As Michael Scrivener notes, her poems are among "the most uncompromisingly militant" poems of the radical and reform press (*Poetry and Reform,* 123). Like others in this vein, they contrast the sacrifices of "the brave revolutionaries of the seventeenth century" with the unprincipled cowardliness of the citizens of the contemporary world. Her "Lines Written by a Female Citizen!" (published by John Thelwall in the *Tribune* in 1795) exhibits several characteristic features of radical discourse, including the conspicuous use in the title of "citizen," which would have immediately suggested *citoyen* to British republican readers.[21] The poem opens with the poet questioning her muse:

> Why slumbers now my Muse? is this a time?
> When savage war depopulates each clime?
> When dire destruction holds her deadly sway,
> And rising horrors blast the face of day?
> When the once fruitful field is crimson'd o'er,
> And earth's pale bosom stain'd with horrid gore,
> While many a weeping peasant's left to mourn,
> His harvest trampl'd, and his hopes forlorn,
> His kindred slain, and his once happy cot,
>
> . . . .
>
> Wrapt in devouring flames, or prostrate laid
> By frantic glory's desolating trade.   (ll. 1–14)

The ravages of war ("frantic glory's desolating trade") depicted here are apparently those that have already transpired on the Continent, since they are reported as having already occurred. But the poem's descriptions hint with foreboding at the consequences for Britons should the conflict spread to English soil, as it was fully expected to do.

Turning from this sad spectacle, the poet, her own human sympathy "oppress'd," assesses the situation in Britain:

> Here as I turn with sympathy oppress'd,
> With indignation rising in my breast,
> My injur'd country's woes demand my care.
> Detested scrowls [scrolls] her ripening fate declare:

Britannia's children droop in galling chains,
And lawless Pow'r her boasted annals stains;
With strides gigantic shakes the trembling land,
And lifts aloft oppression's iron hand!   (ll. 15–22)

The poem strips the conflict's local circumstances of identifiably national signifiers, replacing them with the universal pathos they generate: it is not *Frenchmen* (or Dutch, or Flemings, or Austrians) who are victimized but rather the undifferentiated "peasants" who are simply *people,* whatever their nationality.

This humane and responsive "sympathy," the appeal to which the poem makes in strongly maternalistic, nurturant terms, is the source of the two corresponding emotions delineated in the remainder of the poem: indignation and protectiveness. The latter makes "my injur'd country's woes *demand*" (rather than simply excite or even require) the speaker's care. Moreover, this demand is presented rhetorically as the demand of a child on its mother: it is Britannia's *children* that concern the speaker, who is herself both mother and England within this variation on the familiar nation-family trope. Moreover, the author's choice of Britannia, the female emblem of England, further underscores the "femaleness" of the poem's frame of reference. According to the poem's logic, it is Power—specifically the "lawless" power that a presumably masculinist governing establishment has arrogated to itself in defiance of both the historical civil "laws" of individual and societal rights and the "laws" of nature—that oppresses the nation and stains the "boasted annals" of British liberty. The nation is "injured" not by a foreign adversary but rather by an internal, domestic cancer, and the result is the erosion and finally the death of "each lov'd right and privilege" (the nation's figurative children) as "Freedom from her native seat retire[s]" (ll. 51–52). Although the poem implicitly contrasts the nation's current crisis with that of the revolutionary seventeenth century, the final lines hearken back to the myth of the Anglo-Saxon compact and to

Those sires who dar'd with tyranny contend,
A peoples' [sic] dearest interests to defend,
Anxious their *charter'd liberties* to save,
They scorn'd the life that bore the name of slave!   (ll. 57–60; my emphasis)

Appearing as it does in the poem's penultimate line, the politically and culturally overcoded reference to "charter'd liberties" serves a powerful rhetorical purpose—especially when it is followed immediately by the counterposed image of enslavement—in reminding the readers both of the admirable historical precedent and of what is at stake in the present crisis.

The rhetorical and thematic forces that coalesce in this poem are analogous to those we find in Jacobin fiction of the period; the poem's combination of "political radicalism, concern for the poor, and effusive emotionalism" recalls the fiction of authors like Wollstonecraft and Thomas Holcroft (Stafford, *Socialism,* 43). In F. A.C.'s poem, power is linked with "titl'd Pomp" and "fell Injustice" in the "sinking state, / Where thousands perish for the proud and great" (ll. 24–28). Interestingly, F. A.C. employs the familiar technique of the negative definition to set "greatness" against genuine "worth and virtue" (l. 29), which she thus implies are by default the attributes of the oppressed citizens:

> Virtue must shrink from man's inveterate foe;
> From those who honest industry despoil,
> Fed by the tradesman's and the peasant's toil—
> Their toil who labour for their scanty meal,
> Constrain'd the woes of indigence to feel,
> While the best produce of their daily gains,
> The drones of vice and luxury maintains.   (ll. 30–36)

This passage is remarkable in its anticipation of later poems like Percy Bysshe Shelley's "Song to the Men of England" (1819) that take up both the bee figure of the "drone" (drawn in particular from Mandeville's *Fable of the Bees* [1714]) and the notion of a privileged class that subsists, in defiance of all natural laws, on the labor of an oppressed class whose subjugation has grown so habitual that its unnaturalness is no longer even questioned—by either side. The terrible consequences for humanity of the vampiristic predation worked on them by the powerful, self-serving, and conscienceless materialists explains the particularly strong adjective by which F. A.C. designates them: "man's *inveterate* foe."

Notice, too, that F. A.C. introduces tradesmen into her equation here, joining their cause to that of the peasant. F. A.C. is writing at the dawn of British working-class literature, whose (often satirical) poetry is characterized by "ridicule of the oppressor and uncompromising support for the people" and whose most frequent subjects are abstract qualities like freedom and natural reason. Paul Thomas Murray observes that working-class poems are "almost always political and occasional" (97), a characteristic they share with radical poetry. The alliance of peasant and tradesman suggests the mutual interests that cross lines of class and occupation as well as (by implication) nationality. Radical and working-class writers deliberately blur national, occupational, and class lines to internationalize the issues. This casts the contenders in the drama not as England and France but rather as the oppressors and the oppressed, whose respective interests (on both sides of the channel) establish solidarities along ideological and class lines rather than geographical or strictly nationalistic ones. This is the same internationalization that culminated nearly a century later, in 1871, in "The Internationale," the anthem for leftists written in Paris by Eugène Pottier and Pierre Degeyter. Radical writers typically frame their ideological argument in terms of fidelity to *principle* (reason, liberty, nature, community) rather than to nation, so that a writer like Richard "Citizen" Lee, a member of the London Corresponding Society, could argue in 1795 in favor of a "cosmopolitan" view that disdained as "disorderly passions" the narrowly nationalistic jingoism that disrupts or demolishes the preferred "diffusive spirit of universal affection" (19–28).[22]

Here is where the deliberately constructed female voice of a poet like F. A.C. carries special force, for the sympathetic response (for which "affection" is the ubiquitous token especially in writings dating from the early part of the Romantic period) evoked by "Lines Written by a Female Citizen!" (and others like it) is rooted in the tradition of sentiment and sensibility. The historical association of that tradition with women's experience and women's writing had become increasingly pronounced in the later eighteenth century with the growing perception of the novel as predominantly a woman's literary form, one whose readership was also heavily female. Throughout poems in this tradition, the supposedly "natural" or "instinctive" feminine, nurturant response informs the concern with—and the indignation at—aggressively male manifestations of "lawless Pow'r" like the "strides gigantic" and the "iron hand," both of which shake "the trembling land" (ll. 21–22). Indeed, it is worth considering in this light the pointed ambiguity of "the trembling land." Perhaps the land trembles from the repercussions of that gigantic power figure's strides. But perhaps the land—the nation (historically associated with the female in the gendered rhetoric of political discourse)—trembles with the fear that is characteristic of the often-abused spouse. Or perhaps the land trembles, just as the speaker does, with indignation and with an impending explosion of pent-up energy in revolution. There can be no question that F. A.C. artfully plants all these implications in this powerful poem; the use in the title of the blatantly inflammatory and revolutionary double identifier, "a Female Citizen," anticipates and underscores the several varieties of solidarity among the oppressed that the poem goes on to evoke and explore.

The *Tribune,* operated by John Thelwall after his acquittal in the notorious Treason Trials of 1794, was a major, albeit short-lived, player on the radical scene. So was the *Moral and Political Magazine,* which, like Thelwall's *Tribune,* had its roots in the London Corresponding Society and that likewise lasted less than a year.[23] It is not surprising, therefore, to discover that F. A.C.'s work appeared there as well. Her "Invocation to the Genius of Britain" (reproduced in Scrivener, *Poetry and Reform,* 129–30) takes up similar themes, once again beginning with a lament:

Spirit! brave spirit of a free born race!
Why do'st thou slumber in an evil hour;
E'en now when shame, when ruin, and disgrace,
Are dealt unsparing from the hand of pow'r?   (ll. 1–4)

It was the poet's muse that slumbered in "Lines Written by a Female Citizen!" but
now it is the spirit of Britain that slumbers despite the perfidious conduct of the
powerful. As happens regularly in the millenarian verse of the 1790s with which radical poetry shares so much thematically, rhetorically, and stylistically, and as happens
too in the poetry composed during the later and much altered radical insurgency of
the Regency, the poet implores this "brave spirit" to rouse itself:

Spirit awake! awake! once more inspire,
With glowing energy each Briton's soul,
Teach him to emulate each god-like sire,
And scorn to stoop beneath a base controul.   (ll. 21–24)

The call to wake and to rise echoes again and again in radical writings throughout
the Romantic period; Shelley's exoteric poems of 1819 furnish several memorable
examples. Writer after writer implores her or his readers and auditors to shake off the
repression the established powers have gradually imposed on the populace, repression that that populace now regards not as the unnatural imposition that it is but
rather as the unfortunate but inevitable and even natural state of affairs.

F. A. C.'s "Invocation" recycles material from the "Lines Written by a Female
Citizen!" including the figure of "oppression's giant form" which here again paces
"the trembling land . . . / While abject slav'ry with submissive mien / Stoops low
to kiss the terror dealing hand" (ll. 25–28). This poem further illustrates F. A. C.'s
skill at combining multivalent references: she associates the volatile issue of slavery
with her psychologically astute observation about the tendency of victims of ongoing abuse to defer to—even to become romantically attracted to—their abusers: a
sort of sociopolitical "Stockholm Syndrome." Furthermore, her delight in loaded
language is obvious in her command to the Spirit in the poem's ringing coda:

. . . with a strong and powerful arm
Arrest the dreaded tyrant on his way,
Nor, yielding to the *terror* of *alarm,*
The mandates of despotic pow'r obey.   (ll. 33–36; my emphases)

"Arrest," which on one level means simply "halt" or "stop," resonates on another
level with the suggestion of the unlawful nature of the tyrant's power garb and the

consequently lawful remedy to that usurpation. Likewise, the caution not to be swayed by "the terror of alarm" is easily transposed into a warning not to be so over-wrought at the alarm over the Terror (in France) as to be seduced into supporting the dictates of the unlawful domestic power as a supposedly preferable alternative.

Rhetoric and Nationhood

The sheer rhetoricality of much of radical writing suggests the extent to which authors sought to emulate the dynamics of spoken discourse. Less an affectation than an attempt to convey actual verbal inflection, the abundance of italics and exclamation points in this writing underscores the deliberately auditory aspect of radical verse. David Worrall has written that the ultra-radicals preferred speech to writing because "the oral mode of textuality was less susceptible to scrutiny by the Government's surveillance system" (5). The temporal insubstantiality of *speaking* one's words in public certainly made that mode of utterance safer than physically publishing one's words. There is no question that the poets fully appreciated the effects on a reader—especially a reader who was "sympathetic" in the sense in which I have been using the word here—of the powerful orality of their printed verse. By the later Regency, moreover, the poetry of radical journalists like Wooler and Hone makes it clear that for them the craft of poetry was largely irrelevant; for Hone, "the quality of a poem lies not in its rhyme and rhythm but rather in its political truth and power" (Murphy, 105). It is not surprising, then, that radical poetry gravitates toward "simple" verse forms and familiar rhetorical strategies. The effectiveness of popular forms like the four-line ballad stanza, or of verse expressly designated as song (often with the tune to which it is to be sung stipulated at the head of the poem), in propagating the radical agenda cannot be underestimated. Nor should it be forgotten that these particular poetic *forms* had been resurrected most notably in England in Bishop Thomas Percy's *Reliques of Ancient Poetry* (1767) and in Ireland in Charlotte Brooke's *Reliques of Irish Poetry* (1789) and that they had been popularized thereafter in the work of writers of all stripes. These indigenous forms had been associated by Percy and others with the tradition of the "Saxon bard" and by Brooke with the Celtic bards; works that addressed the people in these simple poetic forms, and in an easily comprehensible language and rhetoric, were understood to possess "powerful political and moral force" (Bennett, *British War Poetry*, 51). In their satires in the *Anti-Jacobin* (November 1797 to July 1798), George Canning and John Hookham Frere (to name the principals) audaciously turned these same poetic models against the same reform-minded poets who had employed them; the effectiveness of this tactic testifies to both those forms' wide currency and their proven effectiveness as vehicles for ideological argument.[24] Indeed, even before the *Anti-Jacobin*'s appearance, Hannah More's Cheap Repository Tracts had demonstrated the efficacy of this strategy for countering radical thinking and radical poetic forms by turning both against themselves in poems she deliberately crafted for mass readerships whose literacy was minimal but whose potential for violent political action was understood to be great. The full title and opening stanza of More's "The Riot" illustrate a number of the features I just mentioned:

> The Riot; or, Half a Loaf Is Better Than No Bread
>   in a dialogue between Jack Anvil and Tom Hod
> To the Tune of—"A Cobbler there was"
> [Written in Ninety-five, a Year of Scarcity and Alarm]
>
>   TOM
> Come, neighbours, no longer be patient and quiet
> Come let us go kick up a bit of a riot;
> I'm hungry, my lads, but I've little to eat,
> So we'll pull down the mills, and we'll seize all the meat:
> I'll give you good sport, boys, as you ever saw,
> So a fig for the justice, a fig for the law.
> Derry down.   (*Works*, 1:334)

The poem proceeds to deconstruct Tom's intemperate attitude as both inappropriate and immoral—and of course unnatural.

Although she may have been unusually outspoken, F. A.C. was certainly not the period's only active radical woman poet. Indeed, women's obvious visibility on the radical scene is indicated by the appearance in the 15 January 1798 *Anti-Jacobin* of "Lines, Written at the Close of the Year 1797" and attributed to "an Englishwoman" (reproduced in Rice-Oxley, 32–33). Driven by the *Anti-Jacobin*'s customary antipathy to authors that the editors regarded as dangerous Jacobins, this smugly nationalistic, reactionary poem answers the sort of rhetoric we see in F. A.C.'s poetry. It cites the same ostensible historical heritage invoked by the radicals but claims it instead for its own side:

>   Yes! unsupported *Treason's* standard falls,
> *Sedition* vainly on her children calls,
> While cities, cottages, and camps contend,
> The King, their Laws, their Country to defend.   (ll. 23–26)

These are not the ancient authorities sacred to the radical ideology, however, but rather those represented specifically by Pitt and contemporary Toryism. That the rest of the poem entrusts British welfare—and indeed the welfare of the entire world—to a "Heav'n" from which "the flame of British courage burns" and to "HIM" "At whose 'great bidding' empires rise and fall" (ll. 35–39) reflects that strain of eighteenth-century British nationalism by which England had designated itself the new Israel and its citizens the chosen people.[25] Within this messianic cultural schema it was the current possessors of power whose interests were to be best served by the secular deification implied in this new Israel, not the disenfranchised and the unenfranchised whom the radicals sought to remind of the putative status and authority (in)vested in them (rather than in any set of rulers) under the Anglo-Saxon compact.

Obviously, not everyone subscribed to that gilded image of an English promised land, and the price of dissent was often considerable, especially for women. I close this chapter not with another poem from the 1790s but rather with one published more than a decade later. The reception accorded Anna Letitia Barbauld's *Eighteen Hundred and Eleven* (1812) is instructive, for Barbauld (who had after all in 1793 published an antiwar prose treatise—*Sins of Government, Sins of the Nation*—anatomizing the state of affairs in England) was widely respected as an educator, critic, intellectual, and poet. Remarkably, the opening of this powerful poem picks up the themes—and even the language—that appear in F. A.C.'s poems some fifteen years earlier. Barbauld itemizes the ways in which "Colossal Power with overwhelming force / Bears down each fort of Freedom in its course" so that

> . . . where the Soldier gleans the scant supply,
> The helpless Peasant but retires to die;
> No laws his hut from licensed outrage shield,
> And war's least horror is the ensanguined field.   (ll. 19–22)

Of course, the political situation in England was very different in 1811 than it had been a decade and a half earlier, when the French Revolution was still recent and its progress still unfolding. Then, neither the excesses of the young republic nor the subsequent rise of Napoleon had yet prompted advocates among both genders to temper or even entirely to recant their initial revolutionary enthusiasm and radical politics.

By 1811, the situation for Britain and her allies appeared bleak indeed. The Peninsular War seemed to be going nowhere, despite Portugal's plucky resistance, while Napoleon had cowed both Russia (in 1807) and Austria (in 1809) into treaties and now dominated continental Europe. He already had his eye on Russia, and had he timed his invasion differently or managed it effectively, Napoleonic France might soon have exercised hegemonic control over the entire continent. Meanwhile, Britain stood on the verge of the war with the United States that finally erupted in 1812 and that threatened to isolate and debilitate the nation still further. At the same time, Britain was daily edging nearer domestic rebellion. The spreading Luddite lawlessness that threatened British manufacturing constituted a dangerous form of civil unrest that probably required little more than a charismatic leader and a coordinated strategy to erupt into full rebellion. The economy, too, was in desperate straits, with innumerable bankruptcies complicating the effects of the weak and inflated currency against which radical journalists like William Cobbett railed. With George III's relapse into madness looking irreversible and his widely despised and unpredictable eldest son the Prince of Wales ostensibly in charge, Britons had little reason for optimism. In *Eighteen Hundred and Eleven,* therefore, Barbauld was merely voicing gloomy sentiments that were widely shared across the boundaries of class, party, and gender. It is not unreasonable to say that the weary nation now saw in the war the larger issue of England's survival, both as a nation and as an abstract, symbolic concept. This is one reason why *Eighteen Hundred and Eleven* elicited such a passionate response. In a very real sense, Barbauld's remarkable poem questions both the temporal worth (and cost) for the nation itself of this protracted struggle and the symbolic worth of England as a functionally depleted emblem of moral, political, and intellectual leadership. Painfully aware of the growing antiwar sentiment, Barbauld's critics, like the Tory government itself, recognized this double point and reacted strongly to what they characterized as her affront to the collective national character. As William McCarthy and Elizabeth Kraft observe, in 1812 the British press was "almost unanimous" in regarding Barbauld's fine poem as "culpably subversive of national morale" (*Poems,* 310). Not surprisingly, the fact that the poetry was itself of high literary quality seemed if anything to compound Barbauld's culpability.

Although Barbauld was a lifelong defender of "independence, of political and personal freedom" (*Poems,* xxv), her poem, written nearly two decades after radical poems of the 1790s, differs from most of them in its Volneyesque vision of a future in which liberty thrives not in the Old World but rather in the New, in the Americas. At the same time, however, the poem shares with them the deep-seated moral conviction of British error, British guilt. Indeed, its vision of the future seems to bear out the predictions of her old acquaintance, Coleridge, who had in his "Ode to the Departing Year" (1796) declared "O Albion! thy predestin'd ruins rise" (l. 146). Coleridge deprecated his country's errors and misplaced priorities in poems like the ode and "Fears in Solitude" (1798), and William Wordsworth had followed suit in his political sonnets of 1802 and then (also like Coleridge) publicly regretted his "un-filial fears" (l. 8) later in the year in a sonnet like "When I Have Borne in Memory." Barbauld does not reverse positions, but unapologetically chastises Britain, declaring that "Thou who hast shared the guilt [for the protracted war] must share the woe" (l. 46). This theme of shared responsibility was often attached to a host of social and political issues. In her "Poverty" of 1794–95, for instance, Sarah Spence wrote about the privileged Londoners' contemptuous dismissal of the Irish poor:

> While thus, *some* inly rave, *others* there are
> Whose ardent pleadings bless our favored Isle:
> Their virtues have a voice that's heard in Heav'n;—
> They say:—Spare—spare this guilty land; avert
> Th' impending storm—pardon the Authors of
> This baleful War;—nor doom to woe our land.   (*Poems,* conclusion)[26]

This suggestion that Britain's immoral conduct invites God's punishment was a familiar feature of poems attacking the slave trade, many of which were addressed to women, like the Dublin Quaker Mary Birkett's two-part *Poem on the African Slave Trade* (1792), which, as its subtitle tells us significantly, is *Addressed to Her Own Sex.* Barbauld deliberately continued to include in her poems rhetorically charged references to "slavery"—whether political, economic, intellectual, moral, or cultural—even when those poems had begun to take up subjects other than abolition.

In its assessment of Barbauld's *Eighteen Hundred and Eleven,* whose considerable literary merit it acknowledged, the *Eclectic Review* reverted back to the very word that Coleridge and Wordsworth had used in the concluding lines of the poems in which they publicly regretted their early republican enthusiasms, remarking of the poem's tone that it is "in a most extraordinary degree unkindly and unpatriotic—we had almost said *unfilial*" (my emphasis).[27] Barbauld's poem echoes sentiments like those Amelia Alderson Opie had expressed in poems such as "Ode, Written on the Opening of the Last Campaign" (1795) and "Ode on the Present Times," in the latter of which Opie laments the misfortune of "FAMINE" (l. 67) that is about to descend on England ("O Britain! ill-starred land" [l. 55]) as a consequence of the nation's orgy of warmaking (reproduced in Bennett, 137–42).[28] The warnings that poets like Spence, Opie, Coleridge, and Wordsworth were sounding in the 1790s, like Barbauld's more than a decade later, were no mere versified nationalistic jingoism. Rather, they were prophetic warnings about the universal effects of indiscriminate war that are visited on both contending parties—and especially on its most innocent victims—and about the moral consequences for the nation as a whole of such inhumane rapacity.

Eighteen Hundred and Eleven marks a moral and philosophical return of sorts for Barbauld. Nearly twenty years earlier, in her anonymous *Sins of Government, Sins of the Nation,* she had castigated the moral hypocrisy—indeed the moral bankruptcy—of Britain's high-minded denunciations of the republican principles and practices of "neighbouring nations" (i.e., France) at the same time it sought to invoke "the blessing of God upon our commerce and our colonies" while nevertheless continuing the commerce in human victims represented by the slave trade. Barbauld was not alone in 1812 in believing that the nation was losing the moral struggle—and with it both its soul and its paradigmatic political and symbolic role—even as it appeared about to lose the military one as well. Barbauld's views place her in the company of those radicals and liberals throughout the entire era who attacked a British national posture and policy that visibly served those socioeconomic forces that consistently worked to the disadvantage of those citizens who had the most to lose—their lives—from the seemingly endless war. It was easy to condemn Napoleon's France after the collapse of the Peace of Amiens and Napoleon's shameful (self-) coronation. His subsequent prosecution of the blatantly imperialist Peninsular Wars especially outraged England, where militant opposition to France was presented as being in the best interests of Britain, the world, and indeed "Liberty" itself. It had become a jihad, a holy war in which the future of the world was said to hang in the balance and in which, therefore, any deviation from whole-hearted and unquestioning allegiance was portrayed as not just unpatriotic but both unnatural and unholy. This is one reason why even in the depressingly bleak circumstances of 1811–12 the hard-pressed British government resolutely refused to sue for peace. If the military and economic situation was precarious, the rhetorical posture had to be made to seem anything but.

The terms of the performative public rhetoric that came into play were familiar enough. The years following the fall of the Bastille had seen the pattern established as reactionary political, social, economic, and intellectual spokespersons cloaked the fears of the variously privileged whose interests they represented within the rhetoric of nationalistic self-justification. A prominent feature of this rhetoric was the figure of England as the bastion of freedom and liberty, most often sanctified by an actual or implied blessing from God that can even offset England's manifest sinfulness. Alternatively, the issue might be reduced to a simple binary: we may be bad, but everyone else is worse, so hooray for us. Shortly after the end of the war, Elizabeth Appleton put it this way in the preface to her novel, *Edgar: A National Tale* (1816):

Hail! my Country! thou England greatly superb and generously tender—guardian of liberty, protector of innocence;—thou who hast for ages immemorial succoured the oppressed, subdued the proud, and wept on the fallen. Fair isle, which hast a tear for every misery, a hero for every exploit, a heart for every sentiment; whose smile is caught up with extacy by surrounding empires, and whose frown causes nations to tremble. Sweet Albion, I salute thee! (1)

This was the sort of rhetoric that had been invoked countless times during the war years to motivate, inspire, and sustain the public in the face of a wearying struggle founded on often ambiguous moral, political, and economic principles. Once Britain had prevailed, it could assume a painfully and at times almost insufferably smug and self-congratulatory air.

Anne Grant's long exercise in this sort of nationalistic self-satisfaction, the analogously titled *Eighteen Hundred and Thirteen,* set about rebutting Barbauld's poem by means of the implied contrast invoked by her poem's name. If Barbauld's poem depicts an aging, declining England superseded by other nations and other empires, Grant's presents the contrary vision of a renewed, powerful, and divinely sanctioned Britain presiding both by might and by example over the world's bright future, from which tyranny (the Napoleonic regime and the French revolutionary experiment that had produced it) has been extirpated. As she says in her preface, "the view . . . of the present state and future prospects of this country, will be considered by many as just and well founded." Grant's Britain is, like Wordsworth's in "It Is Not to Be Thought" (1802), the product of a long cultural heritage:

> Our language, lineage, faith, are still the same,
> The torch that kindled Freedom's holy flame
> To light the western world, from British altars came;
> For them our sages think, our poets sing,
> They quaff, unchanged, the British muse's spring.
>
> . . . .
>
> Island of glory! from each chalky steep
> Thy genius seems to lighten o'er the deep;
> Thy strength of arm, thy magnitude of soul,
> Supports and cheers the weak from pole to pole;
> Wherever Sorrow weeps, or Slavery bends,
> Thy pity softens, and thy power extends:
> In spite of foreign force, or foreign wiles,
> The mountain Goddess here serenely smiles;
> Here guards that shrine which all the just revere,
> And builds her favourite gothic temple here.   (6, 54)

Grant's deliberate overlayering of religious terminology in these passages under-scores her conviction of Britain's divinely ordained destiny, as do the carefully bal-anced images of strength and tenderness.

The conclusion of Grant's poem is as different from that of *Eighteen Hundred and Eleven* as can be imagined. Barbauld's poem traces the passing of Liberty's torch from Britain to the nations of the Western Hemisphere.

> But fairest flowers expand but to decay;
> The worm is in thy core, thy glories pass away;
> Arts, arms and wealth destroy the fruits they bring;
> Commerce, like beauty, knows no second spring.
> Crime walks thy streets, Fraud earns her unblest bread,
> O'er want and woe thy gorgeous robe is spread,
> And angel charities in vain oppose:
> With grandeur's growth the mass of misery grows.
> For see,—to other climes the Genius soars,
> He turns from Europe's desolated shores;
> And lo, even now, midst mountains wrapt in storm,
> On Andes' heights he shrouds his awful form;
> On Chimborazo's summits treads sublime,
> Measuring in lofty thought the march of Time;
> Sudden he calls:—"'Tis now the hour!" he cries,
> Spreads his broad hand, and bids the nations rise.
> La Plata hears amidst her torrents' roar,
> Potosi hears it, as she digs the ore:
> Ardent, the Genius fans the noble strife,
> And pours through feeble souls a higher life,
> Shouts to the mingled tribes from sea to sea,
> And swears—Thy world, Columbus, shall be free.   (ll. 313–34)

In contrast to Barbauld's melancholy portrait of England's (and Europe's) "deso-lated shores," Grant's poem ends with a ringing peroration that leaves England's position of perpetual dominance unquestioned:

> . . . calmly seated on her rocky throne,
> Britannia makes the strength of waves her own;
> With stedfast eye surveys each neighbouring state,
> And, like the chosen minister of Fate,
> Injustice checks, encroaching power controuls,

And sheds celestial light on darkened souls;
No higher boon her better hopes desire,
Nor to a more diffusive power aspire;
To her the best, the holiest power is given,
For noblest purposes, derived from Heaven;
For her celestial muses tune their lyres,
For her Devotion fans her hallow'd fires:
To her fair Freedom gives her sacred cause,
Rejoicing nations bless her lenient laws;
O'er every land her energetic tongue
Conveys the lays her lofty bards have sung;
Her children spread o'er Earth's remote extremes,
Or by Columbia's lakes, or Ganges' streams,
Whether they serve, or suffer, or command,
Led by the Genius of their native land,
Shall at their country's hallow'd altars bend,
And truth and freedom o'er the world extend.

. . . .

That noble fabric, bound with patriot blood,
That long the wonder of the world hath stood,
That sanctuary which Heaven delights to bless,
And make the chosen refuge of distress,
Where Justice guards, and Mercy decks the throne,
O! highly-favoured Britons, is your own.   (144–46)

Not everyone who read *Eighteen Hundred and Thirteen* was as pleased as the critic who declared it to be "a spirited and polished work" that, "if we consider the subject in its proper light, [cannot] fail to rouse the utmost energy of Poetry in every breast devoted to the Muses"; others found it, not surprisingly, "too long" and "tedious."[29] As a resounding rejoinder to Barbauld's gloomy vision, however, there is little question that Grant accomplished what she set out to do.

As soon as Barbauld's *Eighteen Hundred and Eleven* appeared, the staunch Tory reviewer John Wilson Croker excoriated its author with particularly mean-spirited sarcasm in the *Quarterly Review* for her decision "to dash down her shagreen spectacles and her knitting needles, and to sally forth . . . in the magnanimous resolution of saving a sinking state."[30] Little had changed, it appears, for the independent-minded woman writer who intervened in public affairs, speaking both for *and to* her fellow citizens on matters of real import. Like her sisters of two decades earlier, Barbauld is faulted in Croker's review, specifically and explicitly, for what he portrays as her indecorous and short sighted (thus the spectacles) rejection of the emblems of her gender (her knitting needles) and her intrusion into the male arena of political discourse. What Sarah Spence had written about the mutually exclusive, gendered purviews of men and women seemed still to hold firm within the culture as a whole in 1812, when Barbauld's poem appeared. That the strains of radical thought visible in women's poetry of the 1790s were beginning to modulate into something else— something seemingly far more determinedly "domestic"—in the inhospitable climate of the Regency should not surprise us. Abolition was no longer a "hot-button issue," new domestic food shortages and other economic hardships were arising, Luddism signaled a new and dangerous labor-based radicalism, and the old reform movement was headed—along with Samuel Bamford, Orator Hunt, and their colleagues—toward Manchester's St. Peter's Fields and that bloody day in August 1819. Meanwhile, the conclusion of the Napoleonic Wars in 1815 removed one of the principal themes of that variety of oppositional radical discourse that women poets had for some two decades made, in a special way, their own. It left a gap that could not be filled in the same fashion, an opening that invited the playing out in women's poetry of different moral, intellectual, and aesthetic assumptions and practices. What began to emerge was another rhetoric—and another ideology—that would grow increasingly distinct from the male tradition represented by Scott, Byron, Moore, Percy Bysshe Shelley, and Keats. This alternative would take shape around the figures and the literary production of women like Felicia Hemans and Letitia Elizabeth Landon, as what has long been regarded as a predominantly masculinist culture of Romanticism began to reflect an evolving feminized and "domesticized" ethos that traditional literary history customarily associates with Victorian culture.

CHAPTER TWO

Women Poets during the War Years

The Culture of War

From 1 February 1793 through 18 June 1815, Britain was almost continually at war, except for the brief period from 25 March 1802 to 18 May 1803 that marked the ill-fated Peace of Amiens. The rest of these twenty-two-plus years witnessed a succession of variously configured coalitions ranged first against Revolutionary France and subsequently against Napoleon's expanding empire. By 1811, as noted in chapter 1, England stood on the brink of collapse. Battling on virtually alone against France, beset at home by social turmoil and a deepening economic crisis, poised for a new war with the United States, and doubly blasted by having an apparently irreversibly mad king and a throne occupied by his despised eldest son, the nation was indeed in perilous straits. The government had from the start routinely encouraged public displays of nationalism to strengthen both its hand and those of the economic interests who stood to gain the most from war profiteering. Throughout the nation, particularly after the government had begun exploiting people's fears of a French invasion, the public pageant of warmaking took on a theatricality that Linda Colley has described as "sad and revealing" (308). Many men were drawn to military service, despite the obvious risks, by the sheer *excitement* of going off to defeat Boney, whom innumerable caricature prints and anti-Napoleonic harangues alike had convinced them would be no match for them:

> To them, coming forward to defend Great Britain offered a brief chance to attempt something big, some slight opportunity to escape drudgery and mundane obligations and become for a time a person who mattered. . . . For a brief time, they could imagine themselves what so many folklore heroes were—doers of daring deeds, men of destiny, winners not losers. And they relished it. (308)

Driven as it was after 1803 by fear of invasion, British volunteerism swelled; the cause was defense of home and family, nation and heritage. Unlike those troops who had been shipped off to foreign soil in campaigns of liberation, these men saw themselves as the nation's last line of defense, and they were prepared to fight to the end:

> We shall defend our Island, whatever the cost may be, we shall fight on the beaches, we shall fight on the landing grounds, we shall fight in the fields and in the streets, we shall fight in the hills; we shall never surrender, and even if, which I do not for a moment believe, this Island or a large part of it were subjugated and starving, then our Empire beyond the seas, armed and guarded by the British Fleet, would carry on the struggle, until, in God's good time, the New World, with all its power and might, steps forth to the rescue and the liberation of the old.[1]

This was Winston Churchill a century and a half later, but Romantic-era Britons saw the issues in virtually the same way; only the opponent was different.

Nationalistic fervor became street theater. The Tory government built public support by continuing to whip up Francophobia as it had done since the Revolution. This exercise in social control was not without consequences for women, since reactionary moralists and politicians alike had criticized women's interest in public policy and political action as an "unnatural" reflection of their French sisters' objectionable involvement in revolutionary politics. Thus writers like Richard Polwhele, Thomas Gisborne, and Hannah More insisted on the separation of gender spheres to maintain both political stability and moral order in the nation.[2] Women had an appropriate role to play in the nation's defense, according to conventional thinking, but that role was an extension of their traditionally gendered roles as wives, mothers, and nursemaids, as in the case of the many women who formed "committees of clothing" to provide for the troops' needs. But even such activities had far-reaching consequences, for in caring for the needs of military men who were neither spouses nor relatives "women demonstrated that their domestic virtues possessed a public as well as a private relevance," which lent their activities a distinctly civic role (Colley, 261). Women also participated in the many propagandistic public ceremonies and pageants designed to serve as conspicuous manifestations of national resolve. Over sixty thousand citizens attended a "military festival" that included both men and women in Leeds in 1795, for instance, while twenty thousand in Wiltshire witnessed the presentation of the colors to the local yeomanry regiment in 1798; later, in London, more than two hundred thousand citizens watched the king review the volunteers in Hyde Park in 1803 (Cookson, 29).

To understand how Romantic-era women's poetry treated war, we need to consider its historical and demographic contexts. When war was declared in 1793 England was emerging from a period of military engagement that had included the Seven Years' War and, more recently, the war with the American colonies. Although hostilities with the Americans had ceased in 1781, the effects of the protracted exercise continued to be felt, both in economic terms and in human ones, well into the 1790s. Many Britons were therefore initially uneasy about engaging France again, especially since doing so struck many (as had the recent American conflict) as a campaign against citizens engaged in pursuing liberty, however defined. As the French Revolution's original egalitarian principles gradually gave place to Napoleon's imperialist designs, though, the mixed response of the earlier 1790s yielded to greater solidarity with British aims (and British nationalism), as we see in the widespread recantation by male writers like Coleridge, Southey, and Wordsworth of their earlier republican enthusiasm for the revolution. This trend accelerated after the collapse of the Peace of Amiens and Napoleon's subsequent coronation as emperor, which provided both actual and symbolic verification of his totalitarian ambitions. By the time of the Peninsular War, women poets like Felicia Hemans were not only extolling the virtues of the dashing soldiers ("That gallant band, in countless danger try'd") who were waging war against empire builders, but they were in fact marrying them.[3] Many women—including Hemans in the poems of her first decade[4]—wrote and published poems that celebrated both the fallen heroes of the wars and the less famous survivors who managed to return to Britain. Many of them enthused over the cause, too: British women "were more prominently represented among the ranks of conventional patriots in this conflict" than ever before in Britain's history, even though many of them believed "that war was always sinful, or that these wars in particular were wrong and oppressive" (Colley, 254). Like their male counterparts, they were often driven both by chauvinistic convictions about the threat posed by a potential invasion and by the sheer social force of peer pressure. But the women differed from their male contemporaries in the directness and the pathos with which they treated the situations of women and their families whose warriors failed to return—or who returned irreversibly altered. In their poems they thus managed to support the ostensible national interest while further staking out their own discursive territory: no longer confined exclusively to the domestic sphere, they proclaimed their presence in the public sphere, from which they were not to be evicted.

The outbreak of war with France in February 1793 found England alarmingly unprepared for full-scale hostilities.[5] The army's small force of fifty thousand was ill equipped and even worse trained. Half of this number was needed for domestic garrison and police duties, and most of the remaining troops were scattered widely throughout Britain's global empire. One immediate remedy for this manpower shortage was to employ mercenaries, as had been done in the campaign against the American colonies: fourteen thousand Hanoverians and eight thousand Hessians were quickly put on army payrolls to augment the British force. Yet even as late as the beginning of the Duke of York's incompetent campaign in Flanders in April 1793 the regular army still included only some seven thousand native British soldiers, many of them too young or too old to qualify for active service. When it saw action in Flanders, this motley force, supplemented by the often unreliable mercenaries, saw little success and was by May 1795 driven all the way to Bremen by the French general Pichegru. The modest number of men actually killed outright in action during the early Allied campaign, however, told only part of the tale of casualties. For to the number of men killed in action had to be added the many who perished on account of unsanitary conditions on the fields and in the field hospitals, especially during the brutal winter of 1793–94. The nation subsequently learned that those "killed or dead in service"—which figure took in both these categories of casualties without distinguishing between them—numbered an astonishing 18,596. Public disillusionment had already been captured early on in James Gillray's brilliant print, *Fatigues of the Campaign in Flanders* (20 May 1793). Gillray's image effectively contrasts the fat, hedonistic leaders (the Duke of York prominent among them) and their camp bawds with the gaunt, miserable uniformed soldiers who are compelled to serve as mere waiters and valets.

This division between those who "serve" and those who command them on the field or compel them from Crown and Parliament became a recurrent feature in visual and verbal texts alike for the next decade. This class-based distinction was of course most painfully apparent to the working classes, who supplied most of the cannon fodder. The Scottish poet Christian Milne, wife of a ship's carpenter, for example, stated the case this way:

> While tyrants sit enthron'd in state,
> With trophies at their feet,
> And fawning courtiers round them wait,
> With adulation sweet!
>
> Informing them in pompous strain,
> Of feats atchieved [sic] in war,
> That will immortalize their reign,
> And spread their fame afar.
>
> Ah! little reckon they the woe
> To many thousands wrought,

Who bleed and die, to crown their brow
With laurels dearly bought!

They think not of the bitter tears
By soldiers' widows shed,
When round a helpless group appears,
Imploring them for bread[.]

("The Wounded Soldier; A Tale," *Simple Poems,* 101, ll. 1–16)

Casualty figures for the Flanders campaign are not anomalous: they are typical for the period. In reality, for every soldier (and sailor) killed in action during the war years, many more died by other means, most often as a consequence of deficient sanitation, improper medical treatment, inadequate clothing, or insufficient food (or potable water). After the Flanders debacle Britons were for a few years spared comparable shocks from the Continent, since no more British forces landed there for four years. But British troops and noncombatant personnel were deployed elsewhere within the colonial empire, often with depressingly similar results. Their deaths furnish the subjects for numerous memorial poems like the one by the Sheffield poet Barbara Hoole (later Hofland) on the death in the West Indies of a Lt. Radford of the Royal Engineers who succumbed (along with others) to yellow fever in 1802.[6] In other words, war and empire building alike claimed both direct and indirect casualties, and those casualties were often mourned all the more keenly because so often they seemed wholly unnecessary.

By 1801, despite the substantial losses it had sustained in the West Indies and elsewhere, the army had nevertheless reached a force of some 150,000. When the Peace of Amiens was signed in 1802, however, Britain demonstrated its remarkable lack of foresight by reducing its regular army to some 40,000 men, which hasty action the nation rued when the war's resumption in 1803 required mobilizing a whole new armed force. Fears of an invasion, however, coupled with an effective alarmist campaign, enabled England quickly to put in place by 1804 some 75,000 regular infantry, 12,000 regular cavalry, 80,000 militia, and 343,000 yeomanry and state-funded volunteer corps. The yeomanry and volunteer corps were intended for local "home defense," however, and not for service abroad. Still, this left roughly 167,000 men, of whom 87,000 were soldiers of the line specifically designated for the Continental conflict. It has been estimated that in 1804 as many as 20 percent of all adult males in England were serving either in the regular army or in one of the other defense forces, including the volunteers (Christie, 170). In the industrialized areas, volunteerism averaged 35 percent (Colley, 298).

Nevertheless, maintaining and safeguarding an increasingly global empire meant that British forces were spread very thin. By 1809 (the year of the ignominious Convention of Cintra that marked for many the nadir of British military competence) nearly 700,000 soldiers served Britain. The garrison for the United Kingdom alone comprised some 108,000 regular infantry and cavalry, along with 65,000 militia, 200,000 local militia, and 190,000 volunteers. An additional 110,000 troops served abroad, including some 22,000 each in the Mediterranean and the West Indies, 24,000 in India, 4,000 in Ceylon, 8,000 in North America, 6,000 at the Cape of Good Hope (to safeguard this strategic point on the route to India), and 900 in Madeira. An additional 1,300 fighting men were required to guard the penal colonies in New South Wales (Australia). Finally, the troops at sea (who represented both artillery and the corps of engineers) accounted for an additional 18,000, and the expeditionary army in Portugal some 22,000 more. By 1814, the regular troops and the foreign and colonial troops together still numbered more than a quarter of a million.

The navy represents yet another set of numbers. Although the navy had been expanded by some thirty ships of the line during the ten years before 1793, and although large stores had been accumulated to provision them once sailors had been recruited (or impressed) to man them, it was still seriously undermanned. At the war's outset in February 1793, the total number of seamen and marines, including officers of all ranks, was only some 45,000. By October 1801 these numbers had swollen to approximately 135,000. Like the army, the navy unwisely reduced its numbers in the wake of the Peace of Amiens. By the end of 1803 the total number had dropped to about 100,000, and when the war ended in 1815 it was 90,000, although the intervening years witnessed considerable fluctuations. When the fledgling United States complicated matters for England by entering the picture as her adversary in the War of 1812, for instance, the numbers reached some 145,000.

Numbers and statistics like these have an inevitable sanitizing (and perhaps anaesthetizing) effect on nonspecialist historians and commentators who work at some remove from the lived realities that they represent. They permit us to avert our eyes from the distraught faces and ruined bodies of the participants and to contemplate instead only the faceless numbers. We are spared the *actuality,* the individual persons these numbers represent: Private William Wheeler of the Fifty-first Battalion (who survived), Sergeant John Donaldson (the Scot who served with Wellington in the Peninsular War and whose memoirs offer a lively and revealing picture of army life), the young rifleman John Harris who in an extraordinary gesture of pity proposed to the widow of his close friend Cochran who had perished in battle, or the unfortunate Duncan Stewart. Stewart, another Scot, enlisted after being gotten drunk by a recruiting party; his wife Mary was sent for, despite her advanced stage of pregnancy, but upon arriving she learned that she would not be permitted to accompany her husband. The traumatic separation that followed brought on labor, and mother and child both died. Crushed, Stewart sailed with his regiment and was one of the first of that unit to die in action.[7] Tales like these were remarkably common. They provided raw material for poets and prose writers alike, who could capitalize on their pathos precisely because by the time of Waterloo there were few Britons who were not personally acquainted with such stories. Not the stuff merely of sentimental writing or nationalist propaganda, war was a central and inescapable reality of British life, and its victims were real people who suffered and died in remarkable numbers.

The devastation wrought by the deaths abroad of husbands, sons, fathers, and brothers was naturally a common theme among women writers, who appreciated especially well the precarious social and economic situation which such deaths inevitably precipitated.[8] The plight of these victims of war would be traced in large part by women writers who no longer represented the higher, more privileged classes (as the Bluestockings had done) but who instead embodied the voices of the middle and lower classes and whose works therefore more typically reflect the mundane, quotidian realities at the center of their lives.[9]

War, Sentiment, and Rhetoric

Paula Backscheider has noted eighteenth-century women poets' growing public engagement with Britain's expanding empire and its wars around the world. By the end of the Romantic era, she notes, the poetry of writers like the Cumbrian Susanna Blamire "records the stretch of England's wars" and documents "the effects of war on ordinary citizens," even in what are ostensibly ballads about love (20–21). Again and again in this poetry, men die far from home (as Charlotte Smith's son did) and the surviving family suffers irreparable harm. Images of the home are suffused with melancholy, barrenness, and cold, while the fields of battle are depicted as wild, bleak, and drenched with blood:

> How many mothers, widows, orphans, mourn,
> How many brothers from their sisters torn,
> How many weep for faithful lovers slain,
> Whilst thou, Bellona, triumph'st o'er the plain.
>
> ([Mary Panton], "War," *Eloise,* 95, ll. 1–4)

Alternatively, poems portray the often-wretched existence of the veterans who return physically and mentally maimed, as in Catharine Upton's early and originally anonymous *The Siege of Gibraltar* (1781):[10]

If a maim'd soldier meets thy wand'ring eye,
Ne'er turn disgusted, but his wants supply;
Think how he lost his *limbs,* his *health,* his *home;*
Perhaps his *children,* to secure *thy own!*
Could there be found on earth a soul so poor
To turn the crippled vet'ran from his door;
Or think a tear of gratitude too much,
I'd blush that armies ever bled for such. (6)

Upton's poem first appeared a year before Helen Maria Williams's first poem, *Edwin and Eltruda* (1782), and three years before Charlotte Smith's *Elegiac Sonnets* (1784). By 1781, however, Mary Robinson had already published her youthful *Poems* (1775) and *Captivity, a Poem* (1777), and Anna Seward's popular *Elegy on Captain Cook* (1780) was already in its third edition. Poems like these had by 1790 established their authors' authority and influence well before the ascendancy of the male poets traditionally associated with early Romanticism. This fact has obvious significance for the reassessment of British writing during the Romantic era, because it locates British Romanticism's rise well before both 1789 (when according to some accounts "Romanticism" began at the Bastille on 14 July)—and 1798 (when a scarcely noticed, anonymous little volume called *Lyrical Ballads* was published). More important, it illustrates women's early prominence in the intellectual and cultural project undertaken in the verse dating from the years that followed Britain's cessation of hostilities with her former American colonies in 1781.

It is no coincidence that this early period saw poems by women that also examined national issues like imperialist exploration (*Elegy on Captain Cook*) and empire building in the new world (Williams's *Peru* [1784]). Nor is it a coincidence, either, that women continued to examine war's political, economic, and social ramifications even after Waterloo. This fact continues to elude many literary and cultural historians, as is evident for example from William St. Clair's recent study of British reading audiences. On one of the rare occasions when he mentions women poets, he observes that "to write about war, history, and voyages to remote lands, was to venture into the masculine public sphere about which they could be expected to know little. . . . In their celebration of official religious military values the women romantic poets were more unyielding than the men" (215–16). This notion is patently incorrect, both in its assessment of the literary culture and in its blithe dismissal of the actual work produced by significant numbers of women poets over several decades.

War was central to the ideological agenda of radical and reformist women writers like those discussed in chapter 1. They treated war within the framework of their broader cultural critique of egregious violations of the "natural" human rights of citizens—especially considered in terms of that most basic of social units, the family—by the institutions of hereditary power and authority that were historically controlled and directed by men. In the preceding chapter I outlined some of the ways in which Romantic-era women writers—and especially women poets—contested in public, in print, many of the same social, political, economic, and "moral" institutions that were targeted explicitly during the 1790s by radical male writers like Thomas Spence, Daniel Isaac Eaton, and John Thelwall and later, during the Regency, by journalists like Thomas Wooler and William Hone. Those male writers have been the subjects of revisionist studies (like Michael Scrivener's illuminating study of Thelwall, *Seditious Allegories*) that build on such interdisciplinary assessments of the political culture as those of Jon Klancher, Marcus Wood, and Kevin Gilmartin. In this chapter I examine within this broad cultural context how women poets treated war and its effects. Their sophisticated understanding of the dynamics of author-publisher-audience relations—especially when it came to matters of oppositional politics—visibly influenced how they framed their discourse.

To be fair, when measured by the era's total poetic output, the number of poems by women that were published about the war itself or that engaged in extensive explicit criticism *or praise* of the war effort were relatively few. Opponents, even those whose associations with radical and antiwar associations are known, tended to be circumspect and indirect in their approach to the subject—and for very good reason. For even though by 1793 women were firmly established members of the literary community—widely published and widely read—their gender still exposed them to antifeminist attacks like those of Mathias's *Pursuits of Literature* and Polwhele's *The Unsex'd Females,* which used politics as a pretext for attacking women's literary and intellectual activities. More important, though, was the vulnerability that came with most women's legal dependence on men—husbands, sons, fathers, brothers—for their social and financial welfare. For a woman to engage in explicit antiwar writing was as dangerous economically and socially as it was politically; left "on her own" (i.e., widowed, abandoned, or otherwise deprived of male social and economic support), a woman who was known to have voiced strong opposition might find herself denied even the minimal assistance she might otherwise receive from a community prone to interpreting her misfortune as divine retribution for her "disloyalty." In approaching their subjects, then, oppositional women writers often adopted a strategy of indirection or substitution. For instance, they typically stressed the suffering inflicted on private individuals (and their families) by war-making, concentrating on sentiment and pathos to carry their argument against not *this* particular war (and its nationalistic imperatives) but rather against war in general (and its universal consequences). They frequently employed the trope of the nation-family to emphasize by analogy how the devastation of the family parallels the inevitable destruction also of the state, the intimate microcosm of the former figuring the public macrocosm of the latter.

Not surprisingly, then, many poets adopted the sentimental mode as part of their implicit appeal to a shared experience, and their choice of genre often reflected this mode. The lyric was particularly suited, both because of its inherently personal or "interior" nature and because of the expressive qualities that Charlotte Smith had been able to exploit so successfully (and so influentially) in the sonnets and the lyric pieces in her *Elegiac Sonnets, and Other Poems,* which by her death in 1806 had already gone through nine editions while swelling into two thick volumes. That women poets chose to write lyrics also reflected the prevailing gendered notions of the poetic forms particularly suited to women's talents and sensibilities. And yet these poems are often much more than the mere "poetic effusions" that their ostensibly self-effacing authors termed them, displaying considerable rhetorical subtlety and sophisticated audience manipulation. Backscheider observes (144–45) that the large number of specifically religious lyrics—of hymns—produced by eighteenth-century women poets, for example, refutes the notion, voiced by Joshua Scodel, for one, that the "personal lyric" "was not a major form between the early seventeenth-century flowering of the 'metaphysical' lyric and the lyric resurgence of the late eighteenth century and Romanticism" (120). Especially in their hymns, Backscheider notes, eighteenth-century women poets employed a diction and syntax whose departures from the conventional idiom of the "proper" literary lady were regarded as justified by their specifically religious purposes. Indeed, she continues, poets like Barbauld (and Elizabeth Singer Rowe before her) represent points on a continuum of "Nonconformist women poets who used religious verse fearlessly for social and political protest" (146). But if women could participate freely on this field of discourse when they wrote of religious (or spiritual) matters, so too did they enjoy considerable latitude when their subject had to do with matters of the family under circumstances of crisis.

How to address the public sphere was an important consideration for women writers who supported themselves and their (often broken) families in precarious circumstances through their writing. Many of them nevertheless published, typically under their own names,[11] poetry whose often sentimental nature only partially concealed a distinctly counterestablishment ideology. Moreover, these poets represented a broad cross-section of British society: Catharine Upton, for instance, is identified on the title page of the 1784 volume in which *The Siege of Gibraltar* again appeared as "Governess of the Ladies Academy, No. 43, Bartholemew Close." Because many of the poems on war approached their subject in terms of both its immediate and its protracted effects on families, and with an ostensibly maternal inflection of pathos, their rhetorical force could be considerable. The extraordinary numbers of primary and secondary casualties from a war that lasted over twenty years ensured that these poets' readers included many women to whose personal traumas the poems spoke eloquently and who therefore shared an implied bond of experience with the poets. Moreover, both the subject matter and the rhetorical approach of many of the more sentimental poems deflected—and even defused— at least some of the gendered objections of the contemporary masculinist critical establishment by seeming to stick to what was regarded as appropriate territory for women writers. Within this context, it is important to remember that for many of these writers a poem's evocative power was as important as its conventional liter- ary excellence. Many poems that our customary aesthetic judgment deems inferior (sometimes deservedly) warrant our attention nevertheless as barometers of cultural conditions and of women's status as public commentators on them.

Women writers knew what they were doing when they launched preemptive strikes to forestall critical churlishness by pleading everything from lack of educa- tional refinement to straitened economic circumstances to sheer lack of time for "polishing." Upton herself offers a good illustration. Writing about *The Siege of Gibraltar* in the preface to the 1784 *Miscellaneous Pieces, in Prose and Verse,* Upton observes:

[S]ome Critics finding fault with my Poem intitled [sic] The Siege of Gibraltar, induces me to say a few words in my own defence. One gentleman said it was not English; another avowed the versification was bad, as one line in it was a syllable too long. . . .

. . . Errors like these, (if they can be called such) are forgiven in great Poets and learned men, but not in a *woman,* who pretends to no learning at all. Their observations put me in mind of what Dean Swift says of critics, whose utmost ingenuity lies in scanning the verses of others on their fingers [sic] ends, without being able to make a tolerable rhyme themselves during the course of their lives.

If my accusers expect me to write better than Dryden or Pope, they assign me a strange task indeed! But I have done with these, and with much more pleasure ad- dress myself to the candid part of mankind. Far be such vanity from me to suppose that my Miscellany contains no faults; but my avocation as a Governess, will, I hope, plead my excuse! I have but little time to write, or *correct* what I write, and shall ingenuously confess, that I send the following sheets into the world, with a view to *support my children,* not to extend my own fame. (vii)

I have quoted Upton at length because these few words by an almost wholly un-known late eighteenth-century woman poet reveal so much about the actual and rhetorical circumstances within which women of the period so often wrote.

Upton's comments demonstrate her skill at manipulating her reader's sensibili-ties. Supposedly unlearned, she still drops the names of Swift, Dryden, and Pope at strategic points to establish her own authority and her familiarity with mainstream British literary history. Citing Swift's remark signals that she knows not only the names but also the works—including the anecdotal evidence. At the same time, she exposes her critics' lack of aesthetic appreciation and of generosity alike, suggesting that their egocentrism renders them incapable both of overlooking minor surface blemishes (one superfluous syllable) that resulted from her inability, as a harried governess, to spend adequate time correcting texts and of perceiving the essential moral truth that is readily apparent to unbiased readers. At the same time, she at-tributes to her work an ostensibly humanitarian purpose, wanting to "support [her] children" through publication. "My children" neatly embraces both her own two children and the girls in the Ladies Academy, so that her work serves both.[12] To cavil at the execution when the motive is so moral, Upton implies, is to betray one's lack of "sympathy" and candor, and indeed one's lack of humanity. The basic terms of this sort of argument were already becoming familiar by 1781, of course, and indeed pleading prefaces themselves became something of a literary subgenre during the Romantic era. Nevertheless, Upton's words show how women poets might frame issues of author-audience relations rhetorically when the subject was war.

Upton's sympathetic portrayal in *The Siege of Gibraltar* of the devastated war veteran who has sacrificed all for an ungrateful and unfeeling country foreshadows many poems that followed in the next thirty-plus years, by women and men alike. Like Mary Robinson later in "January, 1795," Upton sets up a dichotomy between the privileged and those who have secured or preserved that privilege through their own sacrifice:

> Ye sons of Britain, safe within your ports,
> Immers'd in *pleasure, luxury,* and *sports:*
> Small your idea of the soldier's toils,
> Who fights your causes in all climes and soils;
> Patient in dangers; firm, tho' in want of food,

And only anxious for his country's good.
These! These! Britannia! are thy sure support[.]   (5)

Like many who followed her, Upton reminds her readers that those who suffer most from war are those who benefit least, while those who profit live in a world so insulated from the quotidian reality of the majority of the populace that they are essentially and functionally unaware of that sort of life or of those who are fated to live it.

In Upton's poem the veteran returns to a homeland that is dramatically different from the one he had left, a nation eager to forget its humiliation in North America and hungry for a comforting nostalgic vision of British martial and imperial prowess. Reality, however, was less congenial. Often the veterans' families were dispersed or destroyed when their communities turned away with indifference (or worse) from the soldiers (or sailors) whose sacrifices had safeguarded the nation and its social, political, and economic elite. In an alternative and tragically common paradigm, the military man fails to return at all; after he is slain (most often without pension or death benefit), his family disintegrates, falling into squalor and often dying while the community turns a blind eye to their misery. Although any number of male poets wrote about this social disaster (and the moral disaster of which it was symptomatic), as Wordsworth did in *An Evening Walk* (1793), the subject was especially common among women writers. And yet, as Philip Shaw reminds us, surprisingly few studies have considered war's place in Romantic writing: "Rarely, if ever, do we encounter a reading of Romanticism that takes seriously the impact of war" on the people themselves, both those who served in the military forces and those whose lives were materially affected by that service (Shaw, introduction, 1). As Mary Favret puts it, "war in romanticism seems to flow in channels far below the familiar landscape of poetry, revolution, nation, domesticity and ideological conflict" (539).

The plight of the veteran and his family was abundantly familiar throughout the period, though, because "war was the single most important fact of British life" (Bennett, ix).[13] In the 1780s and 1790s, the war of American independence was still fresh in the British consciousness. That war had pitted both actual and symbolic family members against one another in a filial strife that had produced an unexpectedly powerful aversion to again waging war against those who were seeking liberty and self-determination. Many writers presented their case through analogy, in poems that were ostensibly about the war with the colonies but which were in fact transparently about the new conflict with France; Blake's *America: A Prophecy* operates in just this way. Often these poems achieve their greatest dramatic effects through images of suffering individuals and families rather than of massed troops or fields of casualties. War is about people, not numbers, and the full scope of war's disaster only becomes fully apparent when we add into the equation the families of the wartime dead and when we contemplate the effect of all these numbers (and the real people they represent) on actual communities. Each individual death marks only the most central of the rings of social, political, and economic impact that radiate out from that point of origin through the community and the nation.

Many loyalist writers regarded the protracted wars with France not just as a politically and culturally necessary evil but also as a moral (and even overtly religious) imperative. Eighteenth-century British nationalism frequently fashioned the nation as the new chosen people—as the new elect who would found the new Jerusalem, as Blake put it, "in Englands green & pleasant land" (*Milton,* preface, *Complete Poetry and Prose,* 95). This special view of England's God-given role and destiny, which informs countless paeans to Britain's divine sanction, is floridly voiced by Maria de Fleury:

> BRITANNIA, hail! thou favour'd Queen of Isles,
> Long kindly foster'd by thy Maker's smiles!
> When rising first from Ocean's oozy bed,
> He bade thee rear aloft thy stately head;
> Bade thy white cliffs triumphant o'er the main
> Through all succeeding generations reign.
> When from the grave, victorious, JESUS rose,
> Almighty Conqu'ror over mighty foes,
> Th' ascended SAVIOUR claim'd thee for his own,
> An early jewel planted in his crown,
> And sent his everlasting Gospel down;
> Disperst the shades of Druid night away,
> And fill'd the happy Isle with evangelic day.
> Then, as his crowning gift, from his right hand
> FREEDOM he sent, to bless this favour'd land;
> BRITAIN be free! he said; and FREEDOM then
> Became the darling RIGHT of ENGLISHMEN.
> (*British Liberty Established,* 8, pt. 1, ll. 13–29)

Gerald Newman has written that by the time of the French Revolution English national identity had become "an object of veneration and dogmatic assertion" (145). For de Fleury, England's Freedom is both a divine right and a divinely ordained mission about which the nation is expected to evangelize—by force of arms if necessary. De Fleury's view of Britain's real and symbolic role in the world was widely shared for much of the Romantic period (and afterward, for that matter) among nationalist writers who looked forward to Britain's "natural" world dominance once the fighting ended. In her "Invocation to Peace," which appeared in her 1814 *Poetical Effusions,* for example, Isabella Lickbarrow cried,

> Oh come! on Albion's plains for ever dwell,
> Thy sacred temple let our island be,
> Then arts and manufactures would revive,
> And happy Industry rejoice again;
> Then friendly Commerce would unfurl her sails,
> No hostile natives arm'd with bolts of death,
> Would meet in dreadful conflict on the deep,
> But freighted vessels, laden with the fruits
> Of ev'ry varied clime, would crowd our ports.   (ll. 31–38)

These last lines indicate the assumption—especially common among Regency writers—that British wealth and commerce would increase exponentially, as if the nation were to be granted this extraordinary boon as its heavenly reward for leading the effort against France, and that Britain would emerge as the undisputed moral *and economic* leader of post-Napoleonic Europe.

The most overtly prowar poems celebrate Britain's almost mythic claim to be Liberty's divinely sanctioned defender while demonizing France's—and subsequently Napoleon's—role as Freedom's enemy. Barbara Hoole's 1803 poem is typical:

> 'Tis thine the scorpion-scourge to wave,
>   To bend the mighty bow,
> And doom the humbled wretch thy slave,
>   Who laid the nations low.
>
> Tell him, tho' SWITZERLAND no more
>   Can boast her happy plains;
> And lost ITALIA's mourning shore
>   Partakes BATAVIA's chains;
>
> Yet here amid her ALBION's rocks
>   Sweet Liberty retires;
> And hence his fierce defiance mocks
>   With her avenging fires.
>
> Her standard soon, on GALLIA's coast,
>   By BRITAIN's bands unfurled,

Shall blast the CORSICAN's proud boast,

    And save a sinking world.

              ("Verses on the Threatened Invasion, Written in July, 1803," ll. 13–28)

Prowar poems typically emphasize hearth, home, and women (including the emblematic figure of Britannia) and the need to defend them as much as they stress personal glory, so much so that frequently "war is recast as defense of women—mothers, sisters, wives—not the killing of other men" (Favret, 543). Indeed, the desire to partake in the dangers and sacrifices required by war is generally advanced as what accounts for individual and collective male valor in battle against Britain's historical adversary, France. According to Gerald Newman, "it would perhaps be no exaggeration to say that a consciousness of France as England's military, commercial, and diplomatic enemy was one of the foundation stones of the national mind" (75). This entrenched, bitter anti-Gallicism, which is particularly evident in the caricatures of Gillray, Cruikshank, and others (where its graphic visual language is especially powerful), suffuses loyalist verbal discourse (including poetry) throughout the period.

This anti-Gallicism is evident in Elizabeth Moody's 1790s anti-Napoleonic "On Hearing That Buonaparte Was Landed in Egypt" (quoted in full):

Whilst our hero, brave NELSON, unfurls every sail,

BUONAPARTE, that Comet, to catch by the tail,

The cunning Eluder looks back with a smile,

And nods at our fleet from the banks of the Nile.

BUONAPARTE now landed on Egypt's fair plains,

Say, Muse!—What revenge for our Britons remains?

What revenge she replies—but each shade to invite

To return from the regions of Death and of Night.

Those tormentors of Egypt in annals of yore,

Ah, would they again but revisit that shore!

Could but Pharaoh come forth with his bosom of stone,

And a heart that was harder than ever was known;

Could the grumbling old Israelites fill up his train,

And provoke all the plagues of old Egypt again;

Could but Locusts and Lice once more cover the ground,

And frogs on the stools and platters be found;

Such might prove the effect of this varied vexation,

As would cure BUONAPARTE of Colonization.   (*Poetic Trifles*, 162–63)

Moody's poem replicated the sentiments of many of her fellow citizens (including canonical male poets like Coleridge and Wordsworth) as the war proceeded and as direct criticism of the British government (and the motives that inspired it) diminished in the face of the increasing ferocity of successive French regimes. Principled resistance to war became ever less relevant as the issue at hand seemed increasingly to be the survival of England. Bonapartist "Colonization" had to be crushed in biblical terms; British colonialism need not even be mentioned.

How persistent these themes proved to be in prowar poems is evident from Jane Alice Sargant's 1817 *Sonnets, and Other Poems*, a collection of what she calls "poetic trifles" that "stern necessity compels her" to publish in the wake of "a long and painful illness" that she overcame by turning to "those religious principles which had early been implanted in her heart" (ix–xi). The first of two prowar poems, "Address," is inscribed "The Leader to His Soldiers on the Field of Battle"; its first and last stanzas read thus:

> Soldiers! now's the glorious hour,
> Now, in numbers, swiftly pour;
> Quick, unerring bullets show'r—
>   Rush to death or victory.
>
> . . . .
>
> See the Gallic squadrons fly,
> England wave thy banners high,
> Joy is thine and victory;
>   Theirs defeat and slavery.   (32–34, ll. 1–4, 29–32)

It is not hard to imagine actual speeches of this sort on the field, nor to reckon their capacity to rouse and embolden their auditors. On the opposing side, after all, Napoleon was famous for precisely this sort of seductive battlefield rhetoric. Sargant's officer shrewdly appeals to chivalry, as Edmund Burke had famously done in his account of Marie Antoinette, making it seem almost as if the war were being waged to safeguard the women of England—and womanhood in general. Indeed, Eric Walker has asked "What is war all about?" The answer: "To make the world safe for conjugality" (209).

Sargant's second prowar poem, which follows the first after a brief intervening "Song," is also called "Address," and the poet represents it as "Supposed to Have Been Spoken by an Army Leaving the Coasts of England." "Farewell to old England, our dear native shore, / Where late we so happy have been," the poem begins, with its speakers observing that if a tear falls or a breast heaves a sigh, these betoken affection, not fear:

When he thinks of his babes, and the wife of his heart,
    His breast for a moment will bleed;
And the drops of regret and keen anguish will start,
    Yet Valor disdains not the deed.   (38–39, ll. 13–16)

Sargant alters the familiar trope of the wounded soldier: while Sargant's warrior imagines that perhaps his breast "will bleed," the drops he foresees are those of regret and anguish that stem from his separation and his anxiety that he may not return home. Paradoxically, this premonitory anxiety undercuts the poem's hackneyed nationalistic rhetoric. Conspicuous in Sargant's poem is the *absence* of particularization: *specific* literal objectives or policies are never named. Shipped *out of* their country, the soldiers nevertheless claim to be *defending* "our rights," which are themselves left unspecified. Sargant's unsophisticated collective "Army" has been seduced by the sophisticated rhetoric of its leaders—at all levels—that fills so many poems. While Sargant's univocal army claims that "For our King, for our Country, we fall" (39, l. 24), the emptiness of this rhetoric is underscored by the fact that nothing else in the poem really points to the line. Instead, the poem quickly shifts focus from "old England, our dear native shore" to images of the women for whom the army is understood to be fighting.

Sargant also presents a countervision that is supplied, interestingly, not by war's cheerleaders but instead by its casualties. In a long narrative called "The Disbanded Soldier's Lament" she details how a veteran of Waterloo returns to England, collects his pay, and discards the old uniform cap that is all that he retains from "England's great, eventful hour." The battle over, the war won, the returning soldier's Waterloo honor and glory are eclipsed by the plain day-to-day struggles in a war-weary nation trying to adjust to the troubled peacetime conditions of 1815–16. The war's end is at once the end of his heroic status and the beginning of the painful anonymity that would lead him and many of his peers toward domestic unrest in England and to the bloody action of the Manchester Massacre in 1819. For now, the veteran casts away his cap with the bitter observation that "More kind than man, is wind and snow" (80, l. 126).

A comparable ambivalence also underlies Charlotte Caroline Richardson's post-Waterloo "To-Morrow,"[14] which juxtaposes the external national concord produced by the war's end with the ongoing domestic struggle faced by women who have lost the men dearest to them:

Soft Peace our happy land had blest,
    And Britain's gallant Sons returning,
Each clasp'd some fav'rite to his breast,

And fondly hush'd the voice of mourning.
When lovely Anna, hapless maid!
    Thus pour'd the melting strain of sorrow,
"My Edward, may thy gentle shade
    "Direct my wand'ring steps to-morrow."

The morn that calls a world to joy,
    With grateful sounds of triumph swelling,
Shall see the wretched Anna fly
    Far distant from her peaceful dwelling.
I'll seek the turf that Edward prest,
There sigh my last adieu to sorrow,
And pillow'd on his clay-cold breast,
We'll wake in happier scenes to-morrow.   (88–89)

Richardson's poignant poem illustrates how the deaths of loved ones transformed the domestic scene—the traditional site of tranquility—into a site of intolerable anguish. For Anna there is no returning soldier to embrace. Because his death renders "her peaceful dwelling" (and the nation it symbolizes) intolerable, Anna determines to embrace (whether by suicide or sheer grief) the foreign (and therefore alien) earth with which Edward is symbolically and semantically merged in the penultimate line's figure of "his clay-cold breast." For Anna, only death holds the possibility of happiness. This is not mere hyperbole, however, but a representation of human grieving that is as culturally and emotionally recognizable in our own time as it was in Richardson's.

Richardson's long title poem, "Harvest," begins her volume by celebrating her Muse, who "no more . . . the hostile fields shall rove" because she now joyfully views "the once embattled plain" that has become "a scene of pleasure, love, and harmony" where "peace shall diffuse her blessings on mankind, / And War, detested War, shall be no more!" (1, pt. 1, l. 7). The poem ends with a promise to the "Children of Want" that a restored nature, represented by the allegorical figure of Harvest who appears in fields that now are fertile rather than bloody, will in future years yield blessings that stream unabated from "HIM whose boundless mercy gives us all;— / The God of Harvest! and the God of Peace!" (41–42, pt. 2, l. 307). Here Richardson neatly melds the natural world with God through her allegorical figure of Harvest. Along the way, however, the poem describes the victims of war's pitiless and indiscriminate violence, so that even in this seemingly straightforward Christian celebration of peace and prosperity the reader is not spared the scenes of suffering that have preceded Waterloo and the war's end but is instead repeatedly reminded of them. Peace may produce this new postwar "harvest," but it cannot erase the terrible harvest of lives that has gone before.

Isabella Lickbarrow made the same point some five years earlier and with the war's end not yet in sight. "Written at the Commencement of the Year 1813" looks across time and space as the new year dawns, and Lickbarrow recalls that her entire life seems to have been dominated by the news of war and its casualty-strewn fields:

> E'er since my heart could feel for human kind,
> I've heard of nought but wars and desolation,
> Of cities given to the devouring flames;
> Of once fair countries ravag'd and laid waste;
> Their fertile vallies turn'd to fields of death;
> Where, sad to tell, brothers, and sons, and sires,
> Together fell, and shar'd one common grave:
> Those who surviv'd, when the dread work was done,
> Compell'd to leave their much-lov'd native fields,
> Their wives and children unprotected all—
> To fight and perish in a distant land.   (*Poetic Effusions,* 17–18, ll. 11–21)

Even the fact that English soil itself has been spared the terrible war "[t]hat half unpeoples Europe's fairest realms" is scant consolation when she considers that

> . . . long, on almost ev'ry foreign soil,
> Thy bravest sons have lost their lives for thee;
> And many a beauteous maid and widow mourn
> For the dear objects of their tend'rest love,
> And many a mother for her gallant sons. . . .   (18, ll. 34–38)

War spares none, in other words, and the misery it causes observes neither border nor nationality.

Indeed, Nature herself is stymied by the unnaturalness of warmaking, as the powerful opening of Anna Letitia Barbauld's *Eighteen Hundred and Eleven* demonstrates:

> Bounteous in vain, with frantic man at strife,
> Glad Nature pours the means—the joys of life;
> In vain with orange blossoms scents the gale,
> The hills with olives clothes, with corn the vale;
> Man calls to Famine, nor invokes in vain,

Disease and Rapine follow in her train;
The tramp of Marching hosts disturbs the plough,
The sword, not sickle, reaps the harvest now,
And where the Soldier gleans the scant supply,
The helpless Peasant but retires to die;
No laws his hut from licensed outrage shield,
And war's least horror is the ensanguined field.   (ll. 11–26)

Even Nature is powerless, her maternal abundance notwithstanding, against the senseless killing Barbauld calls "licensed outrage," and she underscores her point by troping the mothers' sons as blossoms and war as harvest, the same imagery that Richardson subsequently adopts.

Even earlier, Amelia Opie traced war's consequences in "Lines Written at Norwich on the First News of the Peace," which appeared in her *Poems* of 1802 (81–86).[15] The poem employs the simple, accessible, and egalitarian ballad stanza that during the 1790s had become a favorite choice for poems of social consciousness and social protest. The peace is that of Amiens, which in 1802 produced joy for those who were reunited with male loved ones whose lives seemed to have been spared through Peace's agency:

And you, fond parents, faithful wives,
Who've long for sons and husbands feared,
Peace now shall save their precious lives;
They come by danger more endeared.   (ll. 29–32)

But Peace is not entirely benevolent in Opie's panoramic scene, either, nor of course could it be, for War always exacts its grisly toll: the one "shrunk form" (l. 34) who appears amid the public general rejoicing enjoys neither joy nor peace. This "poor mourner" declares in her own voice that

"Alas! Peace comes for me too late, . . .
For my brave boy in Egypt died! "   (ll. 39–40)

Only a year earlier the Egyptian expeditionary campaign under Sir Ralph Abercrombie that routed the French forces from Egypt had cost 650 lives at the Battle of Aboukir Bay (7 March 1801) and another 1,500 (including Abercrombie himself) two weeks later at the Battle of Alexandria (21 March). These losses were still fresh in the public mind when the Peace of Amiens was signed in 1802, and Opie's poem poignantly reveals the bitterness that results when one's son (in this instance) is lost so near what seems to be the fighting's end. The bereaved woman's first line says it all: "'Talk not of Peace, . . . the sound I hate'" (l. 37). Opie's description of the woman as "shrunk" (l. 34) functions symbolically, conveying not only her altered physical stature but also her diminished psychological and social status in the world she still inhabits, her loss having reduced her in every possible way.

This sort of bitter and largely inconsolable grief figures prominently in much British writing of the war years. These same elements are prefigured, for instance, in Mary Robinson's "The Widow's Home," which appeared in her *Lyrical Tales* (1800), and are echoed in Mary Leadbeater's 1808 poem "The Widow" (*Poems,* 139–47) and in Dorothea Primrose Campbell's "The Distracted Mother" (another lament for a son killed in battle) and her "The Soldier's Widow, at the Grave of Her Only Child" (which records the double tragedy of two linked losses), both of which appeared in 1816 (*Poems,* 50–52, 53–55).[16] Campbell wrote her psychologically acute poem on the war widow before she was seventeen; she published it and other poems to aid her own family, of which she was the eldest child.[17] Her speaker deplores the uselessness of summer to one whose

> . . . world is yonder little grave,
>   My all its narrow space;
> My only Child reposes there,
>   Lock'd in Death's cold embrace.   (ll. 13–16)

Somewhat surprisingly, when it comes to mourning her lost husband the speaker seems to take death in war as a given and does not even wish him alive again, instead wishing only that he were buried near their child rather than on some distant battlefield where he fell:

> Bless'd had I been had'st thou repos'd
>   Beside our infant son;
> Not buried in a field of strife,
>   Where bloody deeds were done.   (ll. 41–44)

Here again war's inherent unnaturalness is presented within an agrarian, pastoral paradigm, with the bloody "field of strife" supplanting the peaceful earth of home and the domestic scene epitomized in the family unit that might under happier circumstances rest side by side in death as they had in life. Indeed, remarkably few poems from the period are framed in comparable *urban* terms, perhaps because cities—like war—are manmade entities that cannot easily be construed in edenic terms. According to agrarian/pastoral poems in this mode, the fields of the soldier's home and family are left uncultivated and unattended and consequently are unproductive while the fields of war—which are presented as "foreign" and alien, situated outside the soldier's nation and away from the family he is "raising"—are tilled with weapons and watered with blood—and tears. As the working-class poet Ann Candler wrote in 1803, "[t]he fertile fields, the wide extended plain, / Are smear'd with gore, and cover'd o'er with slain" ("Serious Reflections on the Times, Written during the Late War," *Poetical Attempts,* 32, ll. 31–32). Campbell's narrator's blank and deterministic resignation is not atypical: Britain's women fully understood that when their men left home for war, the consequences for all were likely to be severe. So they steeled themselves in advance, learning to cope by expecting the worst. Resignation in the face of actual or anticipated bereavement reflects one strategy—however inadequate—for coping with the seemingly endless cycle of killing and the resulting universal social dysfunction. Campbell's speaker's question,—"Why didst thou go?" (l. 39)—was a familiar one.

Like Richardson's "To-Morrow," Mary Leadbeater's "The Widow" treats the agony of the widow who has to imagine her husband's slow, lingering death abroad and who laments the deceptive illusion of security offered to recruits who imagined that their role in the militia or the volunteers would keep them safely on English soil:

> "Why did he trust the promise vain,
>   "That he should *here* abide;
> "Should stay to guard his native plain,
>   "And guard his hapless bride?"   (ll. 21–24)

Loyal but gullible men like these, it turns out, are betrayed by their own government "'who honour's just demand / So lightly can forego, / Who tear him from his native land'" (ll. 25–27). Leadbeater's angry widow recounts how, having borne a child in his absence and having sold the "garments fair" he had left her to support herself in his absence (ll. 73–74), she is now obsessed with the idea of journeying to India where his regiment had been sent. Having parted even with the "watch of silver fine" that he had admonished her to keep until the very last necessity (ll. 77–80), she mourns from afar the husband who fell on the Bay of Bengal during the 1782–83 Indian campaign, "On Coromandel's coast; / When Cuddolore the force withstood / Of Britain's warlike host" (ll. 114–16).

Leadbeater's poem raises the issue of the global nature of Britain's military involvements during this volatile period. Although the situation in India had begun to stabilize somewhat, Holland's fall to the French in early 1795 required British military force to wrest from French control the formerly Dutch positions in Ceylon and the Cape of Good Hope, the primary staging points on the route to India. Then there was of course the Egyptian campaign and the exertions in the West Indies, to which destination some thirty-five thousand soldiers were sent between August 1795 and May 1796 and where engagements under difficult tropical conditions likewise played havoc with the troops.[18] Despite British military successes in the West Indies and elsewhere outside the Continent, the human toll was terrific. In the eight years between war's outbreak and the Peace of Amiens, for instance, England sent some eighty-nine thousand officers and men to the Caribbean and lost approximately 70 per cent of them (Mackesy, 160). The years 1795–96 alone saw more than forty thousand fighting men discharged as a result of wounds, disease and infirmity, and plain mishap (Gretton, 5:526). One such victim is recounted in the two-part ballad, "The Song at Maria's Grave," that Anne Hunter dramatically placed as the final poem in her 1802 collection (*Poems*, 114–22).[19] The poem recounts its female subject's demise following her beloved's death; her "charms exist no more," we are told, and "soon their memory shall cease" (ll. 11–12). While Hunter reports that her poem is "founded on a true story" that "took place in 1785, or near about that time" (according to her footnote on page 122), its analogous relevance in 1802 is unmistakable.

Falling prey to the seductive illusion of glory in war, Hunter's Henry "[r]esolv'd to dare the hostile wave":

> Dauntless to seek his country's foes,
> And bravely to guard her injur'd rights,
> Warm from the heart his courage flows,
> For love and honour Henry fights.   (ll. 32–36)

"Long absent on the wat'ry waste," Henry succeeded at sea: "[V]anquish'd foes his fame increas'd, / While with his fame his fortune grew" (ll. 57–60). Indeed, Henry's overconfident final letter to Maria ominously intimates that he is tempting fate:

> "For thee I live, for thee could die.
>
> "For thy dear sake I still pursue
> Unceasing toils, and think them sweet;
> For now the time appears in view,
> When we again shall meet."   (ll. 76–84)

The second part of Hunter's poem brings the inevitable: "Gay, glitt'ring hope! How bright you seem, / Gilding some joy beyond the hour!" Hunter writes. But it is all " painted cloud, a fairy dream, / A rainbow in a summer's shower" (ll. 93–96). The winds blow ill, and Henry's vessel is wrecked in a terrible storm that "rises on the water's roar, / And death and desolation brings" as the inevitable result of "[t]he warring elements at strife" (ll. 105–9). Having Henry succumb not to warring armies but rather to warring *elements* (though his fatal attraction for the former is what has placed him at the mercy of the latter) is a clever ironic twist that enables Hunter to reiterate the familiar theme of war's unnaturalness: Nature herself claims the haughty warrior who had violated her law by glorying in the carnage.

Still, the deadly burden of all this worldwide warmaking fell with particular devastation on those least able to cope with it: the poor.[20] For many British men, going to war (on land or on the sea) promised at least a small and temporary financial opportunity for their families, in the form of the enlistment bonus that was variously offered (but never paid) over the course of the war years. Moreover, some veterans were able to turn a profit on their war experiences by publishing memoirs and the like, as the famous Capt. Frederick Marryat of the Royal Navy did with his popular adventure novels portraying life at sea. But these were the exceptions rather than the rule: on the whole the small benefit that came to war's ordinary participants failed by a wide margin to offset the often fearsome losses they and their families sustained.[21] Even when a broader public recognition of the deplorable circumstances that confronted returning British soldiers and seamen (and their families) brought about passage in 1795 and 1796 of legislation that allowed military men to allocate some of their wages directly to their families, usually that money was still woefully inadequate to their domestic needs, especially when foul weather and bad economic policies forced a severe rise in the price of food and other necessities (a fact that informs poems like Wordsworth's "The Female Vagrant," published in 1798 in *Lyrical Ballads*). The aforementioned enlistment bounty figures in the work of many other poets; among canonical male poets, for instance, Wordsworth mentions it in "The Ruined Cottage." Indeed, writers who mention it usually do so to demonstrate that the meager bonus proves of little use, finally, when its recipient is killed, wounded, or otherwise incapacitated. Monetary bonuses, even if they had been paid, were irrelevant anyway to the families of the countless men who fell victim to the ruthless press gangs, leaving their families both impoverished and often ignorant even of the men's fate.[22] Given the state's apparent callous indifference to the suffering endured by military families, it was crucial that other avenues for relieving that suffering be explored. Many writers consequently advocated philanthropy, for example, appealing to the wealthy and powerful to assist the less fortunate. This sort of writing, too, was widely understood to be especially appropriate for women.

Such a philanthropic appeal for war's victims appears in the concluding stanza of Isabella Lickbarrow's "Written after the News of a Battle":

Ye sons of wealth! On beds of down
    Who undisturb'd by grief repose,

Pity the fallen soldier's child,
    Pity his friendless widow's woes.   (*Poetical Effusions,* 106–7, ll. 17–20)

Addressing the moon, Lickbarrow invokes pity not just for the British dead but for *all* of "Europe's sons," all of whom the penultimate stanza invites the reader to regard as the victims (in death as in life) less of one another than of the "sons of wealth":

Oh! turn thee from the dreadful plains
    Where Europe's son's unburied lie,
The view would thy pale lustre stain,
    And give thy beams a crimson dye.   (ll. 13–16)

Like her radical sister poets considered in chapter 1, Lickbarrow levels particular blame against those for whose political, ideological, *and economic* interests protracted wars seem perpetually to be fought, wars fought at the expense of the common soldiers and sailors whose fate does not concern the well-to-do.

Antiwar discourse typically insists that war is being conducted by "an aristocratic class indifferent to the suffering of the poor" (Bennett, 13), a point made already in 1789 in *Adversity; or, The Tears of Britannia,* a biting satire by "a Lady" who signed herself as "Eliza." The poet exposes the base commercial motives of the war profiteers who had dealt in military provisions during the American war. These she epitomizes in the person of one "N—h" (presumably Lord North[23]):

IMMERS'D too deep in private zeal,
He quite mistook the public weal;
Protracts the war, for should it cease,
How will emoluments decrease!
Without their jobs, and contracts too,
Wise statesmen scarce knew what to do;
These *weighty* matters turn the scale,
And o'er *majorities* prevail!
Who ready vote him on supplies,
In hopes to share the golden prize.   (6–7, ll. 83–92)

It is but a short step to the stark dualisms of Mary Robinson's strident "January, 1795."

By mounting a *universal* appeal for pity and compassion for all of war's victims regardless of their nationality, antiwar women writers tried to negotiate the tricky rhetorical situation in which they found themselves. Even the most strident hesitated to condemn the war effort, worrying that their criticism might undermine the morale of the combatants themselves, who are almost never the objects of protest or ridicule. Rather than protest the war's *objectives,* therefore, antiwar writers tapped the widespread hostility to the new conflict by rhetorically and symbolically aligning the experiences of the individual nuclear family with those of the nation-state and arguing by analogy that the destruction of the former is inextricably linked to the erosion of the latter. What Anne Mellor calls "feminine romanticism" constructs on the trope of the "family politic" an image of a nation-state "that evolves gradually and rationally under the mutual care and guidance of both mother and father" (*Romanticism and Gender,* 65). Nothing is more destructive to this healthy partnership, of course, than a long and drawn-out war, which devastates the family and enervates the nation. It produces the bleak prospect that Anna Letitia Barbauld depicts in her *Eighteen Hundred and Eleven,* which foresees the decay of a Britain whose stature and influence have been eclipsed by America.

Despite the pervasive nationalism of many of her poems, Jane Alice Sargant also published a sonnet (subtitled "On Seeing a Soldier's Funeral") that is notable for its ambivalence:

> Borne to the grave by yonder weeping train,
>   The soldier journeys to his peaceful home;
> No more to wield th' ensanguin'd sword again,
>   No more a weary exile sad to roam.
> Cold is the heart that martial glory late
>   Awak'd to noblest deeds of endless fame;
> Nerveless the arm that dealt enerring fate,
>   And lost to all, except a deathless name.
> Perhaps far distant in his native vale,
>   For him a parent mourns with bitter tears—
> A faithful maid, who heard his tender tale,
>   Or sadder still, a widow'd form appears;
> Round whom his hapless orphans feebly cling,
>   And, with unceasing cries, her bosom wring.   (60)

Remarkably, the mourners who bear the soldier to his grave do *not* include his "far distant" parents or other family, indicating that he is not being buried in the family plot—a final disruption of the "natural" order. Sargant can only speculate that *somewhere else* may also be a "faithful maid" (i.e., a fiancée) or perhaps a widow with children ("hapless orphans") like those in Wordsworth's *An Evening Walk* (1793). This fracture of temporal and spatial proximity is one of the most powerful—and chilling—rhetorical effects of Sargant's sonnet.

Elizabeth Moody and War's Universal Horror

Perhaps nowhere are the experiences of war so fully universalized as in the extraordinary poems of Elizabeth Moody. An obscure writer, Moody, whose unmarried name was Greenly, was apparently married to a clergyman and occasionally reviewed novels for the *Monthly Review* between 1789 and 1808 before her death in 1814 (Blain, Clements, and Grundy, 754–55). Ralph Griffiths, who edited the *Monthly* (from 1749 to 1803), hired a staff of experts to review books in their particular fields (Sullivan, 233), which suggests that Moody must have enjoyed some contemporary reputation in arts and letters and in critical discourse. Moreover, the Whiggish *Monthly Review's* oppositional politics seem like a good "fit" for Moody, whose poems offer some of the strongest moral and intellectual opposition not just to England's war with France but to war generally.

In her preface to *Poetical Trifles* (1798), which appeared, ironically, in the same year as *Lyrical Ballads,* Moody writes, "I am well aware that this is no period favourable to the Muse," "when the monster WAR is sounding his terrific alarms;—when the spirit of discord is in the air, and pervades every Atmosphere,—when it not only stimulates the combatants in the field of *battle,* but in the field of *Literature,*—when the fiend POLITICS is sharpening the pen to make it a two-edged sword." "How I presume to ask," she continues, "may the compilation of a few harmless Numbers be expected to engage the public attention?" (i–ii). Moody's self-effacing description of her poetic activity, "the compilation of a few harmless Numbers," belies both the aesthetic sophistication and the intellectual commitment that inform her poems.

Although Moody's engagingly witty preface adopts the familiar self-deprecating rhetoric of later eighteenth-century prefaces (especially by women), few contemporary readers would have regarded a collection that begins (as *Poetic Trifles* does) with a frankly contestatory poem like her "Thoughts on War and Peace" (1–7) as either inoffensive or "harmless." That poem examines the moral issue of European militarism in an age of increasingly entrenched nationalism:

> But chief in Europe flow'd, and ever flows,
> The baneful current of war's crimson tide:
> Where despots heedless of a nation's woes,
> Unsheathe the sword to guard the regal pride.
>   Trophies of victory surround the throne;
> Monarchs survey them with deluded eyes;

Lost is the pageant in the people's groan;
Humanity before ambition flies.   (ll. 21–28)

Moody's "despots" and "Monarchs" identify France's Continental opponents, whose hostility to republican revolution is entirely self-serving. As always, though, it is not the powerful who suffer most but the humble, especially when severe food shortages follow crop failures as they did in 1794–96 and 1799–1801:

When Rapine's cruel unrelenting hand,
Beggars the tenant of each little field;
Bids the poor cottager resign his land,
And his reap'd harvest to a stranger yield.

    Bids hostile troops invade the cultur'd soil,
And desperate steeds o'erwhelm the bearded grain,
Rend'ring abortive agriculture's toil,
And vain the labours of the peasant train.   (ll. 49–56)

Turning from this woeful vision, Moody urges her muse to "[r]everse thy theme to images of Peace, / And let her scenes contrast the scenes of woe" (ll. 67–68). This rosier prospect reveals for Moody, as it would for Lickbarrow in 1814, a flourishing Commerce (allegorically capitalized) that is in turn reinforced by a burgeoning sea trade and a regenerated Agriculture ("Her fertile valleys destin'd now no more / To feed the robber and entomb the slain" [ll. 87–88]). Swords are exchanged for plowshares in this vision, if not actually fashioned into them, and men rediscover their "natural" moral and familial duties:

    Her sons now lab'rers of the peaceful field,
The fearful instruments of War resign;
More pleas'd the tools of husbandry to wield,
Than on their brows the sanguine wreath to twine.   (ll. 89–93)

England is transformed under the aegis of this new peace, directed by two guiding forces:

    Britain shall rise in new refulgent day,
And brightest rays on her horizon shine;
Morals reform'd shall rule with milder sway;
And Genius all her schools of art refine.   (ll. 93–96)

Morals and Genius: the moral/spiritual/ethical anchor of life and the spark of inspiration that at once reflects and builds on that foundation; these two are inextricably linked in Moody's symbolic formulation. The clear implication in Moody's poem and in those of other women considered here is that these are precisely the qualities that are absent in the state of war, which of course explains why war *is* by definition inhumane.

"Anna's Complaint; or, The Miseries of War" anticipates much of the writing on the war for the following two decades in detailing Anna's grief over the death in war of her beloved William.[24] Moody's lyric shrewdly exposes both war's seductive nature and the nationalistic jingoism through which it is promoted by those who stand to gain:

> Alas! full little didst thou know,
> The monster war doth falsely show;
> He decks his form with pleasing art,
> And hides the daggers in his heart.
>
> The music of his martial band,
> The shining halberd in his hand;
> The feather'd helmet on his head,
> And coat so fine of flaming red.
>
> With these the simple youth he gains,
> And tempts him from his peaceful plains;
> And by this pomp was William led,
> The dangerous paths of war to tread.   (ll. 17–28)

"War" cannot do all this alone, however; the powerful, the influential, and the greedy are all complicitous in the deadly seduction of the innocent, the idealistic, the gullible:

> Fair-sounding words my love deceiv'd
> The great ones talk'd, and he believ'd,
> That war would fame and treasure bring,
> That glory call'd to serve the king.   (ll. 29–32)

How many believers were disabused of their heady illusions may be gauged by the rolls of casualties for the next twenty-plus years, by the numbers of displaced, dispossessed, and indigent citizens (widowed, orphaned, or otherwise), and by the haunting images of physically and emotionally maimed individuals (men and women alike, but especially men) who people the omnipresent grim war caricatures created by artists like Gillray, Woodward, Heath, and Cruikshank in the succeeding years. As the famous Civil War battlefield photographs of the American Matthew Brady would do half a century later on the other side of the Atlantic, prints like

Cruikshank's *He Would Be a Soldier* (1793) or Gillray's *John Bull's Progress* (1793) made visible for a popular audience images that would become ever more common in real-life England as the human wreckage of war accumulated everywhere. This thread was still evident as late as 1828, when in a poem called "The Soldier's Daughter" Frances Chadwick gave these words to "a once brave soldier's daughter / Whom misfortune had render'd completely forlorn":

> "My father was slain in the field; 'Twas call'd glory!
>   "But ah! how unlike it it seemed then to be!
> "My mother in agony heard the sad story,
>   And she soon bade adieu to the world and to me."   (*Rural*, 41, ll. 21–24)

Some things never change.

War's Domestic Ruins

And when they died, how were the men remembered at home? Like the larger subject of war's cultural impact generally during this period, that of the fallen warriors' funerals has received surprisingly little critical attention. To be sure, there has been no lack of attention to the memorials for the prominent and the powerful, the Nelsons or the Wellingtons who were publicly apotheosized in the various arts; John Wolffe's *Great Deaths*, for example, traces some of this history. Martha Hanson's sonnet commemorating the death of General Sir John Moore on 16 January 1809 at the battle of Corunna is typical in tone and language. Moore had commanded some thirty-five thousand outnumbered troops that had retreated from Napoleon's much larger army toward the northwestern Spanish port city of Corunna (La Coruna) to be evacuated by the British fleet. The ships were not yet at the harbor when Moore's troops arrived, however, and Moore ordered an ultimately successful counterattack against the French troops under Soult who were harrying his men. Although the French were repulsed, Moore was mortally wounded just at the moment of triumph. In one of the evacuating troops' final acts, members of the Ninth Foot Regiment buried Moore on the city ramparts before boarding their ship to return to England. Addressing the spirit of the "Illustrious Chieftain," Hanson observes that the "weeping sisters," Honor and Valor, now bid the laurel to wave "its deathless boughs":

> Illustrious Moore! though my unpolish'd strains,
>   Can nought of Fame, on Thee, or Praise bestow,

> While Glory's hands, her brightest trophies strew
> Where Spain is hallow'd by thy cold remains;
> The simple lay, may where thy Laurels grow,
> Haply impart, one drop of fresh'ning dew.   (*Sonnets,* 2:110, ll. 9–14)

Undeniably formulaic in language and rhetoric, Hanson's poem nevertheless stands in dialogue with numerous others on similar subjects. Typical, for instance, is the self-effacing posture of the writer who portrays herself as both "humble" and "out of the way" but possessed of sentiments no less sincere nor no less deeply felt than those of more prominent eulogists. Like them, too, Hanson exploits the pathos that particularly attaches to the burial of a war casualty on foreign soil. This phenomenon, which sheer practicality made inevitable, unites the experiences of notable generals like Moore and ordinary "unknown" soldiers (and sailors) whose families and communities were likewise denied the consolation of home burials.[25]

Although the memoirs and reminiscences of those who survived the quarter century of Anglo-French conflict often provide firsthand records of the conflicts themselves, relatively little was written then and has been written since about how ordinary soldiers and sailors were commemorated. This is why contemporary poems (and prose accounts) are so valuable; they situate these many deaths in a historically accurate perspective, for their omnipresence in the daily lives of Britons lent them an awful familiarity. The prolific Barbara Hoole Hofland, who entered the market in 1805 as a poet, published a series of Minerva Press novels about broken families struggling (often with surprising success) to survive the loss of the male head of the family.[26] The first of these, *The History of an Officer's Widow, and Her Young Family,* appeared in 1809 and was reprinted frequently. In this tale the young husband and father of five, Capt. Charles Belfield, is ordered (presumably in 1793) "to join the ill-fated expedition to Holland," where he is wounded. His wife, Maria, travels to Whitby to meet him on his return, only to discover a dying wreck typical of the many wounded who returned home only to perish. Hofland briefly sketches what Charles has endured:

> Having been wounded early in the engagement, and fainted through loss of blood, his wounds had been wholly overlooked, and he had lain for many hours on the sea-sands, exposed to the heat of the mid-day sun, and afterwards the chilling sea-breeze. He had afterwards crawled to a cottage, where he was denied even a drop of water to allay the feverish thirst which preyed upon him, or a rag to defend his smarting wounds from the midnight air. At length his wearied limbs lost their power of motion, and he fell on the ground in the forlorn hope of soon terminating his sufferings by death.

Rescued temporarily by the only person who responds with sympathy and human-ity, a poor woman who tends him "in despite of her own poverty, and the malice of her neighbors," he revives sufficiently to escape by sea.

> But here again misfortune pursued: he was tempest-tost, and obliged, notwith-standing his exhausted state, to work so hard upon the water, that his strength was entirely exhausted, and all that remained of hope was, to see his wife and die. (25–28)

For countless British women, this account was more fact than fiction.

Another view of war's grim toll appears in "The Victims of War," published in 1811 by the blind poet Christian Gray (*Tales*, 34–45), who relates the tragic history of the young rural lovers, Julia and Alexis. When Alexis is ordered to enlist ("The lord of the manor commands, I obey" [l. 61]), Julia, who has previously feigned in-difference to him, now weeps at the prospect of what may lie ahead and resolves to accompany him ("And if, far from his dear native land, / He must sail to the Conti-nent, face the dread foe, / Then to share his every danger shall Julia go" [ll. 72–74]). Such a course of action was not unusual, especially in the years after 1800, when surprising numbers of women (and even children) accompanied their husbands to war.[27] In Wellington's army (for example), although the number of wives permitted to do so was nominally restricted to six per hundred men, chosen by lot, others occasionally managed nevertheless to join the party by one means or another, and once there they were normally allowed to move forward with the army (though they were expected to stay with the baggage so as not to become involved in the fighting itself), rather than being billeted behind (Page, 17, 27, 49, and passim). After battles, however, women frequently wandered amid the carnage, searching for their loved ones. A witness to one such scene at the Battle of Nivelle in November 1813 wrote:

> In one place you could see a lovely young woman supporting the head of her dying husband on her bosom, anxiously awaiting the last gasp of life, then again your eye would meet with one in bitter anguish, bewailing her loss, fondly cling-ing to the cold remains of all that was dear to her, and many more were running about mad, unconscious of where they were going or what they were doing, these had received the news of their husbands' deaths in some distant part of the field. (Wheeler, 160–61)

Many contemporary visual works document terrible scenes of this sort,[28] and Felicia Hemans made one such scene the subject of her 1827 poem, "Woman on the Field of Battle," whose stark alternating dimeter and trimeter lines, as Susan Wolfson notes, "mime the drumbeat of a funeral dirge" (*Selected Poems,* 457n):

Gentle and lovely form,
    What didst thou here,
When the fierce battle-storm
    Bore down the spear?

Banner and shivered crest,
    Beside thee strown,
Tell, that amidst the best,
    Thy work was done!

. . . .

    Why camest thou here?

Why?—ask the true heart why
    Woman hath been
Ever, where brave men die,
    Unshrinking seen?

. . . . . .

But thou, pale sleeper, thou,
    With the slight frame,
And the rich locks, whose glow
    Death cannot tame;

Only one thought, one power,
    Thee could have led,
So, through the tempest's hour,
    To lift thy head!

Only the true, the strong,
    The love, whose trust
Woman's deep soul too long
    Pours on the dust!   (*Selected Poems*, 455–56, ll. 1–8, 36–40, 49–60)

In Gray's poem, Alexis serves for a year (during which time the couple has a child), before he faces an engagement. Refusing to remain behind the lines when Alexis goes into his first combat, Julia "follow'd him ev'n to the fight," and when "a ball pierced his bosom, [and] he sunk on the plain!" she "swoon'd at the sight" (ll. 112–15). Alexis dies, and the disconsolate Julia is borne to a tent; she subsequently attempts to make her way back to England, enduring great hardships in the process. In a scene reminiscent of the middle section of Wordsworth's *An Evening Walk*, published nearly twenty years earlier, she reaches her physical and emotional crisis alone, in the dark, after frequent rebuffs to her pleas for charity:

> Cold charity sometimes her wants did supply,
>   But as often rejected her prayer;
> Till one night, quite exhausted, a storm threat'ning nigh,
> To a forest for shelter the wand'rer did fly;
>   For ah! where can the wretched repair.
>
> The country around was dark, barren, and bleak,
>   And keen darted the thick driving hail;
> She press'd her cold lips to her child's colder cheek,
> But feeling no motion, she utter'd a shriek,
>   O my child! and sunk senseless and pale.   (ll. 126–35)

Julia revives and tries, though distracted, to revive the child, but not even the intervention of a charitable rider who gives her shelter avails, and child and mother perish among strangers, their deaths invisible to the parents and friends in England who "ne'er knew of her fate" (l. 154). In this denouement, Gray invests the familiar theme with the same touching twist we see in Sargant's sonnet on the soldier's funeral: death abroad, unbeknownst at the time to one's family and friends. Usually this fate is reserved in poems for the man, as in Sargant's poem; Gray's unusual decision to attach it to the female figure here reveals her poem's more explicitly woman-centered nature.

It is not surprising that women were anxious to accompany their husbands, even if they understood (which of course many did not) the physical and psychological rigors that they would face. Competition for this dubious privilege was keen, and numerous visual works document both the anguish of parting and the activities of those who did manage to go with their husbands.[29] Anne Hunter's "William and Nancy, A Ballad," suggests the lengths to which some women were willing to go to try to follow their husbands (*Poems,* 81–82).[30] As William embarks for naval duty his wife Nancy, having failed to secure the ticket to accompany her husband ("chance denied the wish'd-for prize, / The envied lot another drew" [ll. 13–14]), watches from the quay. Finally, she risks all in a remarkable gambit: leaping from the quay to the moving ship, "She flew, and with a fearful bound / Dropp'd in her William's arms below" (ll. 17–24). While happy anecdotes like these, recorded in simple songs and rhymes, do occur in the writing of the war years, they are the exceptions to the rule. In reality, the returned veterans were frequently ignored, discarded, forgotten; many ended up in debtors' prisons or in workhouses where their impoverished families struggled to eke out a subsistence existence. Prophetic of the fate of many veterans of unpopular modern wars like Vietnam, their experience was even then not a new phenomenon, as is evident from Maria Barrell's 1788 poem *British Liberty Vindicated,* which laments the fate of the families of war veterans who found themselves imprisoned for debt. Barrell's incarcerated soldier asks the rhetorical question:

> "Did I for this in distant climates bleed? . . .
> "None need my help, and none relieve my woe."   (ll. 282, 284)

So too the sailor's fate:

> For debts contracted in his Country's cause,
> He lives imprison'd by that country's laws!
> For whom he oft had fought and oft had bled,
> For whom he mourns a more than brother dead.
> Nor brother, services, or worth avails,
> His wealth exhausted, all his merit fails:
> In vain the horrors of the war are o'er,
> In vain the sailor hails his native shore.   (ll. 303–10)

Barrell's veterans may be from the American campaign, but the impecunious warrior's fate—and that of his family—was little better twenty or thirty years later.

So, too, does Barrell's early Romantic-era poem anticipate many that followed in its pathetic portrait of the veteran's suffering family:

> His weeping wife with unavailing grief,
> Faithful in sorrow, strives to give relief,
> Till sad affliction rends her parting heart,
> And fixing deep the dire envenom'd dart,
> Helpless she falls, while at her tortur'd breast,
> With fever, woe, and agony opprest,
> A tender innocent, scarce knowing why,
> Sends forth the piteous soul-rending cry.
> And lo! in sad participation see,
> A little cripple trembles at her knee,
> Begging in vain the bread she cann't [sic] receive,
> For her sad parents have it not to give,
> Nor ease the babe, through whose enfever'd veins
> With pestilential force putrescence reigns[.]

Sad though this tale, 'tis literally true,
And equal sorrows daily rise to view.   (ll. 245–60)

No mere rhetorical flourish designed for emphasis, the final two lines were, just as Barrell says, "literally true" in 1788, as they would continue to be for the better part of three more decades.

The poems of Catharine Upton and Maria Barrell from the 1780s with which I have begun and concluded this discussion of war poetry introduce themes that are repeated again and again during the decades that followed, when women's voices joined the public discourse over both the principles and the costs—the human costs in particular—of war. That women writers so often came down on the side of humanity, stressing the bloodletting's human toll, offers an illuminating contrast to the writing of the many male poets who promoted and sensationalized war. On this, as on other subjects, poetry written by British women in this wartime culture consistently engages the quotidian reality that was for so many of them and their countrywomen the *only* reality in a society in which the survival of the persons about whom—and for whom—they wrote was so frequently in question. The antiwar poetry in particular reveals how these poets enhanced the power of their oppositional writing by employing both ubiquitous familiar examples and effective performative rhetorical strategies. From the engaging and accessible poetic forms in which they wrote to the sophisticated rhetorical strategies they employed in their poems, their work demonstrates the considerable literary skills they brought to their task, skills that have only recently begun to be apparent to late twentieth- and early twenty-first-century readers.

CHAPTER THREE

Women and the Sonnet

This is no time for straying in the woods,
    Or sitting idly by the river side,
    No time for poet's dreaming, there's a wide
And troubled view before us;—multitudes
    Murmuring like waves of the incoming tide.
    Oh! for some master spirit now to ride,
Like a strong bark, upon those angry waves!
    Oh that the star of truth at once might rise,
    Shedding its glory through these gloomy skies,
To guide that vessel on!—Men have been slaves
In soul too long—they suddenly awake,
    And find that in their sleep they have been chained,
    And fettered to the earth—now must be strained
The chords, and they, or man's strong heart must break!

              ("Sonnet, Written in 1830")

The author is Mary Ann Browne, who published five volumes under this name and another under her married name, Gray. A prolific producer of both sacred and secular verse, despite her modest financial circumstances, Browne is best remembered as hymn writer.[1] Her poetry traces a remarkable spiritual relationship with the natural world, which she valued almost as much as the scriptures as a guide for mediating one's passage to an individualized "heaven." Deeply meditative, that poetry posits an organic relationship among the individual, the natural world, and an eternal "afterlife" that combines traditional Christian views of Heaven with a Zenlike notion of a place of perfect peace and equilibrium in which one is wholly liberated from all sense of self.[2] Browne's 1830 sonnet nevertheless reflects a very worldly preoccupation with the civic lives of Britons at this transitional moment from what we usually think of as the Romantic era to the dawn of the Victorian. It was, after all, the year in which William IV took the throne that would pass to his niece Victoria seven years later on his death (Victoria's father, Edward, Duke of Kent, having died when she was eight months old). Keats, Shelley, and Byron were dead, and Coleridge would follow two years later; Hemans and Landon were increasingly popular, although they would not survive the decade either. It was also the period during which the groundswell for reform finally proved irresistible, as the Reform Bill of 1832 would demonstrate.

Browne's sonnet exhibits an anxiety akin to that which Wordsworth had expressed nearly thirty years earlier in "The World is Too Much with Us," the same uneasiness over social and cultural changes that seemed to be undermining the nation's traditional strengths and virtues at a historically pivotal moment. Like Wordsworth, who had sought another Milton and found him, by implication, in himself ("London, 1802"), Browne calls for a strong navigator in the perilous times that have enslaved her materialistic countrymen "in soul" for so long that their chains have become familiar costume, fettering them to the earth "in their sleep." The distinction she draws between sleep and wakefulness is noteworthy, for, as noted in chapter 1, Romantic-era radical discourse is peppered with calls to a slumbering citizenry to "awake," to "rise like lions after slumber," as Percy Bysshe Shelley had put it in *The Mask of Anarchy* (1819).[3] Like Wordsworth in "London, 1802," Browne invokes the spirit of the poet as activist. Her sonnet's opening lines do not dismiss poets, but only a particular sort of poet: the idle, self-indulgent, flower-sniffing dreamer. That a different sort of poet exists, "some master spirit" whose advent is signaled (like Milton's—and Christ's) by the appearance of a *star* (here "of truth"), is the clear implication of Browne's lines. She was not yet twenty when she wrote these lines, but they underscore a sense of vocation that is voiced also in another poem, "Written the Day before the Authoress Completed Her Nineteenth Year," from the same volume, *The Coronal* (1833):

> To think how few the brows my power from grief and woe hath cleared,
> To think how selfishly mine own deep feelings have been reared,
> To think how for *myself* the tears have been allowed to start,
> How I have been a passive slave unto my own wild heart;
> And oh! how often I have failed, in thought, and, word, and deed,
> To Him who binds the broken heart, and lifts the bruised reed.
>
> But should it be God's holy will my life should lengthened be,—
> If other nineteen years are still in future store for me,—

Oh! unto other, higher aims, may I my spirit lift,
And try to keep unstained and pure God's great and holy gift;
And thus be able to look back, when I have passed my prime,
Upon a clearer, sunnier track than marks my first spring time!

(160–61, ll. 31–42)

Looking back upon her fanciful and self-indulgent early poetry reminds Browne of the greater social responsibilities that are entailed in "God's great and holy gift." That a young woman expresses at the dawn of the Victorian age this sense of God-mandated cultural responsibility in the sonnet with which I began this chapter tells us something important about the role and function of the sonnet throughout the period. As Milton and Wordsworth had demonstrated, the sonnet could be the poetic vehicle for public, political discourse as much as it could for ostensibly private, personal expression. At the same time, the sonnet provided an uncommonly performative—even theatrical—vehicle for the simultaneous exhibition of seemingly personal and confessional sentiment, on one hand, and deliberate craft and technical virtuosity on the other. Drawing on some familiar names and some, like Browne's, that are less familiar, this chapter traces women's engagement with the Romantic-era sonnet.

Early Luminaries

That the sonnet became a particularly popular—or notorious—form during the Romantic era is well known. Stuart Curran has claimed, moreover, that the rebirth of the sonnet in the early Romantic period in England "coincides with the rise of a definable woman's literary movement and with the beginnings of Romanticism" (*Poetic Form,* 30). More recently, Daniel Robinson and Paula Feldman, documenting the remarkable profusion of Romantic sonnets, have observed that "at the height of the sonnet's popularity, it seemed that nearly everyone wrote them—women and men, the rich and the poor, rural and urban poets, established professional writers and those struggling to make a name for themselves" (3) As Mary F. Johnson, whom I consider later in this chapter, wrote in the preface to her own collection of sonnets (1810), "almost every village produces its Poet, and almost every cottage its Sonneteer" (v). J. R. de J. Jackson's extensive bibliography of poetry by Romantic-era women reveals that no fewer than eighteen separate collections appeared that either were composed exclusively of sonnets or contained a sufficient number of sonnets for the volume's title to advertise their presence there.[4] Countless more sonnets appear within the pages of other collections by women poets. The particular fondness among women poets for the sonnet had much to do with sentiment and with the whole culture of Sensibility "with its heavy emphasis on feeling and mood, and with the need to find a poetic form that was both demanding and accessible, to convey thoughts and feelings in a more natural way than poets previously had attempted" (Robinson and Feldman, 10). Sonnets were written by authors whose names we do not usually associate with the form (or even with poetry)—like the novelist Jane West, whose *Poems and Plays* (1799) contains ten occasional sonnets, gathered together under the group heading of "Ten Sonnets" and including one "To the Moon" that lifts the phrase "Fair planet of the night" directly from Smith's sonnet of the same title (1:195). Others appeared in volumes of poetry by writers whose names have long been forgotten, like the thirteen in Elizabeth Bath's *Poems on Various Occasions* (1806) or the twenty-five among the *Poems* (1808) of the unaccountably overlooked Susan Evance or, later, the eighteen in Anne Blanchard's *Midnight Reflections, and Other Poems* (1822).

Part of the Romantic era's rage for sonnets can be explained by the form's simultaneous openness to innovation and convention, to the apparently spontaneous and the visibly formulaic. The sonnet was at once capable of enormous expressiveness while still retaining in its limited space a place for the "performance" of rhetorical and technical fireworks, which made it a form that seemed to be at once deeply personal and self-reflexively performative. In many respects, the Romantic sonnet is the poetic analogue to the portrait miniature, a visual art form that experienced a parallel popularity during this same era. Like the miniature, the sonnet required compression, exactitude of representation, and expressive skill to capture its subject and convey that subject's "interior" properties—its ethos. At the same time, and like the miniature, to produce an accurate likeness in so small a compass required great technical virtuosity on the artist's part, and this virtuosity—this deliberate artistic "show"—is an inherent feature of the genre. Moreover, the ubiquity of the sonnet during the period ensured that both the form and its conventions were abundantly familiar to an apparently insatiable reading public, so that both writing sonnets and reading them were constituent parts of a very public transaction, no matter how seemingly private the sentiments sometimes expressed in them were. The sonnet was, in other words, a remarkably democratic literary vehicle, available to all sorts of writers and possessing the built-in advantage of brevity that particularly suited them to the daily and periodical press, where they appeared in extraordinary numbers. Particularly prominent among the early sonneteers were Charlotte Smith, Mary Robinson, and Anna Seward, each of whom contributed in important and original ways to the Romantic sonnet tradition.

Charlotte Smith, though neither the first nor the most prolific author of sonnets in the period, is without question the most important figure in the Romantic sonnet revival. Indeed, Paula Backscheider calls her "the best woman poet of the last part of the [eighteenth] century" (317). Already in 1792 John Thelwall had declared in the *Universal Magazine* that Smith's sonnets "display a more touching melancholy, a more poetical simplicity, nay I will venture to say, a greater vigour and correctness of genius, than any other English poems that I have ever seen, under the same denomination: *and I certainly do not mean to except the sonnets of Milton*" (my emphasis). According to Thelwall, Smith was without peer among English sonneteers: "Every province has its separate competitors. Over the epic field, Milton, of all British bards, triumphs without a rival, Shakespeare in the dramatic, and in the sonnet, Charlotte Smith." Beginning as a collection containing only sixteen sonnets when it appeared in 1784, Smith's *Elegiac Sonnets, and Other Essays* evolved during the remaining twenty-two years of its author's lifetime through a sequence of editions—each displaying increasing technical, emotional, intellectual, and aesthetic sophistication—into two volumes whose nearly 250 pages finally included some ninety-two sonnets and nineteen "other poems" of various lengths. Smith's project had a rough start, however. When she approached James Dodsley about publishing her slim volume, he dismissed it as of little interest—to him or to any potential readership. What Dodsley failed to appreciate, however, was that even in these early poems Smith was doing something extraordinary with that venerable old poetic form that would quite literally resurrect the sonnet tradition.

The other important figure in the early Romantic sonnet tradition was William Lisle Bowles. Bowles followed Smith both chronologically and artistically, first publishing (in 1789) a set of poems entitled *Fourteen Sonnets* that grew through nine ever-expanding editions over the sixteen years that followed. In his advertisement to the expanded second edition (now called *Sonnets, Written Chiefly on Picturesque Spots, during a Tour,* also 1789), Bowles credits Smith's skill even as he claims for his own sonnets both priority of composition (and therefore presumably of originality) and sincerity of feeling:

> It having been said that these Pieces were written in Imitation of the little Poems of Mrs. SMYTH [sic], the Author hopes he may be excused adding, that many of them were written prior to Mrs. SMYTH's Publication. He is conscious of their great Inferiority to those beautiful and elegant Compositions, but, such as they are, they were certainly written from his own Feelings. (8)

Bowles's rhetorical gesture of magnanimity in 1789 and the *Universal Magazine*'s lavish praise in 1792 notwithstanding, critical response to Smith's sonnets has always highlighted what it regards as her self-indulgent sentimentalism, a response to which Smith contributed by her habit of advertising in the prefaces to her novels and poems her own straitened personal circumstances. But Smith's great contribution to the sonnet revival lies in the manner in which she exploits the sonnet's potential for self-reflexivity—its deliberate and often transparent artfulness—as a means of both describing *and generating* acts of emotional and spiritual transcendence while also meditating on the role of "art" in such transactions. That is, her sonnets deliberately occupy a ground that is at once that of the "real world" and that of a more rarified or esoteric realm of pure art. Put another way, her best sonnets achieve a delicate and productive balance between deep emotional engagement and detached aesthetic contemplation (or appreciation). Moreover, taken in the aggregate, her sonnets possess a sustained rhetorical and emotional force that is at once personal and universal. Indeed, as Backscheider suggests, the *Elegiac Sonnets* as a whole (at every stage of their expanding number) can usefully be considered as a sonnet sequence in which Smith presents "the voice of an individual who suffers, usually from one cause, and expresses different states of that same condition of suffering at different times" (362).[5] At the same time, though, as Jennifer Wagner reminds us, the late eighteenth-century sonnet was often regarded as "a formal metaphor for the mind, for the 'mental space' in which the work of cognition takes place" (13). When we consider the *Elegiac Sonnets* as a deliberately constructed and psychologically insightful study of melancholy's many moods, we discover just how sophisticated is Smith's understanding of the workings of the human mind.

Because Smith's sonnets have received considerable attention in recent years, I examine only one here, "Written in the Church-yard at Middleton in Sussex."[6] Sarah Zimmerman has observed that in her lyric poems generally "Smith's speaker is characteristically occupied in observing her natural surroundings and pursuing the thoughts they prompt, leaving the reader free to observe her" (109). This sonnet furnishes a good example of how Smith typically situates herself rhetorically in her sonnets as both subject and object, as participant and observer, as engaged subjective agent and detached aesthetic artist.

Press'd by the Moon, mute arbitress of tides,
　　While the loud equinox its power combines,
　　The sea no more its swelling surge confines,
But o'er the shrinking land sublimely rides.
The wild blast, rising from the Western cave,
　　Drives the huge billows from their heaving bed;
　　Tears from their grassy tombs the village dead,
And breaks the silent sabbath of the grave!
With shells and sea-weed mingled, on the shore,

> Lo! their bones whiten in the frequent wave;
> But vain to them the winds and waters rave;
> *They* hear the warring elements no more:
> While I am doom'd—by life's long storm opprest,
> To gaze with envy, on their gloomy rest.   (44)

As she often does, Smith overlays two structural arrangements in this sonnet. The first is the octave/sestet *structure* (but *not* rhyme scheme) common to Petrarchan sonnets, in which the octave sets up the situation to which the sestet then responds. The second is the Shakespearean *structure* characterized by three quatrains and a couplet. Looking at the sonnet through the former structural lens reveals Smith describing in the octave first the sea's tidal surge and then the wind's compounding action on that surge. This is followed in the sestet by a comparable two-part substructure in which the bones of the dead that have been unearthed by the tidal surge are sucked out to sea and rolled back repeatedly on the shore. But this description is dovetailed backward, despite the exclamation point that closes the eighth line, to lines 7 and 8, which introduce the dead. At the same time, the sestet fails to divide neatly into equal three-line segments, but instead breaks *partially* at the ends of lines 10, 11, and 12. "But" (l. 11) introduces a first "turn" in announcing the (natural) insensibility of the dead bones, while the italicized "*They*" (l. 12) announces the speaker's different, sentient status, and the "While" that begins line 13 carries forward the contrast that is introduced in the preceding two lines. At the same time, looking at the sonnet in terms of quatrains reveals a different, though related, arrangement. Under this arrangement, the wind's action is rhetorically separated more definitively from the sea's, which is introduced first. The third quatrain (ll. 9–12) introduces the bones while looping back to include the action of sea and wind that impels their grisly motion. The quatrain then concludes (in line 12) by defusing the grisliness, reminding us (and the speaker) that in fact they feel nothing—that it is the speaker (and the engaged, empathizing reader) who "feels." The couplet concludes by underscoring the dramatic and emotional contrast between observer and observed, enforcing in the process the metaphor of "life's long storm."

The scene that Smith describes is rich with melancholy possibilities, and she seems intent on exploiting them all, from the fierce extremity of the storm to the pseudogothic touch of the graves that are undermined and emptied by the encroaching sea (the authenticity of which Smith highlights with a documentary endnote detailing what her poem describes). Moreover, the emotional excesses delineated both in the speaker's stated contrast and in the language through which its emotional charge is conveyed ("doom'd," "opprest," "gaze with envy," "gloomy rest") further enhance the poem's tone of melancholy. At the same time, though, the poem's remarkable aesthetic touches vitiate the emotional charge by calling attention to the sonnet's nature as a work of artifice, of deliberate craft. For example, the recurrent figure of rolling, of circular motion, is replicated at the level of language through Smith's deft use of the "oo" sound in the final lines ("doom'd," "gloomy"), which circle back to the sound introduced in the first line ("Moon," "mute"). Moreover, Smith loads her language with multiple connotations, as for instance when she describes the land as "shrinking" (l. 4), which is both objectively descriptive of a land mass diminishing beneath the sea's encroachment *and* subjectively suggestive of a frightened figure cowering ("shrinking") before a physical threat. Other equally loaded language contributes to this effect of deliberate artifice: "sublimely" (which brings with it a whole post-Burkean complex of signification), "silent sabbath," and bones whitening (stripped bare but also purified) in the surf. Moreover, the poem is further complicated, rhetorically, at the end by the reference to the speaker's envious gaze. For the grammatical object of that gaze is not the bones but rather "the village dead," whose rest is described as "gloomy." But if they are in heaven, then their "rest" should not be "gloomy"; in fact, the "gloom" is a projected manifestation of the speaker's own internal condition, a manifestation that is itself fraught with artifice—with "demonstration"—in that the speaker "gaze[s] *with envy*" on their "gloomy rest." That is, in effect she envies the tormented condition of heightened melancholy that she is in fact projecting on the object (and the subject—herself) of her contemplation. It is indeed a masterful performance.

Sonnets are by nature two-faced creatures. On one hand, they frequently pose as deeply personal expressions by speakers/writers who for one reason or another are constrained from speaking "aloud" and who therefore voice their emotions and ideas privately, cloistering them within the variety of confidential discourse that the sonnet pretends to be. On the other hand, though, the sonnet is one of the most formalistic, and therefore most public, of all poetic forms, governed as it is by conventions that direct not just content but also the way that content is formulated, deployed, and delivered (packaged, disclosed) to the reader. In other words, while the sonneteer typically maintains the ostensible fiction that her discourse is personal and private, she knows full well (as does her reader) that she is performing this fiction within a formal poetic form that is fully intended for "public-ation"—for being read "publicly" as a nevertheless ostensibly "private" discourse. For every moment that the readers are invited to regard as "confessional" in the Romantic sonnet, there exists a counterinvitation to remember that the disclosure is taking place not in the confessional but in the public square—in the marketplace of the print medium. Under these circumstances, sonnet reading is not the voyeuristic act the conventions of the genre would seem to imply but is rather an act of directed (or orchestrated) connoisseurship by means of which the readers internalize the author's "private" disclosures while simultaneously measuring them both against their own personal experiences and, more importantly, against comparable (or wholly different) disclosures that belong to a long history of communication and revelation within the genre.

If this double nature is apparent in Smith's sonnets once we elect not to read them narrowly as almost wholly autobiographical, it is more so in Mary Robinson's *Sappho and Phaon, in a Series of Legitimate Sonnets,* published in 1796, the year after the seventh edition of *Elegiac Sonnets.* That Robinson's volume attracted a large readership may be deduced from the fact that the first edition was published by the relatively "high-end" West End publishers Hookham and Carpenter, whose specialty was novels, whose clients included many titled men and women, and who also operated circulating libraries (St. Clair, 666, 725). Moreover, the subsequent posthumous "new edition" of 1813 was published by A. K. Newman, who had succeeded William Lane as publisher of the Minerva Press and manager of its immense Leadenhall Street circulating library, which has been estimated to have been the largest during the first two decades of the nineteenth century (St. Clair, 237). When her sequence first appeared, Robinson was, as noted earlier, already generally regarded as the preeminent poet of the early 1790s, on account of both her many poems (under many names) in the periodical press and her successful 1791 *Poems,* which contained fifteen sonnets and had been followed in 1793 by both a second volume and a combined "new edition," as well as separate monodies on Joshua Reynolds (1792) and Marie Antoinette (1793) and a collection of long poems (1793), among others. Robinson's first collection, *Poems,* had appeared some twenty years earlier, in 1775, followed in 1777 by a pair of narratives, *Captivity* (a thinly veiled account of her husband's imprisonment for debt) and *Celadon and Lydia,* bound together. The first volume's predictably immature and formulaic poems show the influence of Anna Letitia Barbauld's popular *Poems,* which Joseph Johnson had published in 1773 and that was by 1774 already into its fourth edition. But her atypical pastoral *Celadon and Lydia* demonstrates Robinson's early interest in gender politics, and, as Feldman notes, the popular poems of her prolific 1790s consistently "champion the plight of the disenfranchised while chronicling the moral bankruptcy surrounding and victimizing them" (*British Women Poets,* 592). The monodies and longer poems reveal her skill at handling more ambitious forms and genres; the shorter poems (including the poems in *Lyrical Tales* [1800]) tightly interweave sensibility, radical politics, and women's issues.

During her long career, Robinson demonstrated her versatility as a sonneteer in poems employing a broad variety of forms and voices. *Sappho and Phaon,* however, presents a strict formal and intellectual regularity: in forty-four Petrarchan sonnets, sensual (and sexual) passion, mediated through the vehicle of sensibility, is deliberately linked both to reason and to a political consciousness that is at once civic and gender minded. As Jerome McGann has observed in his study of Romantic-era sensibility, *Sappho and Phaon* represents Robinson's conviction that the poetry of sensibility itself represents a powerful intellectual force capable of "restructuring the philosophy of literature in terms of the feelings and the passions" (*Poetics of Sensibility,* 104). Robinson set out, as her preface announces, to rescue this venerable poetic form from the abuse it had suffered—especially in recent years—from its careless appropriation by countless poets of dubious quality who had cluttered "the monthly and diurnal publications" with "ballads, odes, elegies, epitaphs, and allegories, the nondescript ephemera from the heated brains of self-important poetasters, all ushered into notice under the appellation of SONNET!" (*Selected Poems,* 146). Robinson's reference to "*heated* brains" signals her intention to detach her sonnets from any such heat and to render their undoubted passion the more effective by means of her poems' deliberate calculation. In other words, like Smith's *Elegiac Sonnets,* Robinson's represent an aesthetic (and a poetic) in which passion and artifice—sentimental content and artistic form—draw particular strength from the fact that poet and reader alike appreciate the delicate intellectual balance achieved therein.

In defending the "legitimate"—that is, the Petrarchan/Miltonic sonnet—Robinson was doing what her contemporaries were doing, in part as a means of positioning their own sonnets in clearer relation to (or distinction from) Smith's. Anna Seward (about whom more shortly), who routinely disparaged the work of the more popular Smith, echoed Robinson in the preface to her own subsequent *Original Sonnets* of 1799, decrying the careless practice of regarding as sonnets any variety of "minute Elegies of twelve alternate rhymes, closing with a couplet, . . . without any other resemblance to that order of Verse, except their limitation to fourteen lines" (iii). Seward and Robinson were only two prominent examples among the many women *and men* who felt called on to counter what they regarded as the deleterious effect of Smith's wildly popular sonnets, although other popular poets (Helen Maria Williams, for example) seem to have shown little compunction about imitating both her rhetoric and her technical strategies (Backscheider, 349).

Like Smith's *Elegiac Sonnets,* Robinson's *Sappho and Phaon* portrays its speaker's evolving state of mind, which runs from initial passionate infatuation through a descending spiral of disappointment and despair that culminates in Sappho's suicide. The logical impossibility of treating Sappho's death from a first-person perspective forces Robinson to construct a narrative frame around Sappho's first-person lyrics, a frame that is completed by the final sonnet ("Sonnet 44: Conclusive"), which immediately shifts into third person:

Here droops the muse! while from her glowing mind,
    Celestial Sympathy, with humid eye,
    Bids the light Sylph capricious Fancy fly,
Time's restless wings with transient flow'rs to bind!   (180, ll. 1–4)

The "muse" is of course the muse of poetry, but the figure subsumes as well those of Sappho and of Robinson, both of whom are memorialized in the sequence.

Because it exhibits several useful parallels to Smith's sonnet on the churchyard at Middleton, the forty-first of Robinson's sonnets is worth examining here:

Yes, I will go, where circling whirlwinds rise,
    Where threat'ning clouds in sable grandeur lour;
    Where the blast yells, the liquid columns pour,
And madd'ning billows combat with the skies!
There, while the Daemon of the tempest flies
    On growing pinions through the troublous hour,
    The wild waves gasp impatient to devour,
And on the rock the waken'd Vulture cries!
    Oh! dreadful solace to the stormy mind!
To me, more pleasing than the valley's rest,
    The wood land songsters, or the sportive kind,
That nip the turf, or prune the painted crest;
    For in despair alone, the wretched find
That unction sweet, which lulls the bleeding breast!   (178)

Here Robinson arrays many of the same elements Smith had and to much the same purpose: high winds, ominous storm clouds, driving rain, tempestuous seas, and the trope of the "stormy mind." Robinson deploys these elements to paint Sappho's despair, which is impervious to the comforting delights of the sheltered valley, finding instead in the tormented natural elements a "dreadful solace" for unrelieved despair. But, like Smith's speaker, Robinson's adds a layer of rhetorical and emotional hyperbole (Robinson had, after all, been a professional actress), positively reveling in the emotional theatrics of melancholy pushed to extremity. Thus the tempest provides a "solace" that is comforting—even pleasant—despite its "dreadful" aspect. Moreover, the conclusion voices the masochistic nature of despair, calling it the sole "unction sweet" that "lulls the bleeding breast." This rhetorical and emotional excess is psychologically credible even as it reflects the wholly theatrical—and therefore calculated—nature of the speaker's (and the poet's) performance.

In other words, Robinson's sonnet presents another example of the sonnet's deliberate artifice. "Robinson's self-identity as a poet was inextricably connected to her capacity to perform," Judith Pascoe has written ("Mary Robinson and the Literary Marketplace," 266). Indeed, as Pascoe argues, Robinson's poems involve deliberate "stagings" of the multiple personae she adopted in her writing through the use of multiple pseudonyms, a technique that would have come especially easily for her in light of her career in the theater. But it is more than just that. As I said earlier, the sonnet is itself an inherently theatrical form; every performance, by every sonneteer, involves an implicit competition with other poems and other poets, all of whom are "present" in some fashion in the subject matter, the language, the rhetoric, and the compositional techniques each poet employs. Like Smith, Robinson enters a very public playing space when she composes *and publishes* a separately titled sonnet sequence, as opposed to merely collecting under a group title (like the ubiquitous *Sonnets, and Other Poems* with which the period is replete) the sonnets she had published in the periodical press and in her collected volumes of verse.[7] Robinson further signals her public intent by taking as her sequence's subject the first and still most famous woman poet, whose own fate—as woman and as poet—is sealed by her unfeeling rejection by the male object of her attentions and affections. If Robinson's subject tempts us—as it did her contemporaries—to read in the poems a commentary on the poet's own personal relationships with her numerous lovers, it is instructive to remember that, like Smith's *Elegiac Sonnets,* the sonnets in *Sappho and Phaon* are nevertheless also just that—*poems*—and as such they need to be studied also with detachment and from a literary-historical and an aesthetic standpoint. To read them narrowly on the merely personal, autobiographical level is to separate them from the rich poetic tradition with which they are at pains to engage in dialogue. In being so blinded—whether by accident or by deliberate intent—by the apparent presence in the poems of Smith and Robinson *specifically as Smith and Robinson* we blind ourselves, too, to the community of sentiment *and of intellect* on which they draw for their full resonance. Through just this sort of—often voluntary—blindness has the literary and cultural history of British Romanticism typically elided the accomplishments of women poets.

Many of the same things might be said, albeit for different reasons, about Anna Seward's sonnets. Seward's published comments and private correspondence both reveal that she bridled at Smith's fame. In the preface to her *Original Sonnets on Various Subjects* (1799), some of which date back to 1771, Seward indicates that the reader who is qualified to read (or to write) sonnets with discrimination is no common, uncultured one, but rather one possessed of substantial intellectual and

aesthetic sophistication: "There is no other order of Verse, upon which so much er-
roneous opinion has gone forth, and of whose beauties the merely common Reader
is so insensible" (v). The sonnet is for Seward a literary form of both intellectual
distinction and technical difficulty that requires a reader of acute and heightened
sensibilities. This is evident from the language with which she concludes her preface: "The Sonnet is an highly valuable species of Verse; the best vehicle for a single
detached thought, an elevated, or a tender sentiment, and for a succinct description.
The compositions of that order now before our Reader, ensued from time to time, as
various circumstances impressed the heart, or the imagination of their Author, and
as the aweful, or lovely scenes of nature, arrested, or allured her eye" (vi). Her intellectual expectations about reader and poem (along with her sheer envy of Smith's
greater fame) helps to explain Seward's spiteful references to "Mrs. C. Smith's everlasting lamentables, which she calls sonnets, made up of hackneyed scraps of dismal-
ity, with which her memory furnished her from our various poets" (*Letters,* 2:162).
Like Robinson before her, Seward draws for authority on male writers, in this case
both the "Mr. White," who discussed sonnets in the 1786 *Gentleman's Magazine,*
and Dr. Johnson, whom she presents as an example of a prejudiced, unsympathetic
reader. Nor was Seward without her admirers. Interestingly, just as Thomas Gent
eulogized Smith, the prolific Thomas Park prefaced his 1803 *Sonnets, and Other
Small Poems* with a laudatory sonnet to Seward, whom he credits in his preface with
"render[ing his poems] less unworthy" "to solicit public notice," despite his use in
them of what Seward had called "rebel-rhyme."[8]

It is instructive to observe how Seward treats the subject matter and imagery we
have already considered in the sonnets by Smith and Robinson. Sonnet 95, which
probably dates from the late 1780s,[9] invests these materials with an entirely different
psychological import:

> On the damp margin of the sea-beat shore
>   Lonely at eve to wander;—or reclin'd
>   Beneath a rock, what time the rising wind
>   Mourns o'er the waters, and, with solemn roar,
> Vast billows into caverns surging pour,
>   And back recede alternate; while combin'd
>   Loud shriek the sea-fowls, harbingers assign'd,
>   Clamorous and fearful, of the stormy hour;
> To listen with deep thought those awful sounds;
>   Gaze on the boiling, the tumultuous waste,
>   Or promontory rude, or craggy mounds

Staying the furious main, delight has cast
   O'er my rapt spirit, and my thrilling heart,
   Dear as the softer joys green vales impart.   (97)

Unlike Smith and Robinson, for whose speakers the tempestuous elements provide a natural analogy for their tormented states of mind and who find in the riotous scenes both a parallel and a goad to the emotional excesses their poems describe, Seward claims that these natural phenomena—which constitute a virtual formula for the Burkean sublime—produce a different result altogether. This experience is thoroughly *positive,* and its product is not despair but rapture. Like Robinson, whose Sappho claims that the tempestuous seaside scene is "more pleasing than the valley's rest" (l. 10), Seward too finds in the clamor of elements a delight that is "dear as the softer joys the green vales impart." But what produces Seward's "rapt spirit" and "thrilling heart" is not some irrational emotional immersion—some pure overload of sensibility—but rather a conscious act of intellect: "to listen with deep thought."[10] This is not to say that what Smith and Robinson describe in their sonnets is not also deep thought; indeed, for all three women what a poem presents as an almost overwhelming imaginative and emotional experience is mediated first through the rational intellect ("deep thought") and second through the act of poetic composition, which "arranges" the experience even as it re-presents it. When Wordsworth later described poetry as "the spontaneous overflow of powerful feelings" that "takes its origin from emotion recollected in tranquility" (*Lyrical Ballads,* 173), he might almost have been describing the poetic and the aesthetic that informs these three sonnets. These three highly visible, early Romantic-era women poets were instrumental in reviving and redirecting the sonnet tradition in Britain. That all three, along with Williams and others, were the subjects or the dedicatees of many subsequent sonnets (and other poems), by women and men alike, testifies to the extent of their currency and their influence on the contemporary literary scene.[11]

Later Lights

If Smith is a transitional poet, as Paula Backscheider claims (366 and passim), whose poems participate in the Miltonic verse tradition even as they help to shape the texture of Romantic verse, her work is especially important for the emphasis it lays on the theme of community with which Romantic literature is characteristically preoccupied. This sense of community is apparent in the many poems she and her female contemporaries addressed to other women or in which issues of interpersonal relationships are integral. The Romantic ethos, whether considered within its narrowly canonical parameters or within the broader ones that a revisionist perspective suggests, revolves around the difficult and often tortured relationship between the individual (or private and solitary) self and the social (or public and community) self. Poems ranging from the intensely private and personal (like those on the death of the poets' children) to the overwhelmingly public and communal (like those on political events and cultural phenomena) again and again draw their emotive *and their rhetorical* force from their authors' effective manipulation of their readers' expectations about the role of community in emotional and spiritual health—whether of the individual or of the nation. The sonnet occupies an ambivalent position in this discourse, as I have already suggested, because it is positioned between private emotion and public expression: a formal artifact that arranges "powerful feelings" for the reader's empathetic coperformance at the same time that it asks that reader to observe and appreciate its *aesthetic* aspects. When it comes to sonnets—and sonnet sequences—by some of the Romantic-era women about whom we know very little, the modern reader is forced to pay proportionally greater attention to formal features and to intuit (or invent) the personal. With that in mind, I wish to turn now to collections by three such poets, Anna Maria Smallpiece, Martha Hanson, and Mary F. Johnson.

These three substantial collections appeared during that first decade of the nineteenth century that traditional masculinist literary history has usually regarded as something of a hiatus in terms of poetic production: *Lyrical Ballads* had appeared in its second edition (1800) along with the first of many editions of Bloomfield's *Farmer's Boy,* followed in 1805 by Scott's *Lay of the Last Minstrel,* in 1807 by Wordsworth's *Poems, in Two Volumes* and Byron's *Hours of Idleness,* and in 1808 by Scott's *Marmion.* Meanwhile, Robinson had died in 1800 and Smith in 1806, while Hemans's first collection, *Poems,* appeared in 1808 under her maiden name of Browne. The first decade of the nineteenth century was in fact a full one, when it came to the production of poetry. No fewer than 1,750 volumes of poetry were published in this decade, among which more than 1,250 constituted first editions or first-time appearances. The following decade, from 1810 to 1819, witnessed an even greater productivity, during which at least 2,200 total volumes (including almost 1,500 first editions or first appearances) were published.[12] Among these were many volumes by women, including the sonnets of Smallpiece, Hanson, and Jackson.

Because these collections are by largely "unknown" poets about whom we have only the scantiest of biographical information, they necessarily entail different strategies of reading than do the works of well-known writers.[13] Neil Fraistat has observed that any collection of poems presents the reader with a collective body of internal evidence and information that he calls "contexture." This evidence, Fraistat suggests, typically encourages readers to "synthesize the subjects, themes, and genres of a contexture into the preoccupations and perspectives of a 'speaker' (present or implied) who is responsible for them all"; this speaker's "voice" is then "revealed" to the reader "in the verbal and imagistic echoes among the poems as well as in their individual rhetorical, metrical, and grammatical structures" (16). In other words, when we know little about the author at the outset, we instinctively "create" an authorial persona out of the textual evidence with which we are presented. Each of us has been conditioned by countless acts of reading to privilege narrative and biography when we read literature and to supply it ourselves when it is not already provided for us. These invented personae are inherently tentative, of course, since we have only the often-unreliable evidence of the printed texts on which to ground our inventions.

The Romantic sonnet is not simply a static artifact, then, but rather a dynamic *site* of readerly activity that is both organized and mediated by the poem's text. Therefore, to read the *poems* in each of these volumes is to trace the serial revelation of a personal *consciousness* (a personal *and poetic self*) that we associate with their author. These revelations come to us as readers in a series of snapshots of that authorial consciousness as it is itself in the process of development. The reader is invited to witness these revelatory insights but not to "participate" in them, for the poems' nature *as texts*—as alternative worlds—precludes that variety of intimacy. The act of reading itself, however, calls into existence a parallel "sympathetic" readerly consciousness that is both *trained* and *exercised* in "sympathizing" by means of the paradigms of sensitivity and expressiveness embodied in the texts of the sonnets. In a sense, then, by creating (or delineating) their "author," the sonnets at the same time *create* their (ideal) reader, "training" that reader in how to read the poems—and therefore the poet.

One reviewer of Smallpiece's *Original Sonnets, and Other Small Poems* observed that "sonnets and other short poems have ever been considered as compositions requiring all the sensibility of highly cultivated genius."[14] The point underscores the tricky relation in the Romantic sonnet between the sheer expressiveness of Sensibility and the performative virtuosity—and therefore the deliberate calculation involved in poetic composition—that characterizes these poems. If a sonnet is intended as an emotional snapshot of the poet in the unguarded immediacy of perception, cognition, and response, the reader also has to appreciate the poem as a formal, intellectually constructed work of art in which the "poet" or persona may be as much a creation—an artifact—as the poem itself. By virtue of their inherently performative nature, sonnets create an illusion for the reader, holding in apparent equilibrium two seemingly incompatible components: (1) an ostensibly spontaneous and therefore unmediated expression of intense *feeling*, and (2) an aesthetic dimension characterized both by a determinate poetic and rhetorical form and by the creative use of harmonious and deliberately heightened diction and syntax. In other words, the sonnet by nature walks a delicate and difficult line between absolute sincerity and shocking insincerity: reading the sonnet, the readers risk investing their emotional and intellectual energy in a transaction that may prove in the long run to be wholly chimerical—a fiction and a fabrication.

The volumes of sonnets published by Smallpiece, Hanson, and Johnson exhibit rhetorical and thematic debts to Smith's popular collection, whose title had evolved into its final form, *Elegiac Sonnets, and Other Poems,* during the 1790s.[15] Smallpiece's title is *Original Sonnets, and Other Small Poems,* Hanson's is *Sonnets, and Other Poems,* and Johnson's is *Original Sonnets, and Other Poems.* These later collections differ from Smith's, however, and from Robinson's, in certain important respects. Because each appeared in only a single edition, for example, there are no revised or augmented editions to furnish additional evidence about their authors. None is a formally articulated sequence in the sense in which Robinson's *Sappho and Phaon* is, nor are they quite the same in nature as Smith's *Elegiac Sonnets.* With a formal sequence like *Sappho and Phaon,* a carefully crafted narrative sequentiality, or linearity, is an integral part of the work as a whole, so that although it is possible to examine individual sonnets, one needs to do so while retaining a sense of those poems' place within the sequence of the larger texture (or contexture) of the "whole" work.

Unlike *Sappho and Phaon,* whose narrative linearity is reinforced by the well-known story signaled by the title, these three collections rely on a cumulative rhetorical and structural device that Barbara Herrnstein Smith has called "retrospective patterning" (119). With a work of this sort, we read "forward," in linear fashion, but at the same time we also read "backward" as we go, continually recollecting, comparing, and refashioning our perceptions and conclusions. Successive poems modify, supplement, and even contradict previous ones—or parts of them—so that reading involves a constant refining and refashioning of our "sense" (as well as our "knowledge") of the collection as a whole, even while we retain a nominal focus on each poem as a discrete unit. Even as we read, we are able to imagine alternative orderings that might produce slightly different pathways to cognition and comprehension without fundamentally altering the cumulative effect of the poems' intertextuality. In the case of Smallpiece's *Original Sonnets,* the fifty carefully interrelated sonnets appear first in the book following a dedicatory sonnet; the remaining poems, which do not rise to the aesthetic level of the sonnets either individually or collectively, occupy the 120 remaining pages.

Like Smith's *Elegiac Sonnets* and Smallpiece's *Original Sonnets,* Hanson's two-volume collection also includes "other poems." Each of the two volumes begins and ends with a set of these "other poems," most of which are called "stanzas," with descriptors that identify them as occasional poems about, or addressed to, friends and acquaintances, national figures like Admiral Nelson or Sir John Nelson, and literary figures like Smith, William Hayley, and Walter Scott. In each volume, these occasional poems bracket a consecutive set of sonnets, thirty-four in volume 1 and fifty-four in volume 2, that include among their number sonnets about both Smith and Robinson. In each volume individual clusters of sonnets are organized along roughly thematic lines, but neither volume (nor their set of sonnets) follows a fully articulated intellectual or aesthetic design.[16]

The organizing principle in Johnson's volume resembles the one that Wordsworth had recently employed in his 1807 *Poems,* where he had used subheadings like "Sonnets Dedicated to Liberty," "Poems Written during a Tour in Scotland," and "Moods of My Own Mind," or that Thomas Rodd had used in arranging his sonnets in categories of "amatory," "descriptive," and "religious." Johnson presents several comparable "gatherings" of sonnets under titles like the undifferentiated "Sonnets" (twenty-six poems), "Personification" (twenty-four poems on abstract qualities like "Discontent" and "Peace"), "Tributes of Respect to Particular Friends, and Addresses to Other Persons" (eleven poems), "Miscellaneous Pieces" (twenty-two sonnets), and "Regular Sonnets," or what Robinson called "legitimate sonnets" (forty-three poems). Johnson explains in her advertisement that the sonnets are of three varieties: "*irregular,* the metrical arrangement of which consists of three successive quatrains, and one couplet," others "in the measure used by Spenser," and still others "in that adopted by Milton" (which she calls "the only legitimate sonnet") ([xii]). The sonnets are followed by eight relatively brief poems gathered under the heading of "Odes" and comprising various poetic forms. Within the discrete gatherings of sonnets we discover numerous thematic and "tonal" linkages and interrelations, both among contiguous poems and among poems that are physically separated. But these links are neither so extensive and systematic *nor so aesthetically significant* as they are in Smallpiece's sonnets.

Anna Maria Smallpiece

Anna Maria Smallpiece's *Original Sonnets* bear evidence of their careful arrangement as a sequence. There are exactly fifty in the sequence, preceded by a dedicatory sonnet, and they make up a psychological record that traces the speaker's inner journey through the melancholy stemming from the loss, through death, of a particularly close female friend. For this melancholy neither the external beauties of nature nor the internal resources of memory provide solace; in fact, both contribute to a temporary and deceptive consolation that "beguiles" (sonnet 8) rather than comforts. Poem after poem relates the narrator's own psychological exile and inconsolable alienation in the wake of her loss, as happens in the sonnet to Muswell Hill:

> As thy green hill, sweet Muswell, I now tread,
> And mourning wander o'er thy shadowy way;
> From each lone shrub some spirit seems to say,
> "Thy hours of peace and joy are ever fled."
> Here, where pale Ev'ning shed her pensive beam,
> Veiling the beauteous landscape from the view,
> On the high grass, bespangled with her dew,
> Reclin'd, and wrapt in fancy's magic dream,
> How oft has Friendship, whispering most sweet
> Her dulcet notes in my deluded ear,
> Beguil'd the time: and still this bliss sincere,
> Amid thy shades, I ever hop'd to meet;
> But now thy trees, thy flow'rs, no pleasure lend,
> They blow around the low grave of my Friend.
>
> ("Sonnet 13: To Muswell Hill," 13)

This poem is prototypical in its presentation of the individual consciousness cut off, isolated from the community of nature and humanity alike. Elsewhere Smallpiece underscores this separation by juxtaposing the beauty of nature and natural phenomena to the traumatic unnaturalness of untimely death. Unlike Mary Anne Browne, who finds in nature both a steadying metaphor for a transcendent eternity and a tangible temporal consolation for loss, Smallpiece sees there a chastening lesson about mutability and the human condition:

> The narrow path deep winding through this wood,
> The Robin's song, that cheers the wint'ry glade,
> How much I lov'd! and O! the silver flood,
> And brook so clear that o'er the pebbles play'd,
> Warbled congenial music to mine ear,
> And sooth'd to peace this agitated heart,
> When Memory rested on a lov'd friend's bier,
> And tender scenes from which 'twas hard to part;
> Here while the cowslip hung its pallid head
> Amid the high grass, chrystaliz'd with dew,
> The primrose peeping from its mossy bed,

Beside the streamlet Spring's first incense threw;
They charm'd me then, and could all care beguile,
But now, alas! in vain does Nature smile.

("Sonnet 36: Composed in Aspley Wood," 36)

Smallpiece liberates her sequence from linear sequentiality and generates contexture by employing that "retrospective patterning" to which I have already referred. Her carefully crafted layering or "interleaving" of recurrent words, images, incidents, tableaux, and rhetorical devices directs one's reading almost imperceptibly along multiple "pathways" through the text. The linear organization that the conditioned reader expects fails to materialize, and what comes instead is a rhetorical constellation, or an array; the reader is invited to draw multiple lines and discover multiple and shifting relationships among poems, thereby destabilizing conventional notions of order and poetic closure. The strategy is too consistent—and too effective—to be anything but the result of conscious design on the poet's part.

This unconventional organization shares with the work of other Romantic-era women writers an interest in exploring alternative ways of "knowing" (and "telling"), paradigms that differ from those that we typically associate with masculinist models and with, as Elaine Showalter puts it, "the linear absolutes of male literary history" ("Toward a Feminist Poetics," 131). We see this particularly in such writing's resistance to empirical, linear organization and its reliance instead on what I have called the constellation or the array. This approach to narrative organizes moments of incident, character, perception, insight, and epiphany into an array that is *variously* (rather than singly or monolithically) constituted and whose full interpretation depends on the reader's willingness and ability simultaneously to pursue multiple threads of information, implication, and signification and to continually revise the resulting "content" as new details are added. Showalter remarks that an approach of this sort enables "feminine values [to] penetrate and undermine the masculine systems that contain them" ("Toward a Feminist Poetics," 131).[17] Of course, all writers ask their readers to become cocreators with them, participating in the reading activity literally by "performing" the author's text. But Smallpiece's sonnets, in common with a striking amount of Romantic-era women's poetry (and in common with only a comparatively small portion of Romantic-era men's poetry), bear out Showalter's notion (which is itself grounded in French feminist theory) of a "female aesthetic" that celebrates an intuitive female approach to experience, an approach that opposes the hierarchical and therefore subordinating style of classification and distinction that is so characteristic of the masculinist style.[18] Indeed, one can legitimately say about the *Original Sonnets* what Jerome McGann says about Smith's *Elegiac Sonnets:*

that they derive their peculiar force from the fact that they are meditations on a general condition rather than from the fact they are elegies for particular persons (*Poetics of Sensibility*, 45). Moreover, this multilayered discursive array includes also a specifically aesthetic (or poetic) dimension: several of the sonnets (like sonnets 1, 7, 19, 27, and 45) are themselves also about the making and consuming of poetry (art) and about its restorative (or at least distracting) powers, both for the artist and for the consumer.

Still, Smallpiece's final sonnet offers a fitting, though somber, culmination to the complex skein of signification woven in the preceding fifty:

Illusion sweet, to all thy sunny days,
That have my paths illum'd, a long adieu;
Unwelcome truth is, now, unveil'd to view;
Ah me! I shudder at her purer rays,
Again would listen to love's thrilling lays,
And would again the dear deceit pursue,
Again believe the heart's effusion true,
And nurse the flame that o'er my bosom plays.
—Ah! idle dreams, by rude experience taught,
Rare is the treasure of a faithful friend;
E'en life itself, consuming at this thought,
Drags its long chain, and languishes to end.
For e'en the self depending soul must bend
'Neath cold neglect, where it warm friendship sought.   ("Sonnet 51," 51)

Throughout the sonnets Smallpiece associates "illusion" variously with self-decep-tion as a temporary palliative to suffering (including the vain but seductive belief that sincere friendships may last forever), with the flattering but ultimately deceitful behavior of others (including the emotional and presumably sexual treachery of false friends), and with the temporary pleasure produced by aesthetic experience (in-cluding the linked activities of writing or reading poetry). Now, in this concluding poem, she renounces all of that, resigning herself at last to the "unwelcome truth" that in the quotidian world of appearances and flattery it is all too easy to be misled and that in such a world faithful friends are all too rare. To make matters worse, such friendships are unusually susceptible to dissolution, whether by physical death or by emotional disruption. However much one might wish to follow the easier path traced by illusion's "dear deceit," the mature mind is required finally to accept the truth that "rude experience" teaches. Worst of all, the beguiling, undermining na-ture of the stark reality that must be faced and accepted can not only sour one's sweet illusions but also subdue even "the self depending soul"—the ostensibly self-sufficient individual—by imposing on it the sad, concluding realization that life "drags its long chain," consuming itself, conditioning the individual soul to the "cold neglect" that is all that remains when the search for "warm friendship" proves a vain one.

Martha Hanson

Unlike Smallpiece, who arranged her richly textured sonnet sequence carefully, Hanson announces forthrightly that her collection is very much a miscellany. The poems, she tells us, "have been produced at different, and distant periods; often, when the prey of lingering illness, the amusement of solitary hours, and sleepless nights" (ix). Hanson professes herself to be sanguine about her prospects for fame:

> Reason tells me, the absurdity of expecting to obtain publick approbation; even did these volumes possess far more merit than they have to boast: while, consciousness that they have but little of that intrinsick value which might stand proof against the rapid stream of Time, (which, hurrying with resistless course, bears with it such Books as have only the fashion of the day in which their Writers lived to preserve them) forbids to hope, that they will survive, to obtain, for their Author, the consideration of succeeding times." (xi)

Nevertheless, the first sonnet in volume 1 is addressed to Fame:

> Oh Thou! whose hand adorns the Conq'ror's brow,
>   With verdant Laurel's ever-blooming sprays,
>   And for the Poet, twines a wreath of Bays;
> While from his Harp seraphick numbers flow.
> I seek not to adorn my humble Lyre,
>   With such proud trophies; though their deathless bloom,
>   Which, with immortal honour, decks the tomb,
> Might well an adamantine breast inspire.
> I only ask, to crown my untaught lays,
>   A simple wreath, my artless Lyre to bind,
>   By sacred Friendship's hallow'd fingers twin'd;
> Whose partial fondness gives its meed of praise.
> Her hands, oh Fame! to thy bright wreaths, impart
> A dearer charm; which binds the Feeling Heart.   ("Sonnet 1: To Fame," 1:82)

Here Hanson immediately plays on the theme of the poets' competition, juxtaposing the male "Poet" and the "seraphick" artistry of his bardic "Harp" with the "untaught lays" that flow from her own "artless Lyre." Not the "immortal honour" signified by the wreath of bay leaves accorded the Poet, Hanson asks instead for the "simple wreath" woven "by sacred Friendship's hallow'd fingers." The male poet's memorial is quantitative, measured in calculated public approbation that "inspire[s]" even the "adamantine breast"; the female poet's is qualitative, grounded in affection and informed by "the Feeling Heart." Hanson's conspicuous capitalization underscores the value she places upon the "partial fondness" that informs this affectional bond. This is not strictly competition, then, but rather an assessment of the conventionally gendered spheres of poetic production and reception. But this distinction is formulated *and published* within a public literary production that inherently competes with all of that poetic production even as it participates in it.

Given both Hanson's judgments about men and women poets and her calculated self-deprecating assessments of her own poetry, it is instructive to consider her memorial sonnet on Mary Robinson:

> Daughter of Genius! while thy tuneful lays
> > Lift my warm spirit from its mortal clay,
> > And bid it soar to realms of endless day,
> In vain I seek thy matchless pow'r to praise.
> Though in the regions of the silent Grave,
> > The tyrant Death has laid thy beauties low,
> > Around thy Urn a Lasting Wreath shall blow.
> Which still the wintry storms of Fate shall brave.
> The Muses cull'd its Never Fading Flow'rs:
> > Which emblematick of thy heav'nly strain,
> > To Time's last moment shall unchang'd remain,
> (Nor feel base Envy's sting, Detraction's pow'rs)
> And bloom for ever, round thy Sacred Name,
> 'Grav'd by the fingers of Eternal Time.
> > > ("Sonnet 14: Occasioned by Reading Mrs. M. Robinson's Poems," 2:74)

Crediting Robinson with a public fame that, like the "Lasting Wreath" on her funerary urn, will "bloom for ever," Hanson installs her in that seemingly exclusively male poetic pantheon celebrated in the sonnet just quoted. Indeed, the Muses fashion the memorial wreath, but "Eternal Fame" engraves Robinson's name on the stony tomb just as Robinson has herself inscribed her name (and herself) on the pages of her poems. If Robinson's poems serve Hanson by lifting her own spirit (which is warmed by the act of reading and recollecting) and by opening for her a prospect of "endless day," though, so too do they bear her down again by reminding her of the vanity of any hope to compete with a predecessor of such "matchless" poetic power. The same sentiment recurs in the poems on Charlotte Smith, including the long "Stanzas, Occasioned by the Death of Mrs. Charlotte Smith," with which volume 2 opens and that Stuart Curran regards as an example of that sort of encomiastic poem that illustrates "one woman looking to a predecessor or contemporary for example or support" ("Romantic Women Poets," 161).[19] That poem's first line attributes to Smith the "Magick Harp" that produced "such heav'nly warbling" at her hand (2:1, ll. 1–2). In conspicuously investing Smith with the same instrument she gives the male Poet in her earlier sonnet, Hanson signals her conviction that Smith's accomplishments, like Robinson's, fully bridge the gender gap.

This conviction is important for Hanson, for, despite her predictable self-deprecation, her work has moments of surprising assertiveness. One such moment comes in the middle of volume 2, where "Sonnet 21" appears without any contextual framework to support its extraordinary message:

> How proudly Man usurps the pow'r to reign,
>   In ev'ry climate of the world is known,
>   From the cold regions of the Northern Zone,
> To where the South extends his boundless main.
> Yet in this wide expanse, no realm we find,
>   To boast a Woman, who the yoke disdain'd;
>   And with Intrepid Soul, that Freedom claim'd,
> Which Heav'n Impartial, gave all human kind.
> With Soul too Proud, to bear the Servile Chain,
>   Or to Usurping Man, Submissive bow,
>   Though poorest of the names, Record can shew,
> Ages unborn, with wonder shall proclaim
> The pride of one Unyielding Female thine,
> Dear Native England! and the name be Mine.   (2:91)

Hanson here conveniently forgets not only Catherine the Great (who had died in 1796) and Elizabeth I (who had died two centuries earlier) but also countrywomen like Wollstonecraft, Smith, and Robinson. Of course, Hanson's point is a largely rhetorical one that may simply reflect her apparently unmarried state, but the universal abstractions she invokes here ("Freedom," "Heav'n," "Man," and "Woman") suggest also a broader cultural view that raises interesting questions about the author's relation to feminists of her day, including Robinson, who had in 1799 published *Thoughts on the Condition of Women and on the Injustice of Mental Subordination.*[20] Interestingly, Hanson constructs a gender equity of sorts rhetorically, by counterposing to the pride of usurping Man "the pride of one Unyielding Female" that enables the woman to claim for herself that noble freedom that "Heav'n Impartial" has apportioned to "*all* human kind" (my emphasis) without prejudice or preference. On this more level plain, she achieves what she claims will be the everlasting "Record" (for "Ages unborn") of her own accomplishment, an accomplishment she further invests with a nationalistic flourish in making it "thine, / Dear Native England."

Mary F. Johnson

Like Martha Hanson's, Mary F. Johnson's sonnets are relatively conventional in subject and approach, and like Hanson she does not attempt the sort of carefully articulated sequence that Smallpiece does. Johnson's sonnets range freely over the conventions of the Romantic sentimental sonnet, with poems addressed variously to the seasons, to moods (melancholy, disappointment, gratitude, tranquility, affliction, fortitude, etc.), to flowers (hyacinth, daisy, etc.), to creatures (butterfly, glowworm, etc.), to persons (her niece, her sister, a friend, etc.), and to particular experiences like reading Mary Robinson's poems (the subject of sonnet 14 in volume 2). Like the poems that bracket them in both volumes, they are presented more as a collection of occasional sonnets than as any programmatically ambitious sequence. Indeed, Johnson remarks disingenuously that composing sonnets was for her something of a form of amusement, a "pleasing escape" from the difficult labor demanded by more extended poetic forms:

> Within the limits prescribed by it [the sonnet form], may be expressed casual and momentary thoughts, at the moment when the feeling and impression by which they are excited are most fresh and lively in the imagination; and the mind, so relieved from a sensible pressure, is left easy and satisfied, and again at leisure to receive new ideas and suggestions, whether from surrounding objects and scenery, or from reflection, books, or conversation. (xi–xii)

Writing in 1811, soon after Johnson's volume appeared, the *British Critic*'s reviewer called Johnson's explanation "the best that we have ever heard said for the sonnet."[21] The congratulatory note is pleasant, of course, but the reviewer appears blithely ignorant of (or perhaps deliberately silent about) what other prominent poets had said on the subject, such as Charlotte Smith, for instance, who in the preface to the first edition of *Elegiac Sonnets* had remarked on the sonnet's particular suitability as a "vehicle for a single sentiment" (vii).

Johnson indicates that composing sonnets is (for her at least) inherently therapeutic: it provides relief from the "pressure" of sensory or intellectual stimulation while restoring (and indeed enhancing) the mind's receptivity to "new ideas and suggestions." Johnson's observation is reminiscent of Wordsworth's comment in the "Intimations Ode" about how that poet's "timely utterance" (presumably in the form of a poem) relieved his own "thought of grief" (ll. 22–24). At the same time, she recognizes that poetry cannot simply be willed but must result from unpremeditated visitations:

> In vain you seek to win th' unwilling Muse;
>   Whene'er she comes to bless, she comes unsought,
> And, with self-sounding shell, Attention wooes [sic],
>   Teaching such strains as Study never taught.
>   She brings the waking dream with rapture fraught;
> Enrobes the dreary scene in vivid hues;
>   Gives life to sentiment, and soil to thought,
> And waning Hope with Fancy's fire renews.
> She—child of Heav'n, and heavn's peculiar gift—
>   Descends t' obliterate, in the chosen breast,
> All Fortune's injuries, and its heart to lift
>   Above the cares that vulgar souls molest.
> She comes—not on her Wealth and Power attends,
> But what she gives the highest boon transcends.   ("The Willing Muse," 137)

As for so many Romantic poets, inspiration depends for Johnson on the poet's receptivity to the muse, whose transformational effects produce an alteration of consciousness that lifts and restores the spirit. Just as Wordsworth had claimed that the poet possesses sensitivities and responsiveness above and beyond the capacity of "other men," so too does Johnson set her poet above the "vulgar [i.e., common, ordinary] souls" and the cares that "molest" such commonplace hearts. Significantly, Johnson makes this the concluding sonnet in her collection, situating it immediately before the eight poems she calls "odes" that complete the volume.

This sense of poetry's inherent power to animate and ennoble poet and reader alike is evident in many of Johnson's sonnets, both in passing and, as here, as the primary subject:

> The teeming earth with vegetation heaves,
>   As melts the rigour of the wint'ry gales,
>   The virgin Spring her bashful face unveils,
> And in the sun her primrose garland weaves.
> Her genial breathings the pale bloom receives,

On zephyr's vagrant wing the odour sails,
    The wand'ring bard th' inspiring air inhales,
And with wild lays his raptur'd mind relieves.
When o'er the daisied lawn the breezes sigh,
    With the sweet cowslip's amber pendents play,
And on the bank of azure violets die—
    On the red evening of an April day:
Frigid and tasteless are his heart and eye,
    Who can without delicious feelings, stray.   ("April Evening," 19)

Since the making of art, the composing of poetry, "relieves" the artist's mind, then, by extension, the reader's mind and "delicious feelings" may also be "raptur'd" through the secondary emotional and aesthetic stimulus of the act of reading, by which she or he "strays" through the poems and therefore through the scenes described in them. Nature holds the key to this almost involuntary sharing of experience, for as Johnson explains in a sonnet called "Poesy,"

. . . Nature, by indissoluble bonds,
    United Feeling and true Poesy.
Where Feeling is not, by no studied lore
    An unblest bard awakes a touching strain;

. . . .

Exalted, genuine Poesy! thy chart
Shows from the head the passage to the heart.   (31, ll. 7–10, 13–14)

Johnson consistently portrays individual unresponsiveness to nature as a "want of heart" ("Subdued Desires" [123, l. 12]) and as a corresponding insensitivity to the organic coherence of the human and the natural spheres, which such unfeeling souls frequently and erroneously view not as reciprocal but rather as unequal, alienated, and adversarial. Indeed, one theme that runs throughout Johnson's sonnets is the "civilizing" influence of a lively reciprocal relationship with nature and the natural world, a relationship that educates the soul in virtue and in tenderness.

The first poem in the book, "To the Public," which functions as a sort of preface, announces Johnson's intention to conceal her personal identity, in effect forcing the reader to judge the poems purely on their aesthetic merit:

Though no puff'd memoir or vignette reveal
    That I am old or young, or fair or brown,
    With smiles, dread Public, these weak efforts crown,
And let me on your tol'rance notice steal.

With candour weigh this diffident appeal
  To yours the sole tribunal of renown:
  Though, if but Pity rise to check your frown,
Spare not—but justice, void of vengeance, deal.
  Yet, Public, if its native strain amuse,
  Can you a guileless confidence abuse,
And crush the bird which shelters in your breast?
  The woodland warbler, timid and unknown
  For brilliant plumage or mellifluent tone,
May rise to fame with your protection blest.   ([xv])

This is of course another version of the familiar pleading preface that begs restraint and tolerance for what the reader finds objectionable. But Johnson's concluding metaphor reveals her belief that the act of reading establishes a sympathetic and participatory pact between poet and reader. There is therefore a double import to "the bird which shelters in your breast." Johnson's metaphorical bird (and both the poem and the collection for which it stands) does more than simply seek shelter in the reader's breast, near the heart, as it were. The phrase also hints that the bird— the poetry and its poet—also *reside* in that breast, where they occur naturally. Like Wordsworth (again), who, although he thought poets had special sensitivities, also had written in the preface to the *Lyrical Ballads* (165) that the poet is "a man speaking to men" (therefore implying that all men are at least potentially poets), Johnson implies that the poetic faculty is equally democratic and universal in its distribution among humanity. Granted, her own success requires "your protection blest," but within the compact of readerly sympathy she invokes with her audience, there no question that Johnson envisions a process of cocreation. This compact of sympathy is unfolded more fully in the poems that follow, many of which deal with the consequences of disappointment, whether of love or fortune, sometimes in poems that take the form of an implied conversation with an unidentified "friend" whom Johnson attempts to rally when love fails her, sometimes in poems addressed to particular individuals (in the "Tributes of Respect to Particular Friends, and Addresses to Other Persons" section), and sometimes in poems that constitute part of an internal colloquy, especially on the subject of poetry.

Johnson also comments specifically on women's poetry in a sonnet called "On the Perusal of the Poems of Miss T——, Published 1808," which seems to be a response to Laura Sophia Temple's 1808 *Lyric and Other Poems*:

Her natural bias woman should correct,
  Not melt her waxen mind at Passion's flame:

With life her purity of thought protect,
   And let her studies brace her mental frame.
If for her pen she frigid subjects choose,
   She makes them with her glowing spirit warm;
Woman's will ever be a tender Muse,
   Which throws in rugged themes a softening charm.
Learn'd Carter, pious Moore [sic], and Barbauld, knew
   To lull the passions while the feelings woke;
Affection's chasten'd sentiments they drew,
   But ne'er in vapid Love's weak jargon spoke.
Men write from thought—our strains from feeling flow—
Then pure as ardent may that feeling glow.   (86)

Johnson's choice of Carter, More, and Barbauld for her exemplars is consistent with her own poetic and with her preference for a poetry grounded in moderation, fortitude (mental and emotional), and abstract, allegorical subjects. At the same time, Johnson advocates intellectual as well as artistic sophistication and distinguishes the appropriate "feeling" in women's poetry from mere quotidian "passions." Her poem also makes clear that she regards women's poetry as coequal, its origins and generic considerations notwithstanding, with men's.

Johnson's explicitly gendered view of men's and women's writing may partially account for the largely positive critical reception that *Original Sonnets, and Other Poems* received. The only unfriendly response seems to have been that of the *Critical Review,* whose reviewer observes acidly that she has addressed "hackneyed" sonnets "to Hope, to Peace, to Love, to Friendship, and to almost every thing else, that has been *sonneted* an hundred thousand times before"; the contemporary sonnet has consequently "become so insipid (not to say stupid) from the frequent recurrence of the same images, that Miss Johnson must not be offended when we tell her she comes in for her share of the same tameness of which we have so often had occasion to complain in others."[22] Her other commentators generally approve both her subjects and her poetics, crediting her with "a great deal of genuine taste and poetical feeling" or with "feeling, taste, accuracy and felicity of description, and a poetical spirit."[23]

I have discussed the sonnets of these three little-known poets to argue that, like the better known Smith, Robinson, and Seward who preceded them, they articulate a feminine aesthetic characterized by constellations or arrays of interrelated insights that invite readers to contemplate the intertextual resonances that emerge from the process of reading. In deliberately rejecting strict linearity of organization, they ask their readers to consider alternative ways of receiving and processing information. Hilde Hein has written that "feminist art merges with and commonly expresses a feminist aesthetics" that is in reality "an aesthetics of experience." But, she continues, all experience is contingent, and the largely masculinist language of theory is inadequate for expressing women's particular experience. Therefore, "if experience is to be more than the inscription of what is momentarily given and gone, it must be aesthetically embodied, that is, given shape through imagery and symbolism," which is the process by which experience gives way to reflection. That reflection, she concludes, "does not flee from experience, but stays close to its source and 'muses at its edges'" (452). Sonnets can constitute just such reflections, and in this most public and performative of poetic forms these three poets muse at the edges of female experience. Within the constrained and carefully controlled spaces of sonnets, they present arrays of interrelated insights through which the reader constructs a metastructure that exists outside and "above" the physical texts represented by the printed pages. Each of these metastructures presents for examination the sensibilities of a real *or imaginary* narrative persona. So the volumes present not just an alternative way of *knowing;* they also demonstrate an alternative way of *telling.* They replace the customary linearity of writing/reading with a seemingly nonlinear array of multiple perspectives whose cumulative effect suggests what we often think of as an "epiphany." In this case, though, that epiphany is shivered into its myriad components in order that we may reconfigure it through our own process of reading and cognition.

Afterglow

The sonnet did not die out in Britain with the coming of post-Napoleonic cultural shifts, but it did move in different directions. The major canonical poets all wrote sonnets, and indeed Wordsworth in particular committed himself resolutely to the form: *The River Duddon: A Series of Sonnets* appeared in 1820, followed two years later by the *Ecclesiastical Sonnets.* Sonnet sequences remained popular and, if anything, their number increased, as did the reputation of the sonnet generally in post-Romantic Britain. As the Regency wound to an end, though, published commentary on the sonnet was not encouraging. One anonymous critic who signed himself as "Aristedes" complained to the editor of the *British Stage and Literary Cabinet* about the "incalculable" numbers of writers producing "amorous" sonnets consisting of "love ditties to Anna Maria, or some other dreary [sic] of the 'inspired writer.'"[24] The *New Monthly Magazine* railed at length against the rampant "sonnet-tomania" gripping the nation in 1821, one critic offering by way of illustration the sad case of "a friend of mine" who was "bitten" by the sonnet infection, with the result that "he has ejected, during the interval, two thousand and odd sonnets,—five hundred to the moon, which sphere, by its universal influence on sonnettomania, completely proves the title of the disordered to be ranked with the unfortunate beings denominated lunatics."[25] As Jennifer Wagner has observed, much of the post-Romantic controversy over the sonnet's status revolved around questions of technical form, although discussions of these technical criteria were often colored by morality and politics (115–22). For example, in an extraordinary display of national-istic poetic jingoism, Robert Fletcher Housman claimed in 1835 that reading a son-net leaves a reader with a decidedly *"un-English* feeling . . . creeping about the heart" because of the form's Italian roots (viii). The question of whether or not a sonnet is "legitimate" likewise took on nationalistic implications as British poets and critics sought to repudiate the imputation that the "English" sonnet was "illegitimate" and therefore a bastard form. Some of this confluence of poetics and politics is evident in two additional collections of sonnets that appeared during the Regency, Jane Alice Sargant's *Sonnets, and Other Poems* (1817), which includes two groups of consecutive sonnets (numbering sixteen and thirteen poems respectively) set among the "other poems," and Mariann Dark's *Sonnets, and Other Poems* (1818), whose forty sonnets are bracketed by eleven poems in other forms.

Jane Alice Sargant's preface attributes the publication of her volume to "stern necessity." "Unforseen events have deprived her of fortune," Sargant writes of her-self in the third person, while "the all-wise Disposer of events" has seen fit "to cloud her days with sorrow, and, to the miseries of the most severe domestic afflictions, to add those of decaying health and a sinking constitution." She has undertaken "to augment and revise her collection of poems," which she presents to the public "as the only means which at present offers of gaining support and independence" (x–xi). The published roster of some 330 subscribers (and the fact that a second edition appeared within a year of the first) suggests that Sargant did indeed garner considerable support from her effort. Sargant, whom we met in chapter 2, was born Jane Alice Smith, in Whittlesea, Cambridgeshire, the favorite sister of Sir Henry (Harry) Smith, whose *Autobiography* records his experiences in the Napoleonic wars and afterward. After joining the Yeomanry Cavalry in 1804, Harry Smith became a lieutenant of the Second Battalion of the Ninety-fifth Regiment Riflemen, a com-mission his father purchased for him, rising to the rank of lieutenant colonel by the time he began his autobiography in 1824. Jane Alice Sargant's close connection with her brother and his comrades is evident from the presence in the list of subscribers of a number of military men, including several specifically designated as members of the Rifle Brigade.[26]

Given Sargant's association with the military, her conspicuous nationalism and her enthusiasm for British militarism are not surprising. Her sonnet to her brother Harry, its melodrama notwithstanding, would have struck a responsive chord with many of Sargant's readers:

> Oh! shall I e'er again the face behold,
>   On which enraptur'd I could ever dwell:
> Again the form in strict embrace enfold,
>   And wak'd to bliss each anxious fear dispel!
> Ah! when the battle glows with bloody hate,
>   On seraph wing, ye angels! hover near,
> Arrest the blow of black impending fate,
>   And save the noble youth—to honour dear.
> But should a cruel hand e'er lay him low,
>   And death in endless sleep his eyelids seal,
> Unnerve the arm that check'd the daring foe,
>   And from his manly cheek the roses steal,—
> Then would I seek the spot where Henry bled,
> And make my grave amid the slaughter's dead.
>
> ("Sonnet 9: To My Brother," 9)

Sargant appeals to community and solidarity in the face of the shared anxiety to which her poem's emotional excesses point, but the suicide pact hinted at in the final line undercuts that resolve.

Sargant's sonnets owe much to Smith's both in manner and in matter. Indeed, "Sonnet 10" (10) from the first set revisits the panoply of natural elements, deploying "surly blasts of Winter drear" (l. 1), "howling tempests" (l. 4), "rushing wave" (l. 5), and "overwhelming billows" (l. 8) in a metaphorical psychoportrait of the melancholy sufferer who "loves upon the whiten'd shore, / To listen to the winds' conflicting rage, / And to the troubled gale her sorrows pour" (ll. 11–13). Likewise, the twelfth sonnet of this group unmistakably echoes Smith's "On Being Cautioned against Walking on an Headland Overlooking the Sea, Because it was Frequented by a Lunatic":

> Mark the poor ideot [sic]! now he laughs aloud,
>   Now wildly sad his tears in torrents flow;
>   Pleas'd then he sees them join the stream below,
> Unmindful of the hard, unfeeling crowd
> That idly gaze, or wanton mock his plight

With finger pointed, and with cruel jest,
Till, rous'd at length, they shun him with affright.
    Poor hapless wretch! than me oh far more blest!
His heart from ev'ry anxious care is free,
    And thought of long-lost bliss affects him not;
His days and years alike unheeded flee.
    Each form forgetting, and by all forgot.
No sad reverse of fate he e'er can know,
Or feel like me—the consciousness of woe.   (12)

The final couplet virtually rewrites Smith's concluding lines: "He seems (uncursed with reason) not to know / The depth or the duration of his woe."

The very fact that Sargant's sonnets rehearse so much that by 1817 was universally familiar can be read—as it was by hostile contemporaries—as the poet's mere indulgence in hackneyed substance (to use the popular pejorative adjective), and in light of the mediocrity of much of Sargant's verse, the judgment is not wholly unmerited. But creative recycling of familiar materials has always been a part of the sonnet tradition. When the poetry (and the poet) is judged excellent, critical commentary celebrates the ingenuity with which the poet infuses these familiar materials with unconventional import and effect; when the poetry (and poet) are deemed inferior, they tend to be branded as hackneyed, derivative, and tedious. As I noted in the introduction, Percy Bysshe Shelley observed at just about this time, in the preface to his *Prometheus Unbound* (1819), that all members of any writing community are unavoidably influenced by "the study of contemporary writings," so that their productions are affected by "the peculiarity of the moral and intellectual condition of the minds among which they have been produced." The "form"—particularly the literary form that is the physical manifestation of those "moral and intellectual" conditions—is, as Shelley says, "the endowment of the age," while that which he calls "the spirit of their genius" is "the uncommunicated lightning of their own mind" (*Shelley's Poetry and Prose*, 207). Sargant's poetry is not lit by artistic or intellectual lightning, but Shelley's point is relevant nonetheless. If Sargant is visibly following in Smith's (and others') poetic footsteps, she can scarcely expect her readers not to notice. Indeed, it is precisely *by noticing* that her readers are drawn into the communal activity of reading, comparing, assessing, and performing the poetic text, a text whose visible intertextuality connects it with other writers (and readers) and thereby reasserts the community both of intellect and of feeling that lies at the heart of the literary enterprise. Moreover, given her subsequent socially committed, community-building literary works, it is all the more reasonable to speculate that Sargant's conspicuous intertextuality is at least in part the product of deliberate design.[27]

Nor are Mariann Dark's sonnets without traces of comparable community build-ing.[28] Not surprisingly, Dark's most overt gestures also involve Smith, who is in-voked specifically as a measure for comparison in two successive sonnets.

> Charlotte! with throbbing heart I read of woes,
>   Warbled in melancholy's plaintive tone;
>   In thine, I lose remembrance of mine own—
> Yet similar our fates; ah! why repose
> Trust in deceiving hope? so oft abus'd.
>   Mistress of magic song! thy melting lay
>   Seems fraught with all the sweets of harmony;
> As on its liquid cadence rapt I mus'd,
> Methought a kindred flame our bosoms warm'd;
>   I dar'd aspire to feelings such as thine!
> And as thy lay the pang of woe disarm'd,
>   I knelt again before Apollo's shrine,
> And earnest pray'd he would impart the charm
>   Of thine own melting melody divine.
>   ("Sonnet 12: On Reading Mrs. Smith's Sonnets," 40–41)

Typically for such poems, the community that the poet discovers with her prede-cessor quickly dissolves in her acknowledgment of the gulf that separates them, whether it be one of experience or—more commonly—of poetic skill and public reputation. Participating at once in both the experience Smith's sonnets record and the community of poetic production, Dark declares herself reinvigorated: she kneels again "before Apollo's shrine"—*again* being the critical word—hoping to fill herself with Smith's "own melody divine," which she intriguingly describes as a "charm." That is, Smith's emotive melodic power constitutes a "charm"—a talisman—that may free and empower her own poetic voice; at the same time, this "charm" also describes Smith's poetic effects. Reading Smith's poetry is for Dark a transformative process, as we see from her claim that doing so "the pang of woe disarm'd." Record-ing this transformation and the resulting empowerment is a prototypically Roman-tic gesture on Dark's part that links her alike with canonical poets (and poems) and little-known ones who trace in their own verse the similar consciousness-altering experiences that result from reading *and from composing* poetry.

Predictably, Dark cannot sustain her elation, and the next sonnet documents the collapse of her high hopes:

To thee? presumptuous! here no Avons glide,
   No Otways warble here, or Hayleys sing;
   No dismal sea-mews dip the feath'ry wing,
And tell the musers, woe will soon betide.
Genius, abash'd and silent, fain would hide
   His drooping head; conceal his with'ring flow'rs;
   Muse o'er the dawning of his earliest pow'rs;
While sad neglect and scorn with him abide.
Charlotte! alas no genial breath of fame,
   E'er call'd the infant buds of genius forth;
I strike the lyre unknown! My very name
   Will soon be blotted from this wretched earth.
Thine, Charlotte; thine, the bright, the genuine flame,
Fosters by fair reward—the mead of worth.

                  ("Sonnet 13: On Reviewing the Preceding," 42–43)

The references to Otway and Hayley recall Smith's sonnet "To the River Arun," which river, according to Smith, "inspired thy Otway's plaintive strain" (l. 9) and now boasts that "Hayley is thine own" (l. 12). Writing in obscurity, Dark laments that there is neither Avon (Shakespeare's stream) nor Arun (Otway's and Hayley's) to inspire and uphold her, nor any appreciative, supportive community (Hayley had been Smith's patron in the 1780s and 1790s). It is a bleak prospect, and it appears to have been an accurate one as well, for there is no record of Dark beyond this single volume of poems.

Fittingly, Dark's collection also includes a sonnet addressed to William Lisle Bowles and another to his wife, as well as one noted as having been composed in his garden. Often regarded as the other crucial figure in the revival of the sonnet in England, Bowles had published a set of sonnets that grew in size in its subsequent editions. His *Fourteen Sonnets* (1789) had swelled from some thirty pages to a length of nearly two hundred by its ninth edition (1805), which included poems in other forms. Bowles's Shakespearean sonnets employ the same basic formula as Smith's, usually beginning with some happy setting or some pleasant memory of the past that is then countered by a sorrowful present beset by the world's hostile realities.[29] Beginning in 1804, Bowles had been the vicar at Bremhill, where Dark and her father resided, and after her father's death in 1817 (Bowles gave the funeral eulogy) she at last took the advice Bowles had given her earlier and sent some of her poems to him (and one to the Marchioness of Lansdowne), who seems to have responded warmly.[30]

Dark's sonnet to Bowles sheds some light on her apparently reclusive nature:

> Bowles! hast thou never known a child of song
>   Rapt in oblivion's veil? whose pensive lay,
>   At eventide might o'er some wild stream play,
> Making sweet melody its reeds among;
> But oh! at morning's earliest blush 'tis gone!
>   Mute is the harp that broke the still of night,
>   For ah! the minstrel shuns the orient light;
> Nor loves to mingle with the busy throng.
> Oh! I would bid thee stretch thy hand to save
>   A simple flow'ret that hath blossom'd wild!
> Though in Castalia's stream it may not lave,
>   Yet, 'tis some ev'ning primrose, faint and mild.
> Thou pour'st a requiem o'er the father's grave,
>   Then from oblivion snatch the mourning child.
>   ("Sonnet 24: To the Rev. W. L. Bowles," 56–57)

Bowles seems not to have intervened in Dark's career beyond whatever private encouragement he may have supplied—plus the two copies of *Sonnets, and Other Poems* (which was published by subscription) for which he subscribed. Indeed, she seems to have received more material support from the Marquis and Marchioness of Lansdowne, who together subscribed for six copies and who may have been influential in securing her volume's distribution by the London booksellers Sherwood, Neely, and Jones. Of particular interest in Dark's sonnet is the posture she assumes: hungry for public acclaim, she nevertheless shuns the public forum, in effect dooming herself to the suffocating "oblivion" from which she prays in her closing couplet for salvation. Her choice of the evening primrose for her own emblem is particularly appropriate, since the individual flowers of the evening primrose are short lived, usually first opening in the evening and then withering the following day.

The fragility with which Dark endows her flower is of course a stock metaphor for the sonnet of sensibility and its poet, but in light of what we can glean about the author's own personal circumstances, it is unusually fitting. It is not surprising, therefore, that in the other sonnet in which Bowles features Dark sketches out the personal and poetic sanctuary she desires:

> Rises a wish presumptuous in my breast,
>   For such an earthly heav'n—such fairy bow'rs,
>   To gender fancy's most bewitching pow'rs,

And give imagination highest zest?
Oh! for such leisure! such secluded rest!
   Here elegance and taste the lawns pervade,
   And climbing shrubs, and bow'ring trees o'ershade,
The sweet pavilion, for the poet drest—
      ("Sonnet 33: Composed in the Rev. W. L. Bowles's Garden," 69–70, ll. 1–8)

This is the edenic ideal sought both in fact and in rhetoric—not just by Mariann Dark but indeed by virtually all of the women who wrote and published sonnets during the Romantic era. The combination of leisure and rest must have held uncommon appeal, particularly for those women who wrote to support themselves and their families. Dark's own terminology provides stark testimony to how elusive such security was for them: her longing for the "fairy bow'rs" of such an "earthly heav'n" she attributes to the "wish presumptuous" to cultivate and nurture her own creativity in order to "give imagination highest zest." But such desires are incompatible with quotidian life, especially when one is consigned to physical isolation and public obscurity.

That many Romantic-era women began their publishing careers writing poetry but then turned to prose helps us to appreciate the economics of writing. For many of them, writing was not a matter of leisure but of necessity, and prose—especially fiction—simply paid better. Sonnet writing by women had decreased by the start of the Victorian era, less because the genre was in any sense "used up" than because other forms came to hold greater appeal—and commercial potential—forms like the long verse narrative and the occasional lyric of the sort in which Hemans and Landon particularly specialized and that was so well suited to the burgeoning market of literary annuals and keepsakes. In many respects, the rhetorically performative nature of the sonnet, in which technical skill and aesthetic artifice are as important as intellectual and emotional content, made the form less suited to the changing tastes of a reading public that was coming to expect a "sincerity" that was increasingly incompatible with the sonnet's inherent showiness.

CHAPTER FOUR

Experimenting with Genre

The Long and the Short of It

In chapter 3 I examined how Romantic-era British women poets worked with a single poetic genre, the sonnet, and I approached that genre "vertically," looking down through the interrelated layers of texts to explore the intertextual conversation among the poets that they reveal. In this chapter, by contrast, I take more of a horizontal approach to survey a broader selection of poets and genres. With each of these subsets, though, it is still possible to pursue the same sort of detailed vertical analysis I have offered of the sonnets. Each of these sets of generically related poems likewise reveals intertextual conversations among authors who were exploring, modifying, and reinventing those individual genres and subgenres. Although I am primarily concerned with poetry written by women, these conversations in print inevitably involve both female and male authors, as well as readers of both sexes. Moreover, even when individual poems ostensibly identify a single or limited target audience (by explicitly addressing or otherwise naming a recipient), the formal act of *publishing* the poems converts these ostensibly private utterances into very public documents in which the poet knowingly both acknowledges and engages a much wider audience.

This section's title suggests one criterion that has governed my selection of poems here: their length. The first part of the chapter treats poems that are for the most part "long" poems. Among these, I begin with a group that I describe as poems of social commitment, poems that engage clearly and deliberately with pressing social and political issues and that are in one way or another polemical in nature (for example, the several poems about slavery and abolition with which I begin). A second category of "long" poems is that of long verse narratives that are neither polemical nor particularly concerned with social or political issues but rather are variations on the tradition of the sentimental verse romance. The last part of the chapter takes up poems that are comparatively "shorter"; these are occasional poems, and the ones I consider here are primarily elegiac in nature. I divide these into two groups, the first consisting of commemorative or memorial poems on public figures and composed on or for public occasions. The second group of poems memorialize more immediately private, personal losses, often of children. The rhetoric of this second set differs from that of the poems on more publicly ostentatious figures in the manner in which the poets make personal loss "public" by creating a shared intimacy among the members of the extended rhetorical families that they create in print. Even the necessarily incomplete picture that emerges from the cursory overview that can be achieved in a single chapter demonstrates that the women poets of the Romantic era followed the lead of their eighteenth-century predecessors in experimenting with the limits of genre, revising, recombining, and restyling generic conventions and creating from these diverse materials new forms, new vehicles, that better suited the voices that they were discovering at the dawn of the modern era.

Poetry of Social Commitment

By 1800, British women poets had made their very substantial presence felt in the market for published poetry, whether their efforts resulted in commercial, for-profit publications like those of Robinson, Smith, and Seward or whether their books were issued by subscription for the more modest and localized benefit of the individual poets. It had become obvious by 1800 that a market existed for both types of books, and it is therefore little surprise that many women writers who published during the next several decades began their writing careers, as Amelia Opie, Barbara Hofland, and Sydney Owenson did, by first publishing one or more volumes of poetry before turning to the generally more lucrative market of prose fiction. Moreover, those decades witnessed the publication of numerous extended narrative poems that constitute a variety of fiction in verse that would culminate most notably in 1857 in Elizabeth Barrett Browning's novel in blank verse, *Aurora Leigh,* often regarded as her magnum opus. In that remarkable tale about the literary career of a woman writer, Barrett Browning examined the responsibilities of the writer both to her art and to the broader social and political worlds, raising the question of the place of women in public life and institutions. *Aurora Leigh* represents an important stage in the development of a variety of poetry whose roots lay in the eighteenth century and that flourished during the Romantic era. These were long poems, most of them explicitly political, social, or economic in orientation and many of them polemical in nature, that employed loose narratives as skeletons on which to construct arguments concerning pressing social and political subjects. Such narratives of social commitment, as I call them here, had been written during the eighteenth century: Helen Maria Williams's *Peru: A Poem in Six Cantos* (1784), for example, exposes the terrible consequences of imperialism for both the conquered and the conquerors to a British nation that was only just beginning the project of empire building that would seize the national consciousness during the nineteenth century.

Indeed, Williams is in some respects prototypical when it comes to such narratives. In 1788 she had published *A Poem on the Bill Lately Passed for Regulating the Slave Trade,* a volume that is only some two dozen pages long but that nevertheless articulates many of the arguments that were then being widely circulated in print about slavery's particularly cruel effects on the slave families, who are portrayed as the hapless victims alike of commerce and of war. Williams praises England for taking the first step toward abolition: "Oh, first of EUROPE's polish'd lands, / To ease the Captive's iron bands!" (ll. 37–38). But the act is incomplete, the triumph only partial. Most of Williams's poem paints with the florid rhetoric of highly wrought sensibility the sufferings of the slaves, first in Africa, then during their dreadful transport, and finally in their alien new home. The dramatic peroration with which she concludes appeals to the nation to end slavery once and for all, both because it is morally right on humanitarian grounds to do so and also, significantly, because enacting abolition will have undeniable propaganda value:

> LOV'D BRITAIN! whose protecting hand
> Stretch'd o'er the Globe, on AFRIC's strand
> The honour'd base of Freedom lays,
> Soon, soon the finish'd fabric raise!
> And when surrounding realms would frame,
> Touch'd with a spark of gen'rous flame,
> Some pure, ennobling, great design,
> Some lofty act, almost divine;
> Which Earth may hail with rapture high,
> And Heav'n may view with fav'ring eye;
> Teach them to make all Nature Free,
> And shine by emulating Thee!   (ll. 315–62)

Much of what Williams says in her poem—and how she says it—finds parallels in the better-known poem of her contemporary, Hannah More. *Slavery: A Poem* also appeared in 1788 and was immediately reprinted in Philadelphia, a center of American antislavery sentiment. More soon revised and expanded her poem, calling it "The Black Slave Trade: A Poem" in later published editions. Written, as Paula R. Feldman observes, "to help [William] Wilberforce with his 1788 opening of the parliamentary campaign against the slave trade," this later version underscored More's argument that slavery and civilization (or a civilized society) are fundamentally incompatible (*British Women Poets,* 470). Despite referring to the black Africans in the era's typically condescending language, More nevertheless "insisted on the common humanity that Africans shared with Europeans" and, like Williams (and Ann Yearsley and Anna Letitia Barbauld, both of whom wrote poems on the slave trade), she presented the strongly feminist argument that slavery's greatest evil lay in its inevitable violation of "the domestic affections."[1] When she turns her mind's eye to Africa, More writes,

> I see, by more than Fancy's mirror shown,
> The burning village, and the blazing town:
> See the dire victim torn from social life,
> The shrieking babe, the agonizing wife!
> She, wretch forlorn! is dragg'd by hostile hands,
> To distant tyrants sold, in distant lands!   (ll. 97–102)

That this vision is grounded in "more than Fancy's mirror"—that is, in widely documented facts—strengthens its horror, and More sharpens that horror still further through her calculated use of the rhetorical devices of heightened sensibility in her long descriptions of the scenes of separation and of the miserable deaths that follow.

British women played a prominent public role in the campaign against slavery, and feminist scholars have argued that their experience in that effort taught them valuable lessons which they subsequently applied to their own experiences as women. Women writers learned how to use most creatively in the cause of their own empowerment those rhetorical and stylistic devices of sensibility (or sentiment) that they had practiced when they portrayed the wretched experience of the slaves; these they applied to the situation of women in ways whose familiarity would make them especially effective with their readers. In mounting their arguments in both areas they typically linked two fields that their contemporary society generally conceded to them—sensibility and familiarity with Scripture—with a third—rational intellect or empirical reason—that was generally *not* conceded to them by the majority of their fellow citizens. In a sense, they staked their claim to the third area by demonstrating their authority in the first two. The importance of this calculated incursion into conventionally masculine matters of world economics and commerce cannot be overstated, for the poems that women published on the slave trade not only demonstrate their authors' sophisticated knowledge of the economic and social implications of colonial imperialism and bourgeois capitalism but also establish for them a position *within* the discourse field defined by their subject matter.

It is worth noting that women often addressed their publications concerning slavery to one another: that is, to an audience of women. Doing so on their title pages, though, was of course something of a rhetorical subterfuge that ostensibly shielded the poets from charges of pursuing in print a supposedly inappropriate subject while permitting them to do just that. The Irish Quaker poet Mary Birkett followed this course in 1792, in *A Poem on the African Slave Trade, Addressed to Her Own Sex.*[2] There she observes with angry dismay

> How little think the giddy and the gay
> While sipping o'er the sweets of charming tea,
> How oft with grief they pierce the manly breast,
> How oft their lux'ry robs the wretch of rest,
> And that to gain the plant we idly waste
> Th' *extreme of human mis'ry* they must taste!   (pt. 1, 2, ll. 21–26)

The remedy, however, that Birkett suggests for this destruction of human life and happiness in service to English luxury (note that it is tea that is consumed and even wasted, along with the sugar that sweetens it, rather than any genuinely essential commodity) ironically subscribes to the fundamental colonialist and imperialist project. When her reluctant British imperialist (who bears the curious classical name of Camillus) asks whether in abandoning the slave trade Britain must also abandon "[t]he wealth abundant which in Afric lies," lest its "fam'd commerce languish and decay" and "no more send fleets for slaves away," Birkett's speaker replies:

> No, wise Camillus, search her fertile land,
> Let the mild rays of commerce there expand;
> Her plains abound in ore, in fruits her soil,
> And the rich plain scarce needs the ploughman's toil;
> Thy vessels crown'd with olive branches send,
> And make each injur'd African thy friend:
> So tides of wealth by peace and justice got,
> Oh, philanthropic heart! will be thy lot.
>
> Plant there our colonies, and to their soul,
> Declare the God who form'd this boundless whole;
> Improve their manners—teach them how to live,
> To them the useful lore of science give;
> So shall with us their praise and glory rest,
> And we in blessing be supremely blest;

> For 'tis a duty which we surely owe,
> We to the Romans were what to us Afric now [sic].   (pt. 1, 12–13, ll. 237–52)

This is the familiar list of Christian moral and commercial imperatives that would justify the whole colonialist enterprise as it has been played out in Africa, Asia, and the Americas for centuries, complete with the implied claim that colonialism—specifically *British* colonialism—is an inherent part of God's design and that in playing her part in the drama Britain not only adds to her economic wealth but also uplifts the colonized people, "teaching" them to be little, black-skinned subalterns to the dominant culture and its supposedly higher and divinely sanctioned values. Furthermore, in admonishing Camillus (and Britain) to "plant" colonies in these "fertile" lands, she fuses the language of eighteenth-century agricultural husbandry with God's injunction in Genesis to cultivate the wilderness, inseparably linking the rewards of commercial profit with moral missionary zeal.

Her built-in imperialism notwithstanding, what distinguishes Birkett's poem is her specific charge to *women* to take the lead in setting matters right:

> Oh, let us rise and burst the Negro's chain!
> Yes, sisters, yes, to us the task belongs,
> 'Tis we increase or mitigate their wrongs.
> If we the produce of their toils refuse,
> If we no more the blood-stain'd lux'ry choose;
> If from our lips we push the plant away
> For which the liberties of thousands pay,
> Of thousands once as blest, and born as free,
> And nurs'd with care, (tho' not so soft,) as we.   (pt. 1, 13–14, ll. 260–68)

Granted, this is hardly a call to march through the streets of Dublin. But it is nevertheless an intriguing early demonstration of the power of informed consumerism, boosted by Birkett's insistent plural pronouns. What Birkett advocates is, after all, a coordinated economic action—a boycott—that she correctly understands holds the potential to make a difference if it can be made sufficiently widespread. Birkett concludes with a vision of a future slavery-free empire governed by a specifically feminine benevolence that is grounded in human sympathy and in the ability to identify with the sufferings of the exploited Africans (who serve the sugar manufacturing) and Indians (who are part of the tea trade). But it is the black African with whom Birkett is most concerned, for their slavery involves an element of physical brutality that far exceeds the economic and cultural oppression of the Indians. Consequently, when the better day arrives,

Such! sisters, such! *will be* the Negro's thought:
His breast with every warm affection fraught.
Nor small the glory which to you belongs,
Whose gentle bosoms mourn'd for all their wrongs,
Wept for their woes, and burn'd with honest shame,
To *know* them sanction'd by an *English* name.   (pt. 2, 20, ll. 424–29)

That reliably activist social conscience, Anna Letitia Barbauld, was no less vocal in support of abolition's cause, and her 1791 verse *Epistle to William Wilberforce* after the resounding defeat of his bill to abolish the slave trade reflects her familiarity with the published accounts of the debate over that bill in Parliament in April 1791. In their edition of Barbauld's poems, William McCarthy and Elizabeth Kraft note that, affected by the force of the *Epistle,* Hannah More wrote approvingly to Barbauld (287), and it is easy to see why, for Barbauld's poem possesses a core of moral outrage that had cooled only slightly twenty years later when she meditated on Britain's coming demise in *Eighteen Hundred and Eleven,* where, as we have seen, she laments much the same failure of moral courage and visionary humanity that she documents in the *Epistle.* Barbauld asks, "not unmark'd in Heav'n's impartial plan, / Shall man, proud worm, contemn his fellow man?" (ll. 44–45). Her answer is unequivocal:

And injur'd Afric, by herself redrest,
Darts her own serpents at her Tyrant's breast.
Each vice, to minds deprav'd by bondage known,
With sure contagion fastens on his own;
In sickly langours melts his nerveless frame,
And blows to rage impetuous Passion's flame:
Fermenting swift, the fiery venom gains
The milky innocence of infant veins;
There swells the stubborn will, damps learning's fire,
The whirlwind wakes of uncontroul'd desire,
Sears the young heart to images of woe,
And blasts the buds of Virtue as they blow.   (ll. 45–56)

The language and imagery in this passage are positively Blakean, resembling as they do passages from *America* and *Europe,* both composed between 1791 and 1794, and perhaps even more so "London," from *Songs of Experience* (published 1794). Indeed that urban visionary may have read them, for Barbauld's poem was published by Joseph Johnson, for whom Blake was working during this period when among his productions were a set of illustrations for Mary Wollstonecraft's *Original Stories from Real Life.*[3] Moreover, the "contagion" that Barbauld mentions is undoubtedly an oblique reference to venereal disease, and the hints about sexual excesses in this whole passage likewise resemble what Blake's female character Oothoon says about the consequences of the repression or perversion of sexual desire in his Wollstone-craftian *Visions of the Daughters of Albion* (1793). Despite Wilberforce's best efforts and high intentions, and despite too the support he had in Parliament from both Charles James Fox and William Pitt, the cause was probably hopeless from the outset, Barbauld declares bitterly, for "[w]here seasoned tools of Avarice prevail, / A nation's eloquence, combined, must fail" (ll. 25–26).

In chapter 1, I discussed Barbauld's *Eighteen Hundred and Eleven,* her dissenting view of Britain's prospects for continued dominance in a postwar world. The poem was widely attacked in the press, most notably in an unusually vicious lambasting by John Wilson Croker in the Tory *Quarterly Review.*[4] Anne Grant and others rapidly published their own verse responses, in which nationalistic flag-waving competes for space with angry denunciation of Barbauld specifically and more generally of the sanguinary view of British fortunes that by 1811 was widely shared among a war-weary populace. Shaken by the depth of animosity that her poem provoked among her critics, Barbauld largely gave up public poetry. After the decisive victory at Waterloo, however, the issue of the war's outcome was settled once and for all, and England, which in the modern period had never suffered the wholesale dev-astation that comes with invasion and occupation and that was all too familiar to continental nations, emerged as the undisputed international military, industrial, and economic superpower. Linda Colley has written that throughout the eighteenth century England had embraced with unusual fervency the notion that Great Britain as a nation was divinely favored and that Britons were the new Israel.[5] Indeed, when in her *Eighteen Hundred and Thirteen* Grant fashioned George III as the Moses of his people she was doing what many others had done in applying to Britain the biblical iconography of divine sanction and deliverance from the infidels.

Despite the social and economic reversals that Britain had endured at both the national level and at that of the individual nuclear family as a result of the protracted war, once that war ended the government engaged in a campaign to exploit that iconography still further, encouraging the nation to regard its victory as a deliver-ance of almost biblical proportions that was destined to reveal that Great Britain was indeed the promised land. This was no easy task, for, as Melesina Trench's comments to her friend Mary Leadbeater reveal, the situation was grim: "At present we have a starving population, an overwhelming debt, impoverished landholders, bankrupt or needy traders, unemployed farmers and labourers; but we have fine balls at the Regent's and a strong spirit of luxury cherished and awakened by the great, and thence descending to the poor through every class of society" (*Leadbeater Papers,* 2:290). The presence of the repellent Prince Regent, who was hissed and booed in the streets with such regularity that he often traveled relatively incognito, avoiding the major thoroughfares, and of his less immediately visible but no less dysfunctional ministry lent the postwar Regency a tone of imminent crisis that culminated in the Manchester (or Peterloo) massacre of 16 August 1819. The citizens suffered through high prices, food shortages, and two of the coldest and wettest summers on record (in 1815 and 1816), and they endured the economic depression and the resulting widespread poverty that accompanied the process of reabsorbing the returning soldiers and sailors while industrial production adjusted from wartime to peacetime production.

Complicating matters further still, the effects of technological change in industry prompted destructive mass action by the working classes of which the Luddite movement is the best-known illustration. When in November 1817 the Regent's daughter and presumptive heir, Princess Charlotte Augusta of Wales, died in childbirth, the nation was deprived of both an infant prince (Charlotte's baby boy was stillborn) and a princess for whom the people had formed an extraordinary affection not unlike that which modern Britain demonstrated for Princess Diana of Wales who died in 1997.[6] Nor could the nation draw much solace from the brilliant but deeply nihilistic writings of its most popular poet, Byron. Facing the prospect of a future directed by the widely despised Prince Regent, as there was no hope for the recovery of the poor, blind, mad king who wandered about the halls of Windsor Castle, and facing too an uncertainty—a failure of conviction, perhaps—about the nation's cultural role in the dawning modern age, Britain was in 1817 more than ready to be inspired.

Into this moment of opportunity stepped the young Felicia Hemans, who was destined to be the nineteenth century's most widely read and most profitable woman poet, and who from the beginning of her career devoted herself to celebrating her nation's virtues: military, economic, artistic, intellectual, and of course domestic. Her first volume, *Poems* (1808), though predictably immature, celebrated British militarism both in the abstract (as in "Patriotism") and in the particular (as in "To My Younger Brother, on His Entering the Army"). Almost immediately Hemans, who was still only fifteen, published *England and Spain; or, Valour and Patriotism* (1808), in which her expressed desire for peace reflected the popular sentiment that attributed England's early reversals in the Peninsular War as much to ministerial mismanagement as to incompetence among the commanding officers. Even granting the conventionality of much of Hemans's early poetry on political subjects, her decision to enter this field so ambitiously at such an early age indicates a level of public social commitment that has often been overlooked in criticism that views Hemans reductively in terms of conservative moral and sociopolitical orthodoxy. Hemans's social (and societal) commitment is likewise apparent in *Modern Greece* (1817), which, like the poem that immediately preceded it, *The Restoration of the Works of Art to Italy* (1816), appears to be concerned with matters of art in society but is in fact preoccupied with much more significant matters of national cultural destiny.

Modern Greece is Hemans's contribution to the then-current controversy over the fate of Lord Elgin's marble fragments from the Athenian Parthenon, which the British government had purchased from him in 1817 for £35,000. The poem's ostensible subject involves Greece's struggle for independence from its Ottoman occupiers; it celebrates the glory of ancient Greece while decrying that nation's decline into its present degraded, occupied state. But just as Barbauld's *Eighteen Hundred and Eleven* culminates in a vision of the future, so too does Hemans's *Modern Greece*. Significantly, though, Hemans looks forward to a British greatness that is still to come rather than celebrating past glories in present decline. Hemans's long poem (1,010 lines in 101 Spenserian stanzas) acclaims the luminaries of ancient Greek culture, her verse buttressed by detailed scholarly notes that establish her authority by demonstrating the wide learning she brings to her project. So strong is the poem's evidence of authorial learning, in fact, that the *British Review*'s critic exclaimed that "we conceived it to be the production of an academical, *and certainly not a female, pen*" (my emphasis).[7] All these characteristic signs of literary and intellectual sophistication lend both credibility and conviction to the poem's remarkable conclusion, which follows the poet's long recitation of Greece's achievements:

> And who can tell how pure, how bright a flame,
> Caught from these models, may illumine the west?
> What British Angelo may rise to fame,
> On the free isle what beams of art may rest?
> Deem not, O England! that by thy climes confined,
> Genius and taste diffuse a partial ray;
> Deem not th' eternal energies of mind
> Sway'd by that sun whose doom is but decay!
> Shall thought be foster'd but by skies serene?
> No! thou hast power to be what Athens e'er hath been.
>
> But thine are treasures oft unprized, unknown,
> And cold neglect hath blighted many a mind,
> O'er whose young ardors, had thy smile but shone,

Their soaring flight had left a world behind!

And many a gifted hand, that might have wrought

To Grecian excellence the breathing stone,

Or each pure grace of Raphael's pencil caught,

Leaving no record of its power, is gone!

While thou hast fondly sought, on distant coast,

Gems far less rich than those, thus precious, and thus lost.

Yet rise, O Land in all but Art alone,

Bid the sole wreath that is not thine be won!

Fame dwells around thee—Genius is thine own;

Call his rich blooms to life—be Thou their Sun!

So, should dark ages o'er thy glory sweep,

Should *thine* e'er be as now are Grecian plains,

Nations unborn shall track thine own blue deep,

To hail thy shore, to worship thy remains;

Thy mighty monuments with reverence trace,

And cry, "This ancient soil hath nurs'd a glorious race!"

(*Selected Poems, Letters, Reception Materials*, 61–62, ll. 981–1,010)

By the poem's end the reader becomes aware of the wordplay embedded in its title, for while the poem ostensibly depicts the state of "modern" (i. e., contemporary) Greece, it is in fact about "the *modern* Greece" (i. e., Great Britain).

Arguing against reading *Modern Greece* simplistically as merely a poem of "nationalist aggrandizement . . . concealing flagrant appropriation as threnody on ancient Greece," Isobel Armstrong explains that Hemans in both *Modern Greece* and in *The Restoration of the Works of Art to Italy* articulates an aesthetic that recalls the views of her contemporary Benjamin Robert Haydon, an aesthetic that regards the creation of all art as a process proceeding "from the inside out"; "The artist's vital energy," Armstrong notes, "comes from inside matter rather than being imposed on it" (221). The formulation is reminiscent of Michelangelo's claim that his monumental figures were already present and complete in the raw marble and that his task as sculptor was merely to remove the obscuring rubble of rock to reveal them. But to suggest that the poem's chief function is to articulate an aesthetics of artistic creation is seriously to narrow (and probably to misrepresent) the full import of Hemans's argument. True enough, Hemans's self-congratulatory nationalistic bias is readily apparent in a line like ""Fame dwells around thee—Genius is thine own" (l. 1,003), which excludes all other nations from the highest rung of the artistic ladder while implicitly discriminating the merely popular from the genuinely great. But the poem participates in a larger conversation about art and society that considers within the context of nationhood in its broadest terms the relation of modern artists both to their contemporaries and to their predecessors, an issue that Percy Bysshe Shelley would further explore in his preface to *Prometheus Unbound* (1820) and his *Defence of Poetry* (1821). The ramifications of this issue are as much political as they are aesthetic, for reasons that are apparent both in Hemans's poem and in Shelley's prose. Specifically, art (including both its production and cultivation) is a visible indicator of moral and spiritual qualities that contribute to any nation's status. Thus, as Gary Kelly notes, Hemans's poem makes the point that state acquisition and exhibition of the Elgin marbles necessarily plays an important part in "the reconstruction of Britain as a modern Athens" by placing "the artistic expression of Athenian republican greatness [the Elgin marbles] at the centre of modern British culture" (25).

That Britain still lacked a strong national tradition in the arts, even half a century after the belated establishment of the Royal Academy of Art in 1768, long after the formation of comparable institutions elsewhere in Europe, was a sore point with Hemans. She laments the lost promise of the many artists who have gone "unprized, unknown" (l. 991) in a culture incapable of valuing and sustaining them. This is a both a national disgrace and a national tragedy, her poem implies, and a continuing blot on the reputation of a nation that in 1817 is otherwise preeminent in all things ("Land in all but Art alone," l. 1,001). How the nation will be judged—both as an environment for the creation of art and as a nation that is *measured* by that art and the culture that nurtures it—depends on whether it will be able to effect a fundamental renovation of contemporary cultural values whose importance is in every respect equivalent to those that have produced Britain's military, economic, and social preeminence. Unlike the rueful, nostalgic conclusion of *Eighteen Hundred and Eleven,* then, Hemans's closing passage is a powerfully assertive call to the nation to cultivate Art as part of a program of national achievement, as a hedge against the sort of decline that Barbauld had envisioned and that in Barbauld's poem clearly owed much to the failure of collective cultural vision. Moreover, like the great works of art that lie concealed in their raw materials until the genius of the visionary artist frees them, so too the greatness of a nation may be comparably hidden, even as it is mistakenly sought "on distant coast" by "fond" (i.e., foolish) citizens and would-be connoisseurs who fail to recognize what riches lie within their own national and cultural raw material. The exemplary Nelson and Wellington were "home-grown"; so too are the still-to-be-acknowledged sublime artists—as Hemans, herself a poet after all, daringly implies.

I have discussed *Modern Greece* at some length because despite its ostensible preoccupation with matters of art and culture it too is a narrative of social commitment. That Hemans ties her sociopolitical agenda to the making and consumption of art reflects an emerging concern in the poetry of the later Romantic era: Keats, for instance, clearly privileges art over nature as a permanent restorative to human misery in his "Ode to a Nightingale" and "Ode on a Grecian Urn," just as his friend Haydon (and the Irish artist James Barry before him) argued passionately for the importance of a monumental, heroic art that would both feed and live up to the grand aspirations of nineteenth-century Britain. Likewise, both Hemans and the phenomenally popular Letitia Elizabeth Landon made art and artistic activity a central preoccupation of their major writings during the 1820s and 1830s. The place of art in a civilized society was crucial—perhaps especially so at the dawn of the industrial age with its deeply dehumanizing aspects. Indeed, art was itself a civilizing force, as most artists agreed, precisely because it was also a fundamentally democratizing force. The more accessible forms of art—prints vs. paintings, songs and ballads vs. esoteric poetry, sensational chapbook redactions vs. extended novels, newspapers vs. specialized journals—all contributed to the democratization of public discourse that is a signal characteristic of British Romanticism. Of course, democratizing any field of discourse requires expanding the rolls of that field's participants, and in this context we may profitably consider two other narratives of social commitment that contributed importantly to Romantic humanitarianism, albeit in quite different ways. The first is Charlotte Smith's *The Emigrants* (1793) and the second is Lucy Aikin's *Epistles on Women* (1810).

Smith's poem appeared at that moment when the ideals of the French Revolution were giving way to the excesses that produced the Reign of Terror. The violence was already spiraling out of control in Paris, and England had in February been drawn into war with France following the execution of Louis XVI. In England, those who had at first supported the revolution enthusiastically were already beginning to recant, especially in light of the government's growing intolerance of dissent and opposition to official policy. The plight of the displaced French loyalists whose circumstances form the subject of Smith's poem was widely familiar in England, but it was even more intimately familiar to Smith herself, who had offered refuge to some of these displaced clergy and aristocrats in her own home. In what Stuart Curran has called "her most sustained public poem" and "the finest piece of extended blank verse between Cowper's *The Task* (1785) and Wordsworth's unpublished initial version of *The Prelude* (1799)" (introduction, xix–xxix; xxiv), Smith exposes the universal anarchy that has been loosed upon the era by an international system of injustice and inhumanity in which the opposing sides have little to distinguish themselves from one another by except their nationality. The displaced French citizens are as powerless to redress their situation as Smith and all sympathetic English citizens are: individual freedom and dignity vanishes when subjected to the undiscriminating instruments of institutional power. *The Emigrants* is therefore profoundly antiwar in the way that the poetry I discussed in chapter 2 is: it condemns both sides for the conflict's fundamental inhumanity, emphasizing at every point how the disruption of individual families parallels the larger disruption of civilized society on both sides of the English Channel. As Kari Lokke notes, "Smith seeks to evoke sympathy in her English readers for their French opponents and to create an internationalist consciousness of the need for reform of both English and French political systems, legal institutions and religious establishments" (92). Throughout her poem, Smith argues that what is truly insupportable is neither the claims of the French revolutionaries nor those of their English opponents; rather, as the tragedy of the émigrés demonstrates, what is intolerable is the institutionalized injustice (what Smith calls "legal crimes" [l. 36]) that governs the political conduct of nations without regard for the welfare of the citizens. That Smith located both the blame and the potential for remedy not with one or the other opposing nation but with both—and therefore with broadly systemic and institutional rather than immediately personal or partisan forces—is evident from her comment to the Irish antiquarian and minister, Rev. Joseph Cooper Walker, that *The Emigrants* "is not a party book but a conciliatory book" (*Collected Letters,* 62).

At the heart of Smith's poem is the emblematic figure of Liberty that embodies two different but related manifestations of freedom. The first involves the long tradition of British liberty that had been celebrated again and again as one of the glories of the English nation, the gift that England was repeatedly lauded for having exported to otherwise benighted and languishing nations. The second, though, is that "liberty" that was part of the watchword of the French Revolution and that was coequal with fraternity and equality. This fundamental spirit unites rather than divides the true patriots in *The Emigrants,* all of whom are victimized by the *false* patriots who invoke this term and others in service to antihumanitarian, materialist, and imperialist ends:

> —Ah! while I adore
> That goodness, which design'd to all that lives
> Some taste of happiness, my soul is pain'd
> By the variety of woes that Man
> For Man creates—his blessings often turn'd
> To plagues and curses: Saint-like Piety,
> Misled by Superstition, has destroy'd
> More than Ambition; and the sacred flame
> Of Liberty becomes a raging fire,
> When Licence and Confusion bid it blaze.

. . . .

May lovely Freedom, in her genuine charms,
Aided by stern but equal Justice, drive
From the ensanguin'd earth the hell-born fiends
Of Pride, Oppression, Avarice, and Revenge,
That ruin what thy mercy made so fair!   (64–66, bk. 2, ll. 410–19, 431–35)

Smith treats the powers of good and evil allegorically here, and she paints them with sufficiently broad strokes to render them descriptive of both warring nations. Significantly, Smith tropes Freedom (and her cognate, Liberty) as a female power (or consciousness) that is notably free of the destructive excesses of passion that pollute the other allegorical forces:

And Liberty, with calm, unruffled brow
Magnanimous, as conscious of her strength
In Reason's panoply, scorns to distain [sic]
Her righteous cause with carnage, and resigns
To Fraud and Anarchy the infuriate crowd.   (42–43, bk. 2, ll. 57–61)

Indeed, throughout the poem Smith genders the allegorical forces of discord, anarchy, and violence in masculine terms while consistently presenting the victims of these forces (French and British alike) in feminine or feminized terms. As Adriana Craciun writes, "Smith's poem shares with its counterrevolutionary counterparts a particular concern for female suffering and female sympathy" (*British Women Writers,* 150).[8] Liberty (or Freedom), troped as female like Britannia, becomes in Smith's poem the feminine redeemer of a dysfunctional polity incapable of accomplishing its own salvation without such external intervention. The antidote to the compounded poison of greed, avarice, and national factionalism that has long ravaged Europe is, in Smith's opinion, a compassion that is grounded in human sympathy. But it is a "just compassion" (31, bk. 1, l. 361); compassion and justice are inextricably connected not just in *The Emigrants* but also in Smith's great political novel of the same year, *Desmond.* There, as Kari Lokke notes, the radical program of inescapable and inscrutable (and of course "blind" or nondiscriminating) justice is given its most powerful voice in the novel's "angelic heroine of sensibility, Geraldine" (96–97) when she defends the activities of the revolutionaries whose actions, however violent, "must still be acknowledged as the hand of justice" (*Desmond,* 311).

By, on the one hand, making justice's spokesperson in *Desmond* and elsewhere female but, on the other, freely praising in *The Emigrants* contemporary male intellectual and political defenders of liberty like William Cowper (to whom she dedicated the poem), Charles James Fox, and James Thomson, Smith underscores her conviction that the powers and principles that regulate human behavior for good or ill as they are manifested in individual persons or communities in the temporal world are not inherently gender-specific. The implication seems to be that although the allegorical forces have come by cultural practice to reflect a gender (or gendered) pattern, those who possess those forces or powers may be of either gender. Furthermore, throughout *The Emigrants* Smith incorporates recognizable biblical imagery to suggest the timeless universality of the melancholy view she articulates. Particularly apropos in this respect is Paula Backscheider's observation that Smith "composes an eternal perspective on the small scene of suffering on the coast that is emblematic, first, of the misery caused by the French Revolution and, second, of humankind that is given to war and avarice" (355). *The Emigrants* is a remarkable and powerful meditation on war and the human condition, made all the more poignant because of the immediacy of experience it embodies both for Smith as its author and for its readers who in 1793 were surrounded by the mounting evidence of man's relentless inhumanity to man.

The contribution that Lucy Aikin's *Epistles on Women* (1810) made to Romantic humanitarianism is of a very different sort. The poem, which has seldom received the critical attention it deserves, is an unabashedly feminist retelling of western history from a female perspective that was an appropriate production of this precocious niece of Anna Letitia Barbauld. Published when the poet was only nineteen, the poem possesses a texture of wit and learning that belies the poet's age and that fully justifies a fuller assessment of Aikin's work. Commentators have frequently noted that Aikin's poem is in part a rejoinder to Alexander Pope's claim in his verse epistle "To a Lady" (1735) that "[m]ost Women have no Characters at all" (l. 2), a remark that Pope's poem in fact attributes to the woman to whom his poem is addressed.[9] But *Epistles on Women* is more than just a reply to Pope (and to Virgil and Milton too[10]); it interacts with a tradition of feminist historiography that includes, on one hand, Catherine Sawbridge Macaulay's radical and influential *History of England,* which "records public-spirited female action with 'infinite pleasure'" (Blain, Clements, and Grundy, 682), and, on the other, Mary Hays's monumental 1803 set of 288 "memoirs" of women, *Female Biography,* and Matilda Betham's *Biographical Dictionary of the Celebrated Women of Every Age and Country* (1804). And it looks forward to later Romantic projects like the biographical verse tales that Hemans undertook most notably in *Records of Woman* (1828) and the one that Mary Shelley contemplated but never took up for a volume of prose about "the Lives of Celebrated women—or a history of Woman—her position in society & her influence upon it—historically considered" (*Letters of Mary Wollstonecraft Shelley,* 2:115). In other words, Aikin's long poem not only enters into conversation with ongoing feminist reconstructions of history and gender relations but also engages the ongoing feminist challenge to ideas about what sort of poetry was appropriate for women to write.

Marlon Ross has identified Aikin as the author of an anonymous review of Wordsworth's *Poems, in Two Volumes* (1807) that criticizes the poet for "the undue importance he attaches to trivial incidents" while still crediting him with "a reflecting mind, and a feeling heart" (50). This review is important, as Ross remarks, because it reminds us of women's presence not just among literature's private consumers but also among its professional critics, which group included Wollstonecraft, Elizabeth Moody, Hays, Barbauld, and others. Given the neoclassical bent of her own verse, Aikin's disapproval of Wordsworth's performance is unremarkable; Wordsworth's poetry struck Aikin as a poetry (and a poetics) of particularities and localisms, of sensibility in service to little more than feeling for feeling's sake—something that Wordsworth might argue was, paradoxically, precisely the point that Aikin was failing to get. For Aikin, though, poetry was a field for greater and more sweeping intellectual enterprises than she saw in Wordsworth, and it required of its poet not an abundance of feeling but rather a grounding in cold hard fact, enlivened and fostered by "Friendship" (Epistle 4, l. 40) or the sympathy of kindred spirits. As Anne Mellor puts it, Aikin conceptualizes the best poetry—which is implicitly also a feminist poetry—as "*conversation* or linguistic mothering, as the creation and nurturing of social intercourse or public opinion" (*Mothers of the Nation,* 84).

Epistles on Women reveals not just its poet's ambitious program but also her strong feminist bent. In rewriting the history of the world, from the Creation to the middle of the eighteenth century, Aikin means to present an alternative perspective to that which has been devised by men and then imposed both on other men *and on women.* Because "history is written by the victors," as Winston Churchill is reputed to have declared, not only has the documentary, institutional, and cultural oppression of women since the beginning of time been written and promulgated by men, but its corollary—the doctrine of women's innate inferiority—has been woven by them into the social and political fabric of Western society. The debate over this issue had heated up particularly during the final quarter of the eighteenth century when many women—and some men—began to question in print the gendered assumptions that had produced the long history of inequality. Indeed, when the poem appeared the *Critical Review* began its lengthy review by observing that

> It is not from a feeling of gallantry, a motive which can scarcely be supposed to
> influence a spectacled reviewer, that we are induced to pay our compliments to
> the literary fair, but because we are happy to see a woman asserting the proper

dignity of her sex, and evincing by her own example that female pretensions are well founded. It is quite time that the doctrine of the natural inequality of the sexes should be exploded: indeed we imagine that most sensible people are of this opinion, especially when we recollect, among many others, the names of Seward, Bailey [sic], Edgworth [sic], Barbauld, Opie, and Hamilton.[11]

Other reviewers took a similar view of poem and poet alike although, predictably, most of them couched their praise in forced and condescending gendered references to "the fair sex," "the softer sex," and women as "ornaments."

Interestingly, the *European Magazine* explicitly situated Aikin's epistolary poem within the context of Virgil's *Georgics* and Thomson's *The Seasons* while comparing its tone with that of both Pope's *Moral Essays* and his *Essay on Man.* Of all the contemporary reviews, this one makes the greatest effort to assess the cultural importance of Aikin's project within the contexts of Wollstonecraft's *Vindication* and Hays's *Female Biography,* both of which the reviewer names. The review is both "literary," then, and literate—and it assumes that its readers are too. Indeed, the reviewer is surprisingly sensitive to the cultural realities attendant on the public reception of this sort of poem, as is evident from the review's lengthy opening passage, which begins by warning that

a Lady undertaking to assert female rights, and to do honour to the female character, places herself in rather a delicate situation. She must expect criticism, and criticism not always of a pleasant kind. She must expect to be informed, by some male critics, that the subject, if thoroughly examined, leads to discussions in which no young lady can engage with propriety, and in which no female could preside. Nor must she be much surprised if some critics of her own sex should be the first to take alarm, and to bestow, if not direct censure, not very liberal praise.

But this should surprise no one, the critic continues, for "Nature, who has placed boundaries in all her works, has also limits and laws, by which each sex is distinguished and characterised, as well in the rational as irrational world."[12] This opening has the effect of laying out most of the objections, specious and otherwise, that conventional ideology might raise to Aikin's project, but the review then pointedly refuses to engage any of them, instead observing that Aikin's subject is a worthy and timely one to which she brings "a well-furnished mind," a "delicacy of sentiment," and considerable "force of poetical language" that results in a poem that "possesses much true poetry, and manifests very fine feelings" (36–37).

Aikin did follow the model of Pope's *Essay on Man,* casting her poem too in the form of a four-epistle verse essay addressed to a woman, in this case her sister-in-law

Anna Wakefield Aikin, the daughter of the Unitarian scholar and controversialist Gilbert Wakefield and "arguably the best educated woman of her day" (Mellor, *Mothers of the Nation,* 84). Aikin begins her poem in Eden with the tale of the Creation and Fall. She attributes Eve's fundamental moral superiority to her mate to her nature as woman and mother; indeed, Aikin even contrives to have Eve "born" not from Adam's side as Genesis has it but rather to have her emerge as the product of Adam's mystical coupling with the "unconscious" Earth: "When slumbering Adam pressed the lonely earth, . . . / Unconscious parent of a wondrous birth, . . . / As forth to light the infant-woman sprung" ("Epistle 1," ll. 76–78).

The remainder of the poem traces women's dubious fortunes over centuries of male-dominated history: "Epistle 2" examines the historically detrimental effects on women generally of the culturally enforced myth of male superiority; "Epistle 3" treats the Western world from the classical era through the Middle Ages; "Epistle 4" brings the record forward to modern Europe. For Aikin, women's progress is directly tied to "the increasing feminization of the public sphere" (Mellor, *Mothers of the Nation,* 84), which is precisely the project her own exercise in versified historiography involves her in. Her poem's ringing conclusion calls for an embrace of those companionate, nurturant domestic affections that will disarm the historical power struggle between the sexes and substitute for that entrenched, masculinist antagonism a feminine (and feminized) system of mutual support, of mutual benevolence, productive of the greatest possible good for all:

> Sons of fair Albion, tender, brave, sincere,
> (Be this the strain) an earnest suppliant hear!
> Feel that when heaven, evolved its perfect plan,
> Crowned with its last best gift transported Man,
> It formed no creature of ignoble strain,
> Of heart unteachable, obtuse of brain;
> (Such had not filled the solitary void,
> Nor such his soul's new sympathies employed,)
> But one all eloquent of eye, of mien;
> Intensely human; exquisitely keen
> To feel, to know: Be generous then, unbind
> Your Barbarous shackles, loose the female mind;
> Aid its new flights, instruct its wavering wing,
> And guide its thirst to Wisdom's purest spring:
> Sincere as generous, with fraternal heart
> Spurn the dark satirist's unmanly part;

Scorn too the flatterer's, in the medium wise,
Nor feed those follies that yourselves despise.   (78–79, ll. 442–59)

That Aikin stresses the coequal nature of feeling and knowledge (l. 452) indicates the productive balance she regards as the birthright of "Man," taken both as a gender-specific noun and as a common noun for members of both sexes. Women were of course customarily understood to be under the particular sway of feeling, or emotion, just as men were thought to be guided by wisdom, or reason; combining them as Aikin does underscores the belief she shares with Charlotte Smith: that these qualities are not innately gender-specific. Furthermore, not only are these qualities not gender-specific, but those persons in whom both are not present and active are in fact incomplete and dysfunctional, as is the society (and its institutions) that they produce.

For women, Aikin prescribes a domestic existence ("Be yours the joys of home, affection's charms, / And infants clinging with caressing arms" ["Epistle 4," ll. 464–65]), but not a slavish one that dulls the intellect and stifles the soul. Cultivate the arts, read widely in poetry and history, she tells them:

Thus self-endowed, thus armed for every state,
Improve, excel, surmount, subdue, your fate!
So shall at length enlightened Man efface
That slavish stigma seared on half the race,
His rude forefathers' shame; and pleased confess,
'Tis yours to elevate, 'tis yours to bless;
Your interest one with his; your hopes the same;
Fair peace in life, in death undying fame,
And bliss in worlds beyond, the species' general aim.
"Rise," shall he cry, "O Woman, rise! be free!
My life's associate, now partake with me:
Rouse thy keen energies, expand thy soul,
And see, and feel, and comprehend the whole;
My deepest thoughts, intelligent, divide;
When right confirm me, and when erring guide;
Soothe all my cares, in all my virtues blend,
And be, my sister, be at length my friend."   (80–81, ll. 480–94)

Equals at last, their equality freely proclaimed by "Man" in terms of a sibling relationship rather than the marital one we might expect, the sexes will enter into that sort of sympathetic relationship in which enculturated, gendered behaviors are replaced by companionate ones that reflect the laws not of society and its manufactured belief systems (religious, political, economic, and intellectual) but rather of nature itself. By freely accepting that this is the correct state of gender relations, and then by actively promulgating it in the public sphere, Aikin argues, "Man" (both men and mankind) announce the advent of a new Eden that fulfills in both the private domestic sphere and the public social sphere the promise of eighteenth-century Enlightenment thinking in a revolution no less monumental—and far more productive of human good—than the American or the French revolutions.

The Long Verse Narrative Tale

The extended verse tale's place in the Romantic-era literary scene in Britain is connected to that of the novel in the period's flourishing and expanding market for prose fiction. Women had established themselves by the latter part of the eighteenth century as the most prolific and successful of novelists, in part because selling their work (often for disgracefully small sums) had made it possible for them to achieve a measure of economic self-sufficiency. Even a conservative count of volumes published in Britain by the end of the eighteenth century reveals more than five hundred active women novelists. Robinson and Smith are merely two of the best known among the many who supported themselves and their children in this fashion (as Felicia Hemans would subsequently do with her poetry) in the wake of disastrous marriages to irresponsible husbands who mistreated or abandoned them. The success enjoyed by many women novelists had to do both with genre and with changing social conditions in England. Although the male literary establishment had for most of the eighteenth century largely ceded to women the province of the novel (with notable exceptions like Richardson, Fielding, and Sterne) once it became apparent that there was both financial profit and social, political, and cultural influence to be garnered, more men entered the arena, so that within less than another century the novel had come to be largely dominated in Britain by male authors.

Romantic-era novels took many different forms, of course, from potboiler sensational gothics turned out to satisfy the customers of William Lane's Minerva Press and others (and the circulating libraries associated with publishers like Lane, James Harris, William Sams and others), to Jacobin political works like William Godwin's psychopolitical *Caleb Williams* (originally titled *Things as They Are; or, The Adventures of Caleb Williams* [1794]) or Charlotte Smith's *Desmond* (1792), to ideological fiction like John Thelwall's 1801 *The Daughter of Adoption* (published under the pseudonym of "John Beaufort"), to variously configured moral and spiritual self-help tomes. Scott's particular contribution, the historical novel, came on the literary scene at about the same time as the rise of a new variety of fiction: a sort of "domestic" novel exemplified by Barbara Hofland's early novel *The History of an Officer's Widow, and Her Young Family* (1809) that pointed the way to the culturally engineered definitions of domestic and gender relations we now associate with the Victorian period. Buoyed on one hand by the expansion of literacy among the populace and on the other by the popularity of circulating libraries, prose fiction moved in this period toward the ascendancy over poetry it would begin to achieve in the commercial market during the Victorian era and that it continues to enjoy—by an even greater margin—in the twenty-first century. Indeed, the poets (canonical and otherwise) were far from impervious to the shift in the tastes of the emerging nineteenth-century readerships.

It is possible, therefore, also to trace in poetry the development of a literary vehicle that aimed to satisfy the rapidly expanding and diversifying public audience's appetite for *narrative*—and for "sensational" (in the joint sense of "spectacle" and "sentiment") narrative in particular. Hence the growth in the numbers of extended narratives like Southey's long poetic tales (*Thalaba the Destroyer* [1801–5], *The Curse of Kehama* [1810], etc.), Byron's "Turkish tales," and Byron's longer poems (*Childe Harold's Pilgrimage* and *Don Juan*, e.g.). Perhaps more importantly, we see also a movement away from such decidedly "literary"—or esoteric and "learned"—efforts as Eleanor Porden's Masonic epic, *The Veils; or, The Triumph of Constancy* (1815) and Shelley's *Prometheus Unbound* and toward more accessible and entertaining works like Thomas Moore's *Lallah Rookh: An Oriental Romance* (1817) and *The Fudge Family in Paris* (1818), Landon's immensely popular *The Improvisatrice* (1824) and Hemans's *The Forest Sanctuary* (1825) and the briefer narratives in her *Records of Woman* (1828). Sometimes these extended narratives took up distinctly historical subjects, like Margaret Holford's *Wallace; or, The Fight of Falkirk: A Metrical Romance* (1809) and her *Margaret of Anjou* (1816), a minor masterpiece that has not been accorded the attention it deserves. Even more ambitious was Porden's long two-volume epic, *Cœur de Lion; or, The Third Crusade* (1822), which won for its author the extravagant praise of the *Monthly Magazine.*[13] In Scotland, the extended poetic narrative flourished as well, often with distinctly indigenous subject matter, in works like Elizabeth Scot's *Alonzo and Cora* (1801), Anne Macvicar Grant's *The Highlanders* (1808), and Margarette Wedderburn's *Mary Queen of Scots: An Historical Poem* (1811). In Ireland, while the nationalist poet and novelist Sydney Owenson (Lady Morgan) achieved instant celebrity for her novel *The Wild Irish Girl* (1806), despite John Wilson Croker's notoriously savage review, her contemporaries published long verse narratives. Among these number Sarah Steele's *Eva, an Historical Poem* (1816), Hannah Maria Bourke's *O'Donoghue, Prince of Killarney* (1830), and, most famously of all, Mary Tighe's *Psyche* (1805).

Some of these romances constitute something of a poetic last gasp for the cult of sensibility. This sort of writing would metamorphose during the coming decades into the melodrama and other forms of "popular" entertainment (some of them not "literary" works at all) aimed at increasingly mass audiences and in the twentieth century would reappear in forms like the fantasy-romance and the soap opera. Rather than attempt to survey the innumerable Romantic-era examples of such poems, I will consider one that stands out to me, perhaps paradoxically, for its sheer typicality. This poem is Caroline Anne Bowles's anonymous first book *Ellen Fitzarthur: A Metrical Tale* (1820), which had been recommended for publication by Robert Southey, whom she eventually married in 1839.[14] This long poem (it runs some 2,800 lines in five cantos of mostly rhymed couplets) uneasily combines the sort of homely rustic setting made familiar in Wordsworth's "Michael" and Joanna Baillie's "A Summer Day" and "A Winter Day" with the rhetorical effects of the sentimental mode of sensibility. Set in the suggestively named Malwood Vale, the poem unfolds retrospectively the pathetic tale of Ellen and her poor old widowed father, whose tragedy begins, after a framing introduction told in the narrative present, when Ellen falls in love with a shipwrecked sailor who is delivered to their door, wounded and exhausted:

> For he was one, whose harassed frame
> From foreign fields of conflict came,
> Languid and weak, and many a scar
> (The recent characters of war)
> He bore, and ill his strength could stand
> This shipwreck on his native land.   (28)

Beginning to recover, the young man—whose name is De Morton—observes Ellen, as a year earlier Byron's young Don Juan had observed Haidee, with growing interest:

> Ah, Ellen! fly that dang'rous gaze,
> Beware its false, bewild'ring rays—
> Alas! poor bird, the serpent spell
> Has fixed its simple prey too well,
> And soon, too soon, thy heedless wing
> Shall drop within the charmed ring.   (28–29)

Bowles's symbolically loaded imagery, reminiscent of an array of precursor texts that include *Paradise Lost* and "Christabel" at one end of the literary spectrum and contemporary sentimental verse tales (including gothic and sensational ones) at the other, quickly tells us all we need to know and explains the pitiful despondency that Bowles attributes to old Fitzarthur in the poem's opening section. Before summer's end (naturally, their relationship begins in spring) the young couple plan to marry, but the bliss they anticipate is jeopardized by worries about whether the "slow consent" to their union can be "wrung" from De Morton's "grasping uncle, cold and proud" (34), on whom his fortune—and consequently their fortune—depends. When the couple propose to Fitzarthur that they marry without the uncle's consent and live with him, he rejects the idea outright:

> No! never shall my Ellen's hand,
>> In secrecy's dark shade be given;
> In open day, and sight of man,
>> Her virgin vows shall rise to Heaven!
> No pois'nous breath of whisp'ring fame,
> Shall ever taint my Ellen's name;
> No mildew stain of doubt shall rest
> On her fair brow, and spotless breast.   (37)

Bitterly disappointed by what he regards as De Morton's deceitful conduct, Fitzarthur proposes to cast him out, making any return conditional on the uncle's consent. So he goes.

Now Ellen haunts the lush woods where she can indulge the melancholy that De Morton's absence has produced. Days pass, then weeks and months, and Ellen's hope grows fainter, "Till quiv'ring like a dying flame, / Its fitful flash, and latent spark / At length expired, and all was dark" (46). The effects of despondency are predictable: "On Ellen's cheek the roses faded, / The lustre of her eyes was shaded" (47). Fitzarthur watches her slow and painful deterioration, and he is moved with pity as she grows ever more unresponsive to the beauties of nature that surround her. But a year later De Morton returns, still without his uncle's permission (indeed we are never told whether he has in fact sought it), to press Ellen once more—this time to leave with him; overwhelmed, she succumbs to temptation and they flee.

This is the familiar scenario of Amelia Opie's famous and much-reprinted tearjerker *The Father and Daughter* (1801) whose echoes throughout the period were many, including Austen's tale of Lydia Bennet and Wickham in *Pride and Prejudice* as well as numerous other romances in prose and verse alike. Seduced by a man whose passion (or lust) outweighs his honor (or virtue), the overmatched woman makes the wrong decision and immediately begins to pay the terrible price extracted by both her own moral conscience and the social mores that have shaped it:

> Since Ellen left her father's cot,
> Her heart, remorseful and unblest,
>   Has sought for peace, but found it not.
> Love in its earliest, happiest hours,
> Strewed not her wedded path with flowers;
> Or if a few were scattered there,
> They thinly hid the thorns of care;
> The thorn of conscience—poison'd dart!
> That rankles deadliest in the heart.   (65)

Cut off now from the father whose forgiveness she cannot bring herself to expect, she soon pays another price, for she not surprisingly learns that

> [h]is love waxed cold, for whose dear sake
> She left a father's heart to break:—
> Kind looks, and gentle words, were changed
> For sullen tones, and eyes estranged,
> And love's assiduous cares were lost
> In cold indiff'rence'[s] killing frost.   (68)

Although the couple has (predictably) never married, Ellen holds to a last hope that the baby she now carries may rekindle her lover's faded affection, but of course her hope is vain: Ellen gives birth to her illegitimate daughter alone and in the dark, for her faithless lover has abandoned her, as she learns weeks later from a final letter from him. She turns to needlework to support herself and her increasingly sickly daughter and, though she has ceased to observe the Sabbath, Ellen at last makes her way through the countryside, where she is welcomed by a kindly rural pastor and his little congregation. Her religious faith is revived and, like Coleridge's Mariner, she finds to her surprise that she can pray once again. When she hears the pastor preach on the prodigal son, Ellen's hope revives further, and she begins to plan a return to her father, vowing to confess her sins and repent of them, confident of his forgiveness.

Approaching her old home, however, Ellen is filled with foreboding, lest her old father be dead and she deprived of any hope of forgiveness or peace. Taken in by the kindly villager at whose home she seeks rest, Ellen sleeps "long and deep" while "fev'rish dreams disturbed her sleep" (102), and when she rises the day is so far advanced that her kindly hostess presses her to stay another night, in the meantime relating her tale of how, years earlier, her own daughter had left her without a word and how she had forgiven her nevertheless. Next day Ellen completes her journey, arriving at her father's cottage well after dark. Entering the darkened cottage, Ellen hears the warning bark of her father's old dog, Carlo, who "feebly creeps [forth], to greet / Her late return—and licks her feet, / And, with low whine, would fain express / His dumb delight" (113). Rather than search further for her father, who has in fact died, Ellen now decides to visit the churchyard where her mother is buried and finds a recent grave strewn with flowers just as she had decked her mother's as a child. In a scene that eerily anticipates the graveyard scene in Dickens's *A Christmas Carol,* Bowles continues:

> The stone
> Faced not her view—its further side
> Bore the Inscription,—agony supplied
> A despr'ate impulse—a despairing haste—
> Yet, for a moment, o'er her eyes she plac'd
> A trembling hand, close prest, as if to gain,
> 'Twixt her and fate, a respite short and vain—
> Short, shudd'ring interval! She fronts the stone—
> The cold hand drops—one glance, and all is known:
> One cry, one fearful cry, of wild despair
> Bursts from her heart—another name is there!   (115)

The shock of finding that this is her father's grave kills Ellen, whose body is found the following morning by a peasant who turns out to be Ellen's foster brother. He also takes her cold but still living child to raise with his own. Bowles's long poem ends unceremoniously, with the poet lamenting that her "Lyre" cannot produce "sweeter lays" in light of all this sorrow.

When we separate the pathos-laden tale from the social and cultural values that undergird it we can glimpse something important about the way that Bowles, like many of the women poets who published poems of this sort, interrogates the prevailing social and cultural norms and exposes the extent to which their powerfully masculinist orientation had historically worked against the interests and the welfare of women. Dennis Low sees in *Ellen Fitzarthur*'s "conservative" plot a "cautionary tale" that "upholds the importance of the family unit, the infallibility of the established church, and the fatal instability of sexual relationships outside marriage" (39). But this conclusion misses the real complexity of the issues that Bowles and others examine in their tales. In *Ellen Fitzarthur,* for example, the catastrophe follows from the postchivalric model of behavior that requires the formal consent of parents or guardians for a couple to be married. In Bowles's poem, significantly, both these guardians are male: Fitzarthur's wife has long been dead, and De Morton is the ward of the uncle whose defeminized (or unfeminized) nature is evident in the hardened personality that Bowles characterizes as "grasping" and "cold and proud." Moreover, the inflexible doctrines of the "established church" are implicit in the social strictures that exclude and shun Ellen (and others like her), denying them both compassion and Christian charity as a consequence of their incautious choices.

Furthermore, issues of class clearly affect the action: the reluctant offstage uncle's apparent wealth suggests that Ellen's humble status poses a serious obstacle to marriage, something that is underscored further in Fitzarthur's unquestioning deferential attitude to the uncle and his status. The poem also revisits—perhaps less obviously—the historical opposition of courtly and rural (or pastoral) cultures in tracing the apparent incompatibility of the two families. Finally, the poem questions the often conflicting, socially enforced obligations that require a woman to repress both her personal independence and her sexuality, often at terrible cost, as the price for her participation in a society that locates not just power and authority but also tangible economic and legal resources almost exclusively in the hands of men. The appearance during the Romantic era of so many verse narratives that replicate the general outlines of the thwarted-love plot, often in sentimental—and fatal—terms, and that raise these same issues of class indicates that class was becoming a much larger factor in the national consciousness and in the nation's poetry, where it had historically figured to a far lesser extent. It also demonstrates that the market for sentimental verse fiction continued to expand well into the 1830s, at which point it began to yield its place to prose in the form of the Victorian domestic romance.

During the tumultuous war years and the unstable ones of the Regency and George IV's reign, the extended verse narrative tale provided for many readers not just diversion but a comforting nostalgia. Many of these poems follow the scripted conventions of the romance tradition, whether they are canonical works like Keats's *Eve of St. Agnes* or noncanonical ones like Louisa Stuart Costello's *Redwald: A Tale of Mona,* with which Keats's poem is contemporary. Because they saw in their fanciful, sanitized images of a glorious past an attractive chivalric alternative to a decidedly unchivalrous present (a vision that culminates most famously in Tennyson's *Idylls of the King* [1859–85]), poets of both sexes turned to the basic form and themes of the quest romance, although for rather different reasons. Fearing that the historically "manly calling" of poetry was in danger of being lost within what Marlon Ross calls "a feminine market enterprise" (268), many male poets embraced the powerful masculinism of the chivalric romance tradition both for the "manly" traits that it emphasizes and, not entirely incidentally, for the social force through which that tradition consigns women to the roles of beautiful but largely recessive inspirers of male action. Interestingly, though, the romance verse narrative offered *women* poets something different, a site on which to investigate "the immanent conflict between masculine and feminine desire embedded within the form" and to examine these competing schemata "without overtly placing men and women in adversarial positions" (Ross, 271). Although they show the late Romantic (or early Victorian) verse narrative moving in the direction of the dramatic monologue's more internalized and more psychologically attuned nature, Felicia Hemans's poems repeatedly stage this conflict of gender and desire. Especially in the protohistorical narratives of *Records of Woman,* as Susan J. Wolfson emphasizes, Hemans emerges not as the conventional voice of Victorian domestic values but rather as the remarkably clear-eyed exposer of "women's devastating struggles against the structures, both domestic and national, in which these struggles are set" ("Felicia Hemans," 222).[15] Unlike the conventional romance, which effectively cancels out the troubling present by placing the reader solidly in a safe and sheltered past that does not resemble the present, Hemans's poetic variations on this model, like those of her contemporary Letitia Elizabeth Landon, offer the reader ostensibly removed situations that are disturbingly familiar. Not quite antiromances, neither are they either romances *or* "Romantic" in the usual ways.

The greatest exception to sentimentalized tales of this sort—and, paradoxically, a revealing complement to them—is also one of the period's very finest poems: Mary Tighe's *Psyche; or, The Legend of Love.* Written in 1801–2 and privately printed in 1805 in an edition of only fifty copies she gave to friends and admirers, the poem achieved great celebrity as it was circulated among other readers. Only after Tighe's death of tuberculosis in 1810 did a larger edition, prepared and edited by her cousin William Tighe, follow in 1811; by 1816 this expanded volume was in its fifth edition.[16] The *British Critic* began its review of the 1811 edition by commenting on the already considerable reputation of poem and author alike: "The elegant poem of Psyche was so long circulated in one or two private editions, that to descant upon it as a new performance would be to repeat only what the majority of our readers already know; and to accumulate superfluous praise, where abundance has already been bestowed."[17] The 1811 volume was widely hailed in the reviewing press; the *Monthly Review,* for example, devoted fully fifteen pages to excerpts and enthusiastic praise:

> For elegance of design and accuracy of execution it much exceeds any poetical composition of the present day. We are so often compelled to deplore the want of a corrected taste among our contemporary writers of acknowledged genius, that, when we see these sister-qualities united in one extraordinary mind, we must be allowed to indulge in unusual congratulation to the country which has produced so rare an example. . . . [O]ur poetess has composed a work which is calculated

to endure the judgment of posterity, long after the possessors of an ephemeral popularity shall have faded away into a well-merited oblivion.[18]

Unusually for the period, the widespread critical praise persisted well beyond both the poem's appearance and the poet's death. As Harriet Kramer Linkin notes, the principal journals and reviews continued for most of the century to number Tighe among the age's greatest women poets, as did the editors and compilers of numerous anthologies published in Britain and America. Notably, Tighe's popular and intensely nationalistic countrywoman Sydney Owenson in 1857 still called Mary Tighe "the first and finest *poetess* of her own or perhaps any country" (quoted in Linkin, introduction, xvii), pointedly reminding readers of Tighe's Irish background. Tighe's poetry exerted a broad and demonstrable influence on the work of male and female writers alike, from contemporaries like Keats, Hemans, Owenson, and Thomas Moore through later writers on both sides of the Atlantic, like Elizabeth Barrett Browning, Christina Rossetti, Emily Dickinson, and Edgar Allan Poe. So profound was Hemans's response that she concluded her *Records of Woman* with her poem to Tighe's memory, "The Grave of a Poetess," which is the volume's only "record" of a contemporary woman (Linkin, introduction, xviii).

Psyche stands in almost polar opposition in both subject and style to sentimental verse narratives like *Ellen Fitzarthur*. An allegorical tale based loosely on Apuleius's tale of Cupid and Psyche in *The Golden Ass, Psyche* is a story of love and the human soul that, as Duncan Wu notes, "aims to value love as a romantic ideal" and that emerges—in part because the poem's emotional sincerity and the sheer beauty of its language—as "one of the great love poems in the language" (*Romantic Women Poets,* 372). But the poem is also deeply interested in the situation of women (including creative women) in society, and this interest links it with the underlying concerns of even poems so apparently different from it as *Ellen Fitzarthur*. That is, it considers women's traditional culturally assigned roles and examines the implications for those women who deviate from these roles, whether by choice or by chance. Tighe's concern in this respect is with "the narrating woman poet who insists on her capacity to compose visionary poetry when Romantic-era culture teaches her to be the muse" (Linkin, introduction, xxiii), expecting her to serve as the instigator or inspirer of (usually) male creative activity rather than to assume the active role of female creative artist. The poem consequently draws a close parallel between its narrator (whom we naturally regard as Tighe, whose physical beauty was universally acknowledged) and Psyche as the familiar mythic object of romantic desire.

But the tale ends unromantically, as is fitting for so thoughtful a meditation on women's circumstances during Tighe's era. Like the tragic women who at the end of

sentimental verse narratives find their lives ravaged by the consequences of disappointed or misdirected love, so too does Psyche reach the end of Tighe's poem only
to discover—much as the narrator does—that the ideal life is indeed only a vision.
In fact, Tighe prepares Psyche (and the reader) for this reversal already in canto 1's final stanza, which foreshadows the disappointment that is inevitable for Cupid both
because that is how the myth of Cupid and Psyche goes and because the pattern of
female experience has been repeatedly inculcated in British art and life alike:

> Her suit obtained, in full contentment blest,
> Her eyes at length in placid slumbers close.
> Sleep, hapless fair! sleep on thy lover's breast!
> Ah not again to taste such pure repose!
> Till thy sad heart by long experience knows
> How much they err, who to their interest blind,
> Slight the calm peace which from retirement flows;
> And while they think their fleeting joys to bind
> Banish the tranquil bliss which heaven for man designed!   (ll. 577–85)

The passage could almost serve as a gloss on the situation of Ellen Fitzarthur and
the deceitful De Morton following their flight from Malwood Vale. As in so many
Romantic-era poems, both the subject character and the author are forced to face
the devastating reality that the beautiful visions of private reverie are incompatible
with the unyielding realities of the public sphere that doom all such idealism. Love
does not win the day, nor does virtue necessarily triumph; more often than not, the
reverse is true. Hence the poem's dark, stark final stanza:

> Dreams of Delight farewell! your charms no more
> Shall gild the hours of solitary gloom!
> The page remains—but can the page restore
> The vanished bowers which Fancy taught to bloom?
> Ah no! her smiles no longer can illume
> The path my Psyche treads no more for me;
> Consigned to dark oblivion's silent tomb
> The visionary scenes no more I see,
> Fast from the fading lines the vivid colours flee!   (canto 6, ll. 532–40)

Like Coleridge in "Kubla Khan" and Keats in "Ode to a Nightingale," both published after her death, Tighe finds herself and her art incapable of sustaining in the
"real world" the vision and passion that had enlivened her private, inspired reverie.

In 1812 the *Critical Review* analyzed *Psyche*'s style, calling it

> delicate, simple, and unaffected (if affectation consist in unsuccessful imitation); the diction for the most part is pure and classical, plain, yet rarely prosaic, never mean; and the verse flows with a liquid and unbroken melody. In a word, the author of Psyche takes a middle flight, between earth and heaven, and preserves an even elevation with unfatigued wing. She seldom thrills, surprises, or deeply engages her reader, but often casts him into a voluptuous and soothing trance; and the effect of the whole may be not unaptly compared to a dream of sweet music.[19]

The reviewer's choice of language here—"voluptuous and soothing trance"—and his analogy of "a dream of sweet music" effectively capture the almost hypnotic effect that Tighe's skillful poetry has on its reader. The verse is richly textured, as is evident in the passage quoted above (and particularly in the remarkable final line), and it flows easily through sonorous, complex and strikingly imaged sentences. Emotion, too, is carefully modulated; Tighe juxtaposes her narrative voice's often almost dispassionate observation with an alternative and intensive sensibility that is signaled by formulaic interjections like "Oh!," "Ah!," "Lo!" and by the heightened emotion with which she infuses the poem's conclusion in particular. That she is able to sustain the demanding Spenserian stanza for over 3,300 lines of lively, lush, and often genuinely moving poetry testifies to Tighe's poetic versatility, her appreciation of voice and rhetoric, and her sophisticated understanding of readerly response.

In fact, *Psyche* is also notable for the remarkably forthright invitation that Tighe extends to her readers to discover the wider field of social and cultural signification toward which her tale points. That is, much of what Psyche says, either to (and about) Cupid or to (and about) herself, delineates not just the allegorical situation in which Psyche finds herself but also, perhaps more importantly, the actual position occupied by Romantic-era women (including women writers) within a culture in which privilege and prerogative customarily resided almost exclusively with men. The woman who sought a public self had to knowingly place herself in both real and rhetorical jeopardy by visibly defying (or "transgressing," as many critics put it) the culturally gendered restrictions on her, her actions, and her community. Thus when late in canto 1 the narrator addresses her readers, her lines comment insightfully on writing in general:

> Oh, you for whom I write! whose hearts can melt
> At the soft thrilling voice whose power you prove,
> You know what charm, unutterably felt,

Attends the unexpected voice of Love:
Above the lyre, the lute's soft notes above,
With sweet enchantment to the soul it steals
And bears it to Elysium's happy grove;
You best can tell the rapture Psyche feels
When Love's ambrosial lip the vows of hymen seals.   (ll. 451–59)

Like Wordsworth who in "Strange Fits of Passion I Have Known" declares that his tale will make complete sense only to "the lover's ear" (l. 3), Tighe here invokes a compact of experience with her readers that likens Psyche's "rapture" under the influence of "Love's ambrosial lip" to the experience of sympathetic reading. One might reasonably assume that she is speaking primarily of women readers, whose supposed susceptibility to sensibility was understood to make them the principal audience for sentimental writing. But, like Charlotte Smith and Lucy Aikin, Tighe carefully avoids gender markers in this and comparable passages, making it clear that responsive readerly sympathy is the exclusive province of neither sex but is, rather, a characteristic of the finest and most discriminating human nature. In this and other respects we may reasonably see in *Psyche,* as we may also see in many of the sentimental verse narratives, a poetry that both addresses *and creates* a community of readers that is grounded in shared experience, inviting those readers "in" even as it demonstrates that they are, in fact, *already* "in."

The Elegiac Occasional Poem

Throughout the Romantic era, women produced a great deal of occasional poetry and poetry ostensibly addressed to other women, whether that poetry explicitly named individual recipients or whether it was directed by implication to a wider audience of identifiably women readers. Among the former category are poems on the deaths (especially) of public figures like politicians, military figures, and clergy. Some of these poems memorialize persons whose "fame" or sphere of influence is relatively local, like poems in honor of notable kinfolk, friends, and local luminaries. Another variety commemorates fellow (or sister) artists, like Joanna Baillie's "Lines on the Death of Sir Walter Scott," Mary Robinson's *Monody to the Memory of Sir Joshua Reynolds,* Hemans's "The Grave of a Poetess," or Landon's "Felicia Hemans." Another, more ambitious, variety includes poems on the death of state figures, like the many poems produced on the death of George III (by women like Mary Cockle, Hemans, or Anna Letitia Barbauld, the last of whose poem on the old king's demise is both touching and haunting) or Mary Cockle's tribute to Queen Charlotte.

One particularly poignant variant occurs in the numerous poems of various lengths that women wrote as part of the national orgy of mourning occasioned by the death in childbirth in 1817 of the Princess Charlotte Augusta, the only child of the Prince Regent's ill-fated marriage to Caroline of Brunswick. Among the many women who produced poems on this occasion were Barbauld, Mary Stockdale, Margaret Croker, Charlotte Richardson, Susanna Watts, Isabella Lickbarrow, Catharine George Ward, and Mary Anne Tiernan. J. Paul Hunter writes that what is usually called "occasional poetry" is "often restricted to poems about *public* occasions or events that drive social conversation"; but Hunter includes in this category "poems about more *private* occasions as well—birthdays, meetings and partings of friends, journeys and arrivals, family events, small episodes in private life and other moments of shared experience that two or more people need to remember together—for these became the logical informal extension of the idea of verbally preserving occasions" (207). Indeed, poems of this sort constituted arguably the most numerous in the eighteenth century, and their popularity continued well into the nineteenth century, where by the 1830s they were a staple of the annuals and other "keepsake" anthologies. I begin by considering some poems on "public" occasions before turning to several on very "private" ones. Rather than trying to include all the varieties of poems encompassed by Hunter's definition, I confine myself to several representative poems on the deaths of individuals, and hence to works in the elegiac mode, which Paula Backscheider contends was "one of the three or four most popular forms of poetry" by the later eighteenth century and one that "had penetrated almost every form" of poetic discourse (271).

The Romantic period furnished ample opportunities to mourn the deaths of public figures and to eulogize their virtues and victories. The most prominent deaths included those of politicians like William Pitt the Younger and Charles James Fox, both in 1806; military heroes like Admiral Nelson at Trafalgar in 1805, Sir John Moore at Corunna in 1809, and Robert Ross at Baltimore in 1814; and George III in 1820, Queen Charlotte in 1818, and Princess Charlotte Augusta of Wales in November 1817. Poems published on these occasions were typically formulaic affairs, and the more poems that appeared, the more similar they tended to be both in sentiment and in expression, so that their very redundancy lent them a ritualistic flavor. The political and ideological agendas informing these poems are readily apparent, as we see in Martha Hanson's "Stanzas, Occasioned by the Death of Horatio Viscount Nelson" (which appeared in her 1809 *Sonnets, and Other Poems* [2:33–36]):

While Gallia's hostile sons insulting boast,
　　That by their arms the gallant Nelson fell;

Britannia mourns her godlike Hero lost,
  Whose actions Fame through ev'ry clime shall tell.
From ev'ry Briton's eye, the gushing tear
  To Gratitude, and fond Affection due,
Falls, as their great Commander's sable bier,
  Cover'd with verdant wreaths they view.

. . . .

Around his brow, her everlasting crown,
  Gemm'd with a nation's tears, bright Honour wove;
While spotless Glory, and Unstain'd Renown,
  Bore him from Death's cold arms, to realms above.   (2:35, ll. 1–8)

These lines, which are entirely typical of the genre, illustrate Hunter's observation that public occasions "usually imply some social, political, or ideological statement or loyalty—and therefore an allegiance to some group or position, often involving national patriotism or pride or some version of identity politics"; hence, these poems appeal to "issues of sincerity and group thinking" (209). The death of any prominent national figure poses a challenge to his or her society that must be overcome by the assertion of some transcending reality that reflects "the shared values and convictions of the group as a whole" (Wolffe, 5). The fondness of the poets for allegory, emphasized by conspicuous capitalization, and for patently theatrical (even melodramatic) demonstrations of collective woe, are hallmarks of this poetry. Such emotional excess, typically frowned on when exhibited by women, was apparently acceptable upon occasions of national civic loss. Indeed, the theatricality—the self-reflexive performative nature—of this variety of public occasional poetry further indicates the extent to which such writing served in a public social ritual meant to stimulate the very sort of *catharsis* that is the objective of formal dramatic tragedy.

This kind of dramatic manipulation of the poet's material for propagandistic purposes is evident early in the period, in Anna Seward's *Elegy on Captain Cook* (1780) and even more so in her *Monody on the Death of Major André* (1781), the second of which largely established the reputation she enjoyed for some years as Britain's national poet. Seward celebrates Major André both for his military prowess and his personal virtue, including the fortitude with which he bears the thwarted love that drives him to enter military service. Seward's poem, which blends the tale of a faithful lover with that of a noble military figure cast in the mold of the great classical heroes, "comes to serve the nation" by reminding Britons of the perfidy of the Americans, whose "betrayal of liberty and its English principles" (Backscheider, 295) required an appropriate revenge.[20] Interestingly, in its final passages Seward's poem moves away from an explicit call for national vengeance and toward an attitude of "philosophical melancholy" that is epitomized in the figure of "Imperial Honour" that bends over André's tomb (Guest, 264). Many—even most—of the poems on the deaths of military figures follow this model in treating their subjects within the dual framework of a personal heterosexual romance (interrupted by the man's departure for war, whether as a result of conscription or because of a hasty decision taken in the heat of romantic rejection) and a variety of national (or nationalistic) quest-romance pursued in service to the nation and the principles for which it is understood to stand. The subject's death in service to the latter cause underscores the pathos of what he sacrifices in leaving the former, private sphere and testifies to the self-sacrifice that marks the "deeds above heroic" that Milton called Jesus's deliberate acts of self-sacrifice in *Paradise Regained* (ll. 1.14–15) and in the fatal but prototypically redemptive temporal ministry toward which that epic points.

George III's long-suffering queen, Charlotte of Mecklenburg-Strelitz, was mourned following her death in 1818, but her relative unpopularity among the British public may account for the comparatively small number of formal elegies that were published. Quite the opposite was true in 1820 when one element of Britain's national tragedy was resolved with the old king's death. Public affection for George III had grown during the Regency, partly owing to the increasing national distaste for the Prince Regent, his associates, and their lavish and insensitive indulgence of luxury amid widespread national suffering. Too, the tragedy of dementia was familiar to many households, and the knowledge that the king had succumbed to this terrible fate brought him and his situation closer to the personal experiences of many of his subjects, so that a bond of compassion linked them to the king precisely at the time that the Prince Regent's behavior was alienating them. The poems that appeared following George's death, therefore, combined formulaic rhetorical elements of mourning ritual with more localized details that reflected the unique and peculiar personal circumstances of the king's final years.

But perhaps nowhere among these public elegiac poems do we find so intense a connection between subject and author (and, by implication, reader) as in the poems that women published in the wake of the wholly unexpected death of Princess Charlotte Augusta of Wales in November 1817. The princess's popularity stemmed from several factors. The only child of her ill-suited and dissolute parents, the now-separated Prince of Wales and Caroline of Brunswick, she had in 1814 pluckily rejected an arranged marriage with Prince William of Orange that her father had attempted to force on her and had subsequently married a man largely of her own choosing, the handsome young Prince Leopold of Saxe-Coburg-Gotha (uncle of Albert of Saxe-Gotha, the future prince consort of Queen Victoria), with whom she had retired to a life of apparent virtue and bliss at their country estate of Clare-mont. The very public example of domestic tranquility and civic virtue that they set provided a happy contrast to the outrageous behavior of the rest of the royal family and offered the prospect of an eventual reign by a seemingly virtuous, enlightened, and humanitarian princess who was already being celebrated for all the domestic characteristics that came to be associated with the Victorian image of woman as nurturant wife and mother. When it became known in 1817 that the princess was pregnant, the nation made elaborate preparations to celebrate the birth of an heir apparent. These hopes were dashed when, after a grueling and protracted labor, the princess produced a stillborn son and, within a few hours, died of complications herself. This calamity became the subject of countless works of literature (including not just poems but also innumerable sermons, memoirs, and other accounts), visual art, sculpture, music, textiles, ceramics, metalwork, and other forms of the domestic and industrial arts.

Melesina Trench's words express how deeply the loss was felt by women through-out the nation:

> The melancholy fate of our lovely Princess strikes with a heaviness of heart like a domestic calamity. So sweet, so spotless, so full of endearing qualities, so firm and ardent in her affections, so nobly bold in asserting them when it seemed her duty, so raised above the faults and follies of her age, sex, and station. . . . I did not think anything but the loss of a dear friend could have given me so much pain. . . . Nothing but having been an actor in the scene, could convey an idea of the state of the kingdom. It seemed as if every family had lost an individual from its own circle, who was more or less dear. All was sorrow, lamentation, regret, varied only in kind and degree. . . . The churches and all places of religious worship were overflowing. All sectarian barriers were broken down by the strong feelings of compassion for the living, reverence and regret for the dead. Indeed, when I say pleasure was laid aside, I express myself improperly, for it seemed never to have been thought of in any shape from the time of this deep disappointment to a generous, a devoted, and an enlightened nation. Had a fast day been appointed by public authority, this affecting expression of general sorrow would not have been so clear a proof of the impression made by one whose name is enshrined within our hearts, and who will be remembered for ever as a model of all that is touching and noble, spirited and affectionate, dignified and condescending. . . . She has been wept in every cottage, and her loss has scarcely *yet* been thought of as a political calamity, it has come so near every heart as a private sorrow. (*Remains,* 372–74)

The poems that women published on this occasion repeatedly treated the national loss in unusually personal terms and by means of this approach functionally reduced the social gulf separating the princess from her female subjects of whatever class, uniting them through the common experience of childbearing. In creating this experiential common ground, the poets humanized the princess, treating her not in her role as royal personage but metaphorically as a sister in experience. This procedure also implicitly dignified and ennobled the status of all women, whose experiences as wives and mothers were thus demonstrated to be essentially no different in human terms than those of the princess. As a consequence, the rhetorically empty and largely ritualistic language of universal mourning that characterizes most of the elegies published by men is either absent or significantly toned down in women's poems, which emphasize other, more human experiences that resonated with women readers.

Mary Stockdale, for instance, reminds readers in her "A Wreath for the Urn" (from the collection by the same title) that at the Regent's orders Charlotte had been forcibly separated from her mother, who in fact only learned of her daughter's death from a newspaper account. "Hard is thy lot, O banish'd Princess! hard!" Stockdale writes:

> Her first-born child, her last:—her only gem:
>   But adverse fate forbade her presence here;
> The beauteous flower is sever'd from the stem,
>   And lands remote must view the mother's tear.   (15)

Like so many of the poems discussed in this book, Stockdale's elegy also addresses the situation of the writer who aspires to participate fully in a public poetic conversation for which she nevertheless fears that she may be unqualified. In the poem's concluding section Stockdale turns this familiar rhetorical device to her advantage, stressing how the unfeigned sincerity of her poem ought to compensate for any formal artistic failings:

> Humble the offering, but it is sincere;
>   My pen but dictates what my bosom feels;
> While down each cheek, the sympathetic tear,
>   The big full drop, in sacred silence steals.
>
> . . . .
>
> While countless voices join in Charlotte's praise,
>   One lowly maid would fain her offering bring;
> Would fain commemorate in artless lays,
>   The darling grand-child of our much-loved King.   (18)

Coming as it does near the poem's end, this reference to the king of course invites the reader's sympathy for George, but it also raises the issue of royal succession, which had unexpectedly become a real national concern. The double tragedy of George's madness and his granddaughter's (and great-grandson's) death underscores not the expected and familiar vision of a happy reunion in heaven that one encounters in most of these poems but, instead, a vision in the final stanza that forces the reader back to the stark reality of mortality—including the mortality that attends all literary texts:

> Yes, they are gone!—no hand had power to save,
>> Those spirits blest shall ne'er to earth return;
> Then take, 't is all I have! to adorn her grave,
>> This humble WREATH, and bind it round her URN.   (18)

In linking Charlotte's fate with George III's, Stockdale did what numerous other women poets did, hinting that these family tragedies represented a heavenly judgment for Britain's "sins" of inhumanity as epitomized not just in the nation's military conflicts but also in the social, political and economic phenomena (like slavery, materialism, and class warfare) that accompanied the nation's imperialist project. Barbauld, who was no stranger to this line of argument, wrote in this spirit in "On the Death of the Princess Charlotte" (1818), a poem that is actually more about George and the empire than about Charlotte.[21] Barbauld juxtaposes the self-indulgent public mourning that was sweeping Britain with the dangerous moral and cultural stagnation from which the citizens self-servingly used this mourning to distract themselves. Britain's "universal population well / In grief spontaneous," Barbauld writes, and "rough unpolished natures learn to feel / For those they envied, humbled in the dust / By fate's impartial hand" (ll. 3–7). Meanwhile, "one there is / Who midst this general burst of grief remains / In strange tranquillity" (ll. 9–11) and who, "struck / By heaven's severest visitation" (ll. 24–25), stands alone, oblivious alike to Charlotte's death and to "living nature / Or time's incessant change" (ll. 29–30). Barbauld's poem subtly but effectively reminds her readers of the continuing national tragedy of the king's debilitating insanity that had been swept from the headlines by the more visible recent royal disaster.

In a comparable vein is Jane Dunnett's poignant 1818 poem, "On the King Being Insensible of the National Loss" (from her *Poems on Various Subjects*), which begins with an invocation to Reason:

> O Reason! thou great cause, etherial spring,
>> By which our noblest actions know to move;

By thee deserted, we behold our king
    Forget the former objects of his love.

. . . .

O sweet delusion! does he still behold,
    And think he feels the sun's soft radiance yet?
His vacant eyes fix on its locks of gold,
    While that bright sun is now for ever set!   (63–64, ll. 1–4, 13–16)

Troping Charlotte as the warm and radiant sun, "now for ever set," is a remarkably effective move that must have cast a reassuringly humanizing light over the old king's situation for Dunnett's readers. The metaphor was widely used, though; in "On the Death of the Princess Charlotte of Wales," for instance, Harriet Rebecca King employs it in more conventional terms:

She, whose sweet taste embellish'd ev'ry scene,
Whom England honour'd as her future Queen,
Whose early loss Britannia must deplore,
Her sun is set—on earth to rise no more.   (33–34, ll. 16–19)[22]

But Dunnett's poem remains unique in the touching intimacy that her metaphor achieves.

The fact that Princess Charlotte was first widely admired and then even more widely lamented, like Princess Diana of Wales nearly two centuries later, testifies to how her contemporaries fused her identities as woman and as potential monarch, accommodating the traditionally feminine characteristics of the wife and mother with the usually masculine ones of national ruler.[23] Her death provides the earliest example in Britain of how a woman might be transformed into a commodity for commercial profit as well as for national catharsis. Indeed, the flood of literary and extraliterary commemorative goods that were produced on the occasion introduced the relatively modern notion that purchasing and possessing such goods created a community of ownership: in owning these commodities, citizens shared a vicarious ownership of Charlotte and the qualities for which she was admired. Thus the nationwide exercises in mourning demonstrated, as they would for Diana in 1997, the "elevating power of sympathetic benevolence" (Schor, 227) that raises their subject to the status of myth at the same time it establishes a community of sentiment that crosses all partisan and class lines.

Elegiac poems on private occasions, on the other hand, function differently, in part because their subjects are *not* widely known and are therefore not regarded as calamitous losses to the nation or even to subgroups within it and in part because their rhetoric is markedly different as a result of the author's assumed familiarity—even intimacy—with the poem's subject. Unlike poems on public figures, these are written as though their audience is limited to the author's circle and that of the subject's acquaintances; often this readership is rhetorically framed as an audience of one, and the poems themselves take on the rhetorical conventions of correspondence. These poems typically share with their readers something quite personal about their subjects, in the process making the reader's relationship with the subject more intimate, *increasing* the sense of privacy by treating this shared knowledge almost as a secret. Sharing this sort of intimate information with a reader, Hunter suggests, "both legitimates their near-intimacy and suggests how much more there is than public appearances can tell" (218).

The poems that women published on the Princess Charlotte's death differ from those published by men in several notable ways, but especially in the rhetorical attitude the authors take toward their subject. Women's cultural conditioning in general made them more comfortable than men when it came to assuming a posture of humility in the face of the enigma of unexpected death, which was more likely to leave men either speechless, on one hand, or resorting to clichéd, melodramatic rhetoric, on the other. Death as a consequence of childbirth was universally familiar to British women, though, as was the death of children of all ages, which they experienced in particularly intimate ways. Indeed, the writings of women from all classes and circumstances are filled with moving accounts of the deaths not just of one child but of many children, often in quick succession. Because those deaths are the subjects of so many Romantic-era poems by women, I conclude this chapter by considering three such poems, both to demonstrate how they differ in substance and in style from poems like those I have just examined and to illustrate the remarkable intensity with which such poems were frequently endowed.

The first is a brief poem by Ann Candler, "a Suffolk Cottager" born in 1740 who, as she tells us, has "had nine children, five sons and four daughters, three of the boys died infants, how it has pleased God to dispose of two of the remaining six I know not, as I have not heard of my eldest son and daughter for many years" (4); two children still resided near her when she published her poems in 1803, having endured an unhappy marriage of nearly forty years and spending time on at least one occasion in the Tattingstone House of Industry, a workhouse near Ipswich. "The Mother's Feelings on the Loss of Her Child" states the situation immediately:

O, Gracious God! I ask'd a son;—
    A son to me was giv'n:

Before six moons their course had run
    The gift return'd to heav'n.   (19, ll. 1–4)

Though her infant son dies in the night while she sleeps, Candler's subsequent maternal grief is tempered by her Christian faith in her son's eternal life, a gift so precious that "monarchs, to partake the joy, / Would freely crowns resign" (20, ll. 31–32). With this intermediate consolation in mind, Candler concludes by turning her personal sorrow into a moral lesson about Christian hope and the rewards of a life well and piously lived:

Cease, foolish mother! cease to grieve,
    And blush to shed a tear;
Endeavour such a life to live
    As thou may'st meet him there.

Oh, gracious God! bow down thine ear,
    And grant me my request:
Oh, heav'nly Father! hear my pray'r;
    Let me with him be blest.

Then shall I, with redoubl'd joy,
    My Maker's name adore:
Then shall I meet my infant boy,
    And meet to part no more.   (21, ll. 33–44)

In the face of the perennially inexplicable—the death of children—poets like Candler convert pathos into piety, albeit uneasily, for they are both poets and mothers, and though they are *making* new creations in the form of their poems, those literary offspring come only at the cost of the real lives of the children whose deaths furnish their subjects.

Poems on the deaths of children are therefore, like those on the deaths of celebrities, necessarily performative in nature, much like sonnets that take ostensibly private moments of heightened sensibility and perform them in writing that is fully intended for public consumption. As soon as these poems are *published* they cease to be what they pretend to be—private expressions intended for strictly limited audiences of known readers—and become instead public communications with readers whose identities and circumstances are necessarily unknown to their authors. Even so, the death of children was such a universally familiar phenomenon that there could be no question that the poets would find sympathetic readers among at least half the population. It is no accident, therefore, that such poems, when they are written by women (and they almost always were), assume a framework of familiarity, of sisterhood, in their treatment of their subjects, both at the level of narrative detail and at that of rhetoric.

How profoundly different such poems are from those much less numerous examples by men is apparent from the difficulties with which scholars have long wrestled in dealing with Wordsworth's Lucy poems, whose emotional and rhetorical features are so uncharacteristic both of Wordsworth's writing and of male-authored poetry on the whole, which has always been uneasy about "the manliness of publicizing displays of emotion" (Schor, 50). One can *admire* the fallen hero (or heroine) and *lament* him (or her), but neither the poet nor the reader typically knows them well enough to *love* them. Therefore the poems that commemorate them assume a rhetorically detached posture (the melodramatic and largely formulaic language of melancholy and woe notwithstanding) that the subjects require precisely because they *are* remote from the common citizen's experience. But the mother who mourns the death of her child presents a very different aspect, the culturally sanctioned and proper response to which is sympathy rather than admiration, consolation and comfort rather than detachment. One of the signal differences between elegies written by men and those written by women, Paula Backscheider observes, is "the construction of the importance and benefits of the relationship between the poet and the dead" (314). Male poets typically wrote poems steeped in literary and rhetorical convention, even when their subjects were relatively personal, so that one is generally conscious of that tradition of the "stiff upper lip" that discourages highly personal (and therefore more emotional) engagement with the material. Indeed, it is not hard to find examples of poems in which the intimate nature of the poet's relationship to his subject is signaled, paradoxically, by the sheer *formality* with which that relationship is treated.

Women's elegiac poems, on the other hand, perhaps because they so often assume the conventions of oral or written conversation (and therefore an ostensible, if feigned, privacy of communication), tend to reduce this detachment dramatically and to embrace immediately familiar elements of women's experience as their basis. Writing about (or to) friends from whom they are separated, women describe physical settings and activities they have shared with those persons and that now provide comfort, consolation, and pleasure that compensate for the inevitable sadness produced by that separation. Their elegiac poems attempt to generate a comparable consolation even in the face of death's irreversible separation. The familiar conceit of the loved one's face being "always before one" is no less emotionally and psychologically realistic for its ubiquity. Their elegies, according to Backscheider, enabled eighteenth-century women to celebrate and prolong relationships and to deny the obliteration of memory that comes with separation: for them, "their relationship, rather than the death, becomes 'the event,' and they create a 'kind of continuous present' that denies that the relationship has been severed or taken on a communal rather than personal meaning" (351).[24] Although this certainly states the case fairly and accurately for many women's elegiac poems, when it comes to poems on children's deaths, the poets did not, I believe, intend to deny that the relationship between mother (and author) and child might take on communal meaning. Indeed, quite the reverse: it is precisely in the achievement of communal meaning that such poems find a universality that balances and reinforces the strictly personal aspects of the experiences of individual mothers (and children) described in the poems. This inscribed community is an essential part of the genre, for it is in that communal meaning that the death of the individual child takes on a fuller, almost mythic, significance, and it is there, too, that the mother (author) finds both consolation (through community) and "fame" for herself and her lost child.

In this light it is interesting to consider Isabella Lickbarrow's "On the Death of an Infant," published in her 1814 *Poetical Effusions.* Lickbarrow, a humble and self-educated poet from the Lake District who was orphaned at an early age and who published to add to her meager income, takes up this familiar subject, but because the child her poem mourns is clearly not her own, the poem lacks the warmth and intimacy of poems like that of even the relatively unlettered Candler. One senses immediately in the opening and concluding stanzas the absence of genuinely personal authorial involvement:

> Sweet babe! how peaceful is thy sleep,
>   That sleep which wakes to pain no more;
> No more thy little eyes shall weep,
>   For all thy sorrows now are o'er.
>
> .   .   .   .
>
> The drooping snowdrop's wither'd bud
>   Shall die and never reach its prime;
> But thou sweet flower transplanted hence,
>   Wilt flourish in a happier clime.
>
> No wintry storms can ever rise
>   To blight thy tender blossom there,
> But one unchanging season smile,
>   And summer gladden all the year.   (81–82, ll. 1–4, 29–36)

Lickbarrow was a good poet whose work may have been known by Wordsworth and Southey, who both subscribed to her volume. But a poem like this one fails to transcend its conventionality of sentiment and expression. The poet's evident lack of personal "connection" with her subject leaves the reader largely unmoved. Nor was even a prolific and accomplished poet like Hemans immune to this danger; "The Child's Last Sleep" (1826), first published in *Friendship's Offering*, a literary annual,[25] is curiously impersonal and formulaic:

> Thou'rt gone from us, bright one!—that *thou* shouldst die,
> And life be left to the butterfly!
> Thou'rt gone as a dew-drop is swept from the bough—
> Oh! for the world where thy home is now!
> How may we love but in doubt and fear,
> How may we anchor our fond hearts here,
> How should e'en joy but a trembler be,
> Beautiful dust! when we look on thee?   (ll. 17–24)

If poems like these seem emotionally detached, the reverse is true of the last poem I consider. In 1816 the young daughter of Dublin-born Melesina Trench, whom her doting mother called "Melesina the Less" and "Bessy," died of croup at the age of four years and three months, following a brief illness that had commenced while her mother was away. Writing to her friend and longtime correspondent Mary Leadbeater, Trench poured out her grief:

> My lovely blossom is now in her little coffin, where I have just kissed her beautiful marble brow; for she was and is beautiful, though I restrained myself from ever talking of her personal perfections. What is more important, she was heavenly minded, as far as four years and three months would admit. Her latest request was to look at the stars. The last thing she learned by heart was, "Lord, now lettest thy servant depart in peace;" and when, two days after her death, I wished to read the resurrection of Lazarus, and could not recollect the place, I found it marked with a little daisy she had put in to preserve. . . . [H]er docility, gentleness, joyousness, piety, patience, affection gave me a practical comment on the words asserting that the angels of little children "do always behold the face of my Father in heaven."
>
>   But that her illness commenced in my absence, and was not immediately encountered on my return with the best medical advice doubles my affliction—barbs and poisons the dart. . . . You know how the loss of an only daughter, who to the weakness of mortal eyes appeared faultless, and who had all the attractions which endear a child to strangers as well as friends—you know how it must darken the remaining years of a mother past the age of hoping for any new blessings, but clinging too eagerly to those she already possesses. God bless you, my

dear, dear friend, and preserve you from such affliction. You can never know such, for you are always the constant companion of your children, and cannot feel the regrets and self-reproach which consume one who often left hers to the care of others. This may be often palliated, but it is never right; and when a misfortune of this kind happens it adds self-reproach, the worst of ills, to every other. (*Leadbeater Papers*, 2:281–82)

It is helpful to compare this passage with Trench's comments on Princess Charlotte's death, quoted earlier. While it shares with that letter an obvious sincerity of feeling and a seemingly personal connection to the event, its differences are dramatically evident. This is now a domestic tragedy, and Trench's resulting tortured emotional state is immediately apparent, as is her natural impulse to remember (and to share) those intimate details peculiar to her own situation, such as the daisy preserved in the Bible. Her letter *includes* Leadbeater in her experience even as it hopes, rhetorically, to shield her from it, for the impulse to share (and be consoled in) one's grief inevitably reminds one of the ultimately solitary nature of grief. Confident of its recipient's knowledgeable sympathy, Trench's letter communicates pathos without affectation. But it is also intensely personal in sharing intimate details like Trench's understandable self-reproach at having left her daughter in another's care and then failing to recognize the seriousness of her symptoms. Her poem "On the Loss of Elizabeth Melesina Trench, an Only Daughter, in Her Fifth Year" is a moving tribute to this much-loved child.[26]

After her first marriage, to Richard St. George, ended with her husband's premature death (she shipped his corpse home to Ireland from Portugal on her twenty-second birthday [Blain, Clements, and Grundy, 1,095]), she had married Richard Trench in 1803. During her two marriages Trench bore eight sons and, apparently, two daughters, one of whom died in infancy before 1806.[27] Bessy's presence had helped her to cope with the loss of her young son Frederick, who had died in 1806 in his third year, as "On the Loss" suggests:

And there was one,—who smoothed my brow,
    Image on earth,—of heavenly joy:
Yes,—there *was* one—where is she now—
    Promise of bliss without alloy.

.   .   .   .

As glides the rose leaf on the breeze
    Impelled by joy, how swift her flight,
Whene'er beneath embowering trees,
    Her mother met her watchful sight.

How happy 'mid her flowers she strayed—
    Herself a living—breathing flower:
What rapture o'er her features played,
    As each new blossom gemmed her bower.   (ll. 13–16, 25–32)

But now Bessy is gone, too, and Trench sees herself in her daughter's life and death:

And when her last sad hour was near
    "Oh let me see the stars"—she cried—
In agony of hope and fear,
    Trembling—I threw the curtain wide;

And thought I saw relenting Heaven
    Smile in those orbs—so clear[28] and bright
And deemed that to my prayer was given
    The star of my approaching night[.]

.   .   .   .

To me—she brought returning youth—
    Fair promise of a second spring—
Fond Fancy's dream—surpassed by Truth.
    Image of love—without his wing.   (ll. 41–48, 65–68)

In death, the child's beauty belies the reality of the physical suffering her mother was compelled to witness during her final hours:

Her shining locks, of richest glow
    Still wore of life, the brilliant hue,
And parted—o'er her brow of snow,
    A gleam of sunny radiance threw.

But, Oh!—her long dark lashes closed
    O'er eyes must beam no more on earth.
In joy they flashed—in hope reposed—
    As ripe for their immortal birth.

Her hand—where Health's gay tints concealed,
    Far nobler beauties than they gave,
Its peerless loveliness revealed—
    To shine within her narrow grave.

She lay—as in a peaceful trance:
    Her snowy garb adorned with flowers,

So grouped—as in the sportive dance
   On Pleasure's robe—in festal hours.

Oh could that cold Perfection live!
   In marble stillness, as it lay—
Is there aught else the world could give
   Might win me from th' inspiring clay.

That silent eloquence might reach
   The inmost foldings of the heart:
Not all the magic power of speech
   Such deep devotion could impart.

It bids me own, though tears will flow—
   My child—how justly Heaven's decree
Calls me to bear this weight of woe
   And endless bliss bestows on thee.   (ll. 85–112)

I have quoted Trench's poem at length not because I believe it possesses unusual literary merit but because it speaks so profoundly to the essential humanity with which the poet responded to her personal tragedy. It is almost a cliché to say that this is a poem that, most probably, only a mother could write; but it is true nonetheless, as is evident from the lack of authenticity (of emotion and of experience) that is evident in so many poems written about other people's children. In a prefatory note to the poem Trench declares that "nothing is exaggerated, either as to incident or description, in the following lines; but they have not attempted to paint the *disposition,* the *heart* of the beloved object: so gentle, affectionate, docile, devoted, and generous as to elude the power of words, and give the fairest prospect of her enjoying and dispensing happiness" (introductory note to "On the Loss," 1). Indeed, there is great poignancy in finding this poem among others in a later bound volume that included Trench's 1815 *Campaspe,* for that earlier volume had been dedicated to Bessy with these words:

My Dear Child, Though you have not yet advanced beyond your alphabet, I dedicate to you this little volume, in the hope, it may meet your eye on some future day, and recall to your memory the affection of your mother. Let it also bring to your recollection the opinion she will endeavour to impress, that every attempt to improve your mind, or exercise your invention, however humble, will be its own reward: and that you will find, in a well directed love for reading, more resources against *ennui,* and surer consolation under disappointment, than in any ornamental accomplishment, or worldly pursuit. ([iii])

Equally poignant is Trench's remark in a letter to her friend Emily Agar conveying the terrible news: "Keep this note. I like to think she will not be forgotten" (Gerard, 132).

Indeed, Bessy was not forgotten, for in another rare hybrid volume Trench "published" several retrospective sonnets on her children, the fourth of which concludes with a vision of the unnamed Bessy asleep in the nursery:

> But in the inmost chamber one reclines,
> A single bird within her downy nest;
> A pearl detached—too precious for the rest.
> Round no fond neck her polished arm entwines,
> Lovely and lone—this sweeter blossom lies,
> Just lent to earth—but ripening for the skies.
> ("Sonnet 4: My Children Sleeping, Continued," ll. 9–14)[29]

Significantly, this sonnet does not mention Frederick, who had died approximately ten years before Bessy. Bessy's death was never far from her mother's thoughts. More than a year later, for example, upon returning home from a dance, she wrote about how seeing on such occasions the "transport beaming from a mother's eye, / When light her daughter's airy footsteps fly" inevitably prompts her to "paint what my Bessy *might* have been, / Since what she *was* I never can pourtray [sic]; / . . . A light from heaven, whose pure, ethereal beam / Threw its long glories over life's dark dream" (Gerard, 133).

Melesina Trench's poem represents but a single eloquent variation on the personal occasional elegy, but the emotional force that the poet marshals in it indicates that the genre was neither static nor outworn by 1816. Indeed, like all the major genres, this one too was evolving in new directions that reflected the changing social conditions of the post-Napoleonic British Empire. The years that followed saw the rise and profusion of literary annuals and illustrated periodicals, all of which would provide a rapidly expanding market for poetry written specifically with these publications' readers in mind. That is, poetry—or at least a significant portion of it— would become "commercial" in ways that it had not been in the previous century, when there did not yet exist what we now think of as a mass market. Inevitably, the poets who wrote for this new market adopted many of the least attractive characteristics of "mass-market literature," including redundant imagery, formulaic plots and dialogue, trite sentimentality, melodramatic staging, and conventional (and generally conservative) moral and intellectual values.

Caught up in a potentially self-destructive cycle in which literary works reflected contemporary cultural assumptions even as they helped to shape them, writers struggled to remain intellectually, politically, and culturally "relevant" while still trying to achieve fame and—they hoped—fortune. More and more the two seemed to be mutually exclusive, and those who failed to achieve fortune tended to denigrate (while still envying them) those who did, often with good reason, as literary reprobates who had purchased their popularity at the sacrifice of their principles: one need only think of the attacks leveled against the later Wordsworth (and Coleridge and Southey, for that matter) by the younger writers who struggled during the Regency and afterward to make their marks. Paradoxically, the two most commercially successful later Romantic women poets, Hemans and Landon, have customarily been criticized for those elements of their works that have seemed to their modern critics to constitute the signs of their own capitulation to the supposedly base, or "common," public taste. And yet, as recent scholarship has begun to demonstrate, the matter is never quite so simple. Wordsworth was no simple turncoat, no matter how he readjusted his coat; his evolution into a Victorian patriarch and sage was neither so simple nor so simplistic as his detractors like to imply. Nor, Frederick Rowton notwithstanding, were Hemans and Landon mere mouthpieces for a comfortable, conservative Victorian orthodoxy of sweet domesticity when it came to women, society, and the public sphere. In the works of these three poets, as in those of countless of their contemporaries, we may observe how committed poets from all points on the social, economic, political, and intellectual spectrum labored to refashion the materials and modes of British poetry, revising and renewing them to accommodate the new realities of the modern world that had experienced revolutions—not just in the streets but also in the press—that had irreversibly transformed the conditions of human existence.

Scottish Women Poets

Women and the Scottishness of Scottish Writing during the Romantic Period

When we come to the poetry of Scotland—and that of Ireland, which is the subject of the next chapter—the inescapable realities of political and cultural history intersect with those of literary history. For while the literary history of England has customarily been sketched in relatively straightforward lines in terms of a dominant "English" national culture, that of Scotland (and of Ireland, and to some extent also of Wales) has had to accommodate the consequences of the shifting relative minority status of its writers and citizens. The Act of Union that brought Scotland together with England and Wales in 1707 under the political umbrella of an ostensibly "United" Kingdom could go only so far in producing the heterogeneity implied by nationalist terms like "Britain" and "Britons," especially when so many of those "Britons" continued to call themselves not "British" but "English." A "united" kingdom was in many respects an illusion in any event, for as Leith Davis observes, ever since the Act of Union of 1707, "Great Britain has been a site of contest—not always on the material level, but certainly on the discursive level—between the nations from which it was constructed" (1). Indeed, recent initiatives in Scotland to reclaim full national political independence, beginning with the establishment of a Scottish Parliament in 1999, illustrate how fierce and ultimately ineradicable is the resistance to such political and cultural forced marriages, which are never egalitarian and companionate but are instead unsteady, artificial arrangements in which violence, abuse, and rape play no small part, as the record of Britain's ongoing experience in Ireland has amply and tragically demonstrated.

As Davis and others have argued, the "nation" that emerged from this first Act of Union, like the more complicated one that was produced a century later by the subsequent Act of Union that added Ireland to the kingdom, involved at least as much cultural fracture, displacement, and dislocation as it did happy combination and assimilation. Some scholars of Scottish literature and culture have read in the title of Linda Colley's important book *Britons: Forging the Nation, 1707–1837* a perhaps unintentional pun:[1] the nation that was "forged" by the acts of union was itself a "forgery" in that it was not a homogeneous national entity but instead one that retained what David Daiches calls a significant "dissociation of sensibility" that reflects incongruent (and frequently incompatible) national cultural practices (21). Douglas Mack has described this complicated union, wherein the participants were never either actual or functional equals, in terms of a business partnership in which "Scotland, as the junior partner in the British Imperial project, took a coloniser's role within Britain's external Empire, but shared with Ireland and Wales the experience of being colonised within a process Katie Trumpener has described as 'British internal colonialism'" (7).

As Mack suggests, England's relationship with Scotland—and with Ireland even more so—was inextricably connected with its imperial aspirations first in the eighteenth-century age of exploration and colonization and then in the nineteenth-century age of capitalism and industrialization. Throughout both centuries the pressure to assimilate with what postcolonial theory identifies as the dominant (English) cultural unit met with varying degrees of resistance among the subaltern (Scottish and/or Irish) unit and its constituent members. Pressed to identify with that dominant culture for reasons of political, social, and economic exigency, the Scots (and the Irish) worried, with good reason, about what abandoning their own cultural identity might cost them. Many were ambivalent at best, while others were fiercely opposed, and these responses are evident in the period's literature. That literature reveals, too, a further division of which the Scots were themselves fully cognizant: the cultural divide between the lowland Scots (epitomized by the culturally literate university cities and by Edinburgh in particular) and the Highlanders (the isolated, apparently backward and culturally alien rural culture). The former became "one of the generative centers of European and north Atlantic literary culture" between 1740 and 1840, while the latter became the locus of a sentimentalized rusticity characterized by vernacular literature, programmatic "wildness" and a pseudomythology of a Scottish national past (Duncan, 2–3). As we shall see, this cultural and linguistic divide figures significantly in the Scottish writing examined in this chapter.

"Can the Subaltern speak?" Douglas Mack asks, echoing Gayatri Chakravorty Spivak's famous question within the context of Scotland and the British empire (1–13). Yes, he seems to reply, but only with difficulty. This difficulty, which arises from any dominant culture's efforts to "block other [cultural] narratives from forming and emerging," paradoxically played a major role in the flowering of Scottish literature during the later eighteenth and early nineteenth centuries, when writers were able to "challenge and subvert some of Imperial Britain's assumptions, by trying to gain a hearing for the subaltern voice" (1–2). Mack's primary concern is with prose fiction, but his point is no less relevant for poetry. Moreover, when it comes to poetry by Scottish women, two varieties of actual or virtual subaltern status are involved: one is grounded in national cultural identity, the other in gender. These separate considerations, though not always either parallel or coequal, necessarily exerted their pressure on the poetry that was published.

Scholarly discussions of Robert Burns and Walter Scott have always been concerned in one way or another with issues of national cultural identity and history, including linguistic issues, but much less attention has been paid to how these issues are represented in Romantic-era Scottish women's poetry. How these women identified themselves in and through their poetry, both as women and as Scots, forms part of the subject of this chapter. For, as Dorothy McMillan reports having discovered while preparing her 1999 anthology of Scottish women's nonfictional writing, "the most interesting thing is how many of the women . . . can call themselves Englishwomen without for a moment forgetting they are Scots" (xiii). Although they write in conventional English and even describe themselves as Englishwomen, writers like Mary Somerville and Charlotte Waldie nevertheless clearly identify with the people and the sentiments of particular Scottish communities. And then there is Anne Macvicar Grant, whose first volume of poems, published by subscription in 1803, bears the unadorned name of "Mrs. Grant." Subsequent volumes, however, including her most popular collection, *The Highlanders, and Other Poems,* which saw at least three editions following its appearance in 1808, bore not only her name but also the name of her Scottish community, Laggan, in Inverness-shire. And yet her *Eighteen Hundred and Thirteen* (1814) strikes a reader as wholly "British" in its rhetorical embrace of nationalism and the British imperial project, its attribution to "Mrs. Grant, of Laggan" notwithstanding. Because this sort of doubled national and cultural identity is rooted in larger historical and cultural experiences, I begin this chapter by examining some of this historical context, tracing the evolution during the eighteenth century of the struggle among writers of both genders to be acknowledged as "British" writers without having to sacrifice their Scottish heritage.

By the Romantic period the Act of Union had been in place for three quarters of a century. Following the failure of the Jacobite rising of 1745, according to J. Mackinnon, "a closer and more sympathetic intercourse" developed between the Scots and the English as both groups recognized the clear potential for both socioeconomic and intellectual improvement that lay in a more companionate relationship (461). Scotland therefore steered a steady course toward ever-greater enfranchisement within Britain, to whose now combined culture Scottish intellectual, economic, and moral traditions contributed in increasingly significant ways. Many Scots saw in that larger national identity unit great practical opportunities for personal advancement that made them less eager to cling to sentimental ideas about Celtic origins and made them question the desirability of absolute Scottish separatism. Indeed, especially by the latter quarter of the eighteenth century, as Linda Colley has written in *Britons,* Scots did "not seem to have regarded themselves as stooges of English cultural hegemony. Far from succumbing helplessly to an alien identity imposed by others, in moving south they helped construct what being British was all about" (125). In Scotland, the literary culture of the lowland Scots in particular reflected this political shift toward assimilation and participation, in part in its embrace of a formal English idiom that reflected, on one hand, the dominant intellectual culture of aristocratic England and its literary heritage and, on the other, the intellectual heritage of the Scottish Enlightenment. It is no accident that while there has long been something known as a "Scottish Enlightenment," the existence of a comparable and contemporaneous English Enlightenment has only recently been argued for in compelling fashion.[2] Scotland had for centuries, after all, been one of the world's great intellectual centers, and one immediate consequence of that had been a vigorous and diverse publishing industry. Moreover, for all their traditional sense of cultural difference, many Scots shared with their Protestant English compatriots an overarching anxiety about the threat posed to them all by "outside" forces, most notably Catholic France. Especially with the coming of the French Revolution, sentiment swung sharply in favor of unified "British" solidarity in the face of this clearly mortal danger. Scottish interests in politics, economics, science, and the arts, it became clear, were likely to be served best by a stronger union with England, and as Scots rose to ever greater prominence (and influence) within the national political and economic establishment, much of Scottish literature began to manifest signs both of "loyalist" sentiment and of a distinctively "British" nationalism.

At the same time, though, there remained powerful elements in Scottish culture—especially the literature and associated culture of the Highland Scots—that resisted assimilation precisely because of the entirely reasonable fear that in becoming "British," Scots would lose irretrievably what they considered to be their essential Scottishness. For many Scots, such thinking informed a proud—even defiant—celebration of Scotland's profoundly Celtic origins. For them, the passion for both political *and cultural* independence implicit in this celebration was not to be snuffed out, even when it might at times be tempered for purposes of exigency. The omnipresence in Scottish thinking of the history of William Wallace, for example, whose death at the hands of the treacherous Scottish nobles elevated him to the status of mythic hero, was merely the most dramatic manifestation of how such beliefs persisted. Indeed, as Kirsteen McCue has written, when by the 1790s the actual physical threat posed by the Jacobites had all but vanished, "Jacobitism became the strongest outlet for Scottish national feeling" (64), an outlet that was especially apparent in the poetry and music of the period. Recent postcolonial theory suggests that a subaltern individual or people may subvert or repudiate her or its oppression not only by overt violent resistance but also—often more tellingly—through more subtle means of enculturation.[3] That is, the oppressive power and authority of an alien presence (which may be an actual invader or occupier or, alternatively, a social, cultural, or ideological *force*) may be effectively countered at the level of everyday experience by the perpetuation among the oppressed or occupied subalterns of indigenous cultural behaviors that the occupying culture seeks to repress, overwrite, or extirpate entirely. The stubborn efforts in Scotland (and Ireland) to resist the government's suppression of indigenous languages furnishes one good illustration of this impulse. Laura O'Connor claims that what she calls "print capitalism"—essentially the commercial publishing trade—"enhanced the cultural prestige of the [standardized English] language and helped to fix an image of an implicitly English 'literate speaker.'" But she notes that in providing such a paradigm for "self-improving Scots and others who endeavored to pass as fully Anglicized Britons" by "extinguishing cultural altereity" (2), the same print culture in fact ensured the survival of the vigorously nonstandard elements of the Highland literary tradition as part of an alternative Scottish national heritage. This indigenous culture is most apparent in idiomatic, vernacular writing (and even more so in the body of works wholly in Gaelic), but it informs a surprisingly large portion of the standard literature as well.

Its overt linguistic distinctiveness marks Scottish vernacular poetry as undeniably *different* from the formal idiom of the mainstream Anglo-Scots literary culture, even when it does not presume to stand entirely outside it. As Agnes Mure Mackenzie observes, "alongside the courtly, highly literate and often only too literary verse there runs a voluminous stream of 'folk' literature, of uncommon force and vigour for the most part, and some of it of extraordinary beauty" (33–34). Central to this vernacular tradition are distinctively *Scottish* tales, legends, myths, and characters, as well as familiar historical episodes, all of which call attention to their essential *Scottishness* not just through their content but also through their *form,* including the language in which they are cast. To this tradition belong earlier male poets like Allan Ramsey and especially Robert Fergusson, an Edinburgh poet equally at home in city and countryside who was blessed with a remarkable ear for poetic language and whose unnaturally short life deprived Scottish literature of the eighteenth century's most proficient vernacular male poet. It was, of course, Robert Burns who brought the vernacular tradition to its greatest prominence. At the same time, though, many Scottish poets wrote with equal facility in both idioms, as did Burns and Scott after him, choosing their idiom with their intended audiences in mind and in the process further underscoring both this literary indicator of national cultural difference and the relative access to formal education and to literate public readerships to which their work unmistakably points.

At the same time, however, a poet like Isabel Pagan, who possessed neither formal education nor a socially elite status, nevertheless could (and did) turn these seeming disadvantages to profit by embracing the "naturalness" of a folkloric idiom characterized by its ostensible orality. For, as Penny Fielding notes in connection with Scott's fiction, orality was widely identified as "a subversive social force" that is "frequently associated with the dangerously female" because of its ties to the irrational and the illegitimate (27). To adopt the vernacular, which signals its orality through the orthography of print as well as through the vehicle of sound, is to perform "outside" of conventional print-discourse writing and to embrace a "natural" idiom for which conventional language and typography offers no comparably natural equivalent. The point is not just linguistic: it is decidedly political within the context of contested culture(s) and nationhood(s).

In the "Account of the Author's Lifetime" that opens her volume, Pagan wrote:

> But a' the whole tract of my time,
> I found myself inclin'd to rhyme;
> When I see merry company,
> I sing a song with mirth and glee,
> And sometimes I the whisky pree,
> But 'deed its best to let it be.
> A' my faults I will not tell,
> I scarcely ken them a' mysel.   (6, ll. 13–20)

No one will mistake this for conventional poetic discourse, nor of course did Pagan intend anyone to.

The poem that immediately follows at once affirms the Highland vernacular tradition as context for her own efforts and states her claim to be reckoned a part of that tradition. The poem is called "On Burns and Ramsey," but it is in fact more about Pagan than either of those male predecessors:

> Now Burns and Ramsey both are dead,
> Although I cannot them succeed;

Yet here I'll try my natural skill,
And hope you will not take it ill.

You know their learning was not sma',
And mine is next to nane at a';
Theirs must be brighter far than mine,
Because I'm much on the decline.

I hope the public will excuse
What I have done here by the Muse;
As diff'rent men are of diff'rent minds,
My metre is of diff'rent kinds.   (6)

Here Pagan simultaneously joins and challenges the company represented by Burns and Ramsey, proposing that their respective works are simply *different* and that if their learning lends Burns and Ramsey an advantage of one sort, *her* advantage is that of "natural"—rather than learned or acquired—skill. It is not the library but nature that shapes and tunes her voice, she claims, implicitly privileging the raw folk-inflected productions of the "natural" domestic versifier over the studied works of the professional poet—even the professional poet working within the vernacular tradition. Maintaining the appearance of such naturalness of voice and vision—the spontaneous genius of the rural Miltons celebrated by many Romantic-era poets and critics—was central to the Romantic aesthetic, in which the juxtaposition of the often competing claims of vision and craft would long remain a central theme.

Eighteenth-century Anglo-Scots poetry frequently reflects the cultural ambivalence—indeed frequently a suspiciousness verging on xenophobia—of the many Scots who feared (not without reason) the threat posed to their cultural identity by a cosmopolitanism that they viewed with some alarm, even though Scotland (and especially Edinburgh) had long enjoyed a reputation as a *European* rather than merely a "Scottish" cultural center. Indeed, the cultural self-consciousness visible in much Scottish literature of the period may stem from what was widely regarded as an inherent competition between London and Edinburgh, the latter of which still functioned after the Act of Union as both a national capital and a provincial cultural center. This was a matter of real import for the new (or, perhaps more correctly, the renewed) Scottish nationalism that was itself an inevitable consequence of the Act of Union.[4] Evidence of this cultural unease is visible in the experience of many of the Scots who migrated south to London in the eighteenth century only to find themselves occupying the uncomfortable position of outsiders, even when they sought deliberately to assimilate with the English culture. A. M. Oliver remarks, for instance, that "their speech was not English, but it was close enough to it to irritate rather than to endear" (120). The explanation for this failure to fit, at least in the view of the essayist for the *Monthly Magazine* for 1797, appeared simple enough: "The chief defect in the Scottish literature of this period was, that the Scots had in general ceased to write their own peculiar dialect, of which they were now ashamed, but had not yet learned to write genuine idiomatic English."[5] Never particularly noted for tolerating cultural difference, the English denigrated and ostracized these would-be mainstream Augustans from the north, making them acutely self-conscious of the extent to which their hybrid idiom was no longer wholly Scottish nor yet entirely English. William Wordsworth, for example, in 1815 excoriated what he called the "insupportable slovenliness and neglect of syntax and grammar" in the work of Scottish writers like James Hogg and Scott, concluding that "neither of them write a language which has any pretension to be called English." As Ian Duncan remarks, Wordsworth's objections on the one hand reveal that he recognized (and resented) the commercial success of contemporary Scottish literature in the marketplace and on the other hand demonstrate his opinion that such nonstandard writing needed to be purged from the national literary canon "on the grounds of a national deficiency, a linguistic unfitness 'to be called English'" (1).[6] Wordsworth's xenophobia typified much of contemporary mainstream critical opinion.

In their effort to counteract the hostile and often resentful English attitudes and prejudices that confronted them, transplanted Scots in the south stuck together in loosely connected enclaves, whether their occupations were commercial, economic, military, intellectual, or literary. And because they were typically skilled at their occupations, they tended to thrive despite the obstacles, prospering in part because of their sheer hard work. As the same 1797 essayist put it with a flourish of hyperbole:

> The Scots began to apply themselves to almost every branch of literature and science, with an ardour and a success which were to awaken a new emulation in their neighbours of England, and to make the *Scottish* rank with the *Grecian,* the *Roman,* the *Italian,* and the *Gallic* names, in the estimation of all the votaries of either profound or elegant learning.[7]

By the century's end, there were sufficiently numerous well-educated, well-placed Scots within the British social, political, and intellectual infrastructure to ease the entry and advancement there of growing numbers of their countrymen, an increasingly sore point among the English natives who found themselves threatened or actually displaced in the emerging meritocracy.

Paradoxically, the Act of Union that had "invented" a new national identity under the banner of "Britain" promoted a rhetoric that served the interests of those who advocated Scottish nationalism while at the same time aiding those who sought to join the mainstream English culture, for, as Colley notes, the most successful transplants were able to "reconcile their Scottish past with their English present by the expedient of regarding themselves as British" (125). This process of cultural acclimatization and accommodation was reflected also in literature, where it seemed to many that Scottish poetry was moving away from the vernacular tradition and toward the ostensibly more "respectable" and "polite" idiom sanctioned by the mainstream English literary-critical establishment. By the time the first book of James Beattie's most famous poem, *The Minstrel; or, The Progress of Genius,* appeared in 1771, for instance, many Scots poets were becoming more comfortable with the mainstream English idiom and poetic forms—and even experimenting with them—and they were in the process abandoning the intellectual conservatism of didactic poetry for something new that would reach its first great flowering in the poetry of Walter Scott, which burst on the scene in 1802 with the first edition of his *Minstrelsy of the Scottish Border* and established itself firmly in 1805 with *The Lay of the Last Minstrel.* Here was a poetry that was decidedly "romantic" in nature: powerful, original writing that delighted in tale telling, in superstition and legend and that exuded a finely detailed sense of name, place, and time, a poetry in which a rich texture of the exotic is generated both through the geographically and culturally specific names of characters, settings, and incidents and through the comparative "wildness" of the narratives themselves. Indeed, as Scott and others soon realized, such poetry was in fact a *commodity* that could furnish for a buying public a lucrative market-ready, sentimentalized, nostalgic vision of a mythic "Scotland" that was more fictional than real. Later critics—and then still later postcolonial nationalists—would come to regard this as a betrayal of true Scottish culture (Duncan, 1–2), but at this early stage of Scotland's participation in the British imperial project it made sense, both economically and culturally.

Before taking up Scottish women's poetry in detail, I want to reflect briefly on the state of "Scottish poetry" as it appeared in the later eighteenth and earlier nineteenth centuries. Certainly the vernacular tradition, to which I have already alluded, represents one aspect of this poetry, especially when one goes beyond the surface level of the idiomatic language and into the distinct cultural heritage reflected in the poetry's subject matter itself. In what was for its time an important formulation despite its unfortunately impressionistic terminology, L. M. Watt proposed in 1912 that Scottish literature in general might be characterized by five distinctive features: romanticism, patriotism, love, humor, and nature. These "telling and original chords" of the Scottish literary tradition he attributed in various combination to Scots poets generally, noting that "great passions and pathos have welled out from all of them at sundry times and in divers manners" (18–19). Watt's formulation is in fact more helpful than its apparent fuzziness and its nearly century-old nature make it seem at first to be. By "romanticism," for instance, he means particularly the romance tradition, which extends back to Scotland's earliest Gaelic roots and that provides an important thread of cultural continuity in the form of a sort of "national tale" that runs through Scottish literature in all the genres. Running parallel to this "romanticism" is what Watt calls "patriotism"—what we may perhaps better understand to be that fierce Scottish nationalism that drives historical romances and lyric verse alike. This "patriotism" takes the form of an essentialist "Scottishness" that suffuses literary works that are staged in unmistakably Scottish physical, psychological, ideological, and intellectual settings and that reminds us repeatedly that these works are grounded in some specifically *Scottish* time, place, and culture. This feature is, for example, characteristic of Scott's best-known work, which is on the whole deeply patriotic (in Watt's sense of the word) without being merely jingoistic.

"Love" appears for Watt to involve not only the interpersonal romantic attachment one normally associates with the term but also a more broadly conceived filial bonding, a working out at the level of the family and the community of the passionate attachment that figures also in one's relation to her or his Scottish national identity. Interpersonal human love and love of Scotland—of both the nation and the land (and its peoples)—function almost as tropes of one another. Once again, Scott's immensely popular writing provides a good illustration of how this element permeates poems—and of course works of prose fiction—that are ostensibly devoted to other subjects altogether. "Nature," by extension, likewise involves the sense of a distinctively Scottish *place,* landscape, or setting (including internal setting), and of an equally distinctive and powerful relationship with that setting, that is fundamental to any specifically national cultural definition of literary works. "Humor," of course, takes many forms, from heady intellectual satire to broad physical comedy, and it operates at linguistic, intellectual, and dramatic levels. Moreover, as is the case with most humor that originates in or reflects the particular cultural experience of an indigenous minority or subaltern population, Scottish (and Irish) humor involves an element of cultural interiority (or "insiderness"). We are made to understand by this humor that both the Scottish characters represented in the literature and the knowledgeable subaltern readers of that literature somehow know more than do the cultural "outsiders" (including outsider readers) who appear naive, innocent, and vulnerable to all manner of pranks and deceptions both within the plots and at the level of the language itself. Benedict Anderson has defined "nation" loosely but usefully as "an imagined political community" (x). It is in precisely this fashion that Scottish nationalism defines the nation in the aftermath of the Act of Union, and Scottish literature (and other artifacts of culture from the most esoteric to the least) follows suit in promoting a subversive, oppositional stance by advertising both overtly and covertly its differences from "Englishness," sometimes even as it claims to be reducing, rejecting, or otherwise vitiating those differences.

Added to these distinguishing qualities would have to be also lyricism, which has always been regarded as a feature that enriches both the Anglo-Scots and the vernacular poetic traditions. Burns, Scott, and Hogg were of course superlative lyricists, whether they adopted the sentimental mode or a more vigorous—even contentious—one, and in Anglo-Scots and vernacular forms alike. But so, too were Anne Hunter (whose lyrics were, after all, set to music by Franz Joseph Haydn) and, in a very different vein indeed, Isabel Pagan. This lyricism figures significantly also in the ballads of women poets. Dorothea Primrose Campbell and the blind Christian Gray, for instance, both produced moving ballads on the subject of war's devastation on families, and the songs of Carolina Oliphant, Lady Nairne, were famous and widely admired even before their author's identity became known.[8]

A historical overview of Scottish women's writing reveals the validity of Dorothy McMillan's point about the remarkable *engagement* with issues both "public" and "domestic" that is evident in the work of Scottish women writers (including prose writers):

> The balance of interest between the public and private spheres is peculiarly female. Women almost always take an interest, even if not a part, in public life and they write about that interest, while at the same time they are almost always committed to creating stable environments in which the public figures may relax and develop more complete senses of self: women provide the fabric of social cohesion. (xiv)

Perhaps *because* of the gendered roles historically assigned them by the culture in which they lived and worked, the works of women writers exhibit a particular sensitivity to the relationship between the public and the private, the sociopolitical and the personal. Because so much of their individual and collective experience often depended on the stability and viability of the domestic sphere—on a "family" life, variously defined—women nearly always found themselves placed in positions of real jeopardy by a variety of real or implied threats to that domestic unit. The seemingly endless orgy of war making that dominated much of the Romantic era was of course the most conspicuous cause of the decimation of countless eighteenth- and nineteenth-century families whose male breadwinners were killed or incapacitated.

A more subtle but no less pernicious devastation began to occur during this same period, though, in the wake of the Industrial Revolution, which produced dramatic social and economic consequences for families whose limited social and economic circumstances made it impossible for them adequately to cope with the impact of large-scale industrialization on the workforce. Class warfare, no less than international warfare, was beginning to wreak its havoc on families throughout the nation. Of such variously configured histories of domestic tragedy Scottish literature—like that of Britain generally—provides numerous examples.

For all the progress that was made in the eighteenth century (on both sides of the border) toward achieving a united and assimilated nationhood, then, the history of Anglo-Scottish relations in the eighteenth and early nineteenth centuries nevertheless furnished numerous instances of disruption and devastation that were made even more poignant by the fact of their being played out within the British nation itself rather than as part of an international conflict like that with France or the American colonies. Mistrust, hostility, and outright violence had played a part in English-Scottish relations for centuries: the Jacobite risings fueled the widespread English hostility toward the Scots and for many on both sides exacerbated these sore relations rather than repairing them. English resentment of the Highlanders' march on Derby in 1745, for instance, was matched by Scottish outrage over the apparently genocidal aftermath of the Battle of Culloden in 1746. These political and cultural disruptions—and the tensions that underlie them—were played out as well within literature, a point that Donna Landry makes in connection with "the Scotch milkmaid," Janet Little, when she observes that in Little's texts "the cultural specificity of English imperialism is articulated with and against an emergent Scottish nationalism." A working-class poet herself, Little draws in her work, Landry argues, on "the critical power of the socially marginal, who remain exorbitant to established literary conventions, but within the discourse of Romanticism will become increasingly conventionalized figures of more or less explicit social protest" (*Muses of Resistance*, 236–37). In Little's poetry—and in that of many of her female contemporaries on both sides of the border—the woman, the woman writer's voice, and the woman writer's poetry functions both as signified and as signifier: as "text" and as sign. Their poems, like their lives, become sites for enacting struggles that are being conducted also on the broader stage of culture as a whole. At the ground level of language, we need to appreciate that whether a poet elects to write in Scottish vernacular or standardized formal English is an act that is at once aesthetic *and political,* no less so than is the choice of subject matter or ideological orientation. One is either working within a tradition or outside it, with or against what it represents and embodies.

Especially relevant in this context is Douglas Mack's observation that in the post-Culloden era "the need to adjust to the new British norms was likely to be most keenly felt by members of the Scottish elite who were closest to the British levers of Imperial power and wealth," while "the impulse to retain and sustain Scottish identity was likely to come most naturally to the poor and the dispossessed . . . with little direct access to the material rewards of Empire" (7). Issues of class are never far from center stage in the period's public discourse (including its literary discourse), in other words, any more than are issues of gender, and one's own "place" on this discursive field is itself frequently a contested one.

The ongoing cultural ambivalences generated by the intranational tensions that developed in Great Britain during the eighteenth century undoubtedly contributed to the characteristic hard edge of much of Scottish poetry—including women's poetry. This is a literature whose impulses are at once assimilationist and oppositional, a literature that copes with the appearance of forged cultural nationhood as a "United Kingdom" without neglecting the glories and the grievances of an independent Scotland that refuses to be erased and assimilated. This situation parallels in important ways that in which women have found themselves over the centuries as a dominant cultural and ideological establishment has pressed them to subject and submerge their independence, their voices, their names, *their selves* to the persons and the interests of others. This is one reason why Scottish literature of the Romantic period, like women's literature generally and like Scottish women's writing of that period in particular, so often discloses a powerfully subversive and oppositional character.

Scottish Women's Poetic Voices

The situation of Scottish women writers during the Romantic era was in some ways comparable to that of their English contemporaries to the south, but as should be apparent from the preceding discussion, there are important differences. As Douglas Gifford and Dorothy McMillan have observed, for instance, what is usually called the "Scottish tradition in literature" has customarily been understood to have been "both male generated and male fixated . . . in ways that are not true of English writing," in part because Scottish women poets have typically been represented not only as secondary to Scottish *male* poets but also, inexplicably, as the "junior literary sisters of English women writers" who were their predecessors and contemporaries (xix). Conventional rosters of Scottish poets of the period usually are populated largely or even exclusively by male authors; on those occasions when such lists have been expanded beyond the familiar luminaries, Robert Burns and Walter Scott, they tend to include one or more other men, like James Beattie, the Ossianic forger James MacPherson, Thomas Campbell, the "Ettrick Shepherd" James Hogg, and James Montgomery. When women poets have been mentioned, it has generally been within the context of some sort of subcategory that carries with it inevitable connotations of second-class status: writers of songs or lyrics (Lady Anne Barnard, Hunter, Oliphant/Nairne), working-class writers (Little), or vernacular poets (Pagan). Joanna Baillie, the sole exception, is usually discussed as a playwright and dramatic theorist and only incidentally as a poet. Seldom have any but the most specialized modern literary histories of the period paid serious and systematic attention to any of the dozens of Scottish women poets who were active at the time and whose work was often familiar to their male contemporaries.

This is not to say that the voices of Scottish women poets have always been ignored, however, for they do in fact figure in earlier literary histories and anthologies, especially those dating from the later nineteenth and earlier twentieth centuries. Like their English (and Irish and Welsh) counterparts, Scottish women poets were frequently recognized and credited in these accounts, but like them too that recognition often came in a bracketed and piecemeal fashion that misrepresented what was for many of them a substantial commitment to their poetry. Moreover, their literary efforts already stood at a double disadvantage within the dominant "British" national literary culture, as is clear from what Gifford and McMillan say about the ways in which those efforts have typically been devalued alongside the work of English women writers. Further still, to the strong cultural bias against a nonstandard idiom that plagued vernacular writers of both genders (as also did, for that matter, comparable biases involving class, race, and religion) were added other constraints concerning form, genre, and subject matter that related entirely to their gender.

Like much of the literary history of the British Isles that was written by the later Victorians and their twentieth-century male successors, that which focused on Scotland historically regarded male authors as the really "legitimate" ones: they were the artists whose careers were understood to have been largely or wholly invested in an art that was both "literary" and philosophical—"serious" poetry, in other words. Moreover, Romantic-era male poets of Scotland—not just Burns and Scott but also the colloquialist Andrew Scott, the classicist John Leyden, the prolific Thomas Campbell, the "Ettrick Shepherd" James Hogg, and the long-suffering James Montgomery—have virtually from the start been discussed in terms of sizable and articulated bodies of published work: whole-cloth records of individual personal and poetic experience that take account of what inspired them, what their composition methods were, where and what they published, and what their reputations were. Indeed, even so recently as 1993 a scholarly book by Peter Murphy bearing the impressive title of *Poetry as an Occupation and an Art in Britain, 1760–1830,* could discuss MacPherson, Burns, Hogg, Scott, and William Wordsworth at length and yet not even *mention* any of their female contemporaries for whom poetry was without question both an occupation and an art. Male poets are understood, in other words, to have had writing *careers:* they were *professionals.*

Scottish women poets of the Romantic period have historically fared differently. Their accomplishments have been recorded, for the most part, in those rhetorical terms traditionally reserved for work that is *tolerated* rather than encouraged, *accepted* rather than rewarded, and *noted* rather than praised. The rhetoric of the criticism that proceeds from such thoroughly gendered intellectual and cultural assumptions consistently minimizes women's accomplishments by presenting them as both exceptions and as curiosities, as brief forays into what is implied to be a virtually exclusively male arena. If they harbored hopes of garnering praise for their poetic accomplishments, women poets were expected to stick to subjects and sentiments deemed culturally appropriate for them. This meant, for the most part, devotional verse (including poetic paraphrases of scripture), moral essays in verse, elegiac verses on the demise of public figures and (perhaps more commonly) domestic relatives and acquaintances. It also meant poetry intended for children and for other "unsophisticated" or "uneducated" and therefore presumably "inferior" readers who were understood to be "beneath" male poets' more exalted voice and regard. Finally, it also meant lyrical verse, whether sentimental or colloquial, and then as now lyric verse was widely regarded as a distinctively "minor" form.[9] This designation also applied to the ballad form, and it is in that area that the achievements of Scottish women poets have traditionally been most widely celebrated, as is evident from the longstanding reputations of poets like Barnard and Oliphant. Catherine Kerrigan has suggested, for example, that "women played such a significant role as tradition bearers and transmitters that it can be claimed that the ballad tradition is one of the most readily identifiable areas of literary performance by women" (2), a point that was in fact frequently acknowledged by poets like Burns, Scott, and Hogg, all of whom credited women as prime sources (though often in an oral rather than a written tradition) for their own material.[10]

But narrative poetry was not without its detractors, either. Writing in 1822 about the poetry of Byron, Wordsworth, and Scott, for instance, one critic suggested that narrative poetry (of which ballads form a major part) had by that date become little more than "a mere apology for digressions—a peg to hang dissertations and description on." Implying that the verse narrative as a genre afforded its practitioners fewer opportunities for virtuoso performances, he observed that "all these authors are men of genius, but they know it too well, and will not trust their reputation to works, the worth of which would seem to the vulgar more owing to the materials than the artist. . . . This peculiar bias in the mind of our poets is a sufficient damper to any hopes of a revival of the ballad style of writing."[11] Perhaps these remarks reflect the extent to which the novel had by 1822 begun to supersede the verse narrative as a vehicle for tale telling. British narrative poetry had in fact begun to assume quite a different form after the early 1820s, in the work of prolific women poets like Felicia Hemans and Letitia Elizabeth Landon, whose poetry signaled a new direction in later Romantic poetry. It was not so much that poets disdained the ballad narrative as a vehicle for poetic virtuosity: they had simply moved on to newer and more challenging vehicles for their productions.

For most of the twentieth century, the traditional literary-historical perspective on Scottish women poets and their work stressed the moral and intellectual chastity of their verse. This was important to J. H. Millar, for example, who observed in 1903 that Lady Anne Barnard and "her sister muses" tended in their poems on the whole to follow "the orthodox or Scottish mode of taking some rude, fragmentary, and not over-decent old Scots song or ballad, cleansing it of its impurities, making it coherent, arraying it in decent apparel, and rendering it fit for decent society. In some cases the result savoured of emasculation. In others, and perhaps the majority, the lyric was all the better for the process" (399). What is particularly interesting about Millar's dated and patently gendered rhetoric is how it situates women poets firmly within the sphere of culturally determined domestic duties: their treatment of their poetic raw material involves cleaning, organizing, clothing, "teaching," and otherwise "civilizing" it so as to suit it to "decent society." Millar's terminology tellingly reiterates the roles traditionally associated in post-Enlightenment Western culture with the recessive, nurturant, and wholly domesticated woman who in Victorian culture becomes Coventry Patmore's famous "angel in the house," a role that implicitly situates her (and her art) in a position subservient to and in service to—rather than in partnership or competition with—her male counterparts (and their art and cultural production). Indeed, the only negative in Millar's comments is reserved for what his pointedly gendered language implies is a significant fault in their work: "emasculation" of the thoroughly male originary Scots material.

Like the passage quoted above, another of Millar's observations reveals more than its author intended a century ago: "Poetical composition, it should be added, was by no means confined to the male sex, and many women, from Earls' daughters to alehouse keepers, it is said, engaged in the pastime" (398). In suggesting that "*it is said*" that women of all ranks composed poetry, Millar implies that the actual documentary evidence does not exist (even though it does) and that the record of women's voices is therefore mere hearsay—rumor—a variety of nonliterary communication that is culturally stigmatized as the unreliable discourse of gossips, who are of course routinely figured as women. The word "pastime" likewise subtly devalues their work, situating it both apart from and decidedly beneath that of male poets, whom Millar elsewhere describes as engaged not in pastimes but rather in professions or careers.

Pseudocritical statements of this sort diminish women's poetry further still by representing it in terms of isolated bits rather than as aesthetic, intellectual, or cultural wholes belonging to a coherent fabric of intertextual literary discourse. Millar credits the prolific Joanna Baillie, for example, with having "contributed to the common stock [of Scottish verse] *The Weary Pund of Tow, Tam o' the Lin,* and *Saw ye Johnny Comin',*" as if the rest of her poetry were a thing wholly apart and not worth mentioning. Likewise, Millar's equivocating language manages to deprecate even as it purports to celebrate the famous "Auld Robin Gray" of Lady Anne Barnard when he calls that poem "probably the most popular (Burns's work apart) of the sentimental ditties with which Scots poetry abounds" (399).[12] Nor was Millar alone in this sort of manipulative critical assessment. His contemporary, L. M. Watt, has this to say about Anne Hunter:

> There is no doubt that, had it not been for the fact that Michael [sic] Haydn had set some of her songs to music, the name of Mrs. Hunter, whose husband was the celebrated surgeon, would have long since found absolute oblivion. But one, at least, of them ["My Mother Bids Me Bind My Hair"], and for the very reason urged, is still familiar. (354)

Although such condescending representations of female artists have long since grown both tiresome and offensive, their rhetorical stratagems nevertheless bear consideration here because they are still present (albeit less blatant) in contemporary discourse. Anne Hunter (who is not lent the dignity of being called by her own Christian name) is placed in the reflecting light of two men, her "celebrated" husband and the famous composer (whom Watt did not bother to notice was *not* Michael Haydn but rather his elder brother Franz Joseph) who set some of her songs to music. More offensive still is Watt's frankly nasty opinion that it is only Haydn's musical setting, and not any inherent aesthetic accomplishment in the poem, that saves Hunter's song from the "absolute oblivion" he implies it would otherwise merit.

Of course, part of the difficulty with such dated but nevertheless influential comments lies in the fact that the early twentieth century was neither especially receptive to, nor appreciative of, the poetry of Romanticism in any case, whether by that expression we mean either the traditional canonical authors only or the broader

literary landscape the term refers to today. Thus Millar spoke for many of his contemporaries when he said of Scottish poetry of the Romantic period generally that
"there was much cry, but very little wool" (562). Nor has the general estimate proven
to be substantially better, at least in some quarters, in more recent times, if we are to
judge from the unenthusiastic comments of scholars like D. A. Low, who as recently
as 1993 assured us that the nineteenth century "was not a good century for Scottish poets," perhaps because what he called Scotland's inability (or unwillingness)
to "offer adequate professional stimulus or outlets to all of her able writers" meant
that in the poetry that did appear "strong originality was lacking" (193). Nor was
the situation much better for the reputation of women writers. In *Scottish Poetry:
A Critical Survey* (1955), for example, Robert Dewar recalls Baillie only in terms of
"Saw Ye Johnie Comin'" and "Woo'd and Married an' a'," and Lady Anne Barnard
(once again) in terms of "Auld Robin Gray"—and all these poems he mentions *in a
single sentence* about vernacular poets who were Burns's contemporaries (208). Even
the popular and prolific Scottish celebrant of the Jacobites, Carolina Oliphant, the
Baroness Nairne, emerges in Dewar's formulation as "a sort of feminine Burns *at
best*" (my emphasis) who participated in the aforementioned "cleansing" activities
associated with women poets by joining with other female contemporaries in a
plan to produce a bowdlerized edition of Burns's songs (208–9). Indeed, this "critical survey" of Scottish poetry places all the women poets of the Romantic era in a
clearly subsidiary relation to Burns by characterizing those individual poems that are
singled out for praise as especially good examples of vernacular poems "in Burns's
manner" (208). Moreover, the exclusion of Isabel Pagan testifies to the additional
element of class discrimination that colors the judgments of Dewar and others.

Interestingly, though, one extensive anthology of Scottish poetry published near
the end of the nineteenth century gave Lady Nairne her poetic due with a critical
generosity that seems to have vanished a decade or so later. Introducing a selection
of her poems, the editor, George Eyre-Todd, used the poetic "yardstick" of Robert
Burns in a rhetorically different fashion, writing that

> with a genius which was equally at home in the pathetic, the humorous, and
> the patriotic, Carolina Oliphant remains not only the sweetest and most famous
> singer of the lost Jacobite cause, but far and away the greatest of all Scottish lyric
> poets of her sex, and in two of her pieces, . . . ["The Land o' the Leal" and "The
> Laird o' Cockpen"], it does not appear extravagant to say, she is not surpassed even
> by Burns himself. (2:295)

But this sort of fair-minded assessment of women's poetry proved to be increasingly
the exception rather than the rule, and what generosity there was in nineteenth-

century literary commentary diminished rapidly in the twentieth century. It is not surprising, then, that wholly overlooked in the 1955 *Scottish Poetry: A Critical Survey* are once-familiar poets like Anne Grant ("Mrs Grant of Laggan") and Anne Bannerman. Absent, too, are colorful poets like the remarkable, dissolute, illiterate whiskey smuggler and private alehouse keeper Isabel ("Tibbie") Pagan, many of whose poems were dictated to an amanuensis, the tailor William Gemmell, who transcribed them and who presumably also tempered their reputedly characteristic bawdiness before having them printed in Glasgow in 1803.[13]

It remained for fairly recent scholarship—especially the work that has appeared in the wake of feminist theory and the far-reaching literary and cultural reassessments it has prompted—to begin in earnest the recovery of the poetry of Scottish women. Catherine Kerrigan's *Anthology of Scottish Women Poets* (1991), for example, collects the work of over a hundred poets encompassing some six centuries of Anglophone and Gaelic verse. The long historical and cultural view provided by Kerrigan's anthology reveals both the striking diversity of Scottish women's poetry (and the voices contained therein) and the remarkable continuity of the literary tradition they represent, a tradition that ranges from conventional devout Christian moralism (including copious numbers of hymns or volumes like Mary McMorine's *Poems, Chiefly on Religious Subjects* [1799]) to rollicking bawdiness (Pagan's poems, for example), from sentimental lyric verse like Anne Hunter's to socially and politically committed poetry like that of the earlier Jean Adam, the precursor to the Romantics whose publication in 1743 of her *Miscellany Poems* did not prevent her eventual destitution and death in a Glasgow poorhouse but whose works set the stage for a poetry of proletarian realism that would emerge by the end of the nineteenth century in the work of poets like Dorothea Maria Ogilvy.

Kerrigan concludes the brief introduction to her anthology by indicating how her own project fits within the larger scheme of the recovery of women's poetic voices:

> My purpose in producing this work was to provide a starting, not a finishing, point for the very real challenge that awaits those who are committed to the reclamation of women's literature. . . . [T]hat literature is not only a strong and vital part of a national tradition, it also belongs to the universal past of women's history and, at last, to our more promising future. (10)

Informed by a comparable sense of the urgency of this challenge, I turn in the remainder of this chapter to the poetry of several significant representatives of the large and diverse body of poetry published by Scottish women during the Romantic period. In limiting my discussion to a relatively few authors I hope to provide, like

Kerrigan, "a starting, not a finishing, point," suggesting some ways further discussion of additional poets might usefully proceed.

Voices, Language, and Genre

I have already introduced Isabel Pagan's poetry into this discussion more than once, and I want to return to her work now in greater detail for several reasons, the chief of which has to do with matters of language and idiom on which I focus in this section of the chapter. Pagan offers an excellent example of a poet whose work exists in a sort of borderland area of literary history. For one thing, her ambiguous reputation illustrates the impact of class on critical opinion. Pagan is considered to be a lower-class poet, although her class status was a matter first of circumstance and then of choice rather than one of birth. Born into a "well-connected family," she was apparently abandoned by that family before she was fourteen and left to fend for herself, which she eventually did by running an alehouse near Muirkirk in Ayrshire after she was abandoned for a second time, this time by her fiancé on the eve of their marriage. Nevertheless, Pagan lived to the surprising age of eighty despite these domestic reversals, her physical disability (a lameness owing to physical deformity), and her notoriously dissolute lifestyle.[14] Living first in a hovel and later in a postindustrial structure, and gaining a reputation for drunkenness, promiscuity, and irreverence to social, political, and religious institutions did not prevent her from acquiring a wide reputation for her witty and satirical songs. Like the remarkable Ipswich-area "itinerant poet" James Chambers who was her approximate contemporary, she was as famous for her poetic improvisations as for the shabbiness of her appearance and surroundings. Like Chambers, too, she became a regional celebrity who was widely remembered in print by friends and acquaintances following her death and her very well-attended funeral.

The social and economic circumstances that forced Pagan to exist on the margins of "polite" society no doubt contributed to the satirical bent of her poems, which celebrate her customers and patrons at the same time that they subject them to satire's sharp instruments. Pagan's establishment was a favorite haunt of well-to-do hunters who assembled in Ayrshire, for grouse hunting in August in particular, and she names many of them in poems like "A Hunting Song" and "The Putting Begins," albeit ostensibly shielding their identities by the familiar practice of substituting dashes for some of their names' letters. The latter poem is tagged with the notation that it follows the tune of the popular song "Bright Phoebus," and its four-line verses alternate with a five-line chorus that is stated in full only at the end of the first stanza:

Now the putting begins, if the weather holds clear,
I hope C— ng — n will shortly come here,
With dogs and attendants the muirfowl to try,
I wish they catch many that they be not shy.
Haste away, haste away, haste away,
It is far more for pleasure than gain;
May friendship and bravery,
And freedom from slavery,
Their Honours maintain.   (5, ll. 1–9)

The designation of the song's tune, the marginal notation for the recurrent chorus, and the interesting scansion (which juxtaposes a regular four-line ballad stanza with an irregular five-line chorus) mark this obviously as a song. That it *is* a song further contributes to Pagan's poetic borderland status, for traditional literary history has never been entirely certain of how to evaluate "songs," whether they be high-art productions or folk materials of the sort that were popularized in England by Bishop Thomas Percy's *Reliques of Ancient Poetry* (1765) and in Ireland by Charlotte Brooke's *Reliques of Irish Poetry* (1789).

Interestingly, in poems like this one Pagan finds ways to bring together matters of biographical interest (the names of particular individuals), Scottish linguistic localisms ("putting" as a term both for pushing and shoving and for hunting, "muirfowl" for the local red grouse), and broader social concern ("freedom from slavery," which may be read in terms of personal independence but also in terms of the contemporary debate over the slave trade) in ways that lend the poems a surprisingly sharp temporality. At the same time, Pagan works her own circumstances into the poem's conclusion in a way that makes her both a member of the happy company and a self-conscious outsider:

I wish that my judgment could clearly express
These gentlemen's bravery, I can do no less;
They're humorous and humble in every degree,
And every man's honour is humility.

                      Haste away, &c.

My name is Pagan, I liv'd at Muir-hill,
My learning's so weak, how can I speak with skill?
But yet I take pleasure these verses to sing,
Success to the hunting, and God save the King.

                      Haste away, &c.   (7, ll. 45–54)

It is a poetry of surprising artistry and immediacy, rendered the more so by the particularity of the imagery and language Pagan employs. These are the poetic materials and techniques characteristic of the Highland Scots tradition, and Pagan acknowledges this Highland heritage in one of her songs, intended to be sung to the familiar tune of "Campbells is Coming":

> Lieutenant C — n I have seen,
> I think he is a decent man;
> I give this song a Highland tune,
> They are an ancient Highland clan.   (16, ll. 13–16)

It is important to note how Pagan's verse, its ostensibly humble and ephemeral nature notwithstanding, participates in the national dialogue on politics, nationhood, and the economy. "A New Song," for example, is clearly in touch with the fears of invasion that swept the nation both before and after the Peace of Amiens, but it is equally sharp sighted about how civil and government corruption contributes to the war's effects:

> The French is in force now,
> Our country to invade,
> And to conquer Britain,
> Great attempts have made.
> But I hope our noble heroes,
> Will pull the usurpers down,
> Success to King George,
> Long may he wear the crown.
>
> . . . .
>
> There's disputes at parliament,
> And bribery at home,
> Such conduct as this
> Makes the war still go on.
> But if truth would bear the sway,
> And make deceit to cease,
> It still might be hoped
> There soon might be peace.   (75, ll. 1–8, 17–24)

Bare boned and oversimplified these verses may seem, but sung as Pagan stipulates to the tune of "Lord Cornwallis" they achieve some of the same surprising effects that Mary Robinson and the unidentified "F. A. C." accomplished in the satirical political verse considered in earlier chapters.

A comparable directness is visible in "The Spinning Wheel," a poem that reflects Pagan's sharp sense of issues of class and gender. In this lively poem grounded in the quotidian experience of a woman (and therefore also of women), Pagan juxtaposes her own personal situation—her modest but comfortable circumstances ("my small occupation"), which the spinning wheel identifies as specifically female—with the world that is controlled by "most *men* of fashion" (my emphasis):

For when around me I do look,
And see the merchants dealing,
For they do triple profit take
For every thing they're selling;
For honesty is grown so weak,
It is so old a fashion,
'Tis not regarded in our day,
'Tis scarce throughout the nation.

Kind Providence sent a good crop
For to support our nation,
But Satan's crew sent it abroad,
Which is a sad vexation,
That e'er such blackguard vagabonds
Should have a habitation
Below our British government,
That takes this occupation.   (13–14, ll. 33–48)

Notably, in poems like this one, Pagan largely drops the colloquialisms that we find in her other verse, suggesting that, like Burns, she could shift idiom when the occasion—and the intended audience—called for doing so.

The relative unwillingness to employ a distinctively Scots idiom typifies the work of most of the Scottish women poets, no doubt as a consequence of the overall domination of the Scottish literary scene by the "English" cultural establishment. A good example of this pressure is supplied by Janet Little, "the Scotch milkmaid," whose popular title might have led readers to expect a homey and colloquial idiom in keeping with her occupation and its implied relation to the tradition of peasant poets like Stephen Duck, Mary Collier, and of course Burns. Yet in her 1792 *Poems* the reader does not encounter anything like a Scots voice until more than a hundred pages into the book, in "Given to a Lady Who Asked Me to Write a Poem." There Little offers her own brief history of poetry and the post-Johnsonian prospect of a democracy of poets in which "ilka dunce maun hae a pen, / To write in uncouth rhymes" as does "[a] ploughman chiel, Rab Burns his name," who "[p]retends to write: an' thinks nae shame / To souse his sonnets on the court" (113–15, ll. 18–23). Like Pagan, she uses the male poets to underscore her own more remarkable efforts:

> But what is more surprising still,
> A milkmaid must tak up her quill;
> An' she will write, shame fa' the rabble!
> That think to please wi' ilka bawble.   (114, ll. 27–30)

Significantly, Little notes that "Burns, I'm tauld, can write wi' ease, / An' a' denominations please" even while imparting "a usefu' lesson to the heart" (115, ll. 35–38), and she observes further that Burns generally escapes critical censure ("Nor dare the critics blame his quill" [115, l. 42]). For her own work, however, Little foresees a grimmer fate at the unsmiling critic's hand so that "[m]y hand still trembles when I write" (116, l. 62). This closing line, with its implied anxiety about publishing, strikes an interesting and certainly very self-aware tone, given that it comes at almost the numerical center of a volume that numbers just over two hundred pages. Indeed, as Donna Landry remarks, "the poet's hand may tremble, but she has not stopped writing" ("Janet Little," [8]). Like Burns, Little melds her Scots idiom with the mainstream idiom in ways that prevent her being read either as wholly Scottish or wholly English, even at the cost of occasional semantic awkwardness like that which is visible in the passages cited above, where phrases like "ilka dunce maun hae a pen" collide with words like "denominations" and "impart." This balancing act is ultimately as much political as it is linguistic, and it is grounded in that national and cultural ambivalence discussed earlier and with which Burns (and the Irishman Thomas Moore) had to wrestle in positioning their works for their various audiences.

Indeed, Burns's shadow seems to fall everywhere in the literary culture of Scottish poetry, especially in the earlier part of the Romantic period. His ability to move with relative ease between the very different cultural contexts—and the very different audiences—suggested by his vernacular poems, on the one hand, and his more conventional English ones, on the other, reflects the realities of the publishing industry. Leith Davis has explained that "the literati of Edinburgh" took the lead in creating in Burns a representative of the common man and the unspoiled rustic world of nature. This meant that Burns, who was viewed as "a more up-to-date and less suspect natural bard than Ossian," had to be perceived by his public as "untutored, unlearned, and unaffected by present-day cares," as a poet whose works could be presented to both the Scottish and the wider "British" audiences as the productions of "innocuous peaceful peasants" (124). Burns played along with this game, of course, for it was profitable to do so. As Jonathan Wordsworth has observed, "the idiom he creates, for an English public and with English sources in mind, could be assimilated without the pastiche implied in copying the broader Scottish poems" ([vi]). But the hybridization of rustic bard and national poet did not come without its liabilities. The editor of the *Edinburgh Review,* Francis Jeffrey, for instance, worried about the consequences of associating the national poet with the lower classes, and so he called for dissociating Burns from a potentially disadvantageous class identification (for Scotland as well as for Burns) and for judging him instead purely on his aesthetic merits. Davis explains that Jeffrey's tactic served a double purpose: he was able to imply that since Burns was such a man of the people, then what was remarkable was "not that Burns became famous, but that the rest of his community did not" (124). Jeffrey's argument ought to remind us of Wordsworth's definition of the poet as "a man speaking to other men," a leveling statement whose clear implication is that *all* men are at least potentially poets.

Nevertheless, the issue of language and idiom was a vexing one for writers and critics alike, for it forced them to confront the disjunction between the "standard" ("king's") English that was the ostensible national tongue and the variant dictions, dialects, and vernacular particularities that identified (in what was generally regarded as an unfavorable light) various cultural, linguistic, and economic subsets of that nation. The often class-inflected intolerance of linguistic variance was already firmly entrenched by the later eighteenth century, when, as William Stafford has demonstrated in *Socialism, Radicalism, and Nostalgia,* in order to be taken seriously in formal public discourse (as in petitioning Parliament, for example) one had to be able to write and to speak correctly in standard English. In fact, Scottish literature of this period exhibits a persistent ambivalence about idiom that parallels the Scottish people's larger questions during this period about their status as *Scots* with a distinctive cultural identity and heritage and as Britons who were now part of a "larger" national structure that discouraged the retention of particularizing characteristics. Writing in the last quarter of the century, James Beattie took pains to instruct his fellow Scots on ways in which they could purge their discourse of the identifiable "Scotticisms" that he felt tended to hold them back within the context of national (i. e., "British") discourse.[15] The full title of Beattie's book illustrates the point: *Scotticisms, Arranged in Alphabetical Order, Designed to Correct Improprieties of Speech and Writing.*

This matter of idiom was naturally a concern for women poets no less than for their male counterparts. The appropriately named Elizabeth Scot addresses it directly in the first poem of her posthumous 1801 *Alonzo and Cora,* "Scotia's Address to Her Sister Anglia." The opening lines nod to conventional hierarchies of gender and of nation:

Hail, happy Sister! great in arts and arms,
In manly valour and in female charms;
Whose classic sons the noblest honours claim,
And shine unrivall'd on the list of fame:
Say, wilt thou deign to mark these humble lays,
And kindly pardon, if thou can'st not praise?
Behold! my timid daughter blushing stands;
Her gift she proffers, but with trembling hands.
In antique garb has SCOTIA's Muse too long
Disguis'd the sweetness of her native song:
Ev'n where her work the seal of genius bears,
The phrase uncouth disgusts your nicer ears.   (1, ll. 1–12)

As visual artists had long done, Scot tropes both Scotland and England as female
(as Irish women poets also frequently do with Ireland as Hibernia) and invokes a
standard of female decorum in requesting that England accept the gift of "my timid
daughter" (Scot) in the spirit in which it is given, forgiving if she cannot praise.
Presumably the "antique garb" refers to the Scottish idiom that has served as an unprofitable disguise for natural beauty that "disgusts" England's "nicer ears." Interestingly, in her poem Scot names only three notable Scottish poets, all male—William
Hamilton, John Home, and Beattie—while suggesting that she could name others.
But not women—at least not so far:

More might I add, who seek the Muses' fane
With equal powers, and equal honours gain.
Such are my sons; no daughter yet of mine
Had dar'd to court the favour of the Nine,
While ENGLAND's fair distinguish'd honour grace,
And high in Fame's bright temple claim a place . . .

. . . .

Your votary rose; and, warm with generous flame,
Strove to secure the meed of honest fame;
To follow where your daughters lead the way,
Last of the train, and listen to their lay:
Her harsher lines attune from their smooth strain;
From their full wreaths one humble sprig obtain;
From dark oblivion's gulf her name to save;
Adorn her life, and dignify her grave.   (2–3, ll. 29–34, 39–46)

This "votary" is of course Scot herself, who seeks to tune her "harsher lines" to the standard set by the work of those *English* women poets who have already attained "honour" and repute. The self-deprecation represented in the "one humble sprig" of laurel Scot hopes to attain is a familiar rhetorical device, but it is important to note that in this case Scot very clearly identifies the troublesome deficiency as one of language—of "phrase uncouth"—rather than of ability or of vision.

The daughter of well-placed parents (her father, David Rutherford, was "Counsellor at Edinburgh") who had a country mansion, Scot was well educated in languages and belles lettres; her mentor was Allan Ramsey, and she corresponded with Burns (some of their verse correspondence appears at the end of *Alonzo and Cora*) and with Helen Maria Williams (preface, *Alonzo and Cora,* xv–xvii). Her poetry illustrates her interest in classical themes: "Leander and Hero; Imitated from Musæus," for example, reveals her knowledge both of Ovid and of the literary tradition of elegiac verse cast in elevated rhetoric. Her rueful comment that no Scottish *woman* poet had yet attained a fame comparable to that of her female English counterparts reflects her sense of the inferiority of vernacular verse, for while predecessors like Lady Grizel Baillie, Lady Elizabeth Wardlaw, Scot's aunt Alison Rutherford Cockburn, and Jean Elliot were well known, it was for just such vernacular verse and not for more esoteric poetry.

Although critical response to *Alonzo and Cora* was mixed, most critics—perhaps because the poet had been dead for more than a decade when the volume appeared—at least approached the work with a generous spirit. The *Monthly Review,* however, was less kind, observing acidly that while "we can entertain no doubt that Mrs. Scot was an interesting object to her friends . . . the virtues of domestic life do not constitute the merit of a writer; and the slight verses now brought before the Public would have been more respectably stationed, had they still dwelt in a private bureau."[16] This critic misses a crucial point, however, for while Scot's poetry is faulted repeatedly on account of what it is *not,* it receives little credit for what it *is.* What it is is, in fact, a relatively sophisticated and effectively detailed poetry that reflects its diverse and often learned literary heritage while exploring new and often unexpected opportunities offered by its subject matter. Poems like "The Deserted Mansion" examine contemporary social themes like the inhospitable character of nature and human society, while *Alonzo and Cora* participates in a complex intertextual conversation with other works. The poem draws on Jean-François Marmontel's 1777 novel, *Les Incas,* which novel had also informed Helen Maria Williams's *Peru: A Poem in Six Cantos* (1784). More than the mere sentimental tale some critics took it for, *Alonzo and Cora* is an insightful examination of psychological and sexual desire between two exotic adventurers in a foreign land. Often lushly detailed despite its being cast in Augustan rhymed couplets, the poem contains extended passages of sensually heightened particulars that strike a modern reader as quite extraordinary.

At a considerable stylistic and substantive distance from Scot's poetry is that of Anne Bannerman, whose poems tend to be absent from many of the standard anthologies of British women poets like Paula Feldman's *British Women Poets of the Romantic Era* (1997) and Duncan Wu's *Romantic Women Poets* (1997) as well as from those devoted exclusively to Scottish poets like Catherine Kerrigan's *Anthology of Scottish Women Poets* (1991). Perhaps this owes in part to Bannerman's decision not to follow the national ballad style that Scott popularized in his *Minstrelsy of the Scottish Border* but to emulate in her verse instead the sensationalistic gothic formulae we associate with writers like Matthew ("Monk") Lewis, a feature of her verse that Andrew Elfenbein has examined especially in terms of lesbianism and same-sex relationships.[17] Although her first volume, *Poems* (1800), was relatively conventional and was received politely, her subsequent *Tales of Superstition and Chivalry* (1802) met with general disapproval among the professional critics despite the favorable comments by no less an advocate than Scott himself.[18] The 1800 collection reveals Bannerman's debts to female contemporaries like Charlotte Smith (there are twenty-eight sonnets, including some explicitly linked to Petrarch and to Goethe's *Sorrows of Young Werther*, just as in Smith's *Elegiac Sonnets*) and Joanna Baillie, whom she praises in her poems. But with the *Tales* of 1802 Bannerman shifted her approach, deliberately emulating both the subject matter and the rhetoric of the male gothic writers and in the process invoking the modern "literary" ballad form that, as noted earlier, balances precariously between the spheres of traditional oral literature and formally printed verse. Bannerman's title unmistakably echoes that of Lewis's 1801 versified *Tales of Wonder*,[19] which had notoriously exploited gothic sensationalism to the point of parody. Moreover, like her contemporary, "Charlotte Dacre" (Charlotte King Byrne, also known as "Rosa Matilda"), Bannerman ventured in this collection into the treacherous territory of the sensational and sexually charged gothic scene that was widely considered to be taboo for women writers. Not surprisingly, Bannerman's decision proved costly; her attempts to support herself through writing—her new subscription edition of her poems in 1807, for example—were insufficient and she had to resort to becoming a governess, eventually dying in poverty. Despite her modest circumstances, Bannerman was at least for a time an intimate of "the most influential literary circle in Edinburgh," where she associated with the likes of Scott, Richard Heber, Thomas Percy (editor of *Reliques of Ancient Poetry*), Thomas Park, and John Leyden (Craciun, "Romantic Spinstrelsy," 217–19). This association seems to have produced few tangible results for her, though, and her failure in this respect provides further evidence of the extent to which any Romantic-era author's fortunes—and especially those of a woman author—were tied to a network of patronage and influence that could circumvent the ordinary demands involved in publishing for profit—*if* that network of patrons chose to intervene in an author's behalf.

The poems in the 1802 *Tales* are, according to Adriana Craciun, almost impossibly self-aware in their studied "literariness" ("Romantic Spinstrelsy," 217–19). They reveal Bannerman's familiarity not only with some of the genre's most prominent male authors and their works but also with the conventions of this genre of deliberately archaic and ambiguous tales. Indeed, the first poem, "The Dark Ladie," directly responds to the fragment that Coleridge had published in the *Morning Post* on 21 December 1799 under the title of "Introduction to the Ballad of the Dark Ladie," and which he subsequently revised for inclusion in the 1800 *Lyrical Ballads* under the title of "Love."[20] Bannerman's choice of title implicitly situates her poem within an intertextual conversation in print; to have been a witness to this conversation, the contemporary reader must have been familiar with Coleridge's poem—which had appeared both in the daily press *and,* in different dress, in book form—and with the contemporary faux-antique ballad form that had by 1802 passed from being all the rage to something that struck the literary (and reading) establishment as increasingly decadent. The poem revels in the exaggerated pathos typical of the genre, as for instance when Bannerman describes (in the words of the tale's unreliable internal narrator) the fate of the unfortunate adulteress, the "Dark Ladie," after she fled her home with her sinister tempter, Sir Guyon, in the conclusion of the poem:

"He told me that, at last, he heard
Some story, how this poor Ladie
Had left, alas! her husband's home
With this dread knight to flee:

"And how her sinking heart recoil'd,
And how her throbbing bosom beat,
And how sensation almost left
Her cold convulsed feet:

"And how she clasp'd her little son,
Before she tore herself away;
And how she turn'd again to bless
The cradle where he lay.

"But where Sir Guyon took her then,
Ah! none could ever hear or know,
Or, why, beneath that long black veil,
Her wild eyes sparkle so.

"Or whence those deep unearthly tones,
That human bosom never own'd;
Or why, it cannot be remov'd,
That folded veil that sweeps the ground?"   (14–16, ll. 141–60)

The passage is of a piece with Lewis's *Tales of Wonder* no less than with Coleridge's *Morning Post* ballad and his *Rime of the Ancient Mariner,* while both the superstitious and clearly unreliable narrator and the poem's open-ended and ambivalent conclusion recall Wordsworth's "The Thorn" in particular. A poem like this one and those that accompany it play on a popular craving for the titillation that accompanies any indulgence in the taboo. In employing the familiar ploy of appending to her poems a set of seemingly scholarly endnotes, Bannerman does no more (and no less) than her contemporaries were doing to insulate themselves as authors from the content of the tales their narrators tell. And this too demonstrates the extent to which Bannerman understood—or thought she understood—the dynamic of the market for such poetry. Her miscalculation and the irreversible decline in her literary fortunes it precipitated only demonstrate all the more poignantly how fragile was the lot of the woman poet who sought to participate in the broader literary culture.

Two other poets, Dorothea Primrose Campbell and Margaret Chalmers, both more obscure than Bannerman, further reveal the diversity of Scottish women's poetry. Campbell, who spent her early life in the Shetland Islands and corresponded with Walter Scott (to whom she dedicated the expanded 1816 edition of her *Poems,* which had first appeared in 1811), suffered through a lifetime of financial disasters, to which her introduction alludes when she states that she has published in "the hope of alleviating the many deep distresses" ([v]) that have followed the death of her father and the family's consequent destitution. Campbell's narrative poems, many of which are cast in ballad forms, reify familiar Scottish legends, including pagan ones, with remarkable vitality—and even carnality. Campbell frames this indigenous subject matter for her readers immediately, in a footnote to the 1816 collection's first poem, "The Sprits of the Hill," where she writes that "[t]he Inhabitants of Zetland suppose their hills to be haunted by certain fantastical beings, whom they denominate Bokies, and Fairy-folk, or Fairies: the former of whom are imagined to be spirits of Evil, and the latter spirits of Good" (1). Folkloric subject matter of this sort recurs also in Irish women's poetry of the period, as we shall see in the next chapter. In poems like "Retribution; or, The Hall of St. Garvin" (a pseudogothic ballad fantasy) and "Agnes and the Water-Sprite" (a pathetic tale of an innocent young woman abducted by a malevolent water spirit who drags her to a watery grave) Campbell evidently revels in the machinery of gothic sentimentalism, but in others, like the moving "To an Old Musical Instrument," with which the volume concludes, she affectingly reflects on the passing of the familiar ethos of late eighteenth-century melancholy.

Margaret Chalmers, who was also born in the Shetland Islands, published her *Poems* in 1813, alluding in her preface, like Campbell, to the economic necessity that has driven her to publish. But Chalmers, who sets herself up as something of an unofficial poet laureate of the Shetlands with poems like "Ode for the Morning of the British Jubilee, 1809," "Congratulatory Lines on the Jubilee, Humbly Addressed to His Majesty," and "Verses on the Death of the Princess Amelia," invites a broader audience whose interest might be awakened by the "novelty" of her subject matter at the same time that she nevertheless stresses the particularly *Scottish* nature of her subject matter ([v]). Indeed, in a shrewd maneuver to disarm potential critics, she pleads her case on nationalistic grounds in "The Author's Address to the Critics":

Since Scandinavia rul'd our Isles,
We ne'er have woo'd the muses' smiles;
    Yet own their power
Oft wheels away, in rapid course,
    The wint'ry hour.

Now in the pure Castalian rill
Dips the first British Thulian quill
    To fame addrest;
In slumber lull'd, the poet's art
    Long lay supprest.   (12, ll. 6–15)

The muses' wheeling course suggests both woman's domestic sphere and the tradition of spinner and weaver poets in the British Isles. Continuing, Chalmers cautions her would-be critics against stifling her own voice, which she implies would be equivalent to suppressing Scotland's voice:

Oh ! meliorate your dread awards
    With lenity.

And think, that in our clime so chill,
The spark borne from the muses' hill,

Fanning requires;
Then do not, with a rigid frown,
 Blow out its fires.

In quenching this my feeble gleam,
You may repress a brighter beam
 And loftier lay;
I rest content to Helicon
 To *point* the way.

If on my simple strains you smile,
Some poet from our northern Isle,
 In future day,
More skilfully may touch the lyre,
 And gain the bay. (13, ll. 19–35)

Chalmers's appeal for critical "lenity" is typical of many of the now obscure poets who wrote and published both away from the customary centers of literary activity and in the midst of those centers. What is less typical is the clarity with which she perceives how the literary and cultural status of an entire national entity may be inextricably linked to the fortunes of even a single author. The fate of the many may, in Chalmers's formulation, depend on the fate of the one, especially in circumstances like those in Scotland (and in Ireland and Wales) where the dominant English cultural establishment was already well launched on the inexorable processes by which a dominant culture subsumes and largely erases subaltern cultures, however unique and irreplaceable they may be. This lesson is, of course, also readily applicable to the fate of the woman poet in a literary field that was still populated primarily by men.

Joanna Baillie and the Poetry of the Larger World

No one questions, today, Joanna Baillie's preeminent position as a Romantic-era dramatist. In a period during which all the canonical male poets (and no small number of their less celebrated male contemporaries) tried their hand at drama, Baillie is now acknowledged to have been of signal importance to the genre, both for her plays themselves—though, with the occasional exception of the best known, *De-Montfort,* they are seldom performed today—and for her "Introductory Discourse" to her 1798 *Series of Plays.* But it was as a poet that Baillie first published, in 1790, and unlike the majority of women poets with whom she was contemporary she did so anonymously, as she did again in 1798 when her plays began to appear in print. I want to conclude this chapter with Baillie because her work represents one viable solution to the difficult questions concerning national, cultural, and aesthetic identity that I have explored in this chapter. For Baillie was herself "an expatriate Scot" who had moved to London in the 1780s and who was for most of the remainder of her life a permanent resident of Hampstead (Bardsley, 139–40). Still, she was widely celebrated for her songs and ballads, most of which bear explicit evidence of their strong Scottishness, both in their idiom and in their subject matter, just as she was known for the cosmopolitan appeal of plays that were staged in Europe and North America. In a real sense, Baillie proves to be an "international" poet in ways that show how and why an author might—and did—surmount the difficulties attendant on being identified as a "regional" writer. Both her poetry and, especially, her dramatic works "forge a link between abstract and concrete, universal and particular" to combine the more localized identity of "Scotland" with the larger and more abstract idea of "Britain" (Bardsley, 147). The poems in her 1790 *Poems* mediate between the distinctive Scottishness of their materials and a broader, universalized human experience, while later poems like her extraordinary "Lines to a Teapot" reveal a sophisticated poet capable of successfully engaging issues of economy, commerce, and empire on a global scale within the context of an ostensibly domestic subject. "Lines to a Teapot" appeared in Baillie's 1840 collection, *Fugitive Verses,* which included among its pages all the poems that had appeared in the 1790 volume. She also published *Metrical Legends of Exalted Characters* (1821), a collection of very polished verse, and, late in her life, *Ahalya Baee: A Poem* (1849), a tale of the Indian queen who watches her sons lose their lives in service of the endless warmaking that supports the patriarchal establishment.

In her introduction to Baillie in her *British Women Poets of the Romantic Era* Paula Feldman points out the considerable debt of Wordsworth (and Coleridge) to Baillie that is evident in their *Lyrical Ballads* of 1798, including the fact that Wordsworth "silently borrowed" from her "Introductory Discourse" when he composed the preface to the 1800 second edition of *Lyrical Ballads* (22). Baillie's work was in fact widely known among Romantic-era writers throughout the period; Byron, for example, worked to have her plays staged at Drury Lane, while a broad spectrum of male and female authors, famous and not, demonstrated their knowledge of her poetry and plays both in their private correspondence (and journals) and in their published works. That she published anonymously may have reflected the hope that she might defuse gender bias among potential readers, perhaps a common tactic at the time for first-time authors whether male or female. At the same time, though, the fact that Baillie's first volume of poetry was published by the well-established and well-connected Joseph Johnson suggests both that she was part of a dynamic and interactive community of writers who knew one another and that she was well aware that in publishing her first book of poetry with Johnson (as Wordsworth did in 1793 with *An Evening Walk*) she was gaining access to a diverse and liberally inclined audience. In other words, she demonstrated early on that she understood literature was in a sense a commodity in a public marketplace.

Moreover, even her earliest poems reveal Baillie's remarkable self-awareness as a writer and as a woman. In "An Address to the Muses," for instance, after tracing the careers of both the already great and the unknown aspiring poets and their debts to their muses, Baillie turns to her own situation:

O lovely sisters! well it shews
How wide and far your bounty flows:
Then why from me withhold your beams?
Unvisited of heav'nly dreams,
Whene'er I aim at heights sublime,
Still downward am I call'd to seek some stubborn rhyme.

No hasty lightning breaks the gloom,
Nor flashing thoughts unsought for come,
Nor fancies wake in time of need;
I labour much with little speed;
And when my studied task is done,
Too well, alas! I mark it for my own.

Yet should you never smile on me,
And rugged still my verses be;
Unpleasing to the tuneful train,
Who only prize a flowing strain;
And still the learned scorn my lays,
I'll lift my heart to you, and sing your praise.   (77, ll. 67–84)

It is hard not to smile at this effective self-deprecation; any writer who struggles to find the right word, anyone who reads with despair what she or he has just written in what had seemed a burst of inspiration and eloquence, will recognize the fundamental reality of what Baillie says here. At the same time, though, Baillie's poem is also "delightfully defiant" (as Paula Backscheider puts it [399]) in its effective depiction of poetry's power to animate its readers despite any individual poet's apparent disadvantages. The unflagging commitment to the notion that one has to keep trying would have struck a responsive chord among many of the era's women poets. Moreover, that element of familiarity—which is grounded in the absolutely authentic psychological realities her poems trace—is one of the hallmarks of Baillie's poetry.

Baillie's anonymous 1790 volume gives early evidence of her profound interest in human behavior as it is affected by various states of mind (or "passions," to use the language of her "Introductory Discourse"). This lifelong interest in human psychology is apparent in the long full title of Baillie's volume: *Poems; Wherein It Is Attempted to Describe Certain Views of Nature and of Rustic Manners; and also, to Point Out, in Some Instances, the Different Influence Which the Same Circumstances Produce on Different Characters.* Most obviously, one series of poems presents in turn the "melancholy lover" (82–85), the "cheerful tempered lover" (86–89), the "proud lover" (90–92), and the "poet, or sound-hearted lover" (93–96). Interestingly, it is the *poet* whom Baillie designates as the "sound-hearted" one. In 1790, amid the general popular rage for Smith's *Elegiac Sonnets* and their pervasive melancholy, it would have been easy (and even customary) to identify the poet especially with melancholy. That she chose to do otherwise tells us something about how Baillie saw herself, of course, but also about how she saw the figure of the poet, something that is borne out further by the volume's first two poems.

Poems opens with the paired poems "A Winter Day" and "A Summer Day." These lively and finely imaged poems reveal Baillie's keen eye for the kind of details that effectively epitomize complex human and natural phenomena, recalling the poetic realism we find in some of William Cowper's poetry, or in George Crabbe's more dour poems. Like many poems with which they are roughly contemporary, the poems unfold the events of a single day, setting them in a carefully particularized locale that nevertheless images Scotland in general. "A Winter Day" begins with the cock's "unwelcome call" that announces the new day to

[t]he lab'ring hind, who on his bed of straw,
Beneath his home-made coverings, coarse, but warm,
Lock'd in the kindly arms of her who spun them,
Dreams of the gain that next year's crop should bring.   (1, ll. 7–10)

Baillie's lovely detail of the peasant pair asleep in one another's arms establishes an intimacy that embraces both the human and the nonhuman players in this rustic drama, all of whom pursue their domestic routines in a landscape that is harsh but neither cruel nor unforgiving. This is simply how it is, Baillie implies without being judgmental. And as the day draws toward its close, when the work is done, the family begins to reassemble for the homey pursuits of the candlelit evening, which includes a visit from the "rev'rend form" of the old war veteran, one of "those who have serv'd their country" (10–11, ll. 186, 194) and who now roams the countryside "with feeble body, bending o'er a staff" (189) (like Wordsworth's Old Cumberland Beggar, whose echoes of this figure are unmistakable). Invited in from the cold by the peasant's wife, "the stranger whines not with a piteous tale, / But only asks a little, to relieve / A poor old soldier's wants" (11, ll. 204–6). Warming himself by the friendly fire, the traditional emblem of sociability and natural love, he entertains the children until his mood alters and his face "lays off its smiles":

> His thoughtful mind is turn'd on other days,
> When his own boys were wont to play around him,
> Who now lie distant from their native land
> In honourable, but untimely graves.
> He feels how helpless and forlorn he is,
> And bitter tears gush from his dim-worn eyes.   (12, ll. 217–22)

Now the peasant himself returns and, seeing the old veteran with pleasure, invites him to stay to share their humble meal, after which neighbors arrive to join the hospitality, "widen[ing] out the circle" while "every one, in his own native way, / Does what he can to cheer the merry group" (13, ll. 242–45), including the old veteran, whose "tales of war and blood" (15, l. 271) may not "cheer" the group although they sober them.

The poem's conclusion is masterful in its realism. After the social group disperses and the household retires for the night, only the peasant remains:

> But long accustom'd to observe the weather,
> The labourer cannot lay him down in peace
> Till he has look'd to mark what bodes the night.
> He turns the heavy door, thrusts out his head,
> Sees wreathes of snow heap'd up on ev'ry side,
> And black and grumly all above his head,
> Save when a red gleam shoots along the waste
> To make the gloomy night more terrible.
> Loud blows the northern blast—
> He hears it hollow grumbling from afar,
> Then, gath'ring strength, roll on with doubl'd might,
> And break in dreadful bellowings o'er his head;
> Like pithless saplings bend the vexed trees,
> And their wide branches crack. He shuts the door,
> And, thankful for the roof that covers him,
> Hies him to bed.   (16, ll. 282–97)

Anyone familiar with the ways of "country folk" will recognize the stark authenticity of this conclusion and the keen insight it reveals about the ways in which such people habitually think and behave.

"A Summer Day," which follows, is equally insightful about the ways of the countryside and its residents. Again, the poem traces the day's events with a delightful particularity, right down to the image of the "idle horse upon the grassy field [that] / Rolls on his back, nor heeds the tempting clover" (21, ll. 72–73). This summer day, whose longer hours of sunlight make it seem so much longer than its wintry counterpart, witnesses the same round of social life, including the community's cheerful and respectful response to the presence of the itinerant old man who "sits upon his seat of turf, / His staff with crooked head laid by his side" (29, ll. 219–20):

> No stranger passes him without regard;
> And ev'ry neighbour stops to wish him well,
> And ask him his opinion of the weather.
> They fret not at the length of his remarks
> Upon the various seasons he remembers;
> For well he knows the many divers signs
> Which do foretell high winds, or rain, or drought,
> Or ought that may affect the rising crop.
> The silken clad, who courtly breeding boast,
> Their own discourse still sweetest to their ears,
> May grumble at the old man's lengthen'd story,
> But here it is not so.   (29, ll. 228–40)

As in "A Winter Day," Baillie skillfully embeds in her poem her pointed social commentary on issues of class, in this case contrasting the behavior of the "cultivated" boors of courtly society with the natural gentility of the poem's rural characters. It is a trait that we find in many of her poems, notably, in her later "Lines to a Teapot."

When the day's outdoor work ends and supper is readying, "cheerful groups at every door conven'd / Bawl cross the narrow lane the parish news" as children play and the wandering peddler appears to entice young and old with his seductive wares (30–31, ll. 245–46). But the poem's final glimpse is not of the peasant, as in "A Winter Day," but rather of the "lover skulking in the neighb'ring copse" who at this late hour

> [c]urses the owl, whose loud ill-omen'd scream,
> With ceaseless spite, robs from his wakeful ear

The well known footsteps of his darling maid;
And fretful, chases from his face the night-fly,
Who buzzing round his head doth often skim,
With flutt'ring wing, across his glowing cheek. . . .   (32–33, ll. 293, 297–302)

Carefully rendered details of this sort lend authenticity and credibility to Baillie's observations, not just on the scene but also on the psychological states and behaviors of her characters.

It hardly needs stating that Baillie's *Poems,* published in 1790, are remarkable precursors of Wordsworth's poems in *Lyrical Ballads.* Baillie's fine details anticipate, for instance, one of the most remarkable details in Wordsworth: his description in "The Old Cumberland Beggar" of what the grotesquely double-bent beggar sees in the dusty roadway: "some straw, / Some scattered leaf, or marks which, in one track, / The nails of cart or chariot-wheel have left / Impressed on the white road" (*William Wordsworth: The Poems,* 1:264, ll. 54–57). We do not normally associate with Wordsworth such careful sensory detail as the marks left by the nails in a wheel rim, but here as elsewhere he seems to have learned from Baillie: one thinks of the way he unfolds the tales in "Michael," "Resolution and Independence," and "The Ruined Cottage," to name only three. Moreover, the careful intertwining of social commentary with the tales (and words) of rural characters in these poems of Wordsworth is likewise reminiscent both of *Lyrical Ballads* and of poems of the 1790s by other authors (like Mary Robinson) who were similarly interested in displaying to a reading public the personal dignity and moral purity of characters who had for generations served more as sources of humor and ridicule than as exemplary individuals in literary works intended for readers of "higher" classes. Within the broad community of Romantic-era writers of her time, Baillie's influence was considerable and enduring. Indeed, as Paula Feldman reminds us, D. M. Moir (the Scots critic and regular contributor to *Blackwood's Magazine,* David Macbeth Moir) made precisely this point in 1851, the year of Baillie's death, when he wrote that the "new code of poetry" associated with Wordsworth and Coleridge in *Lyrical Ballads* was not significantly different from the principles advanced by Baillie, and that therefore "it must be admitted, from published proof," that Baillie had in fact "forestalled—or at least divided—the claim to originality indoctrinated in the theory and practice of Wordsworth."[21]

I want to conclude with a poem that reveals the extent to which all these interrelated intellectual, cultural, moral, and thematic elements continued to characterize Baillie's poetry throughout her life. Her *Fugitive Verses,* which did not appear until 1840, gathered verses from across her writing career, including the poems from the

1790 volume. Taking as its point of departure a simple utilitarian object, "Lines to a Teapot" is a witty and incisive meditation on the decline of manners and breeding in an age of empire and the commoditization of culture. Written probably no later than 1829,[22] the poem postdates the lifetimes of the familiar "second generation" male poets and the most productive years of others, including Coleridge, and it comes in the middle years of the careers of Hemans and Landon, both of whom Baillie outlived. Although its metaphorical relationship to Keats's "Ode on a Grecian Urn" is clear, the poem belongs to an extensive genre of poems, dating back through the eighteenth century, that take domestic objects as their subjects. Needless to say, such poems are characteristic productions of women poets. But Baillie takes her poem far beyond the conventional celebrations of these homey objects, and she does so in what is undoubtedly a deliberate conversation with the poem by Keats, her late Hampstead neighbor.[23]

Briefly, the poem traces the history of a ceramic Chinese teapot, from its creation and decoration by Chinese artisans, through its transportation to Europe as "trade goods" and its initial functional history as the centerpiece of the social rituals of tea, and on to what appears to be its fate in the new materialistic world, where it is being handled by would-be bidders at a collectors' auction. Unlike Keats's urn, the "cold pastoral" that is the enigmatic object of the dispassionate gaze of admirers in what is apparently a museum environment, Baillie's teapot is a functional artifact that initially serves a domestic function within an insistently social, convivial setting where it is *warm*(ed) by the hot tea it contains, by the handling of the woman who pours from it, and by the "warmth" of the social company over whose activities she presides. Each poem gives us some of its subject's history, but Keats stresses his urn's unresolvable riddles (Who are these people? What are they doing? Why?) while Baillie emphasizes what is both known and knowable.

Both vessels depict social activities that reflect the cultures in which they originated. But unlike Keats, when it comes to describing the "fair subject of my rhymes," the "goodly vessel of the olden times" (162, ll. 25–26), Baillie adopts a familiar rather than a formal idiom. Like Keats, she insists that her readers "see" her subject, but she expects us to see the teapot both as an object of decorative art and as a utilitarian object. Moreover, she invites us to envision the scene of the teapot's creation, where the potter surrounded by enthusiastic children is followed by the painter, "slow and patient" (163, l. 38), who decorates the pot. Having been shipped, close packed on some merchant ship, to England, the teapot is auctioned (for the first time) to a company of well-dressed society women who "contend in rival keenness for thy charms" (164, l. 54). Baillie's shrewd description of this transit and public sale metaphorically recalls the conditions of slavery, a subject that had long been of concern to British women who continued to take part in public antislavery activism. Amelia Opie's contemporaneous antislavery poems, *The Negro Boy's Tale, a Poem* (1824) and *The Black Man's Lament; or, How to Make Sugar* (1826), for instance, document this ongoing activism among women poets.

Turning to the formal rituals of the tea table, Baillie describes how the teapot and the woman who pours the tea seem to become one, the woman's gracefully extended and curved arm seeming to become an extension of the pot's own shape (165, ll. 73–74). But the scenes of conviviality come to an unhappy end:

> But now the honours of thy course are past,
> For what of earthly happiness may last!
> Although in modern drawing-room, a board
> May fragrant tea from menial hands afford,
> Which, poured in dull obscurity hath been,
> From pot of vulgar ware, in nook unseen,
> And pass in hasty rounds our eyes before,
> Thou in thy graceful state are seen no more.
> And what the changeful fleeting crowd, who sip
> The unhonoured beverage with contemptuous lip,
> Enjoy amidst the tangled, giddy maze,
> Their languid eye—their listless air betrays.
> What though at times we see a youthful fair
> By white clothed board her watery drug prepare,
> At further corner of a noisy room,
> Where only casual stragglers deign to come,
> Like tavern's busy bar-maid; still I say,
> The honours of thy course are passed away.   (166, ll. 93–110)

Here is the contemporary scene, its vulgar modern crowd having replaced the earlier generation's genteel salon set and their uncultured modern sensibilities having polluted at once the teatime and the public culture as a whole. Hence the teapot is relegated to a corner, where it is served not by the "fair" mistress of the scene but instead by a menial servant who is compared unflatteringly to a mere "bar-maid" in service to a languid, listless crowd that populates the "tangled, giddy maze" that has in turn replaced the gracious and orderly salon.

The final verse paragraph details the teapot's crowning indignity. Unlike Keats's Grecian urn, which stands in the center of the imagination's cool museum space, gazed on (but not touched) by aesthetic connoisseurs, the teapot is subjected to the rapacious gaze of a very different breed of "connoisseurs" (Baillie's word) who "thy parts inspect, / And by grave rules approve thee or reject" (167, ll. 112–16). These figurative anatomists are in fact collectors, not connoisseurs, and they are guided by the market value of the teapot as a commodity rather than by the aesthetic value of the Grecian urn as a work of fine art as are the connoisseurs in Keats's poem. In Baillie's poem, "all the bliss which china charms afford, / My lady now has ceded to her lord" (167, ll. 117–18), yielding the ludicrous spectacle of the *man* as the materialistic proprietor of a china collection that has been acquired for its monetary value (presumably as an *economic* investment) rather than for its social value. Ironically, Baillie's teapot will finish out its days in a way that is distinctly *like* Keats's urn: as a sort of museum piece to be gazed at rather than actually used:

> And now on shelf
> Of china closet placed, a cheerless elf,
> Like moody statesman in his rural den,
> From power dismissed—like prosperous citizen,
> From shop or change set free—untoward bliss!
> Thou rest'st in most ignoble uselessness.   (167, ll. 123–28)

More than simply the history of a teapot, "Lines to a Teapot" is a commentary on the decline of modern British imperial culture, an increasingly scathing portrait of the crass materialism that was rapidly accelerating in the new industrial age. Such was the cost of "progress," and Baillie was but one of many who lamented the consequences for the nation and for "civilization" (in the sense of "civility") of that questionable phenomenon. The elegant eighteenth-century aristocratic culture gives way to the emerging vulgarity of the Victorian bourgeoisie; what is lost is not just a way of life but, more importantly, the refined taste and aesthetic discrimination that mark the cultured, civilized society. This is but one price of imperialism. It would be twenty-five years before Dickens's *Hard Times* would appear, but already in this poem we glimpse the brutally unattractive world of the Josiah Bounderbys of empire, and we see, too, the shadows cast on the future by the increasingly desperate working classes whom Dickens would epitomize most starkly in that same novel's tragic figure of Stephen Blackpool.

Moreover, Baillie's poem opens a window on the different ways that the sphere of literary (and cultural) production were defined along gender lines. Keats's "Ode on a Grecian Urn" represents a masculinist definition that privileges a connoisseurship predicated on sophisticated learning (to comprehend classical and technical allusions), linguistic skill (to appreciate subtle wordplay), and financial resources (to acquire and to possess art objects and to enjoy them within private or semiprivate museums or private collections), and of course the class status that permits one to indulge in all of this. The female paradigm, on the other hand, is characterized by more immediately "public" or "domestic" features, by its grounding in the quotidian world, and by its consequently greater accessibility to a broader audience whose exposure to formal learning and the other aspects of male privilege was far less extensive. Both Keats's ode and Baillie's poem comprise statements about aesthetics and the function of art in society. But whereas the urn is valued for qualities that relate to an intellectualized and generally dispassionate male connoisseurship, the teapot's value is grounded in its physical function within a companionate and essentially feminine social activity. The urn is to be beheld; the teapot is to be *held*. This explains why when at the poem's end the teapot is held and examined by men the tone is largely satirical, in keeping with the ludicrous reversal of roles and values the description conveys.

Baillie represents only one aspect of the literary scene traced by the Romantic era's Scottish women poets. But her longevity and her continued production, taken together with her prominent presence within the British literary landscape—in 1853, two years after her death, Frederic Rowton called her "in many respects the most remarkable of our Female Poets" (287)—testify to the central position occupied in that landscape by women writers, including those from Scotland. Their work constitutes an alternatively inflected Romantic poetic that foregrounds the "difference" produced by their Scottishness in ways that "English" women poets seldom felt any need to do, they being after all the "elder sisters" in the poetic sisterhood. That Scottish women poets like Elizabeth Scot commented explicitly on this relationship of national identities and that they did so to the (for them at least) acknowledged disadvantage of the Scots tells us much about how dominant and subaltern cultures assign to one another (and to themselves) the roles that they often perpetuate to their mutual detriment. That representatives of the subaltern culture feel called upon to genuflect to the supposedly superior standard set by the dominant (or colonizing) culture tells us, too, a good deal about how those standards have historically been built into the ideologies and institutions of the colonizing culture—built in to such an extent that the colonized culture(s) on whom they are imposed come at last to accept them as somehow "natural" and permanent rather than as artificial and therefore temporary. This is one reason why so much of the discourse of early Romanticism in particular is so preoccupied with definitions (both theoretical and applied, or "working," ones) of "nature" and of what is "natural." The word recurs endlessly, as noun, as adjective, and as adverb, and in variant forms also as verb in the period's writing. And while literary and cultural history have often "romanticized" the concept of nature in terms of a sort of pristine primitivism, an edenic and unpolluted mortal state of being, even a poem like Baillie's "Lines to a Teapot" warn us ominously that what is truly natural may very well be truly bestial. That is always the danger of congratulating ourselves on how far we have come, how much we know, how much better we are than those who have preceded us and those whom we have conquered, converted, or assimilated. We should bear this in mind, as the poets did, when we consider how Scottish women poets, like their contemporaries in Ireland who are the subject of the next chapter, took up the image of a sisterhood of poets—and of nations—and reformulated that image by replacing the hierarchical model with the egalitarian one that struck them as so much more "natural."

CHAPTER SIX

Irish Women Poets

Irish Literature and the Romantic Context

Much of what I observed in chapter 5 about the circumstances surrounding the lives, works, and reputations of Scottish women poets is relevant also to their Irish contemporaries. But there are important differences, too, that stem not only from geographical and cultural otherness but also from deeply rooted and passionately held convictions about religion and national identity. Ireland is, after all, an island and not a contiguous landmass, and in the later eighteenth century it was an island of almost exclusively Catholic citizens who were governed by an almost exclusively Protestant power structure. These deep divisions were invoked, on one side of the divide, to justify cultural opposition among the Catholic Irish (especially among the peasantry and working classes, and most tragically in the abortive Rising of 1798) to the hegemony of the colonizing English. On the other side, they were invoked to help justify the unconscionable exploitation of the Irish land and people (and their brutal suppression in 1798) by the wealthy Protestant English colonizers who regarded the native Irish in the essentially subhuman terms that are evident in the ubiquitous English stereotypes of the rustic Paddy.[1] Although the Jacobite conflict in the middle of the eighteenth century bore dramatic consequences for Scotland and for Scottish nationalism, the end result was for the most part a movement toward cultural and economic assimilation with the mainstream "British" society, a movement that promised cultural, social, and economic profit for both parties. The same could not be said of the relationship between England and Ireland, however, the Act of Union of 1800 notwithstanding.[2] The brutal exploitation of the native Irish increased exponentially in the wake of the act, which the ruling English took as license for what was widely perceived—then and now—as state-sanctioned plunder. The Rising of 1798 complicated matters infinitely, for it was a rebellion not about succession but rather about survival. That the rival factions were goaded not just by competing national identities but also by complex economic circumstances and by violent religious prejudices only made matters worse. And while Scotland prospered, on the whole, in the wake of its own inclusion after the Act of Union of 1707, Ireland's situation worsened steadily, culminating in the terrible effects of depopulation wrought in the 1840s by the Great Hunger and by the wholesale emigration of native Irish. It is against the backdrop of these very different political, economic, literary, and cultural differences that we need to assess Irish poetry of the period.

Until recently, mainstream literary scholarship has customarily lumped together Irish and Scottish (and Welsh) literatures under the undiscriminating banner of "British" literature and then, most often, ignored those works—and their distinctive national components—or dismissed them as "minor" or "regional" variants of the more or less standardized "British" literature defined by the works of canonical English writers. But such hierarchical nomenclature largely fails to take account of the historical and cultural record. Stuart Curran pointed out some time ago, for example, that Romanticism in culture and the arts developed in Europe and North America along national lines, and that this development reflected among the various countries "the distinct exigencies of national culture" (*Poetic Form,* 209). More recently, Claire Connolly has made the point that even as Irish Romantic literature of the period participated in the broader thematic and stylistic developments of European Romanticism, it both reflected on and relished its singular differences from the amalgamated mainstream "British" literary culture: "Ireland emerged from this period with a renovated reputation as a naturally distinct national culture; this in turn fostered and supported new theories of nationality and nourished the cultural nationalism of the 1830s and 1840s" (408). Just as Scott popularized among contemporary readers a literary and cultural Scottishness whose elements he carefully manipulated in poetry and prose alike, so did Thomas Moore manipulate the readerly consciousness in his long-running *Irish Melodies,* creating for his readers a sentimentalized but nevertheless sympathetic and engaging portrait of a national culture that was for the most part alien to Moore's predominantly English readers. More important, Sydney Owenson (who would become Lady Morgan) played a crucial role in creating an idealized view of a "romantic" Ireland, first in *The Wild Irish Girl* (1806) and then in her *Lay of an Irish Harp* (1807) and *Patriotic Sketches of Ireland* (also 1807). These three works not only generated both interest in, and a measure of sympathetic response to, Ireland among an English readership but also infused new passion into a reviving Irish nationalism that carried through subsequent writers like the poet Anna Liddiard and on into the Young Ireland writers of the 1840s and the Rebellion of 1848.

In chapter 5 I examined in some detail the poetry of a limited number of authors within the broad cultural and historical circumstances of Scotland's relationship to England and British culture. In this chapter I take a more horizontal view of the literary scene in Ireland, ranging over a larger number of poets but necessarily doing so in proportionally less detail. It was probably inevitable, given their status both as women and as Irish writers, that the poets I consider in this chapter would suffer a double erasure, despite the considerable number of them who were active during the Romantic period.[3] Like their Scottish counterparts, Irish women poets have routinely been neglected, just as Irish literature has historically been isolated (or insulated) from "British" literature (although less so since the advent of the modern period marked roughly by Yeats's birth in 1865). Indeed, conventional accounts of Irish writing imply that women wrote little before the rise of the Young Ireland movement associated with Daniel O'Connell's campaign for repeal of the 1800 Act of Union and the subsequent establishment in 1842 of the repeal-oriented propagandist organ the *Nation,* under the direction of Charles Gavan Duffy and Thomas Davis. Even then, according to Mary O'Dowd, "women usually remained in the background of the [Irish nationalist] movement and continued to express their political views through verse rather than prose" (12). When it comes to poetry published by women during the Romantic era, only Mary Tighe's 1805 *Psyche; or, The Legend of Love* has attained anything like canonical status, and that only recently, while Sydney Owenson is remembered not for her poetry but for popular novels like *The Wild Irish Girl.* The era's women writers cannot be accommodated within gendered and exclusionary paradigms like that within with which Robert Hogan, in the *Dictionary of Irish Literature,* describes Irish writers in general. "There are perhaps two types of Irish writer," Hogan observes. "There is the serious or affirmative *Man* with a cause . . . [and] the frivolous or negative *man* Disillusioned with Causes" (1:11–12; my emphases). This masculinist bias pervades the *Dictionary;* among its more than fourteen hundred pages, as Ann Owens Weekes notes, only Mary Balfour, Mary Leadbeater, Lady Morgan, Mary O'Brien (who gets *one line*), and Mary Tighe are mentioned as poets of the Romantic era (18).[4]

Compounding the problem is the familiar practice of defining "British" Romanticism almost exclusively in terms of "English" writers, which creates a one-dimensional (and often paradoxically provincial) portrait that ignores the era's frequently contested cultural diversity. Indeed, after 1800 Ireland's dilemma was painfully evident in the fused kingdom's bifurcated full title, "the United Kingdom of Great Britain and Ireland," a nonsyncretic identity that rendered the Irish "neither Irish nor English," as Patrick O'Farrell puts it (17). Ina Ferris has observed that Romantic-era Irish fiction reflects the uncertainty and fearfulness that typified this cultural borderland in which Irish writers (like Irish citizens) felt that their incomplete incorporation into British culture (to which they were reminded in various ways that they did not really "belong") deprived them also of their Irishness. Consequently that fiction often manifests a nationalistic, oppositional rhetorical stance that resists the expectations of English Anglophone readers while reminding Irish readers of what has been lost in the imperfect process of union. The point is equally relevant to Irish poetry.

Nor, of course, could Irish women writers escape other gendered assumptions and expectations. Weekes and others have pointed out that until fairly recently Irish women writers were routinely evaluated according to criteria historically devised by—and applied to—male writers. Such evaluations typically proceeded without regard for the implications of gender on (1) the substance or content of their writing, (2) the manner in which that substance was embodied in the text (both form and style), and (3) the often different ways in which male and female readers engaged literary texts. The era's frequent derogatory artistic and literary images of the Irish and the many anti-Catholic stereotypes furnish representative examples of these forces. They help to explain why although Mary Tighe is now recognized as an Irish Romantic poet and the poetry of Sydney Owenson and Mary Leadbeater is now familiar to at least a limited few, that is about the limit. The poetry of spirited nationalists like Henrietta Battier, Hannah Morison, and Mary Balfour and loyalist Tories like Jane Elizabeth Moore, Eliza Ryan, and Frances O'Neill is only now being reassessed, as are the antiwar poems of Anna Liddiard, the nostalgic (but patently nationalist) "harp of Erin" poems of Mary St. John and Mary Balfour, the witty verses of Catharine Quigley, and the earnestly moral poems of the later poets Anna Maria Winter and Elizabeth Blackall that represent a thematic portal to the dominant themes of Victorian moral discourse. Not every Romantic-era Irish woman poet was brilliant, of course; some were mediocre at best. But as I hope to demonstrate in the remainder of this chapter, their works are part of a rich and diverse tradition of Irish women's poetry that diverges from "English" verse as often as it attempts to harmonize with it.

We need to remember from the outset that Ireland was more strictly an "occupied" country than Scotland was, even—and perhaps especially—after the Act of Union of 1800, and the pronounced class differences revealed by this occupation of a "conquered native Catholic nation" (McCartney, 17) militated against sympathetic exploration in literature of discursive common ground. As Ned Lebow puts it, "by the nineteenth century, there were in fact two Irelands: one Protestant, Anglo-Scottish, prosperous and politically influential; the other, Catholic, Irish, and living on the edge of starvation" (60). Irish writers in general had to deal with the complications involved in addressing multiple audiences: male and female, Catholic and Protestant, Irish and English, not to mention various economic, political, and intellectual subdivisions and stratifications within these categories. Nor is the dilemma peculiar to the Romantic period. Even today, as C. L. Innes writes, "it is almost impossible for Anglo-Irish writers to take for granted a common set of assumptions, religious, political or cultural, between themselves and their audiences, while the significance of the writers' subjects as well as the language they write in will be wrestled with over and over by the varying communities to whom or for whom the writers speak" (29).[5] The difficulties involved in defining and addressing variously constituted readerships—actual and virtual—inevitably impacted both what Irish women poets wrote and how they wrote it.

Roman Catholic Irish writers, for instance, faced an entrenched anti-Catholicism among the ruling class that further exacerbated their putative inferior "colonial" status. Before 1770, Catholic women who wrote did so almost exclusively in Irish; their entry into the Anglophone publishing community by the century's end was tied to the developing debate in Ireland about nationhood and patriotism. Not surprisingly, the rhetoric of these writers was frequently oppositional and directed against the cultural mindset inherent in the discourse of the imported (or superimposed) English Anglophone writers. As women writers grappled with the conflicting demands of retaining their Irish cultural identity at the same time that they participated in a cosmopolitan Anglophone discourse field, one characteristic theme began to be apparent: "the tension between feeling included and excluded by society," a tension that is expressed at times as inseparable from "the female condition" and at other times as part of "being Irish"—and often both of these (Kilfeather, 774). Catholic writers publishing in English faced the additional obstacle of the entrenched and violent English anti-Catholicism, as we see for example in the brief and tragic career of the poet Thomas Dermody.

Catholic Irish women poets generally do not address this anti-Catholic bias directly, with the exception of Mary McCoy, whose 1813 satirical verse pamphlet (apparently her only publication) responds squarely to a pamphlet by an anonymous author who had styled himself "a friend" to Irish Catholics while attacking Catholics and Catholic Emancipation alike. This ostensible "friendship" is a rhetorical ploy that had been widely adopted in prose pamphlets that during the run-up to the Act of Union had encouraged the Irish to embrace union as being in their own best interests.[6] McCoy concludes her poem by suggesting that the anonymous pamphleteer is himself so vile and reprehensible that "reasonable" persons will recognize him for what he is and that his vicious campaign will therefore backfire, harming him (and his cause) more than those he has attacked:

But he's a disgrace to human race,
From his caitiff vile intentions;
The beasts of the field more virtues yield,
For they never raise discensions [sic];
But concord, love, and harmony,
Which unites all ranks and stations;
He strives to disturb society,
With insidious calumniations.

But he's some broken down old strutting clown,
Or some low reduced pedlar,
Whose pack is done, and to raise a fund
He's become a censorious meddler;
And a pretty show he would be to go
To the Senate of the nation,
So mournfully to shout and cry,

Ah! don't give them Emancipation!!!
But all praises be to the King of Kings,
For all blessings he bestows us;
And 'tis a blessing great, he can't get into state
With his clamourous lies to oppose us;
So, we'll let this friend do all he can,
For to censure and degrade us;
For our actions best can stand the test,
And at last must serve us. Amen.   (9–10, ll. 265–88)

These rough and robust lines, with their bounding rhythms and probably calculated crudeness, represent in some respects the last blast of the kind of Swiftian satirical rhetoric we see earlier in the period in the poems of Mary O'Brien and Henrietta Battier. Such head-on ideological engagement is in fact atypical of most of the period's poetry, especially in bound volumes of poetry as opposed to poems that appeared in the periodical press (as many of Battier's and O'Brien's did), perhaps precisely because it was difficult for poets to pin down and then address exactly the audience they envisioned.

Moreover, as Michael de Nie demonstrates in *The Eternal Paddy*, every Irish writer, regardless of origin or affiliation, had to contend with the deeply entrenched stereotype of the Irish as brutish, ignorant clowns (indeed the Irish typically served as the butt of crude humor in mainstream British writing and art). Daniel Dewar's

1812 assessment of the root cause of this stereotypical view of the Irish "aborigine" is typical: "As to the original [that is, native] Hibernian, his character has not been well nor generally understood. Few have examined it with friendly disposition, and still fewer have been placed in circumstances favourable to investigation, or have had the qualifications requisite to form a fair and impartial judgment" (22–23). Hasty assertion founded on ignorance and cultural bias, in other words, invariably constructs among the dominant culture false and derogatory images of the subaltern, which are over time enculturated by the majority population in general.

To begin, then, we must briefly consider the historical circumstances of Irish literary culture during the Romantic era. As early as 1793, the *Anthologia Hibernica* was observing ruefully that "were the abilities of the Irish to be estimated by their literary productions, they would scarcely rank higher than those nations who had just emerged from barbarism and incivility." There is no lack of publications in Ireland, we are told, but these publications "are not the works of native writers," in part because "men of letters receive no patronage from the great in this island," a fact that redounds to the disgrace of these recalcitrant patrons who shirk their national cultural responsibility. "If learning . . . softens the ferocity of rude nature, and polishes our manners, we may easily determine the precise state in which the minds of those great are, who suffer learned merit to pine in obscurity and penury."[7] Note that the gendered language here ("*men* of letters") excludes women, just as their gender excluded them also from formal higher education and thus from official "learning." Moreover, the statement overlooks what was already in 1793 a considerable body of work by "native writers," male and female alike.

Implicit in this sort of thinking is the assumption that the Irish lack sufficient pride—or even interest—in their own indigenous culture for them to cultivate a "taste" grounded in that culture. Writing in 1817, the Rev. Samuel Burdy observed that "a prejudice prevails among [the Irish] against every production of their own country, and if any Irishman of talents attains celebrity by his productions, he must have acquired it in England and not at home" (567). More recently Weekes, in a formulation reminiscent of Burdy's, has stated that "the dearth of writing by Irish women in the nineteenth century measures to some extent the lack of devotion of the Anglo-Irish to a literary culture. Unlike their counterparts in England, the inhabitants of the Big Houses in Ireland were not given to intellectual or cultural pursuit and did not see themselves as guardians or promoters of the culture that privileged them" (18).[8]

I begin, then, by sketching some of the ways in which Romantic-era Irish women poets set about negotiating their personal and collective gendered status in relation to their attitudes about Irish nationalism and nationhood, as well as about more commonplace and quotidian subjects, and in relation too to their real and imagined audiences. Women from early in the period (like Henrietta Battier and Mary O'Brien) tend more frequently to be overtly "political" (whether they assumed loyalist or radical nationalist stances) in their poems, something that diminishes after the Treason Trials in England in 1794 and of course even more dramatically so after the suppression of the 1798 rising. Later poets (like Anne Lutton, writing late in the 1820s) treat Irish nationalism (and "Irishness") in more oblique fashion by using recognizably "Irish" settings and contexts to present tales that are in fact less immediately "Irish" than they are universal.

In the middle years of the period come poets whose works reflect the frequently competing pressures exerted by their own strong cultural and sociopolitical sentiments, on one hand, and by their precarious and often ambivalent status as writing women, on the other. Sydney Owenson, for instance, begins her public writing career with a volume of *Poems* (1801) in which she uses the recurrent image of the emblematic Irish bardic harp to rally the Irish cultural identity that was at its nadir in the wake of the 1798 rising. At nearly the same time, however, the clergyman's wife Eliza Ryan had already been writing loyalist poems (not subsequently published until 1816) that cast the 1798 rising in terms of a "pestilence" whose perniciousness was the direct consequence of its apparent "foreignness." By the Regency, energetic nationalist poets like J. S. Anna Liddiard emerged who directly engaged Ireland's political and cultural subjugation, but the greater number of Irish women poets were, as we shall see, steering a less risky course, publishing various types of quasihistorical "tales" that reified a semimythical "old" Ireland and invited their readers to measure the present degraded state of an occupied Ireland against the image of a heroic past. By the 1820s, and even more so during the 1830s, a new strain of Christian moral earnestness becomes evident in the poetry by women in both Ireland and Scotland. This development, which accompanied a rise in women's participation in missionary activities, came at the same time that a more cosmopolitan view of the United Kingdom was becoming apparent in rhetorical figurations of the sisterhood that existed between the twin islands, England and Ireland. Women writers in particular stressed that this sisterhood depended on both parties' recognition that the "sisters" were distinctly different siblings and not mere twins and that the healthiest and most moral relationship was a companionate one of mutual support, respect, and equality.

Private and Public: Quotidian and Contested Subjects

As in Scotland and England, so also in Ireland many volumes were published ostensibly to benefit authors who suffered under a variety of deprivations. The unknown

"Lady," a "Native of Newry," for example, declares in the 1807 preface to her *Poems, on Several Occasions* that "circumstances particularly unfortunate—a long succession of disappointments, uncheered by a prospect of their termination" have forced the unwilling author to publish poems "never meant to meet the Public eye" and that she now begs the stern reader to appraise generously in light of her motive for publishing: "a nobler one than vanity; *the support of orphan helplessness*" (3–4).

> When fate o'er ruling seem'd to lead,
> My steps, a certain path to tread,
>   Nor other way would give;
> And is it thus I sighing said,
> An Author am I doom'd for bread,
>   And verses make to live.
>
> That fortune long hath been my foe,
> Her malice but too well I know,
>   She oweth me a spite:
> And now perhaps I'm but her tool,
> To make me yet a greater fool,
>   She sets me down to write.   (introduction, 5–6, ll. 1–12)

Poverty took a different toll on Eliza Ryves, a member of a prosperous Irish family who was rendered destitute "through the chicanery of the law" (Blackburne, 2:225). To sustain herself Ryves moved to London, where she worked both as a translator and as an author, first writing an unsuccessful comic opera (*The Prude* [1777]), then some poems for the periodical press as well as odes and occasional poems that were published separately, and then a novel (*The Hermit of Snowdon* [1794]). The intersection in her poetry of learning, politics, and national interest is evident even in the formal dress of a poem like her *Ode to the Right Honourable Lord Melton, the Infant Son of the Irish Patriot, the Earl Fitzwilliam.*[9] Toward the ode's conclusion, Ryves admonishes Fitzwilliam to prepare his son for national service as "a firm supporter of his country's cause" so that he may join with "enlightened" leaders like Fox and Burke in opposing England's "inhuman" colonizing enterprises. Having described "the soul-exhaling joy of acting well" that rewards such humanitarian leaders, she offers her wish to the child (somewhat incongruously, given his infancy):

> Such is the prize, and not the gauds of state,
>   Or the short sunshine of a monarch's smile,
> That true ambition seeks, sublimely great,
>   Through tracks high born, impervious to the vile:

Glory is her's [sic], and that resplendent crown,
    Which, nor can envy blight, or time impair:
Then, Melton, learn to look superior down
    On fortune's toys, or favour's transient glare;
For, trust my song, (whate'er the boast of power)
WHO WINS IMMORTAL FAME ON VIRTUE'S WINGS MUST TOWER.

                                           (15–16, ll. 201–10)

Ryves has been called "a refined and educated gentlewoman . . . of vast reading and extraordinary attainments" who, on the retirement of the founder of the *Annual Register,* Robert Dodsley, was put in charge of that periodical's "historical and political department." No amount of literary activity turned enough of a profit, however, nor did Ryves's apparently fatal combination of generosity and impracticality help matters. "Her labours were either stolen or paid for with such a pittance, that it did not suffice to keep body and soul together"; Ryves died in April 1797 "of absolute want, in a miserable lodging in Store Street," a derelict London slum (Blackburne, 2:229–31).

Nor is poverty the only special circumstance offered up as reason for publishing one's work. Physical infirmities inflicted their own terrible imperative, as is evident from the title page of the 1789 *The Blind Poem,* "written by a girl, born blind, and now in her Eighteenth Year" and "dedicated to The World, by the Authoress, MARY BYRNE, of WICKLOW. Price 3s 3d. or such GREATER PRICE as the AFFLUENT choose to bestow on POVERTY." This twenty-page poem, described in the preface as a compilation and rearrangement of Byrne's lines by a well-intentioned "Lady" exerting herself on Byrne's behalf, quickly devolves into familiar moral platitudes. But before it does so we get to hear Byrne's own engaging personal voice and figurative language:

To be a Poet, I've often heard it said
You must be born so—one you can't be made.
What then is Poetry but chosen words?
Taken from Prose, just as from whey its curds,
And as the whey to weak and sick is giv'n,
So Sing-song catches Fools, while Prose is driv'n
Like curds, to those whose strong digestive Pow'rs
Can *Food* from *Solids* take, from *Wit* it's [sic] *Flow'rs;*
Poor simile this you will say I've made,
Whilst others to the depths of Hell would wade;
Call on the Planets and their Stars that wait;

Nay Heav'n itself would finish their Portrait.
But I whom Nature hath not form'd to soar
Past her due Bounds, or her great depths explore,
Will write contented on my curds and whey,
Nor censure those who take another way,
My lines 'tis true, may like my whey appear,
Weak and *insipid*, nor *well-turn'd* nor *clear:*
But when I tell you that *I cannot write,*
Am uninstructed—*and depriv'd of Sight;*
That I ne'er liv'd amongst the wise or great,
Ne'er saw nor heard an Orator once speak,
Nor dream'd of Poets but as they've been read
By Clown unletter'd with a vacant Head,
Perhaps you'll pity first and then despise
My vain Attempts to open other's Eyes. . . .   (6, ll. 1–26)

Byrne's is but one of many volumes dating from this period that appeal to "PUB-
LIC COUNTENANCE and PROTECTION" (iii) for sustenance *and profit.* Another, which
also seems to have been shepherded into print by an interested party, is the little
1792 volume titled *Poems,* of which only forty copies seem to have been printed, attributed on its title page to "Ellen Taylor, the Irish Cottager."[10] The editor's preface
to the volume introduces Taylor as "the daughter of an indigent Cottager, in the
remote part of the Queen's County; who had barely the ability to afford common
sustenance to her and a numerous family during his life-time." Despite her modest
circumstances, Taylor seems to have been not only literate but familiar with the
poetry of Milton and Thomson.[11] The most remarkable of her few poems is called
"Written by the Barrow Side, Where She Was Sent to Wash Linen." In it, Taylor
laments the incompatibility of her heavy domestic duties with her unaffected love
of nature and her aspirations as a poet:

Thrice happy she condemned to move
    Beneath the servile weight,
Whose thoughts ne'er soar one inch above,
    The standard of her fate.

But far more happy is the soul,
    Who feels the pleasing sense;
And can indulge without controul,
    Each thought that flows from thence.

Since nought of these my portion is,
    But the reverie of each;
That I shall taste but little bliss,
    Experience doth me teach.   (9, ll. 25–36)

When she showed some of her "unlettered" work to a would-be benefactor (presumably the editor) who was a visitor in the house near Graiguenamanagh, County Kilkenny, in which she was working as a housemaid at the time she composed the poetry in her book,[12] he professed astonishment.

> It now becomes almost a duty of the generous public, to prevent this beautiful field flower from being buried (like Burn's [sic] mountain daizy [sic],) beneath the oppressive Ploughshare of poverty, and which may be prevented by the sale of her Poems; the profits, and some liberal subscriptions, being intended for her sole use and emolument: and the Public may rest assured that whatever sum may arise from the sale of these Poems, or from the subscription which has been confined to a small circle, will most carefully be laid out in order to procure her some permanent establishment, and rescue her from extreme poverty, which she now experiences in a poor Hut on the Commons of Lyons; where to earn a scanty livelihood she keeps a small day school, and receives a trifling pittance for teaching the poor children in that neighbourhood to read and write. (iv)

In the cases of both Byrne and Taylor, the authors are represented by others who have apparently taken their cases in hand and who invest their own credibility and resources in what they portray to readers and potential buyers as valuable exercises in Christian charity in which they invite subscribers to share by purchasing copies. In involving themselves in collecting, editing, and publishing the works of real and imagined lower-class prodigies like these—and like Stephen Duck, Mary Collier, and James Chambers—they join the ranks of benefactors and benefactresses like Hannah More (acting for Anne Yearsley, a.k.a. "Lactilla, the Bristol Milkwoman") and the dissenting Yorkshire writer and schoolteacher Catherine Cappé (who edited and published Charlotte Richardson's *Poems* [1806][13]).

Appeals for patronage come in various guises; youth is sometime pled, as in the case of the first volume published by the prolific poet, novelist, and miniature painter, Louisa Stuart Costello. The poems in *The Maid of the Cyprus Isle, and Other Poems,* the dedication announces, were "composed Between the Ages of Fourteen and Sixteen" (iii), Costello's age at the time of publication. A more extreme instance is the poetry in *Stanzas* (1834), a sixteen-page collection of hymns and occasional verses "by Miss Berkeley Calcott, Eleven Years of Age." Anne Jane Magrath's *Blos-*

soms of Genius (1834) seems to have been published when the author was about seventeen. She tells us that she composed her poems to distract her from "the condition to which the hand of sickness had reduced her" and that has plagued her "from childhood to the present hour" (i–ii). Despite this uninviting prospect, some of the poems are actually quite striking in the way they combine strong lyricism with sophisticated verbal textures and rhetorical techniques. For the most part, Magrath avoids formulaic posturing about melancholy, evoking instead often-powerful contrasts between ideas and images of beauty and those of reality and mortality. Still, like so many of her historically neglected contemporaries, Magrath has gone unremarked in surveys of both Irish and "British" Romanticism, including surveys devoted exclusively to women's poetry.

Although the poetry published by Scottish women offers many examples of a vernacular idiom, most particularly in the lively poems of Isabel Pagan, there are very few examples of a comparable practice among Ireland's women poets. Indeed, the only poet who consistently writes idiomatic poetry is the largely unknown Sarah Leech, a working-class Ulster poet whom Jane Gray calls "the only spinner who published poems in the tradition of the rhyming weavers" (258). Leech is described in her volume's preface as "a peasant orphan girl, destitute of the opportunities, as well as the means, necessary for the cultivation and improvement of the intellectual faculties" (v). Like some of the poets mentioned above, Leech, was taken up by a well-intentioned patron ("a graduate of Trinity College") who arranged for publication of the poems to raise from their sale "a small sum to assist her in her pilgrimage through life" (vi–vii). Interestingly, Leech's patron explicitly appeals to women in particular to "extend to her that patronage and support, to which her 'wood notes wild' give her an indisputable claim" (vii). Although some of Leech's poems are written in conventional English, her best poems employ the lively idiom that we find in a poem like "On Killing a Mouse in Harvest":

> Poor feckless thing, why did I kill thee?
> The muse sic death could never will thee—
> When some few grains o' oats wad fill thee—
>   The lib'ral han'
> Has often left an ear o't till thee
>   Wi' ripen'd awn.[14]
>
> . . . .
>
> Ye tears flow freely frae ilk e'e—
> How could I use sic cruelty,
> Upon a harmless mouse like thee,

As stopt thy breath—
Thou mad'st a vain attempt to flee,
　　　Impending death.　　(20–21, ll. 1–6, 19–24)

The opening stanzas of another poem, "Address to a Cricket," further demonstrate how effectively Leech matches her language to her quotidian subject:

At gloamin' when the twilights fa'
And songsters to their nests withdraw,
A cricket, snug behin' the wa',
　　　Supplies their place,
And in the corner sings fu' braw,
　　　Wi' unco grace.

When younkers scamper, ane by ane,
And dowie I am left alane,
You cheer my heart wi' hamely strain,
　　　Or shrill toned chirple,
As cozie roun' the warm hearth-stane,
　　　You nightly hirple.　　(24, ll. 1–12)

Her choice to write in both standard English and a Scottish idiom recalls Burns, whose poem on a mouse Leech may have seen in her childhood, during which despite her minimal education she did have access to a variety of books, both religious and secular. Indeed, her deliberate use of a distinctively Scottish patois places Leech in something of a borderline position linguistically, since Michael Montgomery and Robert Gregg refer to her as "apparently the only female who made poetry in Scots in the period" among writers in Ulster (596).

The poems of Frances O'Neill and Catharine Quigley offer two very different illustrations of how Irish women poets handled colloquial language and localized imagery to quite different purposes. They also help define the two distinct groups of Irish poets during the period. The first, represented by O'Neill, is that of working-class Irish writers who left Ireland to seek employment in England—most often in London. Just as many Scots had done earlier in the eighteenth century, Irish citizens migrated to England—and especially to London—to escape poverty and to better their circumstances, even if only marginally so. Claire Connolly remarks that because the Act of Union "created a professional literary culture characterised by movement between and across the two islands," it is therefore necessary to include among "Irish" writers a good many who resided for considerable time in England, published there, and were read there (407). Indeed, for many of these writers in

poetry and prose alike, and of both sexes, the interconnected experiences of dislocation, relocation, and imperfect cultural assimilation provided a recurrent theme.
Their experience often parallels that of poets from a higher social class like the unfortunate Eliza Ryves, whose background was not in fact that of a working-class family
but whose considerable talent and multiple literary connections (which included Dr.
Johnson) could not save her from penury. The second group, of whom Quigley is representative, consists of more thoroughly Irish-identified writers who stayed in Ireland,
wrote about Irish subjects (often from a particular local perspective), and directed
their works at audiences whom they could reasonably expect to be knowledgeable
about and sympathetic to both their subject matter and their literary vehicles.

Frances O'Neill seems to have been a working-class Irishwoman who took up
residence with "a respectable Family" in London in the fashionable Berkeley Square,
where she appears to have worked as a seamstress. Her 1802 *Poetical Essays* appears to
have been her only publication.[15] Like many of the volumes by working-class writers, it was published at her own expense, and like them, too, it contained poems in
a variety of forms, including acrostics, which were a favorite among such writers,
perhaps because they furnished a ready vehicle for profitable flattery. That O'Neill's
relocation to London was not without its disappointments is apparent from "On
My Arrival in London," in which she places her uncertain trust in the conviction
that better, happier days lie ahead:

> Alas! not here I find content,
>   Tho' all my raptur'd soul admires
> The stately town, its vast extent,
>   Its op'ning streets, and shining spires.
>
> . . . .
>
> Yet here my Muse no friendship meets,
>   Her every scheme lies overthrown,
> Since thro' these broad expanded streets,
>   She moves unnotic'd, and unknown;
>
> Tho' oft she thrusts her pensive head
>   Amidst the crowds' tumultuous din,
> No friendly hand extends her bread,
>   No pleasing voice invites her in.   (23–24, ll. 1–4, 9–16)

A reflection on the inhospitality of London to the cultivation of her own verse, these
lines also gloss the broader cultural alienation endured by "outsiders" like O'Neill,
especially when their national origin was known.

But it is her rollicking satirical verse that distinguishes O'Neill's work. The volume opens with three poems detailing the boisterous verbal and physical battles waged in that household between "Mr. Kelly," the butler to the "certain great family" that resides in Berkeley Square and to whom O'Neill refers as a "grinder" (a slang term for one who works for another and who compels still others to work for substandard wages), and "Sangster," the Scottish housekeeper. Their physical violence, including the riotous wrestling match described in "The Contention of Kelly and Sangster" that demolishes the household's kitchen, recalls the wild physicality of Fielding's descriptions of Parson Adams's fights in *Joseph Andrews*. In this poem, for example, they begin by trading insults that reveal their nationalist hostilities. Sangster attacks Kelly in "half form'd accents, and a stamm'ring tongue" (67):

> D—n your red eyes, you noisy grinding rogue,
> Your clownish manners, and your Irish brogue,
> A vain conceited block, a stupid fool,
> An Irish blund'ring butt of ridicule,
> Born, as we hear, on Tiperary's [sic] bog,
> Go cringe to Pocock, go you Irish dog,
> Search England round, could we your equal find!
> So prone to practice, and skill'd to grind,
> 'Tis meet and just your canker'd heart to bear,
> And well the song has term'd you what you are.   (12, ll. 68–77)

At this, Kelly leaps up, seizes a cup of scalding tea, and smashes it over Sangster's head, dousing her "hoary" gray hair and her clothing. Then mayhem erupts:

> She scream'd, he swore, and adding blows to blows,
> Dragg'd her Scotch arms, she pull'd his Irish nose,
> Struggling and bawling both continued long,
> Both in a rage, both hardy, rough and strong;
> Now to the table where they first had place,
> Kelly dragg'd Sangster, Sangster scratch'd his face;
> Kelly was mad, his heart was fill'd with ire,
> He spit, he spurn'd, his red eyes flash'd like fire,
> And just o'erturn'd the teaboard in his rage,
> And all the teaboard's shining equipage;
> Now cups and saucers both had felt his power,
> Swept to destruction in a shining shower. . . .   (12–13, ll. 92–103)

In a ploy reminiscent of Pope's *Rape of the Lock,* a kitchen-dwelling sylph intervenes to try to preserve what has not yet been wrecked, stretching herself over the set of shelves containing "full many a jar and many a vase / Of curious figures, and crystalian frames" (13, ll. 109–10). Not content with this effort, the sylph flaps her wings to distract Kelly and then seizes a needle:

> Now in his nose her needle upright stood,
> She jamm'd his cheek, and shew'd his Irish blood;
> This needle, pilfer'd from, a lady's case,
> She now exert's [sic], and maim'd his ugly face.   (13, ll. 120–23)

Finally, with the crockery shattered and the kitchen in shambles, Kelly cudgels and kicks Sangster, who at last tires and is knocked to the floor. The poem concludes in a welter of colloquialisms:

> All this he saw, rejoic'd at what was done,
> He roar'd for sport, and clapp'd his hands for fun;
> Then rais'd her up, and with a mighty shout,
> Wide opes the door, and fairly bang'd her out:
> Thus, freed triumphant from the dire attack,
> He bang'd the sounding portal at her back;
> Return'd to breakfast, now craunch'd his prog,
> Now clos'd his gauldy eyes, and snor'd like any hog.   (14–15, ll. 152–59)

The physical violence that pervades this poem, like the verbal violence that informs the other two satires ("Kelly's Birth and Education in Ireland" and "Kelly's Song, the Irish Grinder") plays to the coarsest of ethnic prejudices among O'Neill's intended English readers, but it also reveals the national cultural ambivalence that characterizes much of the Irish (and Scottish) poetry that was written for a largely English readership. As Wolfgang Zach notes, such spectacles of gratuitous violence play into the very stereotypes they may be intended to ridicule; further, the stereotype of "a specifically latent proclivity to irrational, barbarous violence in the Irish 'character'" had "serious social and political effects: it served the British colonizers as a handy argument to justify all their measures to crush Irish resistance against colonial rule since the Middle Ages" (x–xi).

O'Neill's portrait of Kelly (and to a lesser extent Sangster) in fact betrays an unattractive willingness to pander to ethnic stereotypes in the interest of amusing readers and currying favor with them; it is the sort of classic "sellout" by which subaltern cultures contribute to their own oppression by participating in—and even subscribing to—the institutional and rhetorical structures that oppress them. What O'Neill does in these three satires is very different from what we saw in the jocular satires of Isabel Pagan. Pagan's rich Scottish patois does not demean herself or her subject, nor does it undercut the ethnic culture it delineates. There is in Pagan's songs and poems none of the strain of genuine meanness that we encounter in O'Neill's satires. It is hard to read O'Neill's poems and not find in them the personal bitterness of the cultural outsider who finds herself trapped in a social, economic, and cultural prison from which escape is unlikely and in which capitulation becomes a viable though unhappy coping mechanism. Seen in this light, the volume's penultimate poem, "My Own Wish," is even more affecting in its poet's fond wish to be "on some mountain, far remote, / Where I might round the distant world descry, / With no companion but the capering goat, / The prospect only bounded by the sky" (59–60, ll. 2–4). There, O'Neill suggests, pleasure might at last be possible:

> For here immerg'd in London's noisy streets,
>> Where to and fro the thund'ring coaches roll,
> Where contemplation's eye no pleasure meets,
>> No calm contentment ever sooths my soul.   (60, ll. 9–12)

Of a very different nature, although also largely and unaccountably unnoticed, are the delightful, witty poems of Catharine Quigley, which in many respects form an Irish counterpart to those of Pagan, her Scottish contemporary. Missing from all standard reference works on Irish women writers, Quigley, who apparently was also an orphan, seems never to have been reviewed nor otherwise noticed by her contemporaries, despite what she says about her own poetry's potential public reception in a poem called "Stanzas to a Young Lady, on Reading Bloomfield's Poems":

> How simple my lays must appear!
>> How rough and unpolish'd each line!
> Ill fitted to please a good ear,
>> Compar'd with a genius so fine.
> But, methinks, that in some I discover,
>> Those gracious perfections of mind;
> Which will lead them, at least, to pass over,
>> The faults, that in mine they [my critics] may find.
>
> When Critics are striving to censure,
>> And Cynics are blasting my fame;
> Perhaps they may candidly venture,
>> With generous warmth to exclaim,
> And not without some indignation:

"This work," (I shall thank them again,)
"Is an Orphan's, whose hard destination,
"Hath sought a support from her pen."   (*Poems*, 6, ll. 9–24)

After her two early volumes, *Poems* (1813) and *The Microscope; or, Village Flies* (1819), Quigley largely vanished for some twenty years, reemerging in 1837 with a self-published volume, *A Gift for the Sanctuary*, a collection of disappointingly formulaic moral and devotional poems taken from the "unpublished Works" that Quigley describes in her preface as being "undertaken for the sole purpose of assisting in the completion of the Wesleyan Chapel, lately erected in the City of Armagh."[16]

Quigley's early poems reward the reader who is fortunate enough to find them with their sense of spontaneous verbal delight. Like her Scottish contemporary Joanna Baillie, Quigley employs a language that is for the most part forthrightly formal English, and her descriptions of rural life and manners possess the lively, localizing particularity that, as we have seen, characterize poems like Baillie's "A Winter Day" and "A Summer Day." The opening of "Hodge and Sue: A Pastoral" offers a good illustration:

The morn was bleak, and snow had clad the hills,
Disguis'd the shrubs, and frozen were the rills;
The lowing herds in coverts lay conceal'd,
And hoary devastations round prevail'd.
When Hodge, whom wind or tide did ne'er prevent,
To visit Sue: along the pathway bent
His course; and whistled whiles, and whiles he sung;
Or now and then, a snow ball round him flung.
Revolving in his mind, the jocund chat,
He'd have with Sue; he sometimes twirl'd his hat:
Or with it chas'd the timid birds away,
That strove in vain to peck the leafless spray.   (33–34, ll. 5–16)

The reader is struck by the authenticity of these details—the twirling of the hat, the random tossing of snowballs, the description of the cattle lying concealed in coverts—which testify to things that the poet clearly has experienced and will speak volumes to the readers to whom they are likewise familiar.

If Quigley's poems represent rural life closely and affectionately observed, so too does a poem like "An Epistle from Dublin, to a Friend in the Country" have a comparable ring of authenticity. Writing to the "dear girl" who has requested an account of what she sees in Dublin, the poet expresses her preference for the peace and congeniality of the countryside:

Not much of the city to me is yet known,
For I'm fond of retirement, and mostly alone;
And trust me my friend, should I speak my thoughts free,
Gay scenes can't afford any pleasure to me.
I would rather be ranging alone in a field,
Than partaking those pleasures the city can yield.
Don't imagine from this that my case must be bad,
That my brains are derang'd, or my muse hath run mad:
For believe me if wit ever dwelt in my crown,
There's more in my pate since I came to this town.   (44–45, ll. 11–20)

How different in tone and attitude this is from Frances O'Neill's self-pitying renunciation of London. Quigley is resigned, to be sure, but her stated preference (like O'Neill's) for simple rural pleasures does not prevent her from enjoying and learning from her urban experience. Nor does it produce a bitter tone but rather a chatty and humorous one. The poem runs for just over six pages, enumerating and commenting on the sights and people of Dublin and on the unattractive social affectation that characterizes the place. But rather than end on a dyspeptic note, Quigley finishes with a disarming stroke that is wholly believable:

But my muse does not like on such subjects to treat,
She thinks them too mean, and besides it is late;
It wants but five minutes of twelve at the most,
And to-morrow I must send this off by the post.   (50, ll. 107–10)

This witty and almost epigrammatic ending caps the poem's good-humored rhetoric while at the same time suggesting that the whole poem is an extempore, composed hastily and with little thought about revision.

Although Quigley is quite capable of producing excellent verse in more formal poems like "Apollo" and "Nelson," the latter a striking variation on the familiar apotheosis theme, she is at her best in less formal productions, where her self-deprecating and often humorous tone is enhanced by her relatively informal diction. The preface to *The Microscope; or, Village Flies,* for instance, again assumes the form of a verse letter to a friend:

While some fictitious themes pursue,
Or mould old subjects into new,
Or, blest with genius, taste and art,
Can charm the ear, and win the heart,
With novel tales,—romantic views,—

Can please the young,—the old amuse;

. . . .

There's many a way of killing time,
And some of mine is killed in rhyme;
For many a moment do I spend,
In scribbl'ing [sic] Nonsense to a friend,
Or chasing notions to their end,
Or tracing some idea back,
Which kept my memory on the rack.
And this, my dear, is just the way
I spend an hour of many a day.   (i–ii, ll. 1–6, 15–23)

Quigley's ability to sustain her humorous tone is nowhere more evident than in a witty poem called "The Broken Saucer: A Pastoral." Here, in a two-part poem that seamlessly blends the domestic, the mock-heroic, and the burlesque, Quigley relates the tale of the demise of an ordinary tea saucer. The opening lines announce the poem's mock-heroic tone:

Alas! my pretty saucer, art thou broke!
Cut off, at once, by an untimely stroke;
My comely, decent, well proportion'd delph,
Which grac'd so neat, the cup-board, tray, or shelf
    Ah! cruel hand, that did the barb'rous deed,
What evil had my harmless saucer done?
    Did it e'er make the meanest insect bleed,
Or do an act which dare not face the sun?
What cruel fury could thy ire provoke,
To cut it off with one remorseless stroke?   (74, ll. 1–10)

The culprit is never specifically identified, although Quigley notes that he is not just male but also "in modish lore unskill'd"; neglecting to let his tea cool, the careless guest "[d]ash'd thy gentle carcase to the ground!" (76, l. 54).

Quigley's poem stands in remarkable relation to Joanna Baillie's better-known "Lines to a Teapot," composed more than a decade later, and it is helpful to think about that poem here and to consider how these two very different poets treated comparable quotidian domestic items. It helps, too, to remember Frances O'Neill's exaggerated description of the aristocrat's tea service (and a good deal else) in Sangster's kitchen. There the scene is treated in rough burlesque, with the violence exaggerated for shock effect in a manner that largely strips the narrative of wit and leaves one only with a distasteful sense of coarse brutality. Quigley, on the other hand, delights her reader with her witty and thoroughly lighthearted account of this domestic tragedy, an account that proves to be, paradoxically, more credible for the reader than O'Neill's overblown one.

Of course, Baillie's teapot is never broken, but it suffers an analogous decline in fortune, as we have seen, in passing from the possession of cultured aristocratic connoisseurs to that of mere vulgar collectors. Like Baillie, Quigley lovingly describes the saucer's physical details:

Thy shade was of the finest, liveliest blue,
And all the rustic figures drawn so true,
Embellish'd o'er with lofty waving trees,
Whose branches rustled in the passing breeze;
A browsing herd on one side struck the eye,
    A shepherd, with his trusty dog and crook,
A chrystal rivulet that murmur'd by,
    A fisher boy, who ply'd with skill his hook.   (75, ll. 21–30)

The alternating painted panels make one think of those more famous ones on Keats's Grecian urn, and in a brilliant stroke Quigley itemizes other details of those panels quite literally piecemeal, describing the now disjointed images on the saucer's broken pieces. Quigley's poem turns a quotidian household object into the subject of a brilliant poetic exercise in both domestic economy and cultural history that is no less worthy of critical notice than Baillie's "Lines to a Teapot"—or Keats's "Ode on a Grecian Urn," for that matter. Among other things, "The Broken Saucer" reminds us of how much superb Romantic-era poetry has typically been overlooked or discounted precisely because it is *humorous* and therefore seems not to square with our cultivated expectations about the serious and elevated nature of "Romantic" poetry. Detaching—and then dismissing—humorous verse like Quigley's from the broad and diverse field of the poetry of Romanticism, as traditional literary-historical criticism has customarily done, perpetuates a historically faulty portrait of the overall *community* of Romantic writing, balkanizing that vital literary diversity by imposing on it an artificial and distorted critical and aesthetic hierarchy.

In this same lighthearted vein are some of the poems of the normally serious Eliza Ryan, whose only volume, *Poems,* appeared in 1816. She was the wife of the learned theologian Rev. Edward Ryan, DD, rector of Donoughmore in County Wicklow and subsequently of St. Luke's, Dublin, and author of *The History of the Effects of Religion on Mankind, in Countries Ancient and Modern, Barbarous and Civilized* (1788) who died in 1818.[17] A good example of Ryan in a lighter mood is this little poem, whose title seems almost as long as the poem itself: "To a Lady Who Invited the Author to Her Country Lodging, Promising to Entertain Her with Potatoes, Butter Milk, Water and Fresh Air":

> Potatoes and butter-milk won't do,
> I must have ham and chickens too;
> Besides at dinner I'll have wine,
> To drink your health whene'er I dine.
> As to your water and fresh air,
> I always like substantial fare:
> Tho' to divinity related,
> I must and will again repeat it!
> That when I go to you to dine,
> I must have meat and drink and wine;
> Join'd to that chearfulness [sic] and ease,
> With which you'r [sic] always wont to please.   (91)

I return to Ryan in a more serious vein later, but I mention this poem here to underscore how important verse correspondence was to eighteenth-century and Romantic-era women poets. These women constituted what Paula Backscheider calls a "longitudinal as well as . . . horizontal community of women poets" whose writing takes one characteristic form in the "friendship poems" they addressed to one another as a means of overcoming social and geographical separation (206). The recurrent rhetorical markers by which these poets explicitly included their correspondents in their poems *by naming them*—whether by name or simply as "my friend" or "my dear"—constitutes a compact of female solidarity that implicitly repudiates and vanquishes the efforts of individual mates (like Rev. Ryan) or collective bodies of men to restrict and deny the formation and perpetuation of women's writing communities.

Nationalism and Irish Women Poets

Daniel Corkery has observed that "every Romantic movement is a national effort to discover for present needs forms other than the Classical forms" (xiv). One way to do so is to mine the riches of the indigenous national culture and its artifacts. Like their Scottish contemporaries, some Irish women poets did just this; like them, too, they occasionally employed an at least partially vernacular verse. Given modern postcolonial theory's claim that vernacular idioms inherently resist and undermine any dominant culture and its regularized idiom, the rhetorical and stylistic choice to employ the vernacular idiom suggests an oppositional authorial strategy calculated to counter and to subvert the dominant (and colonizing) English culture by foregrounding the poetry's distinctively Irish (or Scottish) subject matter and idiom. I do not consider poetry written in Irish here, but there is no question that the publication in 1789 of the scholarly antiquarian poet and linguist Charlotte Brooke's *Reliques of Ancient Irish Poetry,* prepared in deliberate emulation of Bishop Thomas Percy's 1765 *Reliques of Ancient English Poetry* and Joseph Cooper Walker's 1786 *Historical Memoirs of the Irish Bards,* stands as a major moment in Irish cultural history. Not only did the *Reliques* make available to an Irish audience a large number of traditional Irish poems both in Irish and in Brooke's own English renderings; her introduction to the volume is also a ringing assertion of the merit, nobility, and antiquity of Irish verse, despite what Clare O'Halloran describes as the "ambivalent primitivism" present in an Irish cultural establishment that was uncertain about the relations between orality and literacy, and between "barbarism" and civility in "ancient" texts (113–14). Brooke's introduction vehemently defends Gaelic poetry as a body of literature that could restore Ireland's literary reputation because it exhibited "a glow of cultivated genius" and a degree of refinement that she proclaimed to be "totally astonishing, at a period when the rest of Europe was nearly sunk into barbarism" (vii–viii). As she observes, "as yet we are too little known to our noble neighbour Britons; were we better acquainted we should be better friends. The British muse is not yet informed that she has an elder sister in this isle" (vii). Brooke's emphasis on the *elder* status of the Irish muse lent additional weight to her subsequent declaration that "the blood which flows in our veins is rather ennobled than disgraced by the mingling tides that descended from our heroic ancestors" (viii). Her aim in publishing the *Reliques,* Brooke's modest rhetoric notwithstanding, was nothing less than a wholesale renovation of the Irish national cultural identity: "Will [our countrymen] not be benefited,—will they not be gratified, at the lustre reflected on them by ancestors so very different from what modern prejudice has been studious to represent them?" (vii). Brooke's *Reliques* painstakingly documents the ancient pedigree of Irish civilization in order to contest English denials that any such credible civilization existed. It was republished in 1816, during a second wave of interest in native materials and national tales, under a new and sympathetic editor, Aaron Crossly Seymour, whose editorial comments are transparently nationalistic.

Kevin Whelan writes that European Romanticism spawned a "political offshoot," cultural nationalism, that "celebrated the customary, the regional, the particularist, at the expense of the new, the cosmopolitan, the universal" (61). In Ireland, this cultural nationalism tended to assert itself more among Catholic than Protestant writers. Many Protestant writers belonged to that Anglo-Irish faction who signed on to the

"British" imperial project because, as in Scotland, it served their social, political, and economic interests to do so. Irish Catholics, on the other hand, because they were both legally and culturally excluded from the Protestant establishment, gravitated toward the concept of a residual Irish political nationalism (and an Irish national state) that was inherently opposed to the union and the associated imperialist view of a "united" and cosmopolitan kingdom. Charlotte Brooke surely cannot therefore be called a nationalist separatist; Gregory Schirmer calls her a "cultural-unionist" who believed that "the confluence of Ireland's two different cultures [indigenous Irish and transplanted English] will inevitably lead to political harmony among the English, the Irish, and the Anglo-Irish" (65). But as O'Halloran explains, Brooke's position was more complex, as is evident from her many comments about the inadequacy of the English language to the demands of rendering accurate translations of Gaelic originals (118). Brooke's apparent confidence in the 1780s about the potential for poetic and linguistic rapprochement was based on a precarious optimism: like her father, Henry Brooke, she fully expected that revolutionary nationalist politics would pose no threat to efforts like her own that were geared toward helping the colonizer that was trying to understand the colonized. While a native Gaelic tradition existed in both countries, however, as both Romantic-era and modern publishing history reveals, popular anti-Scottish sentiment in England never reached the level of virulence of anti-Irish sentiment that is so prominent in "popular" English prose fiction and public discourse generally, both of which routinely style Irish characters (and Irish citizens) as brutes, clowns, and generally subhuman misfits.

On the other hand, no Scots women poets of the period exhibit the overt, explicit, and contestatory *political* engagement we find in the aggressively partisan poems of the novelist and dramatist Mary O'Brien and the prolific nationalist bluestocking Henrietta Battier. Like Eliza Ryves, both were active *early* in the period. And like English contemporaries such as Helen Maria Williams and Mary Robinson during the 1780s and 1790s, O'Brien and Battier produced poetry that explicitly engaged the public discourse surrounding major political events and issues. In 1785 appeared *The Pious Incendiaries*, O'Brien's self-published satirical attack on the rabble-rousing Lord George Gordon and his followers. Fearing a recurrence of the anti-Catholic Gordon Riots of 1780, O'Brien, an Englishwoman who lived in Ireland for some years during the 1780s and 1790s, enters the fray ostensibly at the behest of some "Men of Polite Literature" among her friends who encouraged her to dismiss her reservations about "going public" and to publish the verses she had (she says) intended only for private circulation (i). Like Battier after her, O'Brien claims that her decision to publish stems not from hope of personal gain but rather from her belief that it is her civic obligation.

A thoroughgoing royalist and "the most Swiftian of the political poets of the period" (Schirmer, 56), O'Brien followed *The Pious Incendiaries* in 1790 with *The Political Monitor; or, Regent's Friend,* a collection of violently anti-Pittite satires that originated in the Regency crisis of 1788–89 and that now appeared with her full name.[18] Addressing her volume to "the Commissioners of the Irish Parliament," O'Brien praises their support of the royal establishment during George III's first bout of madness. Although she does not name him explicitly in her dedication, Pitt is an unmistakable presence:

> The event which called forth your interposition has, much to the joy of every loyal subject, passed away; but the principles to which it gave birth remain, and are nurtured with care by hireling advocates of *that ambitious minister, whose aspiring hand had, on the melancholy occasion, nearly subjugated to his pleasure the whole executive power of the state.* (vi; my emphasis)

O'Brien's rumbustious lyrics characterize Pitt as an unscrupulous and power-hungry schemer eager to employ the impressionable Prince of Wales (and presumptive Prince Regent) as an instrument in his own designs for power. For some of the poems, O'Brien assumes the voice of "Paddy Teague," a sharp-tongued Irishman who refers to Pitt in phrases like "Billy, my dear" (9), shrewdly turning against the English the condescending rhetorical posturing that English writers (and politicians) routinely directed toward the Irish. The first poem in the book, "Paddy's Salutation to the Right Honourable William Pitt," is typical:

> Now Billy, my dear,
>   Accept Teague's salutation,
> For the care of the Prince,
>   And the good of the nation;
> Not forgetting your wits,
>   When in council they sit,
> To make a Prince Regent,
>   While you reign King Pitt.   (9, ll. 1–8)

Against the image of this shifty, scheming minister O'Brien counterposes both the Prince of Wales ("Great prince" [33, l. 6]) and the emblematic figure of simple, stocky, long-suffering, and eminently honest John Bull ("Jackey Bull" [27, l. 12]).

That she is indeed the "Regent's Friend" announced in her collection's title is clear from poems like the "Ode for the Prince of Wales's Birthday." There the figure of Fancy "gains power prophetic" to address the prince in verse "while Liberty attends" (33, ll. 12, 16):

"In thee, O Prince, we Britons own,
"Those virtues that adorn a throne,
"Bold, gen'rous, gracefully refined,
"Mercy and truth united find
   "A seat within thy breast;
"Judgment superior to thy years
"In wisdom's sable vest appears,
    "To blazon round thy crest.["]   (34, ll. 17–24)

This embarrassingly fawning poem reveals O'Brien's firm unionist sentiment. The opening line's phrase, "we Britons," rhetorically embraces not just Ireland and England (including Scotland) but also the allegorical powers of Liberty and Fancy that are named subsequently in the poem and that implicitly include the arts—including poetry. O'Brien contributed often in 1794 to Dublin's *Sentimental and Masonic Magazine,* where among conventional poems like "Love, the Little Tyrant" (July), "Lines to Fortune" (August), and "Atlinia: A Pastoral" (October), we find in the "Original Poetry" section also poems like "An Ode to Freedom" (July) and "An Invocation to Peace" (November) that bear her name.[19]

The poems of Henrietta Battier, though they are related in style and tone to O'Brien's, differ in their ringing Irish nationalism. Battier, whom Andrew Carpenter calls "the author of the best Irish satirical verse of the late eighteenth century" ("Poetry in English," 464), was a protégé of Samuel Johnson and an acquaintance of Thomas Moore. She turned to publishing to support herself and her two children after her husband died in 1794. Like O'Brien, Battier appears also to have published political poetry in the periodical press. Her poem, "Bitter Orange," for example, appeared in the United Irishmen's periodical, the *Press.* She may also have been the author of poems signed by "H. B." and "a Lady" that appeared in Dublin in the *Sentimental and Masonic Magazine* between 1792 and 1795, since her poems appeared also under the same initials in *Anthologia Hibernica* (O'Donoghue, 22).

Battier was associated with the United Irishmen, whose writers cultivated the features of Thomas Paine's democratizing rhetoric: "a plain, blunt style, whose muscular rhythms approximated the spoken voice, and which was designed to be read by the many rather than admired by the few" (Whelan, 71). Battier's rousing poems (which she often styled "odes") are visibly indebted also to the popular style of Peter Pindar (John Wolcot) both in their tone and versification and in their pseudonymous attribution to "Patt. Pindar." The stridently antiministerial poems she included in *The Gibbonade; or, Poetical Reviewer* (1793–94), for example, ask pointed questions like this one:

O Guardian Genius of Hibernia, say,
How long her sons must feel th' oppressive sway
Of *rude prerogative?*—While honest zeal,
And upright efforts for the public weal
Are represented to the Royal ear,
By each *mean placeman,* and *each puppy peer,*
As the effects of some disloyal cause,
Subversive of religion and the laws.   (1st no. [1793], 3–4, ll. 1–8)

The answers are much like this, both in tenor and in substance:

   —United Irishmen, must now forbear
One hope, those blessings they maintain'd to share.
—Proscribed, insulted, in a pillag'd land,
Whose partial parcels feed a hungry band.
—*A servile pack of ministerial hounds,*
Who hunt preferment over falshood's [sic] grounds,
Whose souls no purity of thought retain,
No friend but Interest,—and no god but gain.   (4–5, ll. 17–24)

The implied threat in this poem's concluding lines is unmistakable:

Long, Long, may George parental blessing give,
To Erin's sons, and filial love receive;
And may THAT TITLE, dreadful to the ears
Of evil speakers—and *ignoble* peers,
UNITED IRISHMEN—for ever be,
A Strengthen'd term, for virtuous Liberty.   (28, ll. 387–92)

These and other poems by Battier, who died in poverty and obscurity in Sandymount, near Dublin, in 1813, reveal a committed nationalist who worked hard (like many of her Irish contemporaries) to separate Pitt and the Tory majority from the titular head of the nation, George III, and to excoriate the former while professing warm filial respect and allegiance to the latter. As a rhetorical device, this apparently loyal royalist stance affords the author (especially in the hazardous climate of the early 1790s) at least some measure of insulation against the painful consequences of political opposition by an avowedly ardent Irish patriot.

No such strategy of dividing the opposition marks the staunchly loyalist poems of their contemporary, Jane Elizabeth Moore, the English-born feminist daughter of French parents who was by 1795 living in Ireland. When she traveled to Dublin in

1795 Moore seems to have become acquainted with both Battier and Thomas Moore, the latter of whom seems not to have warmed to her. Despite her demonstrated interest in women's rights (there is a remarkable series of verse letters in her 1796 volume that deal with women's exclusion from the Masonic Society), Moore, who was after all new to Ireland, was no proponent of Irish nationalism. Her 1796 *Miscellaneous Poems on Various Occasions* includes tales and occasional poems as well as loyalist political poems and congratulatory verses (like poems on royal birthdays dating back at least to 1786).[20] Indeed, two of the poems are effusive in their praise of Pitt. "On the Avidity of Mr. Pitt, on the Appearance of a War with France in the Year 1787, When It Was Reported That He Wrote His Own Letters" is followed by one called "Continuation to 1796" that foresees a postwar Britain that a grateful world permits "to arbours cool [to] retire." It concludes with these lines about Pitt:

> Thy fame shall then among the fair resound,
> When home their partners shall again be found;
> Parents and children shall assist the lay,
> And crown with harmony the happy day;
> That shall each drooping soul again revive,
> And cause connubial bliss again to thrive.
> And when the herald to the human race,
> Shall bid thee to his order yield thy place,
> Then shall thy name great as thy Sire's shine,
> And Britons decorate thy marble shrine.   (122, ll. 23–32)

Inevitably, the horrors of the Rising of 1798 ushered in a new tone in many of the poems dating from that period and its immediate aftermath. In a loyalist poem called "At the Time of the Irish Rebellion," for instance, which did not appear in a printed volume until 1816, Eliza Ryan (whom we encountered earlier, in a light vein) writes:

> Oh! Let not discord thus destroy
> The blessings we possess;
> To mar our long and peaceful joy,
> With sorrow and distress.
> Let industry once more return,
> To this once happy land,
> And let each heart with ardour burn,
> To join the loyal band.
> Then peace shall flourish, wealth shall flow,

Amidst our fruitful land;
And heaven its choicest gifts bestow,
To industry's fair hand.   (88)

This is the conservative orthodoxy of the establishment, of course, for whom wealth is the divinely sanctioned reward for a peace that is bred of "industry." Such a peace rejects "rebellion" in all its forms as a threat to the system of empire that is in place—and that is growing daily in power.

In a related poem, "In Time of the Rebellion in Ireland," Ryan draws a xenophobic association between rebellion—and therefore resistance to the status quo—and "foreignness":

In time of danger whither shall I flee?
Where, Oh! my God, for shelter, but to thee;
When foreign foes in formidable band,
And secret enemies infest our land:
Threat'ning at once our fortunes and our lives,
Our sons, our helpless daughters and our wives;
On thy Almighty power I'll rely,
And seek my safe protection from on high.   (52)

The same ideological associations of imperial power with divine protection and approbation appear here: with our fortunes and our lives alike threatened, God alone provides recourse and shelter. Moreover, in linking the rising's militant Irish nationalism with pestilence and infestation by both "foreign foes" and "secret enemies" within, Ryan blasts in calculatedly biblical terms as both pernicious and blasphemous that nationalism and the cultural resistance it represents. It is a familiar rhetorical ploy that is no less common in twenty-first-century political discourse.

The protagonists of the bloody Rising of 1798 had been emboldened by their tragically misplaced faith that they would be supported in their rebellion by forces of Napoleon's France. Poems like Ryan's exhibit thematic parallels with earlier Scottish poems on both sides of the Jacobite rebellion, in which French intervention was also anticipated. Such poems examine the typically disastrous consequences for native peoples of actions perpetrated by nationally or culturally "external" forces within and on a political entity that has been constructed artificially (via acts of union) rather than by any culturally or historically "natural" process. Typically, these loyalist poems (and their authors) downplay or totally ignore—as Ryan does in the poems above—the actual strength of the militant political and cultural opposition that exists within the indigenous populace, or else they scorn it as the nasty work of misguided malcontents.

Irish women poets (and Anglo-Irish ones especially) were often generous in their praise of Britain, its royals, its institutions, and its military heroes—especially when the subjects were not just British but also Irish. Thus Sarah Steele eulogized General Robert Ross, who fell in America during the British advance on Baltimore in 1814 and whose body was borne back to Europe, in "To the Memory of the Much Lamented General Ross":

> Again the warrior comes to rest
> Upon his fervent country's breast;
> And Britain hails Hibernia's son,
> From conquered states and battles won,
> While proudly o'er his brow she throws
> The laurel, and her blooming rose.
>
> .   .   .   .
>
> Britannia long must mourn his loss,
> And long must Erin pour her sighs,
> And think of Ross with weeping eyes.   *(Eva,* 91–93, ll. 31–36, 64–66)

A more gratuitous gush of British imperialism appears in Frances O'Neill's "Ode to New-Year's Day":

> Britannia's arms shall conquer and subdue,
>   Our king shall reign a sov'reign power alone.
> What conquests have we gain'd! what glorious spoils!
> What never fading laurels for our toils!
>
> .   .   .   .
>
> Can you be silent, Muse, while fame resounds?
>   Launch'd from these shores, our barks of traffic roam,
> Ships that have reach'd old ocean's utmost bounds,
>   To bear the spoils of either India home;
> Loaded with treasure to enrich our isle . . .
>
> .   .   .   .
>
> Hail then blest morn, that leads the promis'd years,
>   When Time his future progress shall unroll,
> Britannia's name proud France shall learn to fear,
>   And England's sway shall stretch from pole to pole. . . .
>   *(Poetical Essays,* 27–28, ll. 13–16, 21–25, 31–34)

O'Neill signals her eagerness to submerge her own Irish identity within the "British" imperial identity when she refers with calculated disingenuousness to "*our* isle" (craftily binding plural and singular), a strategy exactly opposite to that of Steele, whose taxonomy carefully distinguishes "Hibernia" and "Erin" from "Britain."

Often a popular anti-Gallicism permeates these paeans to imperial Britain, as in Anna Liddiard's "Address to Peace," which appeared in her 1810 *Poems* and again the next year, slightly revised, in *The Sgelaighe*. There she celebrates Britain's resilience in the face of the "foes to lovely Nature's plan;— / By *Vice* transformed to *Brutes*" (22, ll. 17–18):

> One Pow'r alone can their dire force withstand,
> Unshaken as the rocks that gird their Land!
> Britannia's Isles *alone* may proudly boast
> That the last gleam of freedom gilds their coast:
> Unlike those sons of France, tyrannic race!
> Now stain'd by ev'ry crime;—humanity's disgrace!   (22, ll. 22–28)

For Liddiard, " Power" is apposite with Britain both as a military (and political and economic) force and as a force of Nature herself. Likewise, two lines later her italicized "*alone*" suggests at once both "only" (only Britain can boast) and "by itself" (without assistance, as the nation had congratulated itself on opposing France virtually single-handedly). Unlike O'Neill, whose poem folds Ireland into an undifferentiated, singular "isle," Liddiard insists on a separate Irish identity even as she makes the obligatory nod toward political unity, locating that last bastion of freedom instead in the determinedly *plural* "Britannia's *Isles*" (my emphasis).

In both Scotland and Ireland, women poets frequently approached nationalistic sentiments via cultural—even mythical—nostalgia. In both nations, poets treat native traditions of bards, bardic discourse, and—especially in Ireland—the bard's emblematic instrument, the Celtic harp. These nostalgic poems generally involve "antique" subject matter: often they are poetic romances set in a Scots-Gaelic milieu that is made recognizable more by its place and character names than by any explicit references to contemporary social and cultural realities. In the Irish poems the harper either mourns a lost Irish freedom or is a casualty of the struggle to maintain or regain that freedom. This bardic harper is, of course, both a real and a symbolic stand-in for the contemporary poet, especially if that poet is a nationalist. This fact informs—implicitly if not explicitly—the contemporary poet's subject matter and rhetoric. Mary St. John, for instance, published in 1815 a poem called *Ellauna: A Legend of the Thirteenth Century*, a long historical tale in four cantos with copious notes that is an exercise in reifying the historical *and mythical* Irish past. Likewise, the title poem in Sarah Steele's 1816 *Eva: An Historical Poem* is an eighty-page retelling of an episode from Irish history during the reign of Henry II. Nor was that all. Louisa Stuart Costello, the prolific poet, novelist, travel writer, and miniaturist who had been taken from Ireland to Paris by her mother after her father's death in 1814, published in 1819 a poem called *Redwald: A Tale of Mona.* This sentimental tale is set in the locale of Mona (Anglesey), the site of the druid college that was sacked in 61 CE by the Romans and that had long served as a strategic stop for traders in the gold mined from Ireland's Wicklow Hills. In 1822 came Catherine Luby's *The Spirit of the Lakes; or, Mucruss Abbey,* a long verse narrative set among the Killarney Lakes. This was followed in turn by Vincentia Rodgers's *Cluthan and Malvina: An Ancient Legend, with Other Poems;* the three-canto title poem is another verse narrative of old Ireland, this one set in the time of the war against the Danes. Even as late as 1830 such nostalgic narrative tales continued in productions like Hannah Maria Bourke's *O'Donoghue, Prince of Killarney.* Set, like Luby's *Spirit of the Lakes,* among the Killarney Lakes, Bourke's tale explores another peasant legend grounded in the times of the Danish invasion. Poems of this sort reveal how the verse narrative tale, which remained a favorite form among British women poets generally and that was especially cultivated during this period in England by Felicia Hemans and Letitia Elizabeth Landon, was being adapted to serve a variety of purposes, not least of which was a decidedly nationalistic one.

Nostalgic tales of this sort may strike some modern readers as a politically safe and relatively unobtrusive variety of nationalism. But at the time they appeared, they possessed an implicit social and political charge. There was popular—and therefore political—power in the sentimental nostalgia for an "old Ireland" epitomized in the emblematic harp, a cultural rallying image that recurs in many of the Irish volumes. Anna Liddiard gestured in this direction in her 1810 *Poems* when she included at the end a set of five poems specially composed for the Irish Harp Society. A note to one of these poems concludes with Liddiard's observation that "whatever diversity of opinion there may be as to the perfection of the Irish Harp, there can be none, it is presumed, with regard to the superior merits of Irish Music" (89). In the politically charged atmosphere of the Regency and post-Regency United Kingdom, nostalgic narratives like these, with their suggestive cultural iconography, invited their readers to compare present circumstances with past ones and to recognize both *how much* diminished that present was *and why.* Such literary gestures, no matter how sentimental or nostalgic—indeed perhaps because they *are* sentimental and nostalgic—are effective rhetorical strategies for reminding an excluded people of the reality of their exclusion and of the circumstances and institutions responsible for that exclusion.

Mary Balfour's 1810 poem, "The Fairy Queen" (from her *Hope, a Poetical Essay*), furnishes a good illustration of such readerly consciousness raising:

Harp of Erin, trembling wake
   Thy hallowed chords once more,
Again thy magic wildness breathe
   Around her em'rald shore.
  . . . .
Tell then in loftier, louder strain,
Of Erin's sons on martial plain,
   And in soft dying murmurs tell,
     How Erin's heroes fell!—
Again the gallant theme pursue,
    Hold to view,
How Erin's shamrocks crown the brave,
Her tears bedew their grave.   (163, ll. 1–4, 11–18)

Sydney Owenson had already done something of this sort in *The Lay of an Irish Harp,* where the very first poem asks

Why sleeps the harp of Erin's pride?
Why with'ring droops its Shamrock wreath?
Why has that song of sweetness died
Which Erin's Harp alone can breathe?   (1, ll. 1–4)

The cause, she responds, lies in Ireland's past, when "'tis said *oppression* taught the lay" to Ireland's bard, animating "the *last* of the inspir'd throng" (Owenson's emphases) who had "bask'd in Erin's brighter day" (3, ll. 17–20). His song, she tells us, "deepen'd every patriot woe, / And sharpen'd every patriot pang" (7, ll. 55–56).

Owenson dutifully points out in a footnote that her tale concerns "the persecution begun by the Danes against the Irish bards," which "finished in almost the total extirpation of that sacred order in the reign of Elizabeth" (4). Less than a decade after the bloody Rising of 1798, however, her Irish readers could scarcely have overlooked their own situation in 1807 as forced and co-opted members of an artificially "United" Kingdom nor have ignored the consequences for their national identity of that unequal relationship. Indeed, her poem concludes thus:

Yet, ere he ceas'd a prophet's fire
Sublim'd his lay, and louder rung
The deep ton'd music of his lyre,
And *Erin go brach** he boldly sung.   (7, ll. 57–60)

The famous Gaelic phrase that was the motto of the United Irishmen and that appears in the poem's final line Owenson footnotes conspicuously as follows:

"*Ireland for ever!—a national exclamation, and, in less felicitous times, the rallying point to which many an Irish heart revolted from the influence of despair" (7). Given the political, social, and economic circumstances of postunion Ireland, one can hardly read with anything but wry irony Owenson's characterization of the past as "less felicitous times," nor can one easily imagine that her readers would not likewise see things so. After all, "reverse definitions" like these, which define things in terms of what they are *not,* are staples of radical, oppositional rhetoric, as we have seen frequently in earlier chapters. And yet, as Duncan Wu observes, "no reviewer ever faced up to Owenson's Irish republicanism," the vitriolic comments of reviewers like William Gifford and John Wilson Croker notwithstanding (xxii). Nor has the effect of her republican politics on her readers been adequately assessed by scholars who have routinely noted the great popularity that her works in all genres enjoyed among English readers. Like her countryman Thomas Moore, Owenson contributed in important ways to the gradual revision of the unfavorable stereotypes of Ireland and the Irish among the broad English reading public, just as her contemporaries Anne Grant and Walter Scott were doing with respect to Scottish culture. Even so, there is no question either that Owenson wrote with her Irish readers' eyes (and ears) in mind.

Ten years later, under less immediately volatile social and political circumstances, Hannah Morison left no doubt about the depressed state of Irish affairs in her "Tribute to Erin," from her *Poems on Various Subjects* (1817):

> Oh Erin, my country! I sigh to deplore,
> That the wreath of thy standard blooms lovely no more;
> The rose may expand in a sun-favoured isle,
> And the thistle can flourish in Penury's soil—
> But the shamrock in regions congenial appears—
> The dew of her life's Sensibility's tears.
>
>   Oh land of my fathers! thy feelings I boast,
> Nor blush to acknowledge thy sea-guarded coast,
>
> · · · · · · · · · · · · · · ·
>
> While his [Saint Patrick's] sons are alive to the chain which can bind
> With fetters of roses, the delicate mind—
> A mind that can yield, when to loveliness due,
> Yet firm in what's worthy in man to pursue.
>
>   Rise, Genius of Erin! that scorpion destroy
> That mingles despair with the smilings of joy!

Drive hence, with those reptiles, who erst, at command,
Were scattered, to prove us a favourite land—
Fell Discord that shines with the trappings of zeal,
To nurture Revenge, not in love to our weal.

    May the sons of SAINT PATRICK their ardor maintain,
And the shamrock spontaneously spread o'er the plain—
May his daughters, the love of our country prolong,
By teaching the infants to lisp out the song—
May our efforts still tend Independence to save,
And the wreck of her rights be an Irishman's grave;
That soil be his shroud, to embosom when dead,
Ere blasted the shamrock to fade o'er his head.   (207–8, ll. 1–8, 15–32)

Morison implores Saint Patrick to inspire his modern Irish sons to drive out the occupiers, who are figured here as "reptiles" like those which that ancient saint drove from the island. Morison, who seems to have lived in rural obscurity, wrote moralistic poems that extol Christian hope and fortitude, endurance of loss, repudiation of ambition, and faith in an everlasting life following death. Her poems are not heavily didactic, though, and they are characterized by a surprising humanity that characterizes touching poems like the one on a deranged seaman's widow and another on the death of an infant as well as her remarkable antiwar poem "The Twin Soldiers: A Tale." Most important, though, her poems reveal Morison's proud and persistent Irish nationalism.

The repeated invocations in nationalist poetry of Irish identity (past and present) and the status of contemporary Ireland as an occupied nation would necessarily have fueled nationalist resentment against the hegemony exerted by the dominant occupying culture over the oppressed subaltern, even though these poets virtually never specify any particular course of temporal *action* to redress the many injustices. Seldom do they go beyond the attempt to celebrate and sustain the romantic ideal of national and cultural liberty. But for many, this was itself a thoroughly worthwhile enterprise.

Writing a decade after Morison, in 1828, the Catholic writer John Lennon had this to say about the inherently counterhegemonic qualities of indigenous Irish writing:

I am well convinced, that our rural Irish poets in their native strains, and national anthems, have contributed more to the cause of freedom and independence, than the most refined eloquence and lofty speeches of the sublimest orators; for when the strong arm of power kept the wealthy and great in silence, the rural swains have made vocal the sheltering mountain's brow, and charmed their native bogs and woodlands with inspiring hymns of freedom and independence; and it is them only who have kept that glowing spark alive in the hearts of genuine Irishmen, which will never be extinguished until we obtain our lawful rights. (iii–iv)

This is precisely the cultural and rhetorical force on which poets like Balfour, Owenson, Liddiard, and Morison draw in their poems. As Kevin Whelan observes, by deliberately devaluing the authority of the elite culture (and its learned literary forms) and substituting popular literary forms and vehicles like songs, broadsides, and pamphlets the nationalist movement aimed to democratize literary discourse and the printed word itself (71). The point applies equally to the verse forms, language, and imagery of the poetry being considered here. A comparable rhetorical strategy appears in the numerous Scottish poems of the period, by women and men alike, that call on the legends of William Wallace and the more recent events of the Jacobite uprising to foster among the community of readers a distinctly *Scottish* identity and ethos.

In Scotland, as I indicated in chapter 5, Elizabeth Scot was virtually the only woman poet who wrote about what she regarded as the shortcomings of a seemingly rough and uncouth idiom that violated the expectations of mainstream English-language poetical readers. Nor do many Irish women poets broach the subject of readerly expectations, either. A notable exception is Anna Liddiard, whose 1813 preface to *Kenilworth and Farley Castle* (which is inscribed "To my Friends") is particularly instructive. In a brief review of Liddiard's 1811 volume, *The Sgelaighe,* the *Monthly Review*'s critic had taken Liddiard to task over what strikes a modern reader as a relatively small matter. In the title poem Liddiard describes her personified figure of Ireland's Genius as bearing a "silver Spear" that "like the pale Lightning gleam'd" (49). In a footnote, Liddiard explains that "the Genius, both of Great Britain and Ireland, is drawn leaning on a Spear—intimating, as it were, a reliance on their own strength—Silver is always symbolical of purity—therefore an appropriate device for Hibernia" (49). The critic seized on this detail as the starting point for an attack on the volume as a whole, observing that "although this ingenious compliment may win her the smiles of her Irish readers, those who are unprejudiced will scarcely tolerate the feeble and bombastic strains which occupy this volume."[21] The implication, of course, is that Liddiard's Irish readers are both blinded by (nationalist) prejudice and by a deficiency of aesthetic discrimination—unlike himself and the elite (English) culture on whose behalf he presumes to judge.

Responding in 1813, Liddiard angrily opines that this criticism was motivated not by any objective critical or aesthetic criteria but, rather, by a particularly egregious and nationalistic cultural bias. She begins by stating that "the chief cause of offence" seems to have rested with her decision in the 1811 poem to link poetry and painting and to place "a silver Spear in the hands of Hibernia, as emblematic of her purity; or rather with a view to designate those natural manners, peculiar to her, in common with all other Nations, who, not having arrived at a perfect state of civilization, may be said, in a political sense, to wear the 'manners of the Morn'" (vi). In other words, she explains, the *natural* state of Irish "manners" (and arts) is one of naïveté but nevertheless of grace and purity. This view of natural genius, which recalls Charlotte Brooke's claim that the Gaelic muse predates her more cultured English sister, prefaces the more important point about nation that emerges when Liddiard continues:

> That such is, or lately was, an appropriate device with this Country, no one will deny, who knows any thing of her history, and of that innocent and unsuspecting guile, which makes her vulnerable to the intrigues of more civilized Nations.—Hence the sarcastic observation, "that this might go down in Ireland," &c. &c.
>
> Supposing, what I am by no means inclined to allow, that there was no truth in the assertion, (for, I believe, as to purity, Ireland ranks as high as any of the neighbouring Nations,) was there no allowance to be made for the partiality of Patriotism?
>
> But it is easy to see through this criticism;—it was sufficient for such prejudiced Reviewers, that the subjects of the greater number of my former Poems lay in Ireland, which, to them, was an unpardonable fault; particularly, as I did not sweeten them to their palates, by placing her follies in the most conspicuous point of view, and gratify their illiberal prejudices, at the expense of my own feelings. (vii–viii)

Liddiard's conclusion leaves no doubt of her conviction that her refusal to pander to popular images of the Irish as brutish boors—and their culture as a subcivilization—is what actually motivated the *Monthly Review*'s attack on her work. Her point is that the critic not only *belongs* to the "English" cultural hegemony but also *depends* for his own subsistence on perpetuating among the "mainstream" majority culture the practice of a belittling cultural stereotyping.

Interestingly, when in 1819 the *New Monthly Magazine* reviewed Liddiard's *Mount Leinster; or, The Prospect: A Poem Descriptive of the Irish Scenery,* the reviewer began thus:

> This production of an Irish pen breathes a warm national spirit; and, united as the people of the sister islands are into one great empire, they can have but one interest, one liberty, one rise and fall, one disgrace and glory.[22]

The reviewer goes on, though, to fault the author (to whom he predictably refers always in the masculine[23]) for invoking images of "the dark policy or exterminating cruelties of former generations," which he worries will have the inevitable "ill effect of prolonging the existence of expiring prejudices and national animosities" (454). Liddiard's angry objection to the bias against identifiably "Irish" material of the professional reviewers, whom she accuses of hiding behind their anonymity, is unusual among her female contemporaries.[24] Indeed, more remarkable is the fact that even when treating such subject matter most of the Irish women poets adopt the conventional English idiom without any explanation for their decision to eschew a distinctively contemporary Irish idiom. In this they differ significantly from their Scottish contemporaries. Ironically, for the modern reader who looks for it, that strongly idiomatic language is manifested most dramatically by its conspicuous *absence.* Except for strident nationalists like Owenson, Morison, and Balfour, after 1810 or so most Irish women poets opted for a more universal type of verse characterized by its essentially mainstream English idiom and its frequently generic characters, flavored with just enough touches of "local color" to establish a recognizably Irish atmosphere.

As indicated earlier, however, culturally "native" materials took another form in Irish poetry during the Romantic period (as indeed they do in both Scottish *and English* poetry) in a renewed interest in song and in traditional native lyric verse. Mary Balfour, for instance, concludes her 1810 collection, *Hope, a Poetical Essay, with Various Other Poems,* with some thirty pages of poems gathered under the general heading of "songs," which is followed by this note:

> The preceding songs are all original, except the last, and adapted to the air mentioned at the head of each. They were intended for Mr. Bunting's Ancient Melodies of Ireland: a work entitled to the warm support of the nation, as its compiler is to national gratitude, for having preserved music of the highest antiquity and value, till now dispersed over the different provinces, and on the point of being lost for ever. (192)

Balfour refers here to the musicologist Edward Bunting, who had attended the famous four-day Belfast Harp Festival in 1792 and had noted down the music from the old harpers so that it should not be lost forever. (Indeed, he continued collecting traditional tunes, publishing editions in 1796, 1809, and 1840.) Bunting's project was in some ways analogous to Percy's *Reliques of Ancient Poetry* and Brooke's *Reliques of Irish Poetry* in setting out to preserve a vanishing body of indigenous folk verse and song. Efforts like Brooke's, Bunting's, and Balfour's demonstrate the subtle nationalism of all such collections. Even when the authors claimed to appeal for tolerance and mutual understanding, they nevertheless refocused their readers' attention on the fundamental "Irishness" both of the subject matter and of the latent community of mutual interest. Robert Hogan has observed that "the principal characteristic of writing in Ireland is its Irishness" (1:xi). Russell K. Alspach, though, claims that it was not until the nineteenth century, "when the Irish poets began to use in their poetry this matter of Ireland: the myths, the legends, the superstitions, the countryside," and when they adopted rhythms derived from indigenous speech, that "Irish poetry took on distinction of meaning" (11).[25] Because it lacked a distinctly Irish-oriented Anglophone poetic tradition, Robert Welch explains, and because it typically regarded both its subject matter and its rhetorical vehicles as inferior to those of "English" literary culture, nineteenth-century Irish poetry "would have to be intensely and recognisably Irish before it could be anything else" (15). This reassertion of Irishness is visible not just in the better-known, popular poetry of Thomas Moore but also in the work of many of his female contemporaries.

In this light it is worth considering Balfour's 1810 *Hope* a bit further, for it stands out as unusually "Irish" in nature. It appeared soon after the initial installment of Thomas Moore's *Irish Melodies,* which Patrick Rafroidi calls "the first body of [Irish] poetry that is wholly Romantic and national" (1:111).[26] Balfour's title poem is followed by a long ballad-stanza poem (in 147 stanzas) called "Kathleen O'Neil." This poem, Balfour explains in a prefatory "Argument," is founded on an ancient Irish tradition that she reports is still "current among the natives"; the legend has it that one of the ladies of the O'Neil family, Kathleen, was abducted by the *bean sídhe,* or banshee, rescued, subsequently endowed with immortality, "and became the superintending spirit of her race" (42). Kathleen is in fact a deer slayer whose character combines unusual valor with a prototypical feminine shyness. Balfour's interest in the mythic power of her tale is evident from its evolution into a full-fledged three-act "grand national melodrama" that was performed at the Belfast Theatre on 9 February 1814 and published anonymously later in that year. Like most of the poems in the 1810 book, and like the subsequent stage version, "Kathleen O'Neil" provided Balfour with both an occasion and a vehicle for reminding her readers of their *Irishness* by recalling both traditional Irish songs and traditional Irish subject matter. (It is worth noting that Balfour also published numerous translations of Irish poems.) Moreover, both "Kathleen O'Neil" and other poems in the collection reify a past greatness that has been lost through subjection by cultural outsiders. In "Limerick's Lamentation," for example, Balfour exclaims:

Behold where the heroes of Erin repose,
Who fell overpowered by their conquering foes!   (183, ll. 1–2)

In memorializing Ireland's heroic ancient dead, Balfour does no less than what Mary Leadbeater does in these lines from the moving elegies she published in her *Poems* of 1808 on the victims of the more recent savagery she had observed firsthand in Ballitore in 1798:

> The blood-stain'd earth, the warlike bands,
>> The trembling natives saw with dread:
> Dejected Labour left her toil,
>> And summer's blithe enjoyments fled.   ("To I. S.," 265, ll. 5–8)

> The bow'rs were wrapt in ruthless fires,
>> Prone on their fields the peasants bled:
> The Muses dropp'd their golden lyres,
>> And from the scene of slaughter fled.
>>>> ("The Summer-Morning's Destruction," 286, ll. 21–24)

In claiming in the final passage that the Muses abandoned the scene of the destruction, Leadbeater offers what she knows to be an ironic half-truth, for the poet herself disproves her own claim by writing, and her published poem—which returns the Muses (and both the poet and the reader) to the scene of the slaughter after all—becomes the tangible evidence of this fact.

Like all nationalist memorial poetry, Leadbeater's words generate both "sympathy" (in the eighteenth-century sense of "identification with" the feelings associated with the events) and cultural solidarity (in the sense of engendering a community feeling based on the shared horror and indignation called to mind by both the original event and its reenactment within the poem and within the orchestrated activity of reading). Leadbeater's occasional verses do not belong to the genre of popular national tales that appeared during the first decades of the nineteenth century and to which Balfour's "Kathleen O'Neil" does belong, but they share with those tales some of the genre's characteristic features. Those features, which Claire Connolly says were "the result of efforts by (chiefly) Irish female writers to give fictional shape to an interrelated set of concerns, including history, property, and national conduct," combined the traditionally male bardic verse tradition with contemporary feminist concerns about women's civic and cultural status (415). Because Connolly discusses the national tale primarily in terms of prose fiction, she proposes that "from 1808 to 1814 may be seen as the great years of the national tale" (415); in fact, verse tales grounded in Irish history and national mythology continued to be published for many more years.

The "Irishness" of Balfour's poems is of a very different quality from what we find in a later poem by Anne Lutton, "The Irish Peasant," that appeared in her *Poems on*

Moral and Religious Subjects in 1829, the year in which the Tories finally voted for the Catholic Emancipation bill. This, Lutton's most distinctively "Irish" poem, begins by announcing in its opening line, "My country!—much I love thee" (104). And though she does offer rich physical descriptions of the Irish countryside in which the tale is set, she quickly turns the poem into a moral essay on the Christian dignity of a life lived well, but out of the public eye, by the peasant (whom one assumes was himself a Catholic):

—Oh! happy peasant!—thou may'st pass thro' life—
Unheeded by the Great—but on thy soul
Beams the irradiation of the skies!
Small is thy portion of external sweets,
But rich thy flowing cup of inward bliss.   (107, ll. 71–75)

Lutton's Irish setting is a mere convenience for her moralizing, which comes as no surprise in light of her preface, where Lutton says of herself (in the third person) that as author and poet "she will always esteem it the happiest result of every liter-ary labour, should her efforts prove serviceable to the cause of vital Christianity, by inspiring or cherishing sentiments congenial with its spirit and tendency" (vi).

On the other hand, Agnes Mahony actually reverses the formulaic nostalgic na-tionalism that Lutton was trying to exploit in "The Irish Peasant" when in a poem called "Killarney's Lake," published in 1825 in *A Minstrel's Hours of Song,* she has that poem's alienated, emigrant female minstrel *repudiate* Ireland in favor of the England she has adopted as her home:

Land of the Shamrock, bright and fair!
Thine emerald hills are towering there!
For ever be those hills forgot!
Oh! Emerald Isle, I love thee not!
Land of the Rose, a wreath I'll twine,
And call thy much-lov'd country mine.
And though affliction hangs around
My gentle harp's responsive sound,
Still with a patriot's changeless fire
My spirit wakes the vocal lyre.   (44, ll. 95–104)

By the time we reach the poem's end, its conclusion, which is filled with localizing details, strikes one as remarkably ambivalent. The speaker claims in the final verse paragraph that the mention of "HIBERNIA's name" is so inextricably blended for her with "[t]he recollections of the past, / Life's present hours, and future years" that she

spontaneously weeps "burning tears" (45, ll. 106–10) which tears she then rational-
izes with this ambiguous concluding declaration:

> The cold world may defend the strong,
> Oppress the weak, uphold the wrong;
> Yet shall the Minstrel ever be
> In thought, in act, and spirit, free.   (45, ll. 111–14)

Left ambiguous is whether the penultimate couplet has to do with Ireland's subjugated situation in 1825 (when the poem was published in London), or whether it
aims to present a more universal observation on the state of the modern world in
general, in which the Darwinian model of natural selection (including the destruction of the weak) seems to lurk behind and within these final lines.

The Christian Denouement

The overt, explicit Christian imperative so evident in Anne Lutton's verse was in fact
an increasingly prominent feature of the poetry that women published in Ireland and
Scotland during the 1820s and 1830s. In Ireland, for example, the volumes of poetry
that appeared before 1820 were almost exclusively secular in nature. But Lutton's 1829
collection marked a new trend: among the twelve volumes published during 1830–35,
roughly half are explicitly religious in nature, from the anti-Catholic *Emmanuel*
(1833)[27] and *Life* (1835) of the Cork poet and subsequent missionary E. (Elizabeth?)
Colthurst to Mrs. John G. Guinness's *Sacred Portraiture and Illustrations, with Other
Poems* (1834) and Elizabeth Blackall's *Psalms and Hymns and Spiritual Songs* (1835).
To this same genre belongs also Anna Maria Winter's *The Fairies, and Other Poems*
(1833), whose long title poem is a moral fable thinly disguised as an interview between the narrator and Titania, queen of the fairies, who helps the narrator achieve a
better and fuller moral appreciation of the world. Winter's poem is in many respects
a poetic reformulation of material from her three-volume 1831 didactic prose work
The Moral Order of Nature. Much the same thing was happening in Scotland during
this period, where collections like Mrs. M. A. Reid's *The Harp of Salem* (1827) and
Margaret Patullo's *The Christian Psalter* (1828) appeared. Works like these document
the transition from what we usually think of as high Romanticism to the bourgeois domestic ideology of the Victorian era, with its reassertion of the straitened,
gendered notions that regarded religious and domestic subjects as the particularly
appropriate province of women writers.

At the same time, though, another important feature begins to be evident in

Irish women's poetry during this later period. As noted earlier, by the later 1820s women had begun to return in their poetry to the theme of Ireland's depressed state, a shift that reflected the increasingly widespread national unease about the worsening social and economic conditions in Ireland during the decades preceding the famine years. At the same time, though, as Irish writers in general contemplated during these same years the returning prosperity in England proper, it made little sense to some of them, either politically or economically, to perpetuate historically long-standing antagonisms when wealth and power was increasingly concentrated in English hands and when not just their prosperity but indeed their survival depended on their access to that power's instruments and institutions. Things began to change dramatically in 1829 with the passage of Catholic Emancipation, which seemed at last to signal the potential for genuine reconciliation, assimilation, and progress. Patrick Rafroidi observes, for example, that the enfranchisement of a "Catholic nation" under leaders like Daniel O'Connell produced a new and less bleak view of Irish history in which "history was no longer a sequence of events to be suffered, but rather a present and a future that everyone could and should help to shape" (1:79). Even before 1829 some women writers had already begun to approach the problem of antagonism and reconciliation by replacing the paradigm of competing hostile national identities with an alternative vision grounded in sympathy and benevolence, moral qualities that link their writing on the subject with the overt Christian moralism of some of the volumes mentioned above. The trope of sisterhood that figures in the *New Monthly Magazine*'s comment about "the sister islands," mentioned earlier in connection with Anna Liddiard, is of course a familiar element of the period's political and cultural discourse. But for the women poets it was more than just a rhetorical device. In fact, their work offers a considered alternative paradigm to the troubled political and cultural relationship between Ireland and England historically typified by a belligerent and masculinist hostility, an alternative paradigm that draws its force and presumed effectiveness from behaviors traditionally associated in Western culture with the feminine and with sisterhood.

After 1829 this pattern of figuration became even more evident, perhaps because the mitigating consequences of Catholic emancipation were seen to be no less symbolic than social and political. Mary McDermott's interesting 1832 volume, *My Early Dreams,* for instance, voices the contemporary dilemma in the opening of a poem called "Our Sister Land":

When Erin casts her sorrowing eyes across the green sea wave,
And looketh to her sister land to pity and to save:

Oh! when the sighing of her harp is sent across the deep;
Who is there with that mournful tone in sympathy to weep?
All her wild beauties they are dimmed by sorrow's blanching shade. . . .

(169, ll. 1–5)

The English are not a uniformly heartless people, however, McDermott continues. Some enlightened souls there "feel for her, by sorrow thus oppress'd" and when they look through "the veil which poverty had darkly round her thrown," these sympathetic fellow citizens recognize that "her great and noble soul was kindred with their own" (169, ll. 9–12). At the poem's conclusion Ireland gratefully reciprocates the sympathetic response of these enlightened English benefactors in her song:

And as she bends her sorrowing form, and dews her harp with tears;
Soft as by summer's south wind borne, that tender tone she hears:
Her eyes they brighten thro' her grief, as with the fondest strain,
That gratitude's deep soul can pour, she blendeth England's name.

(170, ll. 17–20)

Notice the terms here: tenderness, softness, teary eyes, and gratitude. All these are ascribed to the specifically *female* figure of Ireland. This gendering of the political relationship is particularly interesting in that the central character of McDermott's poem is a harper, who in most Irish poems is presented as a male bard rather than a female lyricist. At the same time, however, *England too* is gendered as female, as she is in another political poem from the same collection, "The Constitution of Great Britain, in the Year 1829." Although the feminized Britain in the form of Britannia is of course a familiar verbal and visual trope, the doubling of the gender references here underscores the deliberately and specifically gendered vision that McDermott is proposing of how the tortured relationship between the two countries might be amended. That alternative vision turns on the participants' election to adopt impulses and behaviors traditionally associated in cultural paradigms with the feminine and with sisterhood, a gendered alliance that finds many analogues in nineteenth-century visual art.[28]

Coda

In 1866 one Capt. W. Macbay published an extraordinary book called *The United Kingdom Really United (Ireland to England); How to Obtain Good and Cheap Beef and Unfailing Crops.* There he proposed that two great bridges should be constructed to connect Ireland and England:

To bridge over the Irish channel, and so connect Ireland with England, in the same way that Scotland is connected with it, would at once do away with her isolation, introduce a new era of civilization, call forth the energies of that country, to supply England and Scotland with her produce, raise the whole property of Ireland to a level with that of England, and in time smooth away, and blend those great distinctions of a social and national character, that at present exist, to the prejudice of that unfortunate country. . . .

. . . Had Ireland been so connected for the last 50 or 100 years, is it possible she would have been in such a backward, revolutionary condition, as she is at this moment; or, on the other hand, if Scotland had been so unfortunate as to have been separated from this country for a like period, would she have benefited to the extent she has? or, is it not probable that her very isolation would have found her, with her inferior soil, and fewer advantages than Ireland, with a class of agitators, doing their best to promote severance with the Mother country? . . .

. . . [I]t should be borne in mind that Ireland is of greater importance to the Crown, even than her Indian possessions; and if there be one gigantic work, more than another, that she ought to accomplish, she should certainly set about that which would tend to consolidate the three Kingdoms for ever. (7–8)

Fatuous as Macbay's scheme may sound to us today, it nicely reflects both the confidence of Britain in 1866 in its technological prowess and the English nation's wholly undiminished sense of innate superiority to its constituent but unmistakably inferior partners in union. Scotland and Ireland may be "sister" members, but England is styled—with telling finality—as the "*Mother* country" in Macbay's formulation. Moreover, he leaves little doubt that the "great distinctions of a social and national character" that presently exist to Ireland's detriment have to do not with any deficiencies on England's part but rather with the failings of "that unfortunate country."

I conclude this chapter with Macbay not for the striking image with which he presents us so much as for his language, which adopts the same gendered terminology we have seen both in the writings of the Irish women poets discussed in this chapter and in those of many of their critics and commentators, then and since. Macbay's rhetoric demonstrates just how widespread this figuration was by midcentury, and how easy it still was to employ it even while simultaneously articulating a fundamentally masculinist vision of nationhood. What Charlotte Brooke had written already in 1789 in her *Reliques of Irish Poetry* about the seniority of the Irish muse to the English one is also relevant here. While Macbay implicitly affirmed that the inequality of the two nations is unfortunate but natural, given their circumstances, Brooke contended that this inequality is not inherent at all, but that it stems from the faulty historical and cultural perspective that has been perpetuated literally over centuries by the dominant culture and applied retrospectively as if it were fact, not fiction. The bridge that Brooke and her sister poets seek to build with England is not an architectural and engineering marvel but a wonder of a finer sort, a cultural one that will first bridge and then eliminate present antagonisms by replacing the prevailing model of belligerent national and cultural machismo with one of benevolent sisterhood. Its egalitarian principles and its rootedness in human (and humane) sympathy mark all aspects of the poetry of the Romantic-era Irish women poets: cultural, intellectual, and aesthetic. Not a small and obscure body of poetry by a handful of equally obscure writers, that poetry is in fact a substantial body of literary production that played an important role in promulgating the leading characteristics and preoccupations of a distinctively *Irish* literary culture, especially in the decades immediately preceding the rise of the better known women poets who wrote for the Young Ireland movement in the 1840s and for the Fenians in the 1860s.[29] That poetry both presumed and participated in the broader literary community of "British" Romanticism —and its increasingly diversified reading publics—even as it sought to reclaim and retain those unique features that made it Irish.

Conclusion

More than a decade ago, Theresa M. Kelley and Paula R. Feldman concluded their introductory essay to their groundbreaking collection of essays on Romantic-era women's writing with the statement that "on every level, much remains to be done to specify the shape of Romantic women's careers and to situate those careers in something like a general (or particulate) field theory of Romanticism, defined by differences and new instabilities as much as or more than by similarities or by a tightly focused set of attributes" (10). Despite the remarkable volume of scholarship on the subject over the past several decades, what Kelley and Feldman said then remains true today. The proliferation of textual materials in both print and electronic forms has lent new access to the works (and the lives) of many writers whose names had vanished from literary history over the course of some two centuries. The editorial work that has accompanied the recovery of these texts has, moreover, reminded us of the complexity of the social, political, and economic circumstances in which these writers worked, were read, and were reviewed, just as it has helped, too, to draw a clearer picture of the day-to-day details of the publishing industry in Romantic-era Britain.

At the same time, important new research has provided a far more detailed and accurate account of the significant changes that transpired in that publishing industry, changes that wholly altered the nature of "reading" as both a pastime and an avocation. The changes in the demographics of readerships, which were both diversifying and growing larger, were attended by significant changes in what was published, in what form, and by which sorts of publishers, as William St. Clair has documented with particular clarity in *The Reading Nation in the Romantic Period.* Circulating libraries, which had risen to prominence in the 1790s and then grown exponentially through the Regency, played an increasingly important role in reading practices in Britain, where it became less necessary to *own* the books that one read when for a flexible and relatively reasonable fee one could have virtually unlimited access to both the established classics and the latest titles. Finally, periodical publication increased during the period, in terms of both the number of journals that were published and, more important, the number of copies that were produced of each issue. Mechanical and technological advancements made possible the production of quantities of journals—and even more dramatically, newspapers—that were undreamed of three decades earlier, and the production and distribution of books, too, was impacted by comparable advances. Literacy increased as well, in consequence of the wider availability of printed texts, even if many of those texts were not what we usually think of as "literary" in nature so much as didactic (e. g., conduct books and sermons) or occupationally "practical" (e.g., schoolbooks or books on cookery, husbandry, and vocational training). But reading—as publishers and the government both recognized—is an activity that easily becomes habit forming, even addictive. The market expanded as copies became cheaper, as their numbers grew, and as reading communities of all sorts became a major feature of British culture.

Women were active in all of this, both as producers and as consumers, as this book has shown. Recent research on print culture and the history of the book in the eighteenth and nineteenth centuries, as Jennie Batchelor and Cora Kaplan remark, opens fresh perspectives on "the intellectual effects of a widening cultural market" in which women were discovering new and profitable ways to participate (3). But the expansion and diversification of the literary market had its own consequences for *what* was written and published. In *Living by the Pen,* Cheryl Turner demonstrates that the woman who aimed to support herself and her family through her own literary activity had to take into account market factors over which she had little control, whether it be the (usually meager) sums which publishers paid for new works, the vagaries of pricing and distribution that affected sales (or library loans) and hence literary reputation, or the moral and ideological presumptions and biases of her reviewers. At the same time, especially in fiction, women authors were already beginning to be "edged out" of the market—or forced into particular niches of that market—by male authors who perceived that there were substantial profits to be made; the remarkable numbers of popular if undistinguished novels published by prolific Romantic-era men like Francis Lathom and Anthony Frederick Holstein illustrate the point.[1] The changes that transpired in the area of poetry are equally apparent when we consider how different in subject matter, rhetorical approach, and popular public reception the works of poets like Felicia Hemans and Letitia Elizabeth Landon are from those of poets like Mary Robinson and Charlotte Smith who had themselves been celebrated in their own time some three decades earlier. Moreover, as I suggested in chapter 4, the development during the period of the romance-oriented long verse narrative indicates the shift in readerly appetites toward the sort of sentimental escapist fiction that remains popular in our own times, when many readers are comparably hungry for emotionally imaginative alternatives to the depersonalization and harshness of modern materialist culture.

And then there were the literary annuals, which sold very well indeed, were widely read, and were decried by many traditionalist writers (poets and prose writers alike) who saw in them a corrupting commercialization that sacrificed "art" to "entertainment" and permanent fame to transitory celebrity. As Dennis Low reminds us, the editors of the annuals and other gift books "commissioned poems and other literary pieces by the page and often dictated their subject matter," and they marketed them not so much on the strength of their contents as on their sheer physical appeal, which they created with fancy bindings and lavish illustrations (9–10). At the height of her career, Landon, for instance, exerted considerable editorial control over the contents and format of *Fisher's Drawing Room Scrap Book,* for which she often composed poems to accompany engraved illustrations that she had herself selected as potentially attractive to *Fisher's* audience. This was very much literature as commodity, and potential readers—and purchasers—were in fact encouraged to judge these books by their covers. In reassessing the poetry written by women during the Romantic era, then, we need to bear in mind the extent to which their literary output reflected deliberate decisions on their part not just about the content of their poems but also, often at least as important, about the commercial viability—the salability—of those poems. Late in their careers, Hemans and Landon both expressed their unhappiness over the intellectual and artistic compromises they had made in their poetry to satisfy the demands imposed by public market factors, as did less well known poets like Melesina Trench, whose most productive writing years—which essentially encompassed the Regency period—were those during which this sea change in reading and writing practices was becoming apparent to all concerned.[2]

The changing nature of the literary scene and the pressures that increasingly bore on the author who wrote for a living, as opposed to one who enjoyed the leisure afforded by secure patronage, was apparent to all authors, whatever their reputation and level of support. Perhaps fittingly, these pressures were described in 1815 by an obscure and apparently male Irish poet by the name of M. M'Dermot.[3] I want to examine the introduction to *Poems on Various Occasions* here, then, despite its apparently male authorship, because it offers a useful concluding touchstone to many of the issues I have discussed in this book and because it further indicates the extent of the discursive common ground shared by poets of both sexes, thus demonstrating another aspect of the "community" interactivity that linked even poets who were probably unknown to one another. In this eloquent introduction M'Dermot celebrates the status of poets during "the primitive stages of the world," when "the unadulterated youth . . . poured forth the effusions of his soul in notes that accorded to the feelings of his heart":

> Man was not then as he is now, a dependent being; he felt no necessity of sacrific-ing at the unhallowed shrine of adulation, nor recoiling at the frown of indignant haughtiness;—he asserted his own natural rights, and no one sought to dispute his title. . . . Unaccustomed to a revolution of fortune, he was free from the cor-roding influence of apprehension; and, untainted by the poison of luxury, he indulged not in the hopes of future prosperity. . . . [H]e pleased others because he was pleased himself, and reached the heart without making any application to the judgment. (iii–v)

This happy state of affairs, M'Dermot continues, has long since vanished, along with the conditions that enabled it in that more innocent and spontaneous state of society. This early "Poet" derived his happiness not from "the prospect of riches, nor the allurements of patronage," but rather from the private observation of nature and the internal operation of fancy. As a result, "[h]e pursued intellectual pleasures not for the gifts they might procure, but for the gratifications they bestowed" (vi).

The modern world of materialism that Wordsworth had already declared to be "too much with us" had changed everything. Independence, once the "inalienable inheritance of all men," is now "a relative term, that expresses the adventitious state of a small portion of mankind" and that visibly excludes the poet from its "happy community" (vi):

> He is generally destined to rank amid the dependant part of mankind, and doomed to render his genius subservient to the fashion of the times.—He must adapt his own taste to the taste of others; he must feel as they feel, and think as they think; and spite of all the talents which nature has bestowed, and all the obse-quiousness which necessity has exacted, he must probably dwindle into obscurity, behold every endowment of mind which distinguished him from the unthinking multitude, congealed into stoic apathy. (vii)

If the poet is "the son of fortune," he can "be certain of establishing his fame even by a mediocrity of genius" (vii), his economic (class) status assuring that he can indulge his middling talent without significant financial risk.

This is the prospect facing the poet in 1815, M'Dermot explains: "He either sails triumphant, wafted by the auspicious gale of public favor, or is tossed through the broad ocean of life by the dark billows of disappointment" (vii). This precarious situation presents a severe caution to any poet who is not blessed by fortune and who therefore needs to be aware from the outset that "even superior merit cannot insure success, and that the doubtful voyage, even when steered by the unerring helm of moral rectitude, is still obnoxious to the vicissitudes of fortune, and the tempests of adversity" (viii). This grim prospect notwithstanding, M'Dermot declares, no genuine poet can stifle the impulse to express himself or herself, particularly when the muse makes the creative activity so irresistibly attractive. M'Dermot's point is that the true poet is a poet not by design or by practice but rather by nature, and that his or her utterance is therefore the voice of nature, mediated through that poet's art but "natural" nevertheless and therefore "true." "He, therefore, who is a poet by nature, *qui nascitur non fit* [who is born, not made], delights in the language of the inspiring muse," M'Dermot writes (viii). M'Dermot immediately assigns himself to this class of poets, to his own professed dismay, announcing that he is "unhappily, one of those who are, or who believe themselves to be, favoured by the muse" (viii), and he reminds his readers that while the empirical reasoner (he cites Locke as his model) "may censure her [the muse's, and by extension the poet's] effusions, they can never be condemned by the feelings of humanity" (ix).

Evident in all that M'Dermot says is his awareness of the crisis of individuality—or personal artistic independence—with which the poets of the time were discovering they would henceforth have to wrestle. Writing verse might very well begin in individual acts of sheer Kantian expressiveness, in what many poets, including M'Dermot, call "effusions" (typically lyrical and deeply personal) undertaken for the interconnected private pleasure of personal expression and the satisfying exercise of technical poetic skill. But as soon as authors elect to *publish* their poems they sacrifice the illusion of spontaneity, for their verses must now be revised and prepared for the press, which process introduces elements of both critical detachment and empirical calculation. Moreover, to publish at all is to envision both an imagined (or virtual) audience *and* a real one of (presumably) paying consumers whose expectations must be met and whose desires must be satisfied. Despite the familiar protestations in prefatory remarks to countless volumes that the poems were "never intended for publication" (as the poets tended to put it), preparing them for the press *does* "intend" them for publication after all, and the mere fact that the poet does "prepare" the poems indicates that she (or he) is making adjustments to them with those intended audiences in mind. If the poet is in fact aiming at both financial gain and literary reputation (which were increasingly perceived as one and the same), then she or he becomes unavoidably conscious in the process of the extent to which she or he modifies the form, content, and rhetoric of the poems in ways that better suit them to the tastes and expectations of the intended readership. All such adjustments, to the extent that the poet acknowledges that they are undertaken with the reader in mind, represent various sorts of compromises, betrayals, or misrepresentations of what originally constituted (at least ostensibly) distinctively private, personal utterance. The movement toward technical artifice is implicitly a movement away from naturalness (or nature, with or without a capital "n"), and as such it signals a shift of authorial intention away from self-expression and toward consumer satisfaction. It is the commoditization of art, in short, and a harbinger of the multifaceted and frequently troubling nature of the literary culture in the modern world.

The issues that M'Dermot raises troubled others as well, as I have argued in this study, and it is notable that M'Dermot's comments are bracketed, chronologically, by clearly related observations made by Martha Hanson in 1809 (*Sonnets, and Other Poems*) and Mariann Dark in 1818 (*Sonnets, and Other Poems*), both of whose work I discussed in chapter 3. Dark foresaw her own erasure from the literary record when in her sonnets she compared her circumstances (and reputation) to those of the famous and influential Charlotte Smith. Hanson took the less direct route into her real subject, beginning by rejecting the commonplace practice of apologizing for publishing one's work, which publication she regards in her own case not as an imposition on the public but rather as a gift. She observes that in reality "few, if any, works of considerable length, are written, or even begun, with the intention of allowing them to remain in the obscurity of their Author's closet" (ix). But Hanson also acknowledges the folly of hoping for popularity (much less fame), writing ruefully that Britain "recognizes not her Writers, as worthy of regard, till long consigned to the silent tomb"; paradoxically, once they are dead, though, authors are far more likely to achieve the fame that had escaped them in life (x). Hence she regretfully observes of her poems that her consciousness of the fickleness of both critical and popular taste "forbids [her] to hope, that they will survive, to obtain, for their Author, the consideration of succeeding times" (xi).

This is a gloomy prospect, especially when it comes in the introduction to two volumes of poems that comprise nearly four hundred pages. But Hanson's sentiments echo those of Elizabeth Moody, who had written a decade earlier, in a witty and pun-laden passage in the preface to her *Poetic Trifles* (1798), that her own "Muse" stood "a fair chance of remaining some time *stationary*, looking through the bookseller's shop window; whence she may be *removed*, (without Habeas Corpus,) to the pastry cooks; and finally, may take up her everlasting rest at the bottom of a *trunk*" (ii–iii; Moody's emphases). Wit notwithstanding, one feels the chilling seriousness of what follows for Moody:

Can I view without deep-felt sensations of mortification, my *darling* offspring thus deposited? It is true this has been the *family vault* of many a Poet; but a Poet does not love to think of the death of his verse any more than of his own.— It is a painful endeavour in both cases to master the thought, and make it subservient to fortitude and resignation." (iii; Moody's emphases)

It is no coincidence that poets of both sexes—but women in particular—so often linked the erasure of their poetical works and their poetic selves with their own physical dissolution.

I have given the last word to M'Dermot, and, in the process, also to Moody, Hanson, and Dark, both because M'Dermot's comments effectively indicate how the public situation of the poet was changing at this time and because his remarks suggest how he, like Wordsworth in the advertisement to *Lyrical Ballads,* wanted to remove the intermediaries between the poet and the reader(s), so that the poet might speak directly to the *feelings* of the latter and not have to depend for success on the "learned" but inevitably biased opinions of the intermediary professional or pseudoprofessional critic. For the many—indeed the hundreds of—poets like M'Dermot, Hanson, and Dark, who published their poems earnestly and enthusiastically and then watched as their efforts were either disparaged, attacked or, worst of all, simply ignored, M'Dermot's comments reveal with particular poignancy that he fully understood what are today called "market factors" that the poet cannot control and can only try to circumvent by appealing to the individual reader. The era of intimacy between author and reader was coming to a close, and the emerging market of mass readerships would permit no going back. Poets would find in this new world fewer and fewer chances to succeed in the way in which poets often had been successful in the preceding century. That so many of the younger poets could still remember this now lost world only made it harder for them to accept the fact that they could do nothing to bring it back. This may be another reason why so many turned to various sorts of nostalgic forms like the verse narrative romance or, later, to pseudobiographical (and pseudoautobiographical) poems like those in Hemans's *Records of Woman* (1828) and Landon's *The Troubdour* (1825), *The Venetian Bracelet* (1829), and *The Vow of the Peacock* (1835). Both the intimate personal (autobiographical) self and the self-revealing lyric it produces brought with them too much danger of rejection, and the emerging genre of the dramatic monologue offered an attractive measure of insulation, even if it also produced self-isolation for the poet whose own life and circumstances could now be read only analogously, rather than actually, in such poems. The compulsion to "follow the muse," to be a poet and send one's personal voice out into the public sphere, had become a dangerous and often self-destructive one, even when it was not so dramatically so as it had been in the case of famous suicides like Chatterton. Perhaps the protracted death in the midst of silence and neglect, which all these poets feared whether they admitted it or not, really was the worst death of all.

The question that needs to be asked at the end of a book like this one is in some respects disarmingly simple. Why does all of this matter? That is, what can we learn from recovering and reassessing the works of literally hundreds of women poets (and prose writers) whose lives and works had largely vanished from the literary record over the preceding two centuries? What is the point of the project, when classroom teachers, compilers of anthologies (usually intended for those teachers and their students), and scholars (of Romanticism, of women's studies, of British cultural history) so often appear already to be burdened with more material than they can easily or effectively deal with in their normal routines? As Shelley wrote in his *Defence of Poetry* about the superabundance of data, "our calculations have outrun conception; we have eaten more than we can digest" (*Shelley's Poetry and Prose,* 530). Shelley's term, "calculations" offers a useful hint. It is not so much that we need to "recalculate" what we know about Romantic-era poetry and about the various alternative and competing literary canons that the last several decades of scholarship have produced. Rather, we need now to reimagine the Romantic literary community in terms of a broadly interactive and multivocal conversation in which the participants are forthright (with themselves and with their audiences) about acknowledging the presence and influence of the many voices audible in that conversational community. Because literary-historical scholarship requires a grounding in as much primary textual evidence as possible, I have aimed in this book to "name names" and to suggest how and why these women poets (who still represent only a limited sampling) and their works—many of them still all too unfamiliar to any but the specialist— need to be reassessed. This reassessment needs to reappraise them both on their own merits (and demerits) and in terms of the larger landscape of what we will continue to call "British Romanticism." Modern advances in digital and electronic media are all providing scholars with increasing access to texts whose rarity has previously left them largely unexamined, entombed in collections and archives scattered about the globe. The more of this recovered poetry we read, and the more we do so with an openness to both its intrinsic merit and its often conspicuous intertextuality, the clearer the portrait of the literary community we will be able to paint. And this larger portrait needs to be continually redrawn, both today and long into the future, as we become still better acquainted with the lives and works of poets of both sexes who have historically been absent from the picture.

My second aim concerns that larger picture itself. Even though my discussion here has focused primarily on *books* of poems rather than on the countless individual poems that appeared in the periodical press (and although it does not even try to address the vast quantity of writing that exists only in unpublished manuscripts), it is plainly evident that the women poets knew, reflected on, discussed, and materially influenced the nature and substance of the contemporary discourse about war, politics, economics, social justice (and injustice), domestic life, *and aesthetics.* Moreover, it is equally clear that not only did a considerable number of them know and respond to one another's works, creating what Sarah Prescott has described as the sociable and collaborative variety of writing visible already in the early eighteenth century but that they also knew *and responded to* the works of their male contemporaries, with whom they frequently engaged in remarkably egalitarian discussion in their poetry. Further still, it is also apparent that many of these male contemporaries knew the works of the female poets and likewise engaged in a conversation in print with them, whether in the form of scurrilous dismissals like those penned by T. J. Mathias and Richard Polwhele, reviews both friendly and unfriendly like John Wilson Croker's or Leigh Hunt's, poetic dialogues in which poets such as Samuel Taylor Coleridge (for example) engaged with Mary Robinson and Anna Letitia Barbauld, private comments such as Byron's professions of admiration for Joanna Baillie and distaste for Felicia Hemans, and published works such as Thomas Gent's warmly appreciative sonnet on the death of Charlotte Smith (1808), or William Wordsworth's 1833 observation that Smith was a poet "to whom English verse is under greater obligations than are likely to be either acknowledged or remembered." My discussion here invites Romantics scholarship both to acknowledge *and to remember* the debt that English verse owes not just to Charlotte Smith but indeed to all those many women who wrote and published poetry under difficult circumstances, contributing their efforts and their voices in what they clearly regarded as a community-oriented national *duty* to educate and to humanize their British sisters and brothers.

My third aim objective follows from the first two. We have reached a point at which we must collectively rise to another challenge posed to us by the recovery work that has been accomplished to date. This challenge involves reassessing the whole matter of *aesthetics* as it applies to Romantic poetry in Britain. If what Jerome McGann famously called "the Romantic ideology" may now be seen to have been defined (or misdefined) by the scholarly literary-historical perusal of too small a "sample set"—the constellation of male poets that Harold Bloom called "the visionary company" in 1971—then it is undeniably time for scholars to revisit the whole matter and to begin rethinking Romantic aesthetics. The process will be messy, of course, since competing theoretical, formal, social, and political measurements will be applied to the poems, and so all results will be tentative in any case. But that is as it should be. Scholarship not just in British Romanticism but indeed in all areas of literary, artistic, and cultural endeavor has often been hampered by the seeming inflexibility of the terms of its discourse. "Rules," "laws," "principles": whatever we choose to call them, they are customarily designed to exclude more so than to include, so that what does not "fit" is most easily disregarded or dismissed. M. H. Abrams wrote in *The Mirror and the Lamp* that "the endemic disease of analogical thinking is hardening of the categories" (34–35). Writing about Romantic-era literature has often been plagued by a comparable ossification that has yielded a sharply distorted picture. Just as it is hard to look at the moon and *not* see the Man in the Moon there once one has seen his face, so too is it still difficult for many of us to look at "Romantic poetry" and not see what so many of us trained ourselves (or permitted ourselves to be trained) to see there. And to judge it accordingly, excluding all other alternative sites and sights. It is time, then, for us to embrace the alternatives and the discontinuities rather than seeking to minimize or banish them. A more genuinely inclusive approach to Romantic aesthetics (including Romantic poetics) need not be seen as opening the door to critical (or aesthetic) anarchy, though. Rather, it is an invitation to conversation—itself an inherently Romantic form of discourse.

Revisiting Romantic aesthetics will of course be a tough project, fraught with all sorts of political and ideological pitfalls. We shall need a good deal more civility and generosity of spirit than is the norm in these fretful days, when the humanities are under siege by cultural critics (ranging from media pundits to academic administrators) who regard this sort of inquiry as notoriously "unprofitable" in both intellectual and economic terms. Nevertheless, it is clear that we require a new, revisionist aesthetics that is capable of coming to terms with the unwieldy, undisciplined, and seemingly inconsistent body of writing that in fact constitutes British "Romantic" writing. On the way to this new aesthetics we shall have to adjust many of our comfortingly familiar attitudes and expectations. We shall have to temper our perhaps understandable conditioned preference for the Jacobin over the anti-Jacobin, for example, for the dissenting over the consenting, for the radical over the reactionary. Marilyn Butler nudged us all in this direction nearly thirty years ago, but the perennial attraction of leftist politics and aesthetics have made us slow to take up the challenge of addressing what lies there on the right. More recently, Gerardine Meaney has put it this way:

Criticism . . . must remain alert to the pitfalls of conducting literary history as a recruitment drive. Implicit even within the most postmodern and radical readings of the literary past is the desire to identify that which is progressive and attractive, that which vindicates and approximates to the literary and critical values of the present. (768)

As innumerable "casebooks" devoted to well-known texts amply demonstrate, it is possible to pass a text through a variety of sieves in order to sift out evidence congenial to a particular critical or theoretical position and in the process to make that text seem to bear out the individual critic's own ideological agenda. It can be done, and indeed it is done with alarming regularity in a profession in which the inexorable pressure to publish plays so prominent a role. But is it accurate? Is it fair? Indeed, is it honest?

In rethinking matters like these, we shall need to acknowledge, then, more than we have historically done, namely, that while one strain of Romantic thought and expression was at any given moment generally "*going* somewhere"—breaking new ground—another strain was often quite pointedly *not* going there and that, moreover, that recalcitrant, reactionary strain often represented the intellectual and ideological principles—no less than the criteria of "taste"—of the cultural majority. Recognizing and then taking seriously the extent and vigor of this conservative mainstream is crucial both for reassessing Romantic-era writing and for rethinking *why* we customarily assess it as we do—and as we long have done. It may not be amiss, in fact, to consider starting over, beginning anew. Just as the "Romantic canon" has over the last quarter century or so been challenged by anticanons and alternative canons, so too will traditional aesthetics need to be interrogated. Just as its defenders have rallied around the traditional canon, eager to fend off upstarts and challengers of all sorts, so too has a new vigor—and a new vision—emerged in the field of Romantic aesthetics that has begun to generate new contests and open up the sort of new vistas that Blake anticipated when he declared that "[o]pposition is true Friendship" (*The Marriage of Heaven and Hell,* pl. 20, *Complete Poetry and Prose,* 42). The contest is not, after all, about any single canon, nor about competing canons: it is about truth, accuracy, and the history of the ways in which literary and cultural judgments come to be made, enforced, and enculturated. For Romantics studies, it is a matter of seeing the picture that is—and always was—actually there before our eyes rather than the one that so many of us came to think we knew without ever having really looked at it.

Despite the consternation and anxiety they may have awakened among some and the excitement they may have generated among others, the "canon wars" that have been vigorously contested over the course of the last two decades or so have been healthy for Romantics studies. What one regards —and teaches—today as "British Romanticism" is no longer a walled-off, exclusionary pleasure garden like Kubla Khan's erstwhile Eden. For like Coleridge's great Khan, the canon's entrenched defenders have nevertheless heard the inescapable *generational* voices prophesying war—the culture wars, the canon wars. At the same time, we have all learned how ultimately unhelpful (and unhealthy) it is for the revisionists simply to ignore or to insult away the canonicals as unregenerate intellectual Luddites. However the contending parties choose to make their own case(s), they must nevertheless be prepared to occupy the field after they have taken it, and the literary-historical ploughshares they fashion from their critical/theoretical swords will be steel nevertheless, merely refashioned. Moreover, these hard-won positions will themselves be contested in the recurrent culture wars that are the hallmark and the heritage of Romanticism itself. We are at a remarkably good point, then, while things are very much in critical and theoretical flux, to begin to explore alternative ways of defining and assessing "value," ways that may enable us to loosen our accustomed grip on reductive dialectical terms like "good" and "bad" and to experiment with more generous (although no less rigorous or principled) terms like "dynamism," "function," "effectiveness," and "consequence."

The new aesthetics of Romanticism—and there will have to be at least one—will draw on technological resources—the Internet, digital editions, portable and cross-platform texts, increasingly sophisticated computer software—that will facilitate increasingly sophisticated primary textual scholarship. At the same time, nothing will ever replace the acts of individual and collective reading carried on with book in hand and with an appreciation for the purely tactile aspects of dealing with books. But these reading acts will be accompanied by other, more culturally informed acts that go with recovering texts that have long been hidden from view and that will involve making continuous critical adjustments to accommodate each of them to the evolving literary landscape of British Romantic writing. At the very least, we shall gain immeasurably from the contests about "valuation" (however we choose to try to define it) that will inevitably ensue as we continue to devise and to apply an infinitely flexible array of critical, cultural, historical, and rhetorical yardsticks by which we shall attempt to measure both the newly recovered and the thoroughly familiar texts. And so too will the authors and the works that furnish the many fields on which those contests will be played out.

Introduction

1. In the sixth edition of the ubiquitous *Norton Anthology of English Literature* (1993), women's writing occupied only about 5 percent of the pages allotted to Romanticism. And despite announcing that it "includes other figures, especially women, who have been less emphasized in the past" (5), the 1995 edition of David Perkins's familiar *English Romantic Writers* managed to boost their presence to barely 9 percent, and that principally by including prose selections. Even Jessica and Jonathan Wordsworth's *New Penguin Book of Romantic Poetry* (2002) assigns only roughly 14 percent of its space to women poets. By contrast, the third edition of Duncan Wu's *Romanticism: An Anthology* (2006) gives women writers slightly more than 20 percent of the space.

2. Curran, "Romantic Poetry." See also Curran, *Poetic Form and British Romanticism.*

3. The opening date has sometimes been set at the date of the storming of the Bastille and the beginning of the French Revolution (1789) and at other times at that of the anonymous initial publication of Wordsworth's and Coleridge's *Lyrical Ballads* (1798). Most often the closing date has been made to coincide with the passage of the first Reform Bill (1832). In another of the paradoxes of traditional literary history, two of these three dates mark events in the political—rather than the literary—world, even though the traditional literary-historical view of British Romanticism has eschewed serious consideration of the decidedly *political* nature of much of the writing—in all genres—of this period.

4. See especially Davidoff and Hall, *Family Fortunes.*

5. See, for instance, Felski, *Beyond Feminist Aesthetics;* Backscheider and Dykstal, introduction.

6. For Habermas, see especially *The Structural Transformation of the Public Sphere.*

7. For Smith's systematic appropriation of Shakespeare, see especially Currie, "Borrowed Authority, Satirized Genre."

8. See Johnson, preface, *Provincial Poetry,* [v–vii].

9. See Charles Robinson, *Shelley and Byron,* and Behrendt, *Shelley and His Audiences.*

10. St. Clair, *The Reading Nation,* 159; Pascoe, introduction, 19; Dibert-Himes, "The Comprehensive Index and Bibliography to the Collected Works of Letitia Elizabeth Landon." St. Clair notes that the separate publication of Southey's poems in the periodical press had earned him nearly £1,500, which was far more than the book produced for him (159). Pascoe notes that in assuming the post of poetry editor at the *Morning Post* in late 1799 (succeeding

Southey in that role, in fact), Robinson ensured the even wider appearance of her work in that paper's pages (34).

11. See Jackson, *Annals of English Verse.* According to Jackson's conservative figures, which, not surprisingly, fail to record *every* publication, there were some 10,300 volumes, including among them approximately 7,500 "first editions" or first-time appearances. The greatest number of these date from the decade of the Regency (2,213, 1,469 of which were first editions), but the output is fairly consistent over the period, beginning with 1,361 volumes (of which 1,105 were "first" editions) in 1770–79 and then declining to 1,941 (1,300 of which were first editions) in 1820–29.

12. The full title of Hodgson's poem is *Childe Harold's Monitor; or, Lines Occasioned by the Last Canto of Childe Harold, Including Hints to Other Contemporaries.* Curran notes that the poem is erroneously attributed to T. J. Mathias (of *Baeviad* fame) in the British Library catalogue and in a contemporary review that appeared in the *Gentleman's Magazine* (224).

13. Letter to Rose Lawrence, 13 February 1835; quoted in Wolfson, introduction, xxiv.

14. Ashfield, introduction.

15. *British Review* 15 (January 1820): 299.

16. *Quarterly Review* 24 (October 1820): 131; emphases mine.

17. "Sonnet on the Death of Mrs. Charlotte Smith" (53). The sonnet is one of the poems that was added to the second edition; the first edition appeared in Yarmouth in 1805, followed by a London impression in 1806. The poems are dedicated to George Canning, founder of and contributor to the *Anti-Jacobin Review,* whom Gent declares to be "not less distinguished for his attainments as a scholar, than for his talents as a statesman" (dedication). The poem appeared again in Gent's 1820 *Poems,* and in a subsequent "new edition" (London, 1828).

18. *Monthly Magazine,* n.s., 1 (April 1826): 417.

19. In *A Book of Women's Verse,* the editor, J. C. Squire, castigates Rowton—with good reason—as "a thief, a hypocrite, a most oily and prolix driveller" (ix), largely on the basis of Rowton's wholesale, unacknowledged appropriations from Dyce's 1825 *Specimens of British Poetesses.*

20. The phrase was used most notably by Jerome J. McGann, whose important 1983 study was one of the earliest calls for a reassessment not just of what we understand by the term "Romantic" but also of the nature and assumptions of the literary-critical activities by which scholars and others have attempted to understand the literature usually gathered—selectively—under the umbrella term "Romantic." See McGann, *The Romantic Ideology.*

21. See also Mathias, *The Pursuits of Literature.* By 1798 Mathias's satire had grown to a total of four dialogues and was into its eighth edition.

22. *Eclectic Review* 4 (September 1808): 815–16.

23. A prefatory poem, "To R. S., the Literal Translator," explains that the author's father, Richard Shackleton, translated the Latin original; for Leadbeater, "untaught in learned lore, / Maffæus sung in vain; / Nor could my anxious wish explore / The Latin poet's strain" (iii).

24. *Eclectic Review* 4 (September 1808): 819.

25. *Critical Review,* s. 3, 15 (October 1808): 217–18.

26. *Eclectic Review* 9 (March 1813): 221.

27. The online *Encarta Dictionary and Encyclopedia* tags "Romanticism" with these synonym markers: "idealization, fantasy, nostalgia, soft focus, rose-tinted glasses, invention, ide-

alism, naiveté." Meanwhile, the brief entry for "Romantic poets" names only Wordsworth, Coleridge, Byron, Shelley, and Keats (and not Blake), to which it adds Scott.

28. See especially Moers, *Literary Women;* Poovey, *The Proper Lady and the Woman Writer;* Mellor, *Romanticism and Gender;* Curran, *Poetic Form and British Romanticism;* Wolfson, *Formal Charges.* See also Ross, *The Contours of Masculine Desire,* Cox, *Gender, Genre and the Romantic Poets,* and Linkin and Behrendt, *Romanticism and Women Poets.*

29. See, for example, the essays in Sweet and Melnyk, *Felicia Hemans;* Tighe, *The Collected Poems and Journals of Mary Tighe;* Glennis Stephenson, *Letitia Landon: The Woman behind L. E. L.*

Chapter 1 · Women Writers, Radical Rhetoric, and the Public

1. Two important recent studies are Clark, *The Struggle for the Breeches,* and Craciun, *British Women Writers.*

2. The first phrase is from the *True Briton.* The latter hyperbole reflects the thinking of the *Oracle* and the *Morning Post;* see Werkmeister, *A Newspaper History,* 311–12. To be sure, it was not a radical poet to whom these accolades were directed but a Della Cruscan whose *Modern Manners* (1793) was an instant success and whose *Monody to the Memory of the Late Queen of France* (1793) was much admired by the British press generally.

3. See Craciun and Lokke, "British Women Writers," and Miller, "The Politics of Truth and Deception." The first quoted phrase is from the *Critical Review* of September 1792 and the second is from Catherine Dorset's memoir of Smith; both are quoted in Craciun and Lokke, "British Women Writers," 24–25.

4. See Mellor, *Romanticism and Gender,* passim.

5. The former poem appeared in the *Gentleman's Magazine* in January 1797, the latter in the *Morning Post* on 21 January 1795.

6. See, for instance, the arguments developed by Mary Wollstonecraft in her *Vindication of the Rights of Woman* (1792), Mary Darby Robinson (writing anonymously) in *Thoughts on the Condition of Women* (no date, but probably late 1790s), Mary Hays (also writing anonymously) in *An Appeal to the Men of Great Britain in Behalf of Women* (1798), Mary Ann Radcliffe in *The Female Advocate* (1799) and, later, men like William Thompson in his *Appeal of One Half of the Human Race, Women, against the Pretensions of the Other Half, Men, to Retain Them in Political, and Thence in Civil and Domestic, Slavery* (1825).

7. Steedman points out that others had made this point before her, most notably Joan Wallach Scott in *Gender and the Politics of History.*

8. See Landry, *The Muses of Resistance;* Lovell, *Consuming Fiction;* Turner, *Living by the Pen.*

9. On this point, and on *Julia,* see Kennedy, "Responding to the French Revolution."

10. The novel does include a poem, but it is not by Smith; in the final volume Smith attributes to Geraldine Verney a poem that was in fact composed by Smith's friend Henrietta O'Neill: "Ode to the Poppy."

11. Part 1 of Thomas James Mathias's *The Pursuits of Literature* appeared in 1794, parts 2 and 3 in 1796, part 4 in 1797. Thereafter, the poem went through many editions. By 1812, the year of the sixteenth edition, it had grown to a large quarto volume of 542 pages, with copious notes, translations of passages, and a detailed index. Interestingly, after the initial publication of parts 1–3 by Owen, publication was taken over by Becket, who was still involved in its pub-

lication in the 1812 sixteenth edition, where "Becket and Porter" are identified prominently on the title page as "Booksellers to the Prince Regent."

12. Ironically, already in the early nineteenth century women writers were beginning to explore the paradoxically *liberating* and *empowering* consequences for them and their families of the patriarchal male's removal from the domestic circle by his death. Barbara Hofland, who began her publishing career in 1805 with a collection of poems, published numerous novels about widows and their families. In virtually every case the husband's death precipitates a radical reorganization of the surviving family and the priorities of its members, who turn this dramatic reversal into an opportunity to develop and mature, both individually and collectively. More important, Hofland repeatedly shows us that this reorientation and the consequent altered commitment of purpose among the surviving family results in significant financial gain, an aspect of plotting that looks ahead to the materialistic value system we customarily associate with Victorian culture. See Behrendt, "Women without Men."

13. The poem's original title was *Sympathy; or, A Sketch of the Social Passion.*

14. The poem's full title is "Poverty; or, The Irish in London: A Reverie." Although it was not published until 1821, the poem's lengthy subtitle indicates that it was "Written during the Severe, and Long Continuing Frost, in the Winter of 1794–95" (13), which makes it contemporary with Robinson's "January, 1795."

15. First published in the *Universal Magazine* in March 1795, reproduced in Bennett, *British War Poetry,* 149–50.

16. Although no publication information appears, a penciled note on the title page of the British Library copy identifies the author as "George Miller of Dunbar." The title page of this presentation copy also bears this inscription: "Presented by the Author to the editor of the Philanthropist with best wishes that his efforts to put an end to the horrid and barbarous custom of War may be crowned with the most complete success." The editor was Daniel Isaac Eaton; the *Philanthropist* was the more economically and socially oriented successor to his *Politics for the People,* which ceased publication in March 1795, the month in which the *Philanthropist* began a run that lasted forty-three weeks, until early 1796.

Adriana Craciun has pointed out that in December 1797 Mary Robinson adopted this same pseudonym, "Humanitas," for a poem she published in the *Morning Post,* "Verses on the Nineteenth of December 1797" (*British Women Writers,* 77–78).

17. The poem, whose "subtitle" is the date, "27th January 1795," originally appeared in the Norwich press, in the *Cabinet* 2 (1795): 92–94, where it was attributed only to "N."

18. See, for instance, Goodwin, *The Friends of Liberty.* For example, in the industrial northwest the *Manchester Herald,* which began publication in March 1792, rejected both the moderate politics and the reserved rhetoric of the *Sheffield Patriot* (also founded in March 1792), effectively forcing other periodicals like the *Sheffield Register* (established 1787) to adopt greater stridency. As Goodwin shows, similar shifts in tone and ideology characterized the regional press nationwide, and when the central government eventually intervened, it was to suppress the radical press (chapter 7).

19. The Regency Bill, by which the Prince of Wales would rule if the king were incapacitated, was proposed to Parliament in 1789 after George III's first bout of mental illness. The king recovered before the bill could be advanced and passed. A Regency Act was not finally passed until 1811, after the king's last incapacitation.

20. See Judith Pascoe's notes to the poem in *Selected Poems,* 290. Adriana Craciun notes that none of the "Tabitha Bramble" poems were included in the 1806 posthumous edition that Robinson's daughter prepared, the ostensible reason being that those poems represented "lighter compositions." As Craciun points out, these poems were not "light" at all but instead represented some of Robinson's most pointed and biting radical commentary (*British Women Writers,* 79).

21. The poem is reproduced in Scrivener, *Poetry and Reform,* 122–23.

22. Lee's comments are cited by Epstein in *Radical Expression,* 8.

23. The *Tribune* appeared in 1795 and ceased publication in 1796; the *Moral and Political Magazine* ran from July 1795 to June 1796 (Scrivener, *Poetry and Reform,* 108–9, 127).

24. See Rice-Oxley, *Poetry of the Anti-Jacobin.*

25. See, for example, Linda Colley, *Britons,* and Newman, *The Rise of English Nationalism.*

26. Significantly, Spence's little volume (thirty pages) begins with a poem called "The Millennium" which she tells us was also "written in the year 1794 or 5" (v).

27. *Eclectic Review* 8 (May 1812): 474; cited in Barbauld, *Poems,* 310n.

28. A native of Norwich, itself a center of radical dissent, Opie (née Alderson) had many radical friends, including both Wollstonecraft and Godwin.

29. *Gentlemen's Magazine* 84 (November 1814): 458; *Eclectic Review,* n.s., 2 (July 1814): 101.

30. *Quarterly Review* 7 (June 1812): 309.

Chapter 2 · *Women Poets during the War Years*

1. Winston Churchill, speech to House of Commons, June 4, 1940.

2. See, for instance, Polwhele, *The Unsex'd Females;* Gisborne, *Enquiry into the Duties of the Female Sex;* More, *Strictures on the Modern System of Female Education.*

3. See, for instance, "To My Eldest Brother, with the British Army in Portugal," from which line 27 is quoted here. This poem was placed, significantly, just before the long poem, "The Domestic Affections," with which the collection of that title concludes. In 1812 she married Capt. Alfred Hemans, himself a veteran of the Peninsular Campaign.

4. See, for example, other flag-waving poems from *The Domestic Affections* like "To My Younger Brother, on His Return from Spain, after the Fatal Retreat under Sir John Moore, and the Battle of Corunna" and "The Wreath of Loyalty" ("Written for the Jubilee of the 25th Oct. 1809" commemorating the fiftieth year of George III's reign).

5. The figures in the following paragraphs are derived from a number of sources, including Traill and Mann, *Social England,* vol. 5; Christie, *Wars and Revolutions;* Emsley, *British Society and the French Wars;* Mackesy, "Strategic Problems of the British War Effort."

6. The poem, titled "Stanzas, Occasioned by the Death of Mr. S. Radford, Lieutenant in the Royal Engineers, by the Yellow Fever, in the West Indies, in 1802," appears in Hoole's 1805 *Poems,* 165–68. She names other casualties in a note and concludes with this statement: "These Officers went out together, and were all victims to the yellow fever, after about four months' residence on the Island. About the same time also the civil Engineer to the Island died" (167).

7. Stewart's story is related by Glieg, *The Subaltern,* 9–19. Harris recounts his proposition in *Recollections of a Rifleman.* See also Donaldson, *Recollections of an Eventful Life,* and Wheeler, *The Letters of Private Wheeler.*

8. Patricia Y. C. E. Lin has examined this issue in her doctoral dissertation, "Extending Her Arms," where she discusses the British government's efforts to create the nation's first social welfare system to assist the families of common soldiers and seamen.

9. Marlon Ross observes that this shift also marks a move whereby British authors, who had tended before this time to occupy the peripheries of political discourse, began to immerse themselves in politics and social service (*The Contours of Masculine Desire,* 192).

10. *The Siege of Gibraltar* was subsequently included in *Miscellaneous Pieces.* Upton was married to a lieutenant in the army and had firsthand experience with coming under fire; in 1781 she published a prose pamphlet about the siege in the form of a journal addressed to her brother. Not disillusioned by her husband's or her own experience, she declares in her preface that she has "returned to England with a firm resolution to educate my son to arms" (4). See Jackson, *Romantic Poetry by Women,* 355–56. A will dated 15 October 1781 was recorded at Canterbury for "Jonathan Upton, Lieutenant of His Majesty's Ship Thunderer": whether this is Catharine Upton's husband is unclear. That she was by 1784 employed as a governess in a girls' school suggests that he did not survive the siege (which took place between 24 June 1779 and 7 February 1783), during which 333 British citizens were killed, 911 were wounded, and 536 died from disease.

11. See Feldman, "Women Poets and Anonymity in the Romantic Era," 279–89.

12. In her 1781 prose pamphlet Upton repeatedly refers to her very young daughter Charlotte and her somewhat older son Jack.

13. Bennett's collection of some 350 poems drawn from the literally thousands published during the period on various aspects of war remains a rich resource. See also Scrivener, *Poetry and Reform.*

14. In *Harvest.* Richardson published a poem called *Waterloo,* a brief verse narrative called *Isaac and Rebecca,* and *Ludolph, or the Light of Nature,* as well as a novel, *The Soldier's Child; or, Virtue Triumphant.* She is not to be confused with another Charlotte Caroline Richardson, who married a shoemaker in 1802 and who, upon the deaths of him and their daughter in 1804, opened a school in York. With the sponsorship of her influential patron, Mrs. Newcome Cappé (Catharine Cappé), she published in 1806 a collection called *Poems Written on Different Occasions* that saw a second edition in the same year; this was followed in 1809 by a second volume, meant as a companion to the first and bearing the telling title of *Poems, Chiefly Composed during the Pressure of a Severe Illness.* See Jackson, *Romantic Poetry by Women,* 268–69.

15. On Opie's antiwar rhetoric, see also Mahon, "In Sermon and Story."

16. A later edition of Campbell's poems was published in London by Baldwin, Cradock, and Joy in 1816.

17. This information comes from the preface, which declares that the publisher (presumably J. Young, who first published the poems in 1811) was so impressed with the naive beauty of the poems and so struck by his "feeling for the helpless situation of one who seemed so unconscious of their value" that he published the poems for Campbell's sole benefit (7–9).

18. See also Duffy, "War, Revolution, and the Crisis of the British Empire," where deployments to Ireland are considered in addition to those to the Americas.

19. A second edition of Hunter's collection appeared in 1803.

20. H. T. Dickinson observes that this disproportionate burden on the lower classes often

significantly affected both the poor rates and overall public order. See his introduction to *Britain and the French Revolution,* 16.

21. See, for instance, Emsley, *British Society and the French Wars.*

22. Among the later fictional works that examined some of the consequences of the press gangs' activities was Elizabeth Gaskell's 1863 novel, *Sylvia's Lovers.*

23. Lord North served as chancellor of the exchequer from 1767 to 1782 and First Lord of the Treasury from 1770 to 1782. Having cultivated an image of himself as "the leader of a government that was going to teach the rebels a lesson," North found that by the time of Cornwallis's surrender at Yorktown in 1781 he was widely viewed as heavily responsible for England's unsuccessful campaign. He resigned in the spring of 1782. See Steven Watson, *The Reign of George III.*

24. The poem first appeared in the *Universal Magazine* in March 1795 and in the *Scots Magazine* in May 1795; it was subsequently published in Moody's *Poetic Trifles* (1798). It is reproduced in Bennett, *British War Poetry,* 149–50.

25. In a particularly ludicrous variation on this theme, Eliza Mary Hamilton later published a poem called "On Receiving a Leaf, Brought from the Weeping Willow That Is Planted at Waterloo Where the Marquis of Anglesey's Leg Is Buried" (*Poems*).

26. Hofland's maiden name was Wreakes; her first husband (the merchant Thomas Bradshawe Hoole) died in 1798, leaving her with an infant son, whom she supported by operating a boarding school. In 1808 she married the artist Thomas Hofland and began adding to their household income through her many publications. I have discussed *The History of an Officer's Widow,* along with other of Hofland's tales about widows, in "Women without Men."

27. Mary Robinson's rollicking, noisy poem, "The Camp," published in the *Morning Post* in August 1800 under her pseudonym "Oberon," effectively captures the chaos these camp-followers endured (albeit often willingly) already before 1800.

28. William Blake, for instance, includes such a scene at the base of the title page of his illuminated poem *America: A Prophecy* (1793) and in the background of a painting known as *A Breach in a City, the Morning after a Battle* (c. 1790–95).

29. See, for instance, the engraving of the melancholy parting of a uniformed man from his wife and three children (one of whom wears a child's replica of the uniform), who have not secured a ticket to follow him (not surprisingly, having children worked against wives' petitions to follow their husbands), or the prints of activity along the march, reproduced in Page, *Following the Drum,* between pages 40 and 41.

30. A prefatory note announces that the poem is "Founded upon an interesting incident which took place on the embarkation of the 85th Regiment for Holland at Ramsgate, August 10, 1799."

Chapter 3 · *Women and the Sonnet*

1. Andrew Ashfield notes that Browne "lived in some poverty," even after her marriage in 1842 to James Gray following her move to Dublin in 1839. Ashfield also refutes the rumor that Browne was a relative (possibly the sister) of Felicia Browne Hemans (*Romantic Women Poets,* 226).

2. The fullest examination of Browne's poetry is found in Deuk Ju Jeon, "Nature and Poetry."

3. Written in Italy during the volatile days of reformist unrest in Britain that culminated in the massacre at St. Peter's Fields in Manchester on 16 August 1819, Shelley's poem (see *Shelley's Poetry and Prose*, 315–26)—which he sent to Leigh Hunt, whom he hoped would publish it in the *Examiner*—was suppressed until 1832, after the passage of the first Reform Bill. Shelley's rallying stanza, which occurs early in his poem and reappears, verbatim, as the final stanza reads:

> "Rise like lions after slumber
> In unvanquishable number—
> Shake your chains to earth like dew
> Which in sleep had fallen on you—
> Ye are many—they are few."

4. I have not counted subsequent editions of works like Smith's *Elegiac Sonnets* (which saw multiple editions), even when they are substantially different from the original works.

5. Backscheider credits the original idea to Michael Spiller, as elaborated in *The Sonnet Sequence.*

6. The sonnet first appeared in the fifth edition (1789), where it was the forty-fourth of forty-eight sonnets; the text follows this edition. Unlike the previous editions, published by Dodsley, the fifth—the first to contain engraved illustrations—was published by the important bookseller Thomas Cadell, whose bookshop on the Strand was described as "the first in Great Britain and perhaps in Europe" (Timperley, *A Dictionary of Printers and Printing,* 814–15.) Cadell maintained an extensive list of novelists and had in 1788 published Smith's first novel, *Emmeline, the Orphan of the Castle.* This edition was issued by subscription, which enabled Smith to secure financing in advance and, more important, to insert with the front matter a list of 817 subscribers that spans eight pages of double-column type and includes the names of dignitaries (like William Pitt, Horace Walpole, and William Cowper) and "unknowns" (such as a young Cambridge student by the name of William Wordsworth) alike—. In acknowledging in the new, brief preface to this fifth edition "so many notable, literary, and respectable names" (vii), of course, Smith implicitly authorized herself also by her association with them.

7. Robinson's *Poems* of 1791, for instance, includes fifteen variously titled sonnets, while the second volume (1792) includes another thirteen.

8. In his sonnet Park asks, "Will SHE with friendship's veil / Shield 'rebel-rhyme,' ev'n while her hands prepare / To shew that studious art and taste refin'd, / Can make our rugged language graceful wear / Ausonian chains" (i, ll. 8–12). Park footnotes the term "rebel-rhyme" thus: "A term poetically applied, by Miss Seward, to verses which assume the title of Sonnets, without having the essentials required to rank them properly in that order of composition" (113). That Park was no mere slavish follower of Seward's dicta, however, is indicated by the presence in his volume of an enthusiastic sonnet to Charlotte Smith (sonnet 6, 6). Park's collection begins with thirty sonnets.

9. Some of the sonnets bear composition dates, and these are distributed throughout the volume in chronological order. Sonnet 92 is dated March 1790, while a note to sonnet 74 contains a reference to spring 1789.

10. See Backscheider, *Eighteenth-Century Women Poets,* 339–40, who also sees in this son-

net a clear echo of Smith's imagery and who observes that the poem demonstrates "the signs of an experienced poet willing to break with the most conservative formula with, for instance, dependence on sight rhymes and unexpected uses of indentation" (340).

It is worth considering what Mary Tighe did with these same elements in a sonnet of her own, "Written at Scarborough" (*Psyche*, 220), composed in 1799:

As musing pensive in my silent home
    I hear far off the sullen ocean's roar,
    Where the rude wave just sweeps the level shore,
Or bursts upon the rocks with whitening foam,
I think upon the scenes my life has known;
    On days of sorrow, and some hours of joy;
    Both which alike time could so soon destroy!
And now they seem a busy dream alone;
While on the earth exists no single trace
    Of all that shook my agitated soul,
    As on the beach new waves for ever roll,
And fill their past forgotten brother's place:
    But I, like the worn sand, exposed remain
    To each new storm which frets the angry main.

11. Stuart Curran enumerates some of these poems in *Poetic Form and British Romanticism*, 225–26, nn. 7–9.

12. These conservative numbers are from Jackson, *Annals of English Verse*.

13. I have speculated in print, in some detail, about Smallpiece's identity in "In Search of Anna Maria Smallpiece." In correspondence, Andrew Ashfield has shared his own research that suggests that Smallpiece was one of three sisters whose maiden name was Rogers; she seems to have married John Smallpiece (probably in London, where her children were baptized) and died in Wokingham in 1842, at the age of 76. Martha Hanson is at least equally obscure; she seems to have grown up in Sussex before publishing her two-volume collection, which seems to be dedicated to the Countess Tankerville, who—like the count—subscribed for two copies. Little is known about Mary F. Johnson either. Her volume's preface suggests that she resided on the Isle of Wight. She appears to have published only this one volume, apparently at a relatively young age, while Robinson and Feldman note that an inscription in one copy says that she later married George Moncrieff and died in 1863 less than a year after the death of a daughter (introduction, 138).

14. *General Review of British and Foreign Literature* 1 (January 1806): 90–91, 90.

15. The title first occurs in this form in an American edition: *Elegiac Sonnets, and Other Poems* (1795); this edition is set from the sixth English edition (1792), whose full title is *Elegiac Sonnets, with Additional Sonnets and Other Poems*.

16. For example, see "To the Rising Sun" and "To the Setting Sun" (vol. 2, nos. 44, 45) or "To the Midnight Hour," "To Night," and "To the Moon" (vol. 2, nos. 25, 26, 27), which three are followed—without thematic ties—by "To Melancholy," "To the Primrose, " and "Gratitude" (nos. 28, 29, 30).

17. This is, of course, a key principle of what is generally called Gynocriticism, which

includes among its emphases "the psychodynamics of female creativity," "linguistics and the problem of a female language," and "the trajectory of the individual and collective female literary career" (Showalter, 128).

18. The concept is most fully developed in Showalter, *A Literature of their Own.*

19. Curran also discusses Mariann Dark's responses to Smith's life and works.

20. Robinson's long pamphlet initially appeared under the pseudonym of "Anne Frances Randall," but the second edition's title page (also 1799) lists Robinson as author, while an advertisement following the title page explains the fiction of the initial pseudonym and acknowledges her as the work's author.

21. *British Critic* 38 (October 1811): 401–2, 402.

22. *Critical Review,* s. 3, 23 (August 1811): 411.

23. *British Critic* 38 (July 1811): 81; *Poetical Register, and Repository of Fugitive Poetry, for 1810–11* [8] (1814): 569–70.

24. "Sonnet-Writers," *British Stage and Literary Cabinet* 4 (November 1819): 67–68.

25. "Sonnettomania," *New Monthly Magazine* 1 (June 1821): 645–46.

26. In 1800 the British Army formed the Experimental Corps of Riflemen, a select, hand-picked corps that by 1803 had been renamed the Ninety-fifth Regiment, or Rifle Regiment. In 1803 it was joined briefly by the Forty-third and Fifty-second regiments to form the Light Brigade, commanded by Sir John Moore. It served under Wellington at the siege of Copenhagen (1803) and in the Peninsular War (1808–14) as well as at Waterloo. In 1816 the unit was taken out of the numbered regiments of the line and given the title Rifle Brigade, by which name its members are designated in Sargant's list of subscribers. See http://www.royalgreenjackets.co.uk/framesetpages/mainpages/regimentalheritage/95.htm.

27. Evidence about Sargant's life is scanty. She appears to have continued to support herself through writing, publishing conduct books (as early as 1820), two novels, *Ringstead Abbey* (1830) and *Charlie Burton* (1849), as well as eight volumes of *Home Tales* (1853–61). She also wrote Sunday-school books, including *But Once* (1853) and *Shades of Character* (1853), as well as the intriguingly titled *The Broken Arm: A National School Story* (1847). She was the apparent author of numerous pamphlets on social issues, including *An Address to the Females of Great Britain, on the Propriety of Their Petitioning Parliament for the Abolition of Negro Slavery* (1833), authored as "An Englishwoman," and published first in the Tory periodical *John Bull,* and another on the Marriage Law (1849).

28. Mariann Dark was christened Mary Ann Stiles in 1801, in Calne, Wiltshire, although she was apparently born sometime before 1795. Her father was Henry Stiles, a longtime resident of Wiltshire. Her father's death and burial in Bremhill, Wiltshire, in January 1817 is central to her collection of poems. Her mother, the former Winifred Howell, survived until 1826; she was also buried in Bremhill. Mary Ann seems to have been the youngest child; she apparently had two older brothers and two older sisters, all of whom lived until midcentury; another sister, Elizabeth, died in 1790.

29. On Bowles's relationship to Smith, see Curran, *Poetic Form and British Romanticism,* 32–34.

30. See Dark's comments in her "Brief Memoir of the Late Henry Stiles, of Whitley, in Wiltshire," *Sonnets,* xxxii–xxxiv.

Chapter 4 • *Experimenting with Genre*

1. See Mellor, *Mothers of the Nation,* 75. Yearsley, *A Poem on the Inhumanity of the Slave-trade;* Barbauld, *Epistle to William Wilberforce.*

2. A second edition also appeared in 1792, in Dublin.

3. See Easson and Essick, *Plates Designed and Engraved by Blake,* 9–12. The first edition was published in 1791; a second appeared in 1796.

4. [John Wilson Croker], anonymous review, *Quarterly Review* 7 (June 1812): 309–13.

5. See *Britons,* especially chapter 1, "Protestants."

6. I have examined the circumstances of Princess Charlotte's death and its impact on the material culture of Great Britain—including the extraordinary literary production associated with the event—in *Royal Mourning and Regency Culture.*

7. *British Review* 15 (January 1820): 299.

8. As Craciun notes, the plight of French émigrés was addressed in many works published at the time, including pamphlets like Hannah More's *Considerations on Religion* (1793) and Fanny Burney's *Brief Reflexions Relative to the Emigrant French Clergy* (1793), works for children like Lucy Peacock's *The Little Emigrant* (1799), Mary Pilkington's *New Tales of the Castle; or, The Noble Emigrants* (1801), and the widely circulated *The Young Exiles* (1799) which was an English translation of Mme. de Genlis's *Les petits émigrés* (1798), and another long poem, Maria Julia Young's thoroughly counterrevolutionary *Adelaide and Antonine; or, The Emigrants* (1793).

9. The poem's opening line, "Nothing so true as what you once let fall," implies that the line about women's characters, which is enclosed by quotation marks in Pope's poem, had first been spoken by the woman to whom the poem is addressed (Pope, *The Poems of Alexander Pope,* 560).

10. See Anne Mellor, who suggests that Aikin also responds to Virgil's injunction in the *Æneid* by singing "the Fate of Woman," to Milton's proposal in *Paradise Lost* by justifying "the ways of god" to women, and to Pope's plan to show in the *Essay on Man* that "whatever is, is not yet right for women" (*Mothers of the Nation,* 80).

11. *Critical Review,* s. 3, 23 (August 1811): 418–26, 419.

12. *European Magazine* 60 (July 1811): 35–39, 35.

13. See the *Monthly Magazine,* n.s., 1 (April 1826): 417: "The authoress of 'The Veils,' and that *splendid epic,* 'Cœur de Lion,' has only lately winged her way to a higher world. Miss Porden's epic has been neglected. Every noble whose ancestors fought in the Holy Land is bound in honour to see their deeds recorded; and when they have been nobly sung by a woman, let chivalry save her poetry from perishing unnoticed and unknown."

14. As Dennis Low demonstrates, Southey actively advocated the work of numerous women writers of his acquaintance; in Bowles's case, he not only recommended her work to readers and publishers but also secured professional introductions for her; see *The Literary Protégées,* 35–68.

15. See also Wolfson, *Borderlines,* especially chapter 2, "Felicia Hemans and the Stages of 'The Feminine.'"

16. The first edition (1805) contained 222 pages; the 1811 and subsequent editions, to which William Tighe added additional poems, ran roughly 330 pages. For the full history of Tighe's poems, see Tighe, *The Collected Poems and Journals of Mary Tighe.*

17. *British Critic* 38 (December 1811): 631–33, 631.

18. *Monthly Review* 66 (October 1811): 138–52, 139.

19. *Critical Review,* s. 4, 1 (June 1812): 607.

20. See Backscheider, *Eighteenth-Century Women Poets,* 293–95. Backscheider notes that Seward carefully avoids dealing with the fact that André, who had unsuccessfully courted her friend Honora Sneyd, seems to have died largely as a consequence of his own ineptitude as a military man, this biographical fact being in any case almost irrelevant to the larger political point she wishes to make.

21. Written in 1818, Barbauld's poem appeared in the *Annual Register . . . for the Year 1818,* which was published in 1819. There it was titled simply "Elegy" and signed "Mrs. B——d." It was retitled in 1825 in *The Works of Anna Letitia Barbauld, with a Memoir by Lucy Aikin.*

22. King's *Poems* was another subscription volume undertaken for the financial relief of the author, who begins her preface by telling her reader that she "has for many years been afflicted with nervous deafness" and wishes now to share (for profit, of course) the poems which she publishes "at the solicitation of partial friends" and which "are nothing more than mental exercises, entered on as a refuge from repining thought, and often pursued in the midst of society, or in the various avocations of life" (iii).

23. Esther Schor discusses some of the many writers, including Felicia Hemans, who located both sets of characteristics "in the context of her anticipated reign" in *Bearing the Dead.*

24. The embedded quotations are from Schenck, "Feminism and Deconstruction: Re-Constructing the Elegy," 23–24.

25. Hemans republished "The Child's Last Sleep" in *The Forget-Me-Not* for 1829 as "The Sculpted Children: On Chantrey's Monument at Lichfield." Sir Francis Chantrey's 1812 sculpture in the cathedral Church of St. Chad, Lichfield, commemorates the death of two young girls who are depicted as if sleeping. See Hemans, *Selected Poems, Prose, and Letters,* 344–45.

26. The poem appears in a "hybrid" copy of Trench's *Campaspe* in the New York Public Library. This copy bears on its title page an inscription in Trench's hand: "not published." The elegy was in fact simply inserted between two of the "other poems," "To Lady —— on Reading Lord ——'s Farewell" (41–44) and "Turkish Song" (45–46), which also explains how a poem treating a death in late 1816 could be present in a volume dated 1815. In fact, *most* of the volumes by Trench in the New York Public Library's collection bear similar "not published" inscriptions, and many of them are also filled with annotations and corrections in Trench's hand, as are other "hybrid" volumes to be found in other libraries. In those volumes, too, the irregular pagination in particular suggests that Trench had her works printed for private circulation and that she frequently assembled "books" from these various print impressions and then annotated and corrected them. Complicating matters further still for the textual scholar, the annotations are themselves inconsistent, varying from copy to copy, which further suggests the "made-to-order" nature of Trench's presentation copies.

27. When Trench wrote in 1806 to Charles Manners St. George, her son by her first marriage, to inform him of Frederick's death, she mentioned the earlier loss of "my infant daughter" who "was merely a little bud," unlike Frederick, who "had safely passed all the earliest dangers." Her letter indicates that by 1806 she had lost another child as well. See *Remains of the Late Mrs. Richard Trench,* 200.

28. Corrected in New York Public Library copy to "pure."

29. The poem appears in a very rare "hybrid" or composite volume in the Library of Congress (Washington, D.C.) that bears the tentative title of *The Plague Fiend [, and Other Poems]*. Undated and irregularly paginated, this volume appears to be another ad hoc production that Trench pieced together and annotated for some particular recipient. Trench's four sonnets on her children (54–57) name four sons, Francis, Richard, Philip, and William, the only sons whose names appear in *Burke's Peerage and Baronetage,* 106th ed.; there is no mention of Trench's daughter. The poem that follows the sonnets is titled "On Reading Coleridge's Christabel," which suggests a date no earlier than 1816, when "Christabel" was published. If Trench's four sonnets, which move ambiguously and inconsistently between present and past tenses, date from late 1816 or afterward, then Bessy was already dead and the sonnet's ending is a description of fact rather than a vision of fancy. The final line's phrase, "ripening for the skies," is borrowed from Anna Letitia Barbauld, whose 1773 poem "A Summer Evening's Meditation" includes the phrase "ripen for the skies" (l. 120).

Chapter 5 · Scottish Women Poets

1. See, for instance, Bardsley, "Joanna Baillie Stages the Nation."

2. See, for example, Porter, *The Creation of the Modern World.*

3. See, for instance, Bhabha, *The Location of Culture.*

4. See also Landry, *The Muses of Resistance,* especially chapter 6: "Other Others: The Marginality of Cultural Difference."

5. "Account of the Former Progress and Present State of Literature and Science in Scotland," *Monthly Magazine, and British Register, for 1797,* 4:261–64, 357–61, 443–45, 358.

6. Duncan quotes Wordsworth's letter to R. P. Gillies (14 February 1815).

7. "Account," *Monthly Magazine, and British Register, for 1797,* 358.

8. She wrote nearly a hundred songs based on traditional Scottish airs, publishing them under the pseudonym of "Mrs. Bogan of Bogan." Only after her death was her identity revealed when her *Lays from Strathearn* was published in 1846.

9. Thus, for example, when the editors of the ubiquitous *Norton Anthology of English Literature* elected at last to include in the sixth edition (1993) some Romantic-era women poets, they inserted them (along with several men) under the subheading of "Romantic Lyric Poets," a gathering of some 27 pages that was placed (deliberately and strategically) *after* the 862 pages devoted primarily to the canonical Romantic authors.

10. See also Brown, "Old Singing Women." Brown writes that "women have been among the primary performers and consumers of the form" and that "gender—and more particularly, gendered life experiences—have had something to do with the choices of songs—both to know and to perform, as well as to hear" (51).

11. W. W., "Scottish Literature," *Edinburgh Magazine and Literary Miscellany,* n.s., 10 (June 1822): 735.

12. The poem was in fact translated into many languages and became the subject of many paintings and engravings—and even of several plays.

13. See Feldman, in *British Women Poets,* 539–42; see also Bold, "Beyond 'The Empire of the Gentle Heart,'" 246–61.

14. See Feldman, *British Women Poets,* 539–42.

15. See Davis, *Acts of Union,* 9–10, 74–75.

16. *Monthly Review* 38 (August 1802): 436–37, 436.

17. *Romantic Genius;* see especially chapter 6: "Lesbianism and Romantic Genius: The Poetry of Anne Bannerman."

18. The best discussion of Bannerman's work and its reception among the male critical establishment is Adriana Craciun's "Romantic Spinstrelsy: Anne Bannerman and the Sexual Politics of the Ballad."

19. Byron did something comparable in 1808 with the title of his *Hours of Idleness,* which clearly echoes that of Charlotte Dacre's *Hours of Solitude.*

20. See Coleridge, *Samuel Taylor Coleridge,* 247–49, 275–78, and 525.

21. Feldman, *British Women Poets,* 26, quoting D. M. Moir, *Sketches of the Poetical Literature of the Past Half-Century.* See also Nolte, "David Macbeth Moir as Morgan Odoherty," 803–6. More recently, Claire Connolly asserts that "Odoherty" was the Cork-born Irish satirical writer and acquaintance of William Maginn (437–38).

22. In correspondence with me, Judith Bailey Slagle has suggested a tentative date of 1829, noting that in *Fugitive Verses,* which is arranged in generally chronological fashion, the poem comes immediately after "Lines to a Parrot," which is known to date from 1829.

23. I have discussed this poem and its relation to Keats's ode in greater detail in "An Urn, A Teapot, and the Archeology of Romantic Reading."

Chapter 6 · Irish Women Poets

1. On the recurrent figure of Paddy, see especially de Nie, *The Eternal Paddy.*

2. The Act of Union created the schizophrenically named "United Kingdom of Great Britain and Ireland." It is sometimes called the Act of Union of 1800 and sometimes the Act of Union of 1801; the Act of Union dissolved the Irish Parliament in August 1800 and declared a legislative union, but it did not officially go into effect until 1 January 1801. For consistency, I use the 1800 date in this discussion.

3. Patrick Rafroidi's detailed examination of English-language Irish literary publications of the period lists some 246 authors, but identifies only 11 women who published one or more volumes between 1789 and 1835. Traditional literary histories routinely overlook the work of women poets of that era; Patrick Power's 1967 *Story of Anglo-Irish Poetry,* for instance, seems blithely unaware of any Irish women poets before Katherine Tynan and Lady Gregory. In 1996 Anne Ulry Colman's more specialized bibliography of nineteenth-century Irish women poets still identified only 14. Even J. R. de J. Jackson's extensive 1993 bibliography of Romantic-era poetry by women did not catch everyone. In 1998 Gregory Schirmer included among Romantic-era poets three women—Mary O'Brien, Charlotte Brooke, and Mary Balfour—but omitted Tighe and Owenson. Most recently, an extensive reference work on Irish women writers edited by Alexander Gonzalez includes *only one* Romantic-era poet: Mary Tighe. See Rafroidi, *Irish Literature in English;* Power, *The Story of Anglo-Irish Poetry;* Colman, *Dictionary of Nineteenth-Century Irish Women Poets;* Jackson, *Romantic Poetry by Women;* Schirmer, *Out of What Began;* Gonzalez, *Irish Women Writers.*

For a clearer sense of the actual picture, see Stephen C. Behrendt, *Irish Women Romantic Poets;* this electronic database includes volumes of poetry published by more than fifty women poets from the Romantic era. In selecting poets for inclusion, I followed the definition of "Irish" authors offered by Margaret Kelleher and Philip O'Leary in the *Cambridge History of Irish Literature:* "Our primary criterion for inclusion has been that authors were born on the island of Ireland or lived a significant and formative period of their lives there" (4).

4. Although Weekes's primary concern is with prose fiction, her point applies to women's poetry as well; paradoxically, her comment reveals her own neglect of the considerable volume of productions in that genre by early nineteenth-century Irish women.

5. Innes's comments on this point are as relevant to the Romantic period as they are to the early modern that is her principal focus.

6. The nature of such pro-union propaganda is apparent from one title among many: *A Letter to the People of Ireland, Which They Can All Understand, and Ought to Read,* signed "a Real Friend." His language dripping with a pompous condescension that anticipates modern talk radio and that fails to mask his cultural contempt, this author claims he wishes to save the impercipient Irish from themselves, for "if ever a people had reason to be undeceived, to see and repent their folly and their crimes, you of Ireland, my Friends, are that people" (6).

7. *Anthologia Hibernica: or, Monthly Collections of Science, Belles Lettres, and History* 1 (January–June 1793): 295–96.

8. Weekes is writing about fiction here, but even she seems unaware of the volume of writing that was actually being produced and published by women.

9. The poem was printed at the author's expense. The half-title page of the copy in the British Library bears Ryves's signature, as well as several corrections to the text, also in her hand.

10. See Carpenter, "Poetry in English," 300.

11. Taylor mentions reading both poets in "This Poem Address'd to a Gentleman, Who Had Lent Her Some Books" (6–7).

12. Andrew Carpenter, in *Verse in English,* 473n.

13. This is *not* the same Charlotte Richardson whose *Harvest* (1818) and other works I discuss in chapter 2.

14. In an appended glossary, "awn" is defined as "the beard of corn" (70).

15. The introduction reports that the poems are published "at the ardent request of the Authoress['] intimate Friends" (3).

16. By 1837 Quigley may have been working on some sort of collection of moral and religious poems that never appeared; *A Gift for the Sanctuary* includes several poems about church bells and a number of poems related to particular times of day, while other poems are referred to as extracts from "The Sanctuary at Noon" and poems. The circumstances of her orphaning are recounted in *The Microscope,* in a poem called "Extempore: Putting on Mourning for my Father" (44–46); Quigley provides no information about how old she was at the time of her father's death.

17. Ryan mentions this work by name in the title of the poem that appears on page 94: "On Edward's History of the Effects of Religion on Mankind."

18. Few copies of *The Political Monitor* appear to survive. The book was unfavorably reviewed by both the *Critical Review* (August 1790) and the *Monthly Review* (January 1791); see Ravens, Forster, and Bending, vol. 1 of *The English Novel, 1770–1829,* 507, where it is incorrectly attributed to Sarah Green.

19. *Sentimental and Masonic Magazine* (July–December 1794).

20. A second edition, with minor changes and additions, appeared in Dublin in 1797.

21. *Monthly Review* 67 (March 1812): 323.

22. *New Monthly Magazine* 12 (November 1819): 454.

23. Ironically, the editors of *The Feminist Companion to Literature in English* say that *Mount Leicester,* which is usually attributed to Liddiard, is probably by her husband, William (658). In 1816 the Liddiards published a set of three poems, two by William and one by Anna.

24 . In the preface to *Kenilworth and Farley Castle* in which she makes her accusations, Liddiard seconds Anna Seward's opinion that the literary establishment should "oblige, by a law, the Authors and Compilers of such publications, to prefix their names to their criticisms. This would, she thinks, be the only 'guard for their integrity.' The world might then know how to form a proper estimate, how far they ought to depend upon the opinions of the several Critics, while Spleen and Envy would in consequence be disarmed of their insidious weapons" (xii–xiii).

25. Alspach devotes an entire chapter to Charlotte Brooke, whose poetry and scholarship he much admired.

26. *Irish Melodies,* whose poems were intended to be sung to familiar Irish airs, continued in installments through 1834. Their consistent theme is Ireland past, present, and to come.

27. Although her editor, the Rev. Henry H. Beamish, observed in his notes to *Emmanuel* that Colthurst is "an eminently devoted Christian lady," he remarked that she lives "in a retired but beautifully romantic district of the South of Ireland, *the benightment of whose deluded inhabitants she mourns,* and whose best interests she ardently desires to promote" (iii; my emphasis). This circuitous comment about benightedness and delusion would easily have been read as a reference to Catholicism.

28. This visual trope persists throughout the century. Popular periodicals like *Punch* regularly included illustrations featuring Britannia and Hibernia as women. Hibernia is generally characterized in these prints by her helplessness and passivity and by her racial similarity to Britannia (as opposed to the visible racial "otherness" of exotic allegorical figures like Africa and, later, India). See Innes, *Woman and Nation,* 9–25. Innes points out that although these images of Hibernia epitomize "the extreme of angelic femininity" in their grace, beauty, spirituality, and passivity, the Irish "Hibernians" represent "the extreme of masculine bestiality": they are dirty, ugly, loutish, and violently aggressive (14).

29. See Schirmer, *Out of What Began,* 71, 150–60.

Conclusion

1. See Tuchman and Fortin, *Edging Women Out.*

2. Trench wrote in 1820 that "I should write much better if I had ever been criticized. . . . [M]y little attempts *can* have no merit but that of showing to those who love me, what I might have done, had I not been deprived of the advantages of classical learning; had I not been flattered in my youth, as one to whom mental acquirements were unnecessary; had I not been the fond mother of nine children, and the troublesome wife of one whom I do not much like to have out of my sight; four very unfavourable circumstances to the cultivation of

any art or science whatever" (*Remains of the Late Mrs. Richard Trench,* 432–33). Trench voices here the familiar rueful sense of what the woman writer necessarily sacrifices as an artist in the interest of her obligations as wife and mother, including both education and leisure.

3. The volume is inscribed *Poems on Various Occasions.* The copy in the National Library of Ireland has had a second "T" written in by hand at the end of the author's surname. Despite being indicated only by the initial "M." the author's Christian name is occasionally given in catalogues as "Mary," perhaps because another volume, *My Early Dreams* (published in Belfast in 1832; also at the National Library of Ireland), has been attributed to "Mary McDermott." Internal evidence indicates that this later volume is not by the same poet as the 1815 one, but even the actual name of the 1832 volume's author is questionable, for she is identified on the title page only as "M. McD." Moreover, internal evidence in the 1815 volume suggests that its author is male, not female. In the preface to an apparently no longer extant 1814 production called *The Vale of Verna,* which is inserted in the 1815 book after the author's introduction, for instance, the author refers to that poem and observes that "of its poetical merit *he* must be silent," and that "*he* shall only say, that it was written before *he* thought of making it public, and that *he* obeyed consequently, the impulse of *his* feelings, and not the directions of *his* judgment" (xii; my emphases). Although women may choose, for various reasons, to refer to themselves with masculine pronouns, *Poems on Various Occasions* also contains poems whose subjects seem decidedly masculine, like "The Miser's Paternal Advice" (53–57), which comments on everything from studying science to selecting a good wife. Moreover, the appended long list of subscribers (which contains the names of more than a dozen other individuals named "M'Dermot," including a Dr. H. M'Dermot of Coolavin, who is subscribed for five copies) includes the names of only a very few women, which is itself atypical of volumes authored by women. Kaye Kossick, in correspondence about this volume, agrees that it is more likely the production of a male poet.

PRIMARY WORKS

Aikin, Lucy. *Epistles on Women, Exemplifying their Character and Condition in Various Ages and Nations, with Miscellaneous Poems.* London, 1810.

Appleton, Miss [Elizabeth]. *Edgar: A National Tale.* 3 vols. London, 1816.

Baillie, Joanna. *Ahalya Baee: A Poem.* London, 1849.

———. *Fugitive Verses.* London, 1840.

———. *Joanna Baillie: Poems, 1790.* Edited by Jonathan Wordsworth. Oxford, UK: Woodstock Books, 1994.

———. *Metrical Legends of Exalted Characters.* London, 1821.

———. *A Series of Plays, in Which it is Attempted to Delineate the Stronger Passions of the Mind, Each Passion Being the Subject of a Tragedy and a Comedy.* 3 vols. London, 1798–1812.

Balfour, Mary. *Hope; a Poetical Essay, with Various Other Poems.* Belfast, 1810.

———. *Kathleen O'Neil: A Grand National Melodrame, in Three Acts, as Performed at the Belfast Theatre.* Belfast, 1814.

Bannerman, *Poems.* Edinburgh, 1800.

———. *Tales of Superstition and Chivalry.* London, 1802.

Barbauld, Anna Letitia. *Eighteen Hundred and Eleven: A Poem.* London, 1812.

———. *Epistle to William Wilberforce, Esq., on the Rejection of the Bill for Abolishing the Slave Trade.* London, 1791.

———. *The Poems of Anna Letitia Barbauld.* Edited by William McCarthy and Elizabeth Kraft. Athens: University of Georgia Press, 1994.

[———]. *Sins of Government, Sins of the Nation; or, A Discourse for the Fast, Appointed on April 19, 1793.* London, 1793. Signed "A Volunteer."

———. *The Works of Anna Letitia Barbauld, with a Memoir by Lucy Aikin.* Edited by Lucy Aikin. 2 vols. London, 1825.

Barrell, Maria. *British Liberty Vindicated; or, A Delineation of the King's Bench.* London, 1788.

Bath, Elizabeth. *Poems on Various Occasions.* Bristol, UK, 1806.

Battier, Henrietta ("Patt. Pindar"). *The Gibbonade; or, Poetical Reviewer,* no. 1 (1793–94).

Beattie, James. *The Minstrel; or, The Progress of Genius: A Poem in Two Books.* Edinburgh, 1771.

———. *Scotticisms, Arranged in Alphabetical Order, Designed to Correct Improprieties of Speech and Writing.* Edinburgh, 1787.

Betham, Matilda. *Biographical Dictionary of the Celebrated Women of Every Age and Country.* London, 1804.

Birkett, Mary. *A Poem on the African Slave Trade, Addressed to Her Own Sex.* Pts. 1 and 2. Dublin, 1792.

Blackall, Elizabeth. *Psalms and Hymns and Spiritual Songs.* Dublin, 1835.

Blake, William. *America: A Prophecy.* London, 1794.

———. *The Complete Poetry and Prose of William Blake.* Rev. ed. Edited by David V. Erdman. Berkeley: University of California Press, 1982.

———. *Europe: A Prophecy.* London, 1794.

———. *Milton: A Poem in 2 Books.* London, 1804.

———. *Songs of Experience.* London, 1794.

———. *Visions of the Daughters of Albion.* London, 1793

Blanchard, Anne. *Midnight Reflections, and Other Poems.* London, 1822.

Bourke, Hannah Maria. *O'Donoghue, Prince of Killarney: A Poem in Seven Cantos.* Dublin, 1830.

[Bowles, Caroline Anne.] *Ellen Fitzarthur: A Metrical Tale.* London, 1820.

Bowles, William Lisle. *Fourteen Sonnets, Elegiac and Descriptive, Written Chiefly on Picturesque Spots during a Tour.* Bath, UK, 1789.

———. *Sonnets, and Other Poems . . . to Which is Added Hope, an Allegorical Sketch on Recovering Slowly from Sickness.* 9th ed. London, 1805.

———. *Sonnets, Written Chiefly on Picturesque Spots, during a Tour.* Bath, 1789.

Brooke, Charlotte. *Reliques of Irish Poetry, Consisting of Heroic Poems, Odes, Elegies, and Songs, Translated into English Verse, with Notes Explanatory and Historical, and the Originals in the Irish Character, to Which is Subjoined an Irish Tale.* Dublin, 1789.

Browne, Felicia Dorothea. *The Domestic Affections, and Other Poems.* London, 1812. See also, Hemans, Felicia.

Browne, Mary Ann. *The Coronal: Original Poems, Sacred and Miscellaneous.* London, 1833.

Browning, Elizabeth Barrett. *Aurora Leigh.* London, 1857.

Burdy, Samuel. *The History of Ireland, from the Earliest Ages to the Union.* Edinburgh, 1817.

Burney, Frances. *Brief Reflexions Relative to the Emigrant French Clergy.* London, 1793.

Byrne, Mary. *The Blind Poem.* Dublin, 1789.

Byron, George Gordon. *Hours of Idleness: A Series of Poems, Original and Translated.* Newark, UK, 1808.

Calcott, Berkeley. *Stanzas.* Dublin, 1834. Signed "Miss Berkeley Calcott, Eleven Years of Age."

Campbell, Miss D. P. [of Zetland]. *Poems.* Inverness, Scotland, 1811. 2nd, exp. ed., 1816.

Candler, Ann. *Poetical Attempts, with a Short Narrative of Her Life.* Ipswich, UK, 1803. Signed "Ann Candler, a Suffolk Cottager."

Chadwick, Mrs. [Frances]. *Rural, and Other Poems.* London, 1823.

Chalmers, Margaret. *Poems.* Newcastle, UK, 1813.

Coleridge, Samuel Taylor. *Samuel Taylor Coleridge: The Complete Poems.* Edited by William Keach. London: Penguin, 1997.

Colthurst, E. *Emmanuel, with a Recommendatory Preface by the Rev. Henry H. Beamish, M. A.* Edited by Henry Beamish. London, 1833.

———. *Life: A Poem, by the Author of "Emmanuel," with Explanatory Notes.* Cork, Ireland, 1835.

Costello, Louisa Stuart. *The Maid of the Cyprus Isle, and Other Poems.* London, 1815.

———. *Redwald: A Tale of Mona, and Other Poems.* Brentford, UK, 1819.

Dacre, Charlotte. *Hours of Solitude: A Collection of Original Poems, Etc.* London, 1805.

Dark, Mariann. *Sonnets, and Other Poems.* London, 1818.

de Fleury, Maria. *British Liberty Established, and Gallic Liberty Restored; or, The Triumph of Freedom: A Poem, Occasioned by the Grand Revolution in France, 1789, with a Prospect of the Glorious Time When True Religion and Civil Liberty Shall Shed Their Benign Influences over the World.* London, 1790.

de Genlis, Madame, *Les petits émigrés.* 1798. Translated as *The Young Exiles.* London, 1799.

Dewar, Daniel. *Observations on the Character, Customs, and Superstitions of the Irish, and on Some of the Causes Which Have Retarded the Moral and Political Improvement of Ireland.* London, 1812.

Dickens, Charles. *A Christmas Carol.* 1843. Ed. Richard Kelly. Peterborough, Ontario: Broadview Press, 2003.

Donaldson, John. *Recollections of an Eventful Life.* Edinburgh, 1852.

Dunnett, Jane. *Poems on Various Subjects.* Edinburgh, 1818.

Dyce, Rev. Alexander. *Specimens of British Poetesses, Selected and Chronologically Arranged.* London, 1825.

"Eliza." *Adversity; or, The Tears of Britannia: A Poem.* London, 1789. Signed "a Lady."

Evance, Susan. *Poems, Selected from Her Earliest Productions to the Present Year.* London, 1808.

Fielding, Henry. *Joseph Andrews* (1742). Edited by R. F. Brissenden. London: Penguin, 1977.

Finch, Mrs. B. *Sonnets, and Other Poems, to Which are Added Tales in Prose.* London, 1805.

Gent, Thomas. *Poetic Sketches: A Collection of Miscellaneous Poetry.* 2nd. London, 1808.

Gifford, William. *The Baeviad.* London, 1797.

Gisborne, Thomas. *Enquiry into the Duties of the Female Sex.* London, 1796.

Glieg, G. R. *The Subaltern.* Edinburgh, 1825.

Grant, Mrs. [Anne Macvicar]. *Eighteen Hundred and Thirteen: A Poem in Two Parts.* Edinburgh, 1814.

———. *The Highlanders, and Other Poems.* London, 1808.

———. *Poems on Various Subjects.* Edinburgh, 1803.

Gray, Christian. *Tales, Letters, and Other Pieces, in Verse.* Edinburgh, 1811.

Guinness, Mrs. John G. *Sacred Portraiture and Illustrations, with Other Poems.* Dublin, 1834.

Hale, Mrs. [Sarah Josepha]. *The Ladies' Wreath: A Selection from the Female Poetic Writers of England and America, with Original Notices and Notes, Prepared Especially for Young Ladies.* Boston, 1837.

Hamilton, Eliza Mary. *Poems.* Dublin, 1838.

Hamilton, William. *Poems on Several Occasions.* Edinburgh, 1760.

Hanson, Martha. *Sonnets, and Other Poems.* 2 vols. London, 1809.

Harris, James. *Recollections of a Rifleman*. London, 1848. Rpt., London: Peter Davies, 1928.

Hays, Mary. *An Appeal to the Men of Great Britain in Behalf of Women*. London, 1798.

———. *Female Biography; or, Memoirs of Illustrious and Celebrated Women of All Ages and Countries*. 6 vols. London, 1803.

Hemans, Felicia. *Felicia Hemans: Selected Poems, Letters, Reception Materials*. Edited by Susan J. Wolfson. Princeton: Princeton University Press, 2000. See also Browne, Felicia Dorothea.

———. *Felicia Hemans: Selected Poems, Prose, and Letters*. Edited by Gary Kelly. Peterborough, Ontario: Broadview Press, 2002. See also Browne, Felicia Dorothea.

———. *Records of Woman, with Other Poems*. Edinburgh, 1828. See also Browne, Felicia Dorothea.

Hodgson, Francis. *Childe Harold's Monitor; or, Lines Occasioned by the Last Canto of Childe Harold, Including Hints to Other Contemporaries*. London, 1818.

Hofland, Barbara. *The History of an Officer's Widow, and Her Young Family*. London, 1809. See also Hoole, Barbara.

Holford, Margaret. *Margaret of Anjou: A Poem in Ten Cantos*. London, 1816.

———. *Wallace; or, The Fight of Falkirk: A Metrical Romance*. London, 1809. Signed "M. H."

Home, John, Rev. *Douglas: A Tragedy*. London, 1770.

Hoole, Barbara. *Poems*. Sheffield, UK, 1805. See also Hofland, Barbara.

Housman, Robert Fletcher. *A Collection of English Sonnets*. London, 1835.

Hume, David. *A Treatise of Human Nature*. Edited by L. A. Selby-Bigge. Oxford, 1888.

Hunter, Ann. *Poems*. London, 1802.

Johnson, Mary F. *Original Sonnets, and Other Poems*. London, 1810.

King, Harriet Rebecca. *Poems*. Salisbury, UK, 1823.

"Lady, A." *Poems, on Several Occasions*. Newry, Ireland, 1807. Signed "a Native of Newry."

Landon, Letitia Elizabeth. *The Improvisatrice, and Other Poems*: *Poetical Works of Letitia Elizabeth Landon*. 2 vols. London, 1867.

Leadbeater, Mary. *The Leadbeater Papers: The Annals of Ballitore, with a Memoir of the Author, Letters from Edmund Burke Heretofore Unpublished, and the Correspondence of Mrs. R. Trench and Rev. George Crabbe with Mary Leadbeater*. 2 vols. London, 1862.

———. *Poems, to Which is Prefixed Her Translation of the Thirteenth Book of the Æneid, with the Latin Original, Written in the Fifteenth Century, by Maffæus*. Dublin, 1808.

Lee, Richard. *A Summary of the Duties of Citizenship, Written Expressly for Members of the London Corresponding Societies*. London, 1795.

Leech, Sarah. *Poems on Various Subjects*. Dublin, 1828. Signed "Sarah Leech, a Peasant Girl."

Lennon, John. *The Mirror of Tolerance: Poems, Principally Dedicated to the Cause of Freedom, Most Gratefully Inscribed to John Lawless, Esq., the Enlightened and Unchangeable Irish Patriot*. Belfast, 1828.

Lewis, Matthew G. *Tales of Wonder, [in Verse]*. 2 vols. London, 1801.

Lickbarrow, Isabella. *Poetic Effusions*. Kendal, UK, 1814.

Liddiard, J. S. Anna. *Kenilworth and Farley Castle, with Other Poems*. Dublin, 1813.

———. *Poems*. Dublin, 1810.

[———]. *Mount Leinster; or, The Prospect: A Poem Descriptive of the Irish Scenery*. London, 1819.

———. *The Sgelaighe; or, A Tale of Old, with a Second Edition of "Poems," Published in Dublin, and Additions*. Bath, UK, 1811.

Luby, Catherine. *The Spirit of the Lake; or, Mucruss Abbey: A Poem in Three Cantos.* London, 1822.

Lutton, Anne. *Poems on Moral and Religious Subjects.* Dublin, 1829.

Macaulay, Catherine. *The History of England.* London, 1763–83.

Macbay, Capt. W. *The United Kingdom Really United (Ireland to England): How to Obtain Good and Cheap Beef and Unfailing Crops.* London, 1866.

Magrath, Anne Jane. *Blossoms of Genius: Poems on Various Subjects.* Dublin, 1834.

Mahony, Agnes. *A Minstrel's Hours of Song.* London, 1825.

Mathias, Thomas James. *The Pursuits of Literature; or, What You Will: A Satirical Poem in Dialogue.* London, 1794–97.

McCoy, Mary. *A Poem, in Answer to an Anonymous Pamphlet, in Three Letters, Called Friendly Hints to Catholic Emancipation.* Belfast, 1813.

McDermott, Mary. *My Early Dreams.* Belfast, 1832.

M'Dermot[t], M. *Poems on Various Occasions.* Belfast, 1815.

[Miller, George, of Dunbar]. *War a System of Madness and Irreligion, to Which Is Subjoined by Way of a Conclusion, The Dawn of Universal Peace, Wrote on the Late Fast Day, 1796.* c. 1796. Signed "Humanitas."

Milne, Christian. *Simple Poems, on Simple Subjects.* Aberdeen, Scotland, 1805.

M'Mullan, Mrs. [Mary Anne]. *The Naiad's Wreath.* London, 1816.

Moir, D. M. *Sketches of the Poetical Literature of the Past Half-Century.* Edinburgh, 1851.

Moody, Mrs. [Elizabeth]. "Anna's Complaint; or, The Miseries of War, Written in the Isle of Thanet, 1794." *Universal Magazine* 96 (March 1795): 205–6.

———. *Poetic Trifles.* London, 1798.

Moore, Jane Elizabeth. *Miscellaneous Poems on Various Occasions.* Dublin, 1796.

More, Hannah. *Considerations on Religion.* London, 1793.

———. *Slavery: A Poem.* London, 1788.

———. *Strictures on the Modern System of Female Education.* 2 vols. London, 1799.

[———]. *Thoughts on the Importance of the Manners of the Great to General Society.* 6th ed. London, 1788.

———. *The Works of Hannah More.* 18 vols. London, 1818.

Morison, Hannah. *Poems on Various Subjects.* Newry, UK, 1817.

[O'Brien, Mrs. Mary]. *The Pious Incendiaries; or, Fanaticism Display'd: A Poem.* London, 1785. Signed "a Lady."

———. *The Political Monitor; or, Regent's Friend, Being a Collection of Poems Published in England during the Agitation of the Regency, Consisting of Curious, Interesting, Satyrical, and Political Effusions of Poetry.* Dublin, 1790.

O'Neill, Mrs. Frances. *Poetical Essays, Being a Collection of Satirical Poems, Songs and Acrostics.* London, 1802.

Opie, Amelia Alderson. *Poems.* London, 1802.

Owen, Robert. *A New Vision of Society; or, Essays on the Principle of the Formation of the Human Character and the Application of the Principle to Practice.* London, 1813.

Owenson, Sydney. *The Lay of an Irish Harp; or, Metrical Fragments.* London, 1807.

———. *Patriotic Sketches of Ireland, Written in Connaught.* 2 vols. London, 1807.

———. *The Wild Irish Girl: A National Tale.* London, 1806.

Pagan, Isabel. *A Collection of Songs and Poems on Several Occasions.* Glasgow, 1803.

[Panton, Mary]. *Eloise, and Other Poems on Several Occasions.* Leith, Scotland, 1815. Signed "a Young Lady."

Patullo, Margaret. *The Christian Psalter: A New Version of the Psalms of David, Calculated for All Denominations of Christians.* Perth, 1828.

Park, T[homas]. *Sonnets, and Other Small Poems.* London, 1803.

Peacock, Lucy. *The Little Emigrant.* London, 1799.

Percy, Thomas, ed. *Reliques of Ancient English Poetry, Consisting of Old Heroic Ballads, Songs, and Other Pieces of Our Earlier Poets . . . Together with Some Few of a Later Date.* 3 vols. London, 1767.

Pilkington, Mary. *New Tales of the Castle; or, The Noble Emigrants.* London, 1801.

Polwhele, Richard. "On the Dissipation of Fashionable Women." In vol. 2 of *Discourses on Different Subjects.* London, 1788.

———. *The Unsex'd Females: A Poem, Addressed to the Author of "The Pursuits of Literature."* London, 1798.

Pope, Alexander. *The Poems of Alexander Pope.* Edited by John Butt. New Haven: Yale University Press, 1963.

Pratt, Samuel Jackson. *Sympathy: A Poem.* London, 1781. Alternative title, *Sympathy; or, A Sketch of the Social Passion.*

Quigley, Catharine. *A Gift for the Sanctuary, from Unpublished Compositions.* Armagh, 1837.

———. *The Microscope; or, Village Flies, in Three Cantos, with Other Poems, Never Before Published.* Monaghan, Ireland, 1819.

———. *Poems.* Dublin, 1813.

Radcliffe, Mary Ann. *The Female Advocate.* London, 1799.

"Real Friend, A." *A Letter to the People of Ireland, Which They Can All Understand, and Ought to Read.* Dublin, 1799.

Reid, Mrs. M. A. *The Harp of Salem: A Collection of Historical Poems, from the Scriptures, Together with Some Reflective Pieces.* Edinburgh, 1827.

Richardson, Charlotte. *Poems, Chiefly Composed during the Pressure of a Severe Illness.* York, UK, 1809.

———. *Poems Written on Different Occasions, to Which is Prefixed Some Account of the Author, Together with the Reasons Which Have Led to Their Publication, by the Editor, Catherine Cappé, Published by Subscription for the Benefit of the Author.* York, UK, 1806.

Richardson, Charlotte Caroline. *Harvest: A Poem in Two Parts, with other Poetical Pieces.* London, 1818.

———. *Isaac and Rebecca.* London, 1817.

———. *Ludolph; or, The Light of Nature: A Poem.* London, 1821.

———. *The Soldier's Child; or, Virtue Triumphant.* London, 1821.

———. *Waterloo: A Poem, on the Late Victory . . . to Which Is Added, Truth, a Vision.* London, 1815.

Robinson, Mary. *Captivity, a Poem, and Celadon and Lydia, a Tale.* London, [1777].

———. *Lyrical Tales.* London, 1800.

———. *Mary Robinson: Selected Poems.* Edited by Judith Pascoe. Peterborough, Ontario: Broadview Press, 2000.

———. *Monody to the Memory of the Late Queen of France*. London, 1793.

———. *Monody to the Memory of Sir Joshua Reynolds*. London, 1792.

———. *Poems*. London, 1775.

———. *Poems*. Vol. 2. London, 1793.

———. *The Poetical Works of Mrs. Mary Robinson*. [Edited by Maria E. Robinson]. 3 vols. London, 1806.

———. *Sappho and Phaon, in a Series of Legitimate Sonnets, with Thoughts on Poetical Subjects, and Anecdotes of the Grecian Poetess*. London, 1796.

———. *Sight, The Cavern of Woe, and Solitude. Poems*. London, 1793.

———. *Thoughts on the Condition of Women*. London, [n.d.].

Rodd, Thomas. *Sonnets, Amatory, Descriptive, and Religious; Odes, Songs, and Ballads*. London, 1814.

Rodgers, Vincentia. *Cluthan and Malvina: An Ancient Legend, with Other Poems*. Belfast, 1823.

Rowton, Frederic. *The Female Poets of Great Britain, Chronologically Arranged, with Copious Selections and Critical Remarks*. 1853. Facsimile ed. Edited by Marilyn L. Williamson. Detroit: Wayne State University Press, 1981.

Ryan, Mrs. Edward [Eliza]. *Poems on Several Occasions*. Dublin, 1816.

[Ryves, Eliza]. *Ode to the Right Honourable Lord Melton, Infant Son of Earl Fitzwilliam*. London, 1787.

St. John, Mary. *Ellauna: A Legend of the Thirteenth Century in Four Cantos, with Notes*. Dublin, 1815.

[Sargant, Jane Alice]. *An Address to the Females of Great Britain, on the Propriety of Their Petitioning Parliament for the Abolition of Negro Slavery*. London, 1833. Signed "an Englishwoman."

———. *The Broken Arm: A National School Story*. London, 1847.

———. *But Once*. London, 1853.

———. *Charlie Burton*. London, 1849.

———. *Home Tales*. 8 vols. London, 1853–61.

———. *Ringstead Abbey*. London, 1830.

———. *Shades of Character*. London, 1853.

———. *Sonnets, and Other Poems*. London, 1817.

Scot, Elizabeth. *Alonzo and Cora, with Other Original Poems, Principally Elegiac*. London, 1801.

Scott, Walter. *Minstrelsy of the Scottish Border, Consisting of Historical and Romantic Ballads*. 2 vols. Kelso, Scotland, 1802.

Seward, Miss [Anna]. *Elegy on Captain Cook, to Which Is Added, an Ode to the Sun*. London, 1780.

———. *Letters of Anna Seward: Written between the Years 1784 and 1807*. Edited by A. Constable. 6 vols. Edinburgh, 1811.

———. *Monody to Major André, to Which Are Added Letters Addressed to Her by Major André in the Year 1769*. Lichfield, UK, 1781.

———. *Original Sonnets on Various Occasions, and Odes Paraphrased from Horace*. London, 1799.

Shelley, Mary. *The Letters of Mary Wollstonecraft Shelley.* Edited by Betty T. Bennett. 3 vols. Baltimore: Johns Hopkins University Press, 1983–88.

Shelley, Percy Bysshe. *The Complete Poetical Works of Percy Bysshe Shelley.* Edited by Thomas Hutchinson. London: Oxford University Press, 1961.

———. *Shelley's Poetry and Prose.* 2nd ed. Edited by Donald H. Reiman and Neil Fraistat. New York: W. W. Norton, 2002.

Smallpiece, Anna Maria. *Original Sonnets, and Other Small Poems.* London, 1805.

Smith, Charlotte. *The Collected Letters of Charlotte Smith.* Edited by Judith Phillips Stanton. Bloomington: Indiana University Press, 2000.

———. *Elegiac Sonnets, and Other Essays.* London, 1784.

———. *Elegiac Sonnets, with Additional Sonnets and Other Poems.* 5th ed. 1789.

———. *Elegiac Sonnets, and Other Poems.* 6th ed. Worcester, MA, 1795.

———. *Elegiac Sonnets, and Other Poems.* 8th ed. London, 1797.

———. *The Emigrants: A Poem in Two Books.* London, 1793.

———. *Emmeline, the Orphan of the Castle.* London, 1788.

———. *The Poems of Charlotte Smith.* Edited by Stuart Curran. New York: Oxford University Press, 1993.

Spence, S[arah]. *Poems, and a Meditation.* Colchester, UK, 1821.

———. *Poems and Miscellaneous Pieces.* Bury St. Edmunds, UK, 1795.

Steele, Sarah. *Eva: An Historical Poem, with Illustrative Notes, Accompanied by Some Lyric Poems.* Dublin, 1816.

Stockdale, Mary. *A Wreath for the Urn: An Elegy on Her Royal Highness Princess Charlotte of Wales and Saxe-Cobourg, with Other Poems.* London, 1818.

Taylor, Ellen. *Poems.* Dublin, 1792. Signed "Ellen Taylor, the Irish Cottager."

Temple, Laura Sophia. *Lyric and Other Poems.* London, 1808.

[Thelwall, John]. "An Essay on the English Sonnet, Illustrated by a Comparison between the Sonnets of Milton and Those of Charlotte Smith." *Universal Magazine* 91 (December 1792): 408–14, 408–9, 414.

Thompson, William. *Appeal of One Half of the Human Race, Women, against the Pretensions of the Other Half, Men, to Retain Them in Political, and Thence in Civil and Domestic, Slavery.* London, 1825.

Tighe, Mary. *The Collected Poems and Journals of Mary Tighe.* Edited by Harriet Kramer Linkin. Lexington: University Press of Kentucky, 2004.

———. *Psyche; or, The Legend of Love.* London, 1805.

———. *Psyche, with Other Poems.* 5th ed. London, 1816.

Trefusis, Elizabeth *Poems and Tales.* 2 vols. London, 1808.

Trench, Melesina. *Campaspe: An Historical Tale, and Other Poems.* Southampton, UK, 1815.

———. *The Remains of the Late Mrs. Richard Trench, Being Selections from Her Journals, Letters, and Other Papers.* Edited by Richard Chenevix Trench. 2nd rev. ed. London, 1862.

Upton, Mrs. [Catherine]. *Miscellaneous Pieces, in Prose and Verse.* London, 1784.

———. *The Siege of Gibraltar, from the Twelfth of April to the Twenty-seventh of May, 1781.* London, [1781].

Walker, Joseph Cooper. *Historical Memoirs of the Irish Bards.* Dublin, 1786.

West, Jane. *Poems and Plays.* 2 vols. London, 1799.

Wheeler, William. *The Letters of Private Wheeler*. Edited by B. H. Liddell Hart. Boston: Houghton Mifflin, 1952.

[Williams, Helen Maria]. *Edwin and Eltruda: A Legendary Tale*. London, 1782. Signed "a Young Lady."

———. *A Farewell, for Two Years, to England: A Poem*. London, 1791.

———. *Letters Written in France*. Edited by Neil Fraistat and Susan S. Lanser. Peterborough, Ontario, Broadview Press, 2001.

———. *Peru: A Poem in Six Cantos*. London, 1784.

———. *A Poem on the Bill Lately Passed for Regulating the Slave Trade*. London, 1786.

———. *Poems on Various Subjects, with Introductory Remarks on the Present State of Science and Literature in France*. London, 1823.

Williams, Jane. *The Literary Women of England, Including a Biographical Epitome of All the Most Eminent to the Year 1700, and Sketches of All the Poetesses to the Year 1850, with Extracts from Their Works and Critical Remarks*. London, 1861.

Winter, Anna Maria. *The Fairies, and Other Poems*. Dublin, 1833.

———. *Thoughts on the Moral Order of Nature*. 3 vols. Dublin, 1831.

Wollstonecraft, Mary. *A Vindication of the Rights of Woman*. London, 1792.

Wordsworth, William. *An Evening Walk*. London, 1793.

———. *The Poetical Works of William Wordsworth*. Ed. E. de Selincourt and Helen Darbishire. 5 vols. Oxford: Clarendon Press, 1947.

———. *William Wordsworth: The Poems*. Edited by John O. Hayden. 2 vols. New Haven: Yale University Press, 1977.

Wordsworth, William, and Samuel Taylor Coleridge. *Wordsworth and Coleridge: Lyrical Ballads, 1798*. 2nd ed. Edited by W. J. B. Owen. Oxford: Oxford University Press, 1969.

Yearsley, Ann. *A Poem on the Inhumanity of the Slave-Trade*. London, 1788.

Young, Maria Julia. *Adelaide and Antonine; or, The Emigrants*. London, 1793.

SECONDARY WORKS

Abrams, M. H. *The Mirror and the Lamp: Romantic Theory and the Critical Tradition*. New York: W. W. Norton, 1953.

———, ed. *The Norton Anthology of English Literature*. 6th ed. New York: W. W. Norton, 1993.

Alspach, Russell. K. *Irish Poetry from the English Invasion to 1798*. 2nd rev. ed. Philadelphia: University of Pennsylvania Press, 1959.

Anderson, Benedict. *Imagined Communities: Reflections on the Origin and Spread of Nationalism*. New York: St. Martin's, 1991.

Armstrong, Isobel. "Natural and National Monuments—Felicia Hemans's 'The Image in Lava': A Note." In Sweet and Melnyk, eds., *Felicia Hemans*, 212–30.

Armstrong, Isobel, and Virginia Blain, eds. *Women's Poetry in the Enlightenment: The Making of a Canon*. New York: St. Martin's Press, 1999.

Ashfield, Andrew. Introduction. In Ashfield, ed., *Romantic Women Poets*, xi–xviii.

————, ed. *Romantic Women Poets, 1770–1838: An Anthology.* Manchester, UK: Manchester University Press, 1995.

Backscheider, Paula R. *Eighteenth-Century Women Poets and Their Poetry: Inventing Agency, Inventing Genre.* Baltimore: Johns Hopkins University Press, 2005.

Backscheider, Paula R., and Timothy Dykstal. Introduction. In *The Intersections of the Public and Private Spheres in Early Modern England,* edited by Paula R. Backscheider and Timothy Dykstal, 1–40. London: Frank Cass, 1996.

Bainbridge, Simon. *British Poetry and the Revolutionary and Napoleonic Wars.* Oxford: Oxford University Press, 2000.

Bardsley, Alyson. "Joanna Baillie Stages the Nation." In Davis, Duncan, and Sorensen, *Scotland and the Borders of Romanticism,* 139–52.

Barthes, Roland. "From Work to Text." *Image—Music—Text.* Translated by Stephen Heath, 155–64. New York: Hill and Wang, 1977.

Batchelor, Jennie, and Cora Kaplan. Introduction. In *British Women's Writing in the Long Eighteenth Century: Authorship, Politics and History,* edited by Jennie Batchelor and Cora Kaplan, 1–16. Houndsmills: Palgrave Macmillan, 2005.

Baylen, Joseph O., and Norbert J. Grossman. Vol. 1 of *Biographical Dictionary of Modern British Radicals.* Hassocks, UK: Harvester Press, 1979.

Behrendt, Stephen C. "In Search of Anna Maria Smallpiece." *Women's Writing* 7.1 (2000): 55–74.

————. *Royal Mourning and Regency Culture: Elegies and Memorials of Princess Charlotte.* London: Macmillan, 1997.

————. *Shelley and His Audiences.* Lincoln: University of Nebraska Press, 1989.

————. "An Urn, a Teapot, and the Archeology of Romantic Reading." *CEA Critic* 67.2 (Winter 2005): 1–14.

————. "Women without Men: Barbara Hofland and the Economics of Widowhood." *Eighteenth-Century Fiction* 17.5 (April 2005): 481–508.

————, ed. *Irish Women Romantic Poets.* Alexandria, VA: Alexander Street Press, 2008.

Bennett, Betty T., ed. *British War Poetry in the Age of Romanticism: 1793–1815.* New York: Garland, 1976.

Bhabha, Homi. *The Location of Culture.* London: Routledge, 1994.

Blackburne, E[lizabeth] Owens. *Illustrious Irishwomen, Being Memoirs of the Most Noted Irishwomen from the Earliest Ages to the Present Century.* 2 vols. London, 1877.

Blain, Virginia, Patricia Clements, and Isobel Grundy, eds. *The Feminist Companion to Literature in English.* New Haven: Yale University Press, 1990.

Bloom, Harold. *The Visionary Company: A Reading of English Romantic Poetry.* Rev. ed. Ithaca: Cornell University Press, 1971.

Bold, Valentina. "Beyond 'The Empire of the Gentle Heart': Scottish Women Poets of the Nineteenth Century." In Gifford and McMillan, eds., *A History of Scottish Women's Writing,* 246–61.

Bourke, Angela, Siobhán Kilfeather, Maria Luddy, Margaret Mac Curtain, Gerardine Meaney, Máirín Ni Dhonnchadha, Mary O'Dowd, and Claire Wills. *Irish Women's Writing and Traditions.* Vol. 5 of *The Field Day Anthology of Irish Writing.* Cork, Ireland: Cork University Press, 2002.

Brown, Mary Ellen. "Old Singing Women and the Canons of Scottish Balladry and Song." In Gifford and McMillan, eds., *A History of Scottish Women's Writing*, 44–57.

Burke's Peerage and Baronetage. Edited by Charles Mosley. 106th ed. 2 vols. London: Fitzroy Dearborn, 1999.

Butler, Marilyn. *Romantics, Rebels and Reactionaries: English Literature and its Background, 1760–1830.* New York: Oxford University Press, 1981.

Carpenter, Andrew. "Poetry in English, 1690–1800: From the Williamite Wars to the Act of Union." In Kelleher and O'Leary, eds., *Cambridge History of Irish Literature*, 1:282–319.

———, ed. *Verse in English from Eighteenth-Century Ireland.* Cork, Ireland: Cork University Press, 1998.

Chandler, James. *England in 1819: The Politics of Literary Culture and the Case of Romantic Historicism.* Chicago: University of Chicago Press, 1998.

Christie, Ian R. "Conservatism and Stability in British Society." In Philip, ed., *The French Revolution and British Popular Politics*, 169–87.

———. *Wars and Revolutions: Britain, 1760–1815.* Cambridge, MA: Harvard University Press, 1982.

Clark, Anna. *The Struggle for the Breeches: Gender and the Making of the British Working Class.* Berkeley: University of California Press, 1995.

Cole, Lucinda, and Richard G. Swartz. "'Why Should I Wish for Words?' Literacy, Articulation, and the Borders of Literary Culture." In Favret and Watson, eds., *At the Limits of Romanticism*, 143–69.

Colley, Linda. *Britons: Forging the Nation 1707–1837.* New Haven: Yale University Press, 1992.

Colman, Anne Ulry. *Dictionary of Nineteenth-Century Irish Women Poets.* Belfast: Kenny's Bookshop, 1996.

Connolly, Claire. "Irish Romanticism, 1800–1830." In Kelleher and O'Leary, eds., *Cambridge History of Irish Literature*, 1:407–48.

Cookson, J. E. "War." In McCalman, ed., *Oxford Companion to the Romantic Age*, 26–34.

Corkery, Daniel. *The Hidden Ireland: A Study of Gaelic Munster in the Eighteenth Century.* 4th ed. Dublin: Gill, 1956.

Cox, Philip. *Gender, Genre and the Romantic Poets.* Manchester, UK: Manchester University Press, 1996.

Craciun, Adriana. *British Women Writers and the French Revolution: Citizens of the World.* London: Palgrave Macmillan, 2005.

———. "Romantic Spinstrelsy: Anne Bannerman and the Sexual Politics of the Ballad." In Davis, Duncan, and Sorensen, eds., *Scotland and the Borders of Romanticism*, 204–24.

Craciun, Adriana, and Kari E. Lokke. "British Women Writers and the French Revolution, 1789–1815." In Craciun and Lokke, eds., *Rebellious Hearts*, 3–30.

Craciun, Adriana, and Kari E. Lokke, eds. *Rebellious Hearts: British Women Writers and the French Revolution.* Albany: State University of New York Press, 2001.

Curran, Stuart. Introduction. In Smith, *The Poems of Charlotte Smith*, xix–xxix.

———. *Poetic Form and British Romanticism.* New York: Oxford University Press, 1986.

———. "Romantic Poetry: The I Altered." In Mellor, ed., *Romanticism and Feminism*, 185–207.

―――. "Romantic Women Poets: Inscribing the Self." In Armstrong and Blain, eds., *Women's Poetry in the Enlightenment,* 145–66.

―――. "Women Readers, Women Writers." In *The Cambridge Companion to British Romanticism,* edited by Stuart Curran, 177–95. Cambridge: Cambridge University Press, 1993.

Currie, Joy M. "Borrowed Authority, Satirized Genre: Appropriations of Shakespeare in Charlotte Smith's Poetry and Novels." PhD diss., University of Nebraska, 2006.

Dabundo, Laura, ed. *Jane Austen and Mary Shelley and Their Sisters.* Lanham, MD: University Press of America, 2000.

Daiches, David. *The Paradox of Scottish Culture: The Eighteenth-Century Experience.* London: Oxford University Press, 1964.

Davidoff, Leonore. *Worlds Between: Historical Perspectives on Gender and Class.* New York: Routledge, 1995.

Davidoff, Leonore, and Catherine Hall. *Family Fortunes: Men and Women of the English Middle Class, 1780–1850.* Chicago: University of Chicago Press, 1987.

Davis, Leith. *Acts of Union: Scotland and the Literary Negotiation of the British Nation, 1707–1830.* Stanford: Stanford University Press, 1998.

Davis, Leith, Ian Duncan, and Janet Sorensen, eds. *Scotland and the Borders of Romanticism.* Cambridge: Cambridge University Press, 2004.

Decker, Catherine H. "Women and Public Space in the Novel of the 1790s." In Lang-Peralta, ed., *Women, Revolution, and the Novels of the 1790s,* 1–24.

de Nie, Michael. *The Eternal Paddy: Irish Identity and the British Press, 1798–1882.* Madison: University of Wisconsin Press, 2004.

Dewar, Robert. "Burns and the Burns Tradition." In Kinsley, ed., *Scottish Poetry,* 185–211.

Dibert-Himes, Glenn T. "The Comprehensive Index and Bibliography to the Collected Works of Letitia Elizabeth Landon." PhD diss., University of Nebraska, 1997.

Dickinson, H. T., ed. *Britain and the French Revolution, 1789–1815.* London: Macmillan, 1989.

―――. Introduction. In Dickinson, ed., *Britain and the French Revolution,* [x–xxv].

Duffy, Michael. "War, Revolution, and the Crisis of the British Empire." In Philip, ed., *The French Revolution and British Popular Politics,* 118–45.

Duncan, Ian, with Leith Davis and Janet Sorensen. Introduction. In Davis, Duncan, and Sorenson, eds., *Scotland and the Borders of Romanticism,* 1–19.

Easson, Roger R., and Robert N. Essick. *Plates Designed and Engraved by Blake.* Vol. 1 of *William Blake, Book Illustrator: A Bibliography and Catalogue of the Commercial Engravings.* Normal, IL: American Blake Foundation, 1972.

Elfenbein, Andrew. *Romantic Genius: The Prehistory of a Homosexual Role.* New York: Columbia University Press, 1999.

Ellison, Julie. *Delicate Subjects: Romanticism, Gender, and the Ethics of Understanding.* Ithaca: Cornell University Press, 1990.

Emsley, Clive. *British Society and the French Wars, 1793–1815.* London: Macmillan, 1979.

Epstein, James A. *Radical Expression: Political Language, Ritual, and Symbolism in England, 1790–1850.* New York: Oxford University Press, 1994.

Eyre-Todd, George, ed. *Scottish Poetry of the Eighteenth Century.* 2 vols. Glasgow, 1896.

Favret, Mary A. "Coming Home: The Public Spaces of Romantic War." *Studies in Romanticism* 33.4 (1994): 539–48.

Favret, Mary A., and Nicola Watson, eds. *At the Limits of Romanticism: Essays in Cultural Feminist and Materialist Criticism.* Bloomington: Indiana University Press, 1994.

Feldman, Paula R., ed. *British Women Poets of the Romantic Era: An Anthology.* Baltimore: Johns Hopkins University Press, 1997.

———. Introduction. In Feldman, ed., *British Women Poets of the Romantic Era,* xxv–xxxiii.

———. "The Poet and the Profits: Felicia Hemans and the Literary Marketplace." *Keats-Shelley Journal* 46 (1997): 148–76.

———. "Women Poets and Anonymity in the Romantic Era." *New Literary History* 33.2 (2002): 279–89.

Feldman, Paula R., and Theresa M. Kelley, eds. *Romantic Women Writers: Voices and Countervoices.* Hanover, NH: University Press of New England, 1995.

Felski, Rita. *Beyond Feminist Aesthetics: Feminist Literature and Social Change.* Cambridge, MA: Harvard University Press, 1989.

Ferris, Ina. *The Romantic National Tale and the Question of Ireland.* Cambridge: Cambridge University Press, 2002.

Fielding, Penny. *Writing and Orality: Nationality, Culture, and Nineteenth-Century Scottish Fiction.* Oxford: Clarendon Press, 1996.

Fraistat, Neil. *The Poem and the Book: Interpreting Collections of Romantic Poetry.* Chapel Hill: University of North Carolina Press, 1985.

Gerard, Frances A. *Some Fair Hibernians, Being a Supplementary Volume to "Some Celebrated Irish Beauties of the Last Centuries."* London, 1897.

Gifford, Douglas, and Dorothy McMillan. Introduction. In Gifford and McMillan, eds., *A History of Scottish Women's Writing,* ix–xxiii.

———, eds. *A History of Scottish Women's Writing.* Edinburgh: Edinburgh University Press, 1997.

Gilmartin, Kevin. *Print Politics: The Press and Radical Opposition in Early Nineteenth-Century England.* Cambridge: Cambridge University Press, 1996.

Goodwin, Albert. *The Friends of Liberty: The English Democratic Movement in the Age of the French Revolution.* Cambridge, MA: Harvard University Press, 1979.

Gonzalez, Alexander G., ed. *Irish Women Writers: An A-to-Z Guide.* Westport, CT: Greenwood Press, 2005.

Gray, Jane. "Gender and Plebian Culture in Ulster." *Journal of Interdisciplinary History* 24.2 (Autumn 1993): 251–70.

Guest, Harriet. *Small Change: Women, Learning, Patriotism, 1750–1810.* Chicago: University of Chicago Press, 2000.

Habermas, Jürgen. *The Structural Transformation of the Public Sphere: An Inquiry into a Category of Bourgeois Society.* Trans. Thomas Burger and Frederick Lawrence. 1989; Cambridge, MA: MIT Press, 1998.

Hein, Hilde. "The Role of Feminist Aesthetics in Feminist Theory." In *Feminism and Tradition in Aesthetics,* edited by Peggy Zeglin Brand and Carolyn Korsmeyer, 446–63. University Park, PA: Pennsylvania State University Press, 1995.

Hogan, Robert, Introduction. In *Dictionary of Irish Literature,* edited by Robert Hogan, 1–19.

————, ed. *Dictionary of Irish Literature*. Rev. and exp. ed. 2 vols. London: Aldwych Press, 1996.

Hunter, J. Paul. "The Poetry of Occasions." In *A Concise Companion to the Restoration and Eighteenth Century*, edited by Cynthia Wall, 202–25. Malden, MA: Blackwell, 2005.

Innes, C. L. *Woman and Nation in Irish Literature and Society, 1880–1935*. Athens: University of Georgia Press, 1993.

Jackson, J. R. de J. *Annals of English Verse, 1770–1835: A Preliminary Survey of the Volumes Published*. New York: Garland, 1985.

————. *Romantic Poetry by Women: A Bibliography, 1770–1835*. Oxford: Clarendon Press, 1993.

Jacobus, Mary, ed. *Women Writing and Writing about Women*. London: Croom Helm, 1979.

Janowitz, Anne. "'A Voice from across the Sea': Communitarianism at the Limits of Romanticism." In Favret and Watson, eds., *At the Limits of Romanticism*, 83–100.

Jeon, Deuk Ju. "Nature and Poetry: An Ecocritical Approach to Modern Poetry (from the Romantic Age to the Ecological Age)." PhD diss., University of Nebraska, 2004.

Johnson, C. R. *Provincial Poetry, 1789–1839: British Verse Published in the Provinces, the Romantic Background*. London: Jed Press, 1992.

Jones, Vivien. "Women Writing Revolution: Narratives of History and Sexuality in Wollstonecraft and Williams." *Beyond Romanticism: New Approaches to Texts and Contexts, 1780-1832*, edited by John C. Whale and Stephen Copley, 178–99. London: Routledge, 1992.

Kelleher, Margaret, and Philip O'Leary, eds. *The Cambridge History of Irish Literature*. 2 vols. Cambridge: Cambridge University Press, 2006.

Kelley, Theresa, and Paula R. Feldman. Introduction. In Feldman and Kelley, eds., *Romantic Women Writers*, 1–10.

Kelly, Gary. Introduction. In Hemans, *Felicia Hemans: Selected Poems, Prose, and Letters*, 15–85.

Kennedy, Deborah. "Responding to the French Revolution: Williams's *Julia* and Burney's *The Wanderer*." In Dabundo, ed., *Jane Austen and Mary Shelley and Their Sisters*, 5–12.

Kerrigan, Catherine. Introduction. In Kerrigan, ed., *An Anthology of Scottish Women Poets*, 1–11.

————, ed. *An Anthology of Scottish Women Poets*. Edinburgh: Edinburgh University Press, 1991.

Kilfeather, Siobhán. "The Profession of Letters, 1700–1810." In Bourke et al., eds., *Irish Women's Writing and Traditions*, 772–77.

Kinsley, James, ed. *Scottish Poetry: A Critical Survey*. London: Cassell, 1955.

Klancher, Jon. *The Making of English Reading Audiences, 1790–1832*. Madison: University of Wisconsin Press, 1987.

Landry, Donna. "Janet Little." In *Scottish Women Poets of the Romantic Period*, edited by Stephen C. Behrendt and Nancy J. Kushigian. Alexandria, VA: Alexander Street Press, 2002.

————. *The Muses of Resistance: Labouring Class Women's Poetry in Britain, 1739–1796*. Cambridge: Cambridge University Press, 1991.

Lang-Peralta, Linda, ed. *Women, Revolution, and the Novels of the 1790s*. East Lansing: Michigan State University Press, 1999.

Lebow, Ned. "British Images of Poverty in Pre-Famine Ireland." In *Views of the Irish Peasantry, 1800–1916,* edited by Daniel J. Casey and Robert E. Rhodes, 57–85. Hamden, CT: Archon Books, 1977.

Lin, Patricia Y. C. E. "Extending Her Arms: Military Families and the Transformation of the British State, 1793–1815." PhD diss., University of California, Berkeley, 1997.

Linkin, Harriet Kramer. Introduction. In Tighe, *Collected Poems and Journals,* xv–xxiii.

———. "Recuperating Romanticism in Mary Tighe's *Psyche.*" In Linkin and Behrendt, eds., *Romanticism and Women Poets,* 144–62.

Linkin, Harriet Kramer, and Stephen C. Behrendt, eds. *Romanticism and Women Poets: Opening the Doors of Reception.* Lexington: University Press of Kentucky, 1999.

Lokke, Kari E. "'The Mild Dominion of the Moon': Charlotte Smith and the Politics of Transcendence." In Craciun and Lokke, eds., *Rebellious Hearts,* 85–106.

Lovell, Terry. *Consuming Fiction.* London: Verso, 1987.

Low, D. A. "Literature in the Nineteenth Century." In *The New Companion to Scottish Culture,* edited by David Daiches, 192–94. Edinburgh: Polygon, 1993.

Low, Dennis. *The Literary Protégées of the Lake Poets.* Aldershot, UK: Ashgate, 2006.

Mack, Douglas S. *Scottish Fiction and the British Empire.* Edinburgh: Edinburgh University Press, 2006.

Mackenzie, Agnes Mure. "The Renaissance Poets: (1) Scots and English." In Kinsley, ed., *Scottish Poetry,* 33–67.

Mackesy, Piers. "Strategic Problems of the British War Effort." In Dickinson, ed., *Britain and the French Revolution,* 147–64.

Mackinnon, J. *The Union of England and Scotland: A Study of International History.* London, 1896.

Mahon, Penny. "In Sermon and Story: Contrasting Anti-War Rhetoric in the Work of Anna Barbauld and Amelia Opie." *Women's Writing* 7.1 (2000): 23–38.

McCartney, Donal. "The Quest for Irish Political Identity: The Image and the Illusion." In *Image and Illusion: Anglo-Irish Literature and Its Contexts,* edited by Maurice Harmon, 13–22. Dublin: Wolfhound Press, 1979.

McCue, Kirsteen. "Women and Song, 1750–1850." In Gifford and McMillan, eds., *A History of Scottish Women's Writing,* 58–70.

McGann, Jerome J. *The Poetics of Sensibility: A Revolution in Literary Style.* Oxford: Clarendon Press, 1996.

———. *The Romantic Ideology: A Critical Investigation.* Chicago: University of Chicago Press, 1983.

McMillan, Dorothy. Introduction. In *The Scotswoman at Home and Abroad: Non-Fictional Writing, 1700–1900,* edited by Dorothy McMillan, xi–xiv. Glasgow: Association for Scottish Literary Studies, 1999.

Meaney, Gerardine. "Women and Writing, 1700–1960." In Bourke et al., eds., *Irish Women's Writing and Traditions,* 765–71.

Mellor, Anne. K. *Mothers of the Nation: Women's Political Writing in England, 1780–1830.* Bloomington: Indiana University Press, 2000.

———. *Romanticism and Gender.* New York: Routledge, 1993.

———, ed. *Romanticism and Feminism.* Bloomington: Indiana University Press, 1988.

Millar, J. H. *A Literary History of Scotland.* New York: Charles Scribner's Sons, 1903.

Miller, Judith Davis. "The Politics of Truth and Deception: Charlotte Smith and the French Revolution." In Craciun and Lokke, eds., *Rebellious Hearts,* 337–63.

Moers, Ellen. *Literary Women: The Great Writers.* 1963. Rpt., New York: Oxford University Press, 1976.

Montgomery, Michael B. and Robert J. Gregg. "The Scots Language in Ulster." In *The Edinburgh History of the Scots Language,* edited by Charles Jones, 569–622. Edinburgh: Edinburgh University Press, 1997.

Murphy, Peter T. *Poetry as an Occupation and an Art in Britain, 1760–1830.* Cambridge: Cambridge University Press, 1993.

Murray, Paul Thomas. *Toward a Working-Class Canon: Literary Criticism in British Working-Class Periodicals, 1816–1858.* Columbus: Ohio State University Press, 1994.

Newman, Gerald. *The Rise of English Nationalism: A Cultural History, 1740–1830.* New York: St. Martin's Press, 1987.

Nolte, Eugene. "David Macbeth Moir as Morgan Odoherty." *PMLA* 72.4 (1957): 803–6.

O'Connor, Laura. *Haunted English: The Celtic Fringe, the British Empire, and De-Anglicization.* Baltimore: Johns Hopkins University Press, 2006.

O'Donoghue, D. J. *The Poets of Ireland.* Dublin: Hodges, Figgis, 1912.

O'Dowd, Mary. "The Political Writings and Public Voices of Women, c. 1500–1850." In Bourke et al., eds., *Irish Women's Writing and Traditions,* 6–12.

O'Farrell, Patrick. *Ireland's English Question: Anglo-Irish Relations, 1534–1970.* London: B. T. Batsford, 1971.

O'Halloran, Clare. *Golden Ages and Barbarous Nations: Antiquarian Debate and Cultural Politics in Ireland, c. 1750–1800.* Notre Dame, IN: University of Notre Dame Press, 2004.

Oliver, A. M. "The Scottish Augustans." In Kinsley, ed., *Scottish Poetry,* 119–49.

Page, F. C. G. *Following the Drum: Women in Wellington's Wars.* London: Andre Deutsch, 1986.

Pascoe, Judith. Introduction. In Robinson, *Mary Robinson: Selected Poems,* 19–62.

———. "Mary Robinson and the Literary Marketplace." In Feldman and Kelley, eds., *Romantic Women Writers,* 252–68.

Perkins, David, ed. *English Romantic Writers.* 2nd ed. Fort Worth, TX: Harcourt Brace, 1995.

Philip, Mark. "Revolution." In *An Oxford Companion to the Romantic Age: British Culture 1776–1832,* edited by Iain McCalman, 17–26. Oxford: Oxford University Press, 1999.

———, ed. *The French Revolution and British Popular Politics.* Cambridge: Cambridge University Press, 1991.

Pocock, J. G. A. "Political Thought in the English-Speaking Atlantic, 1760–1790." In *The Varieties of British Political Thought, 1500–1800,* edited by J. G. A. Pocock, with Gordon J. Schichet and Lois G. Schwoerer, 246–301. Cambridge: Cambridge University Press, 1993.

Poovey, Mary. *The Proper Lady and the Woman Writer: Ideology as Style in the Works of Mary Wollstonecraft, Mary Shelley, and Jane Austen.* Chicago: University of Chicago Press, 1984.

Porter, Roy. *The Creation of the Modern World: The Untold Story of the British Enlightenment.* New York: W. W. Norton, 2000.

Power, Patrick C. *The Story of Anglo-Irish Poetry (1800–1922).* Cork, Ireland: Mercier Press, 1967.

Prescott, Sarah. *Women, Authorship, and Literary Culture, 1690–1740.* Houndsmills: Palgrave Macmillan, 2002.

Rafroidi, Patrick. *Irish Literature in English: The Romantic Period (1789–1850).* Atlantic Highlands, NJ: Humanities Press, 1980.

Raven, James, Antonia Forster, and Stephen Bending, eds. Vol. 1 of *The English Novel, 1770–1829: A Bibliographical Survey of Prose Fiction Published in the British Isles.* Oxford: Oxford University Press, 2000.

Rice-Oxley, L., ed. *Poetry of the Anti-Jacobin.* Oxford: Basil Blackwell, 1924.

Robinson, Charles. *Shelley and Byron: The Snake and Eagle Wreathed in Fight.* Baltimore: Johns Hopkins University Press, 1976.

Robinson, Daniel, and Paula R. Feldman. Introduction. In *A Century of Sonnets: The Romantic-Era Revival, 1750–1850,* edited by Paula R. Feldman and Daniel Robinson, 3–19. New York: Oxford University Press, 1999.

Ross, Marlon. *The Contours of Masculine Desire: Romanticism and the Rise of Women's Poetry.* New York: Oxford University Press, 1989.

Russell, Gillian. *Theatres of War: Performance, Politics, and Society, 1793–1815.* Oxford: Oxford University Press, 2000.

Schenck, Celeste M. "Feminism and Deconstruction: Re-Constructing the Elegy." *Tulsa Studies in Women's Literature* 5.1 (1986): 13–27.

Schirmer, Gregory A. *Out of What Began: A History of Irish Poetry in English.* Ithaca: Cornell University Press, 1998.

Schor, Esther. *Bearing the Dead: The British Culture of Mourning from the Enlightenment to Victoria.* Princeton: Princeton University Press, 1994.

Scodel, Joshua. "Lyric Forms." In *The Cambridge Companion to English Literature, 1650–1740,* edited by Steven N. Zwicker, 120–42. Cambridge: Cambridge University Press, 1998.

Scott, Joan Wallach. *Gender and the Politics of History.* New York: Columbia University Press, 1988.

Scrivener, Michael. *Poetry and Reform: Periodical Verse from the English Democratic Press, 1792–1824.* Detroit: Wayne State University Press, 1992.

———. *Seditious Allegories: John Thelwall and Jacobin Writing.* University Park: Pennsylvania State University Press, 2001.

Shaw, Philip. Introduction. In Shaw, ed., *Romantic Wars,* 1–12.

———. *Waterloo and the Romantic Imagination.* New York: Palgrave Macmillan, 2002.

———, ed. *Romantic Wars: Studies in Culture and Conflict.* Aldershot: Ashgate, 2000.

Showalter, Elaine. *A Literature of their Own: British Women Novelists from Brontë to Lessing.* Princeton: Princeton University Press, 1977.

———. "Toward a Feminist Poetics." In *The New Feminist Criticism: Essays on Women, Literature, and Theory,* edited by Elaine Showalter, 125–43. New York: Pantheon, 1985.

Smith, Barbara Herrnstein. *Poetic Closure: A Study of How Poems End.* Chicago: University of Chicago Press, 1968.

Spiller, Michael. *The Sonnet Sequence: A Study of Its Strategies.* New York: Prentice Hall, 1997.

Spivak, Gayatri Chakravorty. "Can the Subaltern Speak?" In *Marxism and the Interpretation of Culture,* edited by Cary Nelson and Larry Grossberg, 271–313. Urbana: University of Illinois Press, 1988.

Squire, J. C. *A Book of Women's Verse.* Oxford: Clarendon Press, 1921.

Stafford, William. *English Feminists and Their Proponents in the 1790s: Unsex'd and Proper Females.* Manchester, UK: Manchester University Press, 2002.

———. *Socialism, Radicalism, and Nostalgia: Social Criticism in Britain, 1775–1830.* Cambridge: Cambridge University Press, 1987.

Starr, G. Gabrielle. *Lyric Generations: Poetry and the Novel in the Long Eighteenth Century.* Baltimore: Johns Hopkins University Press, 2004.

St. Clair, William. *The Reading Nation in the Romantic Period.* Cambridge: Cambridge University Press, 2004.

Steedman, Carolyn. "The Price of Experience: Women and the Making of the English Working Class." *Radical History Review,* no. 59 (Spring 1994): 109–19.

Stephenson, Glennis. *Letitia Landon: The Woman behind L. E. L.* Manchester, UK: Manchester University Press, 1995.

Sullivan, Alvin, ed. *British Literary Magazines: The Augustan Age and the Age of Johnson, 1698–1788.* Westport, CT: Greenwood Press, 1983.

Sweet, Nanora, and Julie Melnyk, eds. *Felicia Hemans: Reimagining Poetry in the Nineteenth Century.* Houndsmills, UK: Palgrave, 2001.

Timperley, Charles H. *A Dictionary of Printers and Printing.* London, 1839.

Traill, H. D., and J. S. Mann, eds. *Social England: A Record of the Progress of the People.* 5 vols. London: Cassell, 1914.

Trumpener, Katie. *Bardic Nationalism: The Romantic Novel and the British Empire.* Princeton: Princeton University Press, 1997.

Tuchman, Gaye, with Nina Fortin. *Edging Women Out: Victorian Novelists, Publishers, and Social Change.* New Haven: Yale University Press, 1989.

Turner, Cheryl. *Living by the Pen: Women Writers in the Eighteenth Century.* London: Routledge, 1992.

Ty, Eleanor. *Unsex'd Revolutionaries: Five Women Novelists of the 1790s.* Toronto: University of Toronto Press, 1993.

Vogler, Richard A., ed. *Graphic Works of George Cruikshank.* New York: Dover, 1979.

Wagner, Jennifer Ann. *A Moment's Moment: Revisionary Poetics and the Nineteenth-Century English Sonnet.* Madison, NJ: Fairleigh Dickinson University Press, 1996.

Walker, Eric C. "Marriage and the End of War." In Shaw, ed., *Romantic Wars,* 208–26.

Watson, J. R. *Romanticism and War: A Study of British Romantic Period Writers and the Napoleonic Wars.* New York: Palgrave Macmillan, 2003.

Watson, J. Steven. *The Reign of George III, 1760–1815.* Oxford: Clarendon Press, 1960.

Watt, L. M. *Scottish Life and Poetry.* London: James Nisbet, 1912.

Weekes, Ann Owens. *Irish Women Writers: An Uncharted Tradition.* Lexington: University Press of Kentucky, 1990.

Welch, Robert. *Irish Poetry from Moore to Yeats.* Totowa, NJ: Barnes and Noble, 1980.

Werkmeister, Lucyle. *A Newspaper History of England, 1792–93.* Lincoln: University of Nebraska Press, 1967.

Whelan, Kevin. *The Tree of Liberty: Radicalism. Catholicism and the Construction of Irish Identity, 1760–1830.* Notre Dame, IN: University of Notre Dame Press, 1996.

Withey, Lynne. E. "Catharine Macaulay and the Uses of History: Ancient Rights, Perfectionism, and Propaganda." *Journal of British Studies* 16.1 (1976): 59–83.

Wolffe, John. *Great Deaths: Grieving, Religion, and Nationhood in Victorian and Edwardian Britain.* Oxford: Oxford University Press, 2000.

Wolfson, Susan J. *Borderlines: The Shiftings of Gender in British Romanticism.* Stanford: Stanford University Press, 2006.

———. "Felicia Hemans and the Revolving Doors of Reception." In Linkin and Behrendt, eds., *Romanticism and Women Poets,* 214–41.

———. *Formal Charges: The Shaping of Poetry in British Romanticism.* Stanford: Stanford University Press, 1997.

———. Introduction. In Hemans, *Felicia Hemans: Selected Poems, Letters, Reception Materials,* xiii–xxix.

Wood, Marcus. *Radical Culture and Print Culture, 1790–1822.* Oxford: Clarendon Press, 1994.

Wordsworth, Jonathan. Introduction. In Baillie, *Joanna Baillie: Poems, 1790,* [iii–xii].

Wordsworth, Jonathan, and Jessica Wordsworth, eds. *The New Penguin Book of Romantic Poetry.* New York: Penguin, 2001.

Worrall, David. *Radical Culture: Discourse, Resistance, and Surveillance, 1790–1820.* New York: Harvester Wheatsheaf, 1992.

Wu, Duncan. Introduction. In Wu, ed., *Romantic Women Poets,* xix–xxviii.

Wu, Duncan, ed. *Romantic Women Poets: An Anthology.* Malden, MA: Blackwell, 1997.

———, ed. *Romanticism: An Anthology.* 3rd ed. Malden, MA: Blackwell, 2006.

Zach, Wolfgang. Introduction. In *National Images and Stereotypes.* Vol. 3 of *Literary Interrelations: Ireland, England and the World,* edited by Wolfgang Zach and Heinz Kosok, ix–xii. Tübingen: Gunter Narr, 1987.

Zimmerman, Sarah M. "'Dost Thou Not Know My Voice?' Charlotte Smith and the Lyric's Audience." In Linkin and Behrendt, eds., *Romanticism and Women,* 101–24.

BRESCIA UNIVERSITY
COLLEGE LIBRARY